PEARSON EDUCATION
TEST PREP SERIES
FOR AP® PSYCHOLOGY

FOR

PSYCHOLOGY
FOURTH EDITION
AP® EDITION

Saundra K. Ciccarelli
Gulf Coast State College

J. Noland White
Georgia College

William Elmhorst
Marshfield High School,
Marshfield, WI

Boston   Columbus   Indianapolis   New York   San Francisco   Upper Saddle River
Amsterdam   Cape Town   Dubai   London   Madrid   Milan   Munich   Paris   Montreal   Toronto
Delhi   Mexico City   São Paulo   Sydney   Hong Kong   Seoul   Singapore   Taipei   Tokyo

Pearson Education Test Prep Series for AP® Psychology 4e AP® Edition

Please visit our Web site at www.PearsonSchool.com/Advanced

AP® is a trademark registered and/or owned by the College Board, which was not involved in the production of, and does not endorse, this product.

PEARSON

ISBN 10: 0-13-385608-9
ISBN 13: 978-0-13-385608-8

8 18

CONTENTS

The purpose of this section of the test preparation guide is to give you ideas and tips on preparing for the AP Psychology exam. The material in this section is drawn from years of classroom and AP exam grading experience. Preparation for the exam will involve many steps along the way, and this guide will help you focus on the appropriate topics and materials as you progress from chapter to chapter. In Part One of this section, you will learn about the format of the AP Psychology exam and how it is scored to help you make good decisions and maximize your potential exam score. In Part Two you will read practical advice on preparing for the exam that will help you understand and remember key concepts as you use this guide to prepare for the exam. Finally, in Part Three you will read about a number of do's and don'ts for exam day that will help you avoid common mistakes and work toward a successful exam taking experience.

Part One

At the beginning of every year, one of the questions many students have is, "What is the AP Psychology exam?" The answer to this question is complex, so let us begin with the format of the exam, then move on to describe how the exam is graded, and finish by going over how your exam score is calculated.

To begin, the exam consists of two parts. Part One is made up of 100 multiple-choice questions and is weighted as two-thirds of your grade. You have 70 minutes to complete the multiple-choice exam, and most students find the 70 minutes a comfortable amount of time. Part Two of the exam consists of two Free Response Questions (FRQs), and each question makes up one-sixth of your grade. HINT: An FRQ is not a formal essay question and does not require a traditional five-paragraph essay response.

The 100 multiple-choice questions are designed to cover 14 topics, and each topic is weighted according to the amount of content it requires to cover the topic. For example, History and Approaches is 2 to 4 percent of the exam while Research Methods is 8 to 10 percent of the exam. HINT: By paying attention to the differences in weight given to a topic, you can distribute your study time accordingly, spending more time on the greater percentage topics, and best prepare for the exam (see Table 1). The multiple-choice questions are designed to determine if you understand a psychological term, assess general understanding of the scientific method, assess knowledge of findings from major research studies, and apply concepts in psychology. You can see how the difficulty of the questions will vary depending on the type of question. Typically, identifying a term will be easier than showing your understanding of findings from major research studies. Psychology is a very broad discipline, and there is always a good chance that you will see questions assessing topics that you are not familiar with. Remember to keep in mind that this is the case for most students. Make note of the question and move on to the next one. You can always come back later for a second look, and other questions in the test might prompt you to remember more information. There is no penalty for incorrect answers, and you should try to answer all the questions as best you can. Be sure to budget your time, and you should be done with at least 50 questions after the first 35 minutes of the exam. When the time has expired, you will then move on to the Free Response Question (FRQ) part of the exam.

Table 1: Topics and Percentage of AP Psychology Exam

History and Perspectives	2–4%	Developmental Psychology	7–9%
Research Methods	8–10%	Personality	5–7%
Biological Basis of Behavior	8–10%	Testing and Individual Differences	5–7%
Sensation and Perception	6–8%	Abnormal Psychology	7–9%
States of Consciousness	2–4%	Treatment of Psychological Disorders	5–7%
Learning	7–9%	Social Psychology	8–10%
Cognition	8–10%		
Motivation and Emotion	6–8%		

Part Two of the exam consists of two FRQs, and you have 50 minutes to write your responses. The FRQs require students to draw information from across several topics, integrate the information in a relevant manner, and apply the information in a "cogent argument." This means that you have to do more than list information or make an outline. Writing in full sentences is expected, and "bullet point" answers will not score, so be sure to write out your response in complete sentences.

After many years of teaching AP and preparing students for the exam, there are a few things that come to mind about the FRQs. First, there is little value in trying to predict the questions. The test design committee is formulated from the "best of the best" teachers of psychology, and the questions they develop are always challenging. A better use of your time is to spend it on thorough preparation of all the topics. Second, there is a chance you will find that a part of the question may be something you have never heard of before. This could happen simply because no single textbook or class can be comprehensive enough to cover every aspect of psychology in an introductory psychology course, so don't be upset or become anxious if you find some unfamiliar terms or concepts in the FRQs. Concentrate on the parts of the question you know, and work on the unfamiliar parts last. Finally, you are better off attempting an answer, even if you are guessing, because there is no penalty for incorrect answers. On occasion students "back into" a point and score on the rubric, improving their overall score. However, you must make sure not to contradict yourself in your answer because by making such a contradiction you have not demonstrated a cogent argument.

> Example: *The dog owner used positive reinforcement by giving the dog a treat when training the dog to roll over. The dog owner used negative reinforcement by giving the dog a treat when training the dog to roll over.*

These sentences clearly contradict each other, and the student is trying to score a point by answering both ways. An exam reader would not score this point because they are contradictory sentences, and the student is not making a cogent argument or showing understanding of the concept.

This test preparation guide includes practice FRQs for each chapter. Be aware that these practice FRQs are focused on the content in each chapter. FRQs on the AP exam tend to draw from several topics and assess a broad base of understanding of concepts in psychology. The practice FRQs will familiarize you with the general style of questions you will see on the exam. The sample scoring guides should be taken as examples of how to respond to the question and score on a possible rubric for a possible AP exam question. Keep in mind that the rubrics for the FRQs on the AP exam will be comprehensive and may give credit to several approaches to each part of an FRQ. If your responses are accurate, relevant, and similar to the sample responses provided with the FRQ rubrics, you are on the right track with your answers. Below is Sample FRQ 1. Notice that the question has several parts and that the subparts of the question come from various topics in psychology.

Sample FRQ 1

Linus lives near a noisy airport and has difficulty sleeping at night. Explain how each topic might be relevant when living near an airport and then explain how it applies to the difficulty Linus is having sleeping.

> Availability heuristic
> Classical conditioning
> Operant conditioning
> Evolutionary psychology
> Tinnitus

Notice that the FRQ includes some broad topics as well as a few specific and challenging topics. When answering an FRQ it is important to first answer the parts that you know and then move on to those that are less familiar. In addition, since you only have 50 minutes you need to budget your time and move on to the next question while you still have sufficient time to write your second response. In the event that you have time at the end, you can come back and work on the first question. <u>HINT: It is a good idea to</u>

format your response in a reader-friendly manner. Leave one blank line between your response to each part, underline the concept or term you are writing about, write in complete sentences, use the language of the discipline, and use legible handwriting.

Now that you have completed your exam, it has to be graded. The multiple-choice scanner sheets will be graded by a computer. Be sure to erase any errant marks cleanly, make only one mark per question, and make the mark of your choice on each question dark and completely filled in. HINT: Be careful with the marking of your sheet. It will help you to minimize clerical errors. Your written responses to the FRQs will be graded by an AP Psychology teacher or a college psychology professor. Great care is taken to ensure that your exam receives a fair and accurate grade. In order for the grading process to be consistent, a rubric is developed by a committee, and the rubric becomes the standard by which all exams will be graded. Below is an example of a rubric for sample FRQ 1

Sample FRQ 1 Rubric

10 points

- Availability heuristic
  - Point 1
    - Relates seeing a plane crash on TV or in a newspaper and thinking that plane crashes occur more than they actually do
  - Point 2
    - Applies to insomnia because the availability heuristic results in a heightened perception of the threat of a plane crash resulting in difficulty sleeping

- Classical conditioning
  - Point 1
    - Relates a startling noise from the airport being associated with a stimulus related to sleep (example—bed covers, pillow, darkness) resulting in a conditioned response
  - Point 2
    - Applies to insomnia because the presence of the conditioned stimulus leads to a conditioned response of a startle

- Operant conditioning
  - Point 1
    - Relates to sleeping behavior being modified in some way
  - Point 2
    - Applies to insomnia because it elicits a reinforcement or punishment (examples—getting sympathy or attention from other people, getting days off from work, getting docked pay, or being fired)

- Evolutionary psychology
  - Point 1
    - Relates to safety and security caused by vigilance toward the noise of the airport
  - Point 2
    - Applies to insomnia because of the need for safety or survival is threatened by the noise of the airport so it is difficult to sleep

- Tinnitus
  - Point 1
    - Relates to the noisy airport because it could cause hearing loss
  - Point 2

- Applies to insomnia because tinnitus is a bothersome ringing or noise in the ears that could make sleep difficult

It is important to note that FRQs often have multiple points for each part. <u>HINT: Be sure to answer all parts of the question. Students often neglect parts of the question and miss points.</u> Also, because the FRQ rubrics are comprehensive, there are usually multiple ways to score a point. <u>HINT: Be sure to write all you know about a topic, and always give an example to illustrate your point.</u>

In calculating your final score there are several factors to consider, including the difficulty of the exam, your multiple-choice score, and the score of the two FRQ responses. First, the difficulty of the exam is determined by comparing the performance of your cohort (all the students taking the exam the same year) with the performance of previous cohorts. When the difficulty of the exam is determined, the next step then is to determine cut scores to establish the levels for AP grades (1–5). Once the cut scores are determined, your score can be calculated. The following formula is an example of how your score is determined.

Calculating Your AP Exam Score

(<u>Number Correct on the Multiple Choice</u>) = MC Score
Note: this number is already a percent because there are 100 possible points on the MC exam.

Next, your FRQ grade will be calculated by totaling the points you scored on each of the two rubrics.

Example: FRQ 1 has 8 rubric points, and you scored 6. FRQ 2 has 8 rubric points, and you scored 5. In this case there are 16 rubric points possible, and you scored 11.
Note: the number of possible rubric points changes from question to question.

Finally, your composite score can now be calculated.

As mentioned before, the multiple-choice section is weighted at two-thirds of your score and the FRQ section is weighted at one-third of your score, so a final calculation must be made.

(Multiple-Choice Percent) × 1.00) = (Multiple-Choice Weighted Score)

(FRQ Percent) × (.33) = (FRQ Weighted Score)

(Multiple-Choice Weighted Score) + (FRQ Weighted Score) = (AP Score)

MC 73 × 1.00 = 73

FRQ 1: 6 × 3.125 = 18.75
FRQ 2: 5 × 3.125 = 15.62

FRQ 1 + FRQ2 = 34 (do not round to the nearest whole number.)

MC Weighted Score (73) + FRQ Weighted Score (34.375) + AP Composite Score (107)
(round to the nearest whole number.)

Now that you have your AP Score calculated, it will be applied to the cut scores to determine your AP Grade. Keep in mind that due to the variation in the difficulty levels of the exams from year to year, the cut scores move around a little. That being the case, you should consider the following chart an approximation of the possible cut scores for an AP Psychology exam.

Approximate AP Exam Cut Scores	
5	108–150
4	90–107
3	71–89
2	62–70
1	0–61

These are approximate cut scores and they can vary from exam to exam.

In this case, the AP Score of 107 earns an AP Grade of a 4, and you are eligible to earn credit for your score at many colleges and universities. If your score fell a little below 71, your score is considered "possibly qualified," and with more preparation you could test well enough to move into the "qualified" range.

As indicated earlier, the question "What is the AP Psychology exam?" requires a complex answer, and there are many factors to consider before an exam grade can be determined. While the calculations and rubrics are complicated, the task of preparing for the exam is not. The next part of this section will go over a number of suggestions on how to prepare for the exam and will help position you for a successful testing experience.

Part Two

Effective test preparation is a long-term process, and the following suggestions are intended to be implemented over your course of study. As you prepare for the exam, you will need to integrate these suggestions into your daily routines and make them part of your habits of mind. This section will help you in pacing your studies and maximizing the results of your study time, offer suggestions on quality resources for studying, go over in detail a number of mnemonic devices to help remember content, and end with a set of proven test-taking tips. Like many other tasks in life, a "one size fits all" approach is not always useful, especially when it comes to learning; therefore, it is important for you to reflect on your learning preferences and make appropriate choices with your study time.

Students often ask, "How should I review for the exam?" and the answer is usually not what the students hope to hear because the answer is "CONSTANTLY!" Best practices in pacing your study time indicate that short and distributed study sessions are more effective than a long cramming session at the end of a semester or year. AP students normally carry heavy class loads and need to make careful choices about their time. First, when you get to class, instead of spending the time chatting and socializing, spend five minutes reviewing at the beginning and end of class. Second, keeping your notebooks, note cards, handouts, and textbook handy will make taking advantage of short review sessions more likely, so try not to leave them in your locker or at home. Third, establish a study group. Having a reliable "accountability group" helps raise everyone's commitment to studying. Fourth, study in a quality learning environment at home. It is important to avoid studying in front of the TV, Internet, social networking sites, or while texting back and forth to friends. Also, long grueling sessions of studying are counterproductive. Short sessions of reading and studying distributed over the days of the week are more effective and help you to avoid the late-night cramming sessions that leave you more fatigued and less effective as a learner the next day.

There are a number of techniques to employ when studying that will help you maximize your study time, but be sure to factor in your learning preferences when selecting from the various strategies. Let us first talk about one of the greatest challenges in learning psychology: learning the language of psychology. Like every area of study, psychology has a set of terms and phrases called the "language of the discipline." This language can be confusing and inconsistent. Some estimates of the number of these terms in psychology run into the thousands, but for the purpose of the AP exam, the number can be limited to the most common and high-profile terms. Yet by the time you get through 14 topics you will still be challenged to remember all the terms, so it is best to take such a large task and break it down into the smaller parts of chapters and sections. HINT: Note cards are an effective way to help learn the large number of terms in psychology; however, writing out note cards should be meaningful and not just an exercise. When making note cards, you need to include four things: the term or phrase; a breakdown of the term, when possible, into its prefix, root, and suffix with a note about the word's origins; three or more synonyms for the term; and a relevant context sentence that elaborates on the meaning of the term. Certainly not every term or phrase will fit this format, but the closer you strive toward this model the more information you will have available to understand the terms. Another helpful strategy is note taking while you are reading your text. In this case working in front of a computer is a good idea because if you have a search engine handy you can look up names and terms to learn more about the topic. HINT: Note taking does not mean transcribing paragraphs from the textbook into a notebook. It is better to take a paragraph of reading, summarize the paragraph into a sentence that answers the question "What is the most important idea in this paragraph?" and make a short note about the most important idea in your notebook. This is not "speed reading" and it will take more time to complete, so be sure to break up your "slow reading" into small blocks of time. Finally, using a study group is helpful in making efficient use of your study time. Breaking up a term list or reading assignment into smaller parts and working together on the task can shorten the time needed to complete the task. HINT: Be sure to make your own meaning out of the terms you read and not cheat by handing in your study partner's version of the assignment. Handing in another person's work as your own is unethical, qualifies as plagiarism, and will likely result in severe discipline procedures. You may have noticed that these suggestions are time intensive and require considerable work and effort by the student. The fact of the matter is that in order to be successful you will have to make a commitment to your studies because there are no shortcuts to quality learning. Now, while there are no shortcuts to learning, there are a tremendous number of resources available to students that can make learning a little more fun.

The purpose of this section is to point you toward a number of "teacher approved" online resources that will help you prepare for the exam. The first resource on the list is your textbook's Web site, MyPsychLab. You will find a number of self-assessment tests as well as multimedia resources including audio, video, simulations and animations that are designed to support your learning. These resources are specifically designed to accompany your textbook, so you can be confident you are getting high-quality, accurate content. It is important to note that the resources available in MyPsychLab are organized around the topics you need to study to best prepare for the AP exam. The vastness of the Internet can result in students spending time on interesting, entertaining, and dramatic activities that have no bearing on their ability to be successful on the AP exam, so stick close to the recommendations of your teachers whenever you use resources from the Web.

Another quality resource is the APA Online Psychology Laboratory (OPL can be found at http://opl.apa.org/). Students can participate in a large number of demonstrations and analyze data. OPL is supported by the American Psychological Association, and your teacher will need to set up an account for your class so you can participate in the demonstrations.

A third, and very relevant source, is the College Board Web site for AP Psychology. Through this Web site, students can access topic outlines, information about the exam, past exam FRQs, scoring guidelines, and sample multiple-choice questions. AP Central for students is also available and provides numerous resources for AP students.

The final area to look for resources on the Web is AP Psychology teacher Web sites and blogs. These teacher-built Web sites vary in focus and style, but they often contain some of the most valuable materials for students. AP Psychology teachers are "in the trenches" with their students, and they have a keen eye for quality and relevance. On many occasions teacher sites contain contact information, and a quick email can be rewarded with a lengthy reply explaining a concept or answering a question about AP Psychology. HINT: Look for Web sites developed by teachers who have experience as an AP exam reader. AP Psychology teachers tend to be in agreement that participating as an AP exam reader is the best experience they can have when it comes to going back and helping their students prepare for the exam. As an exam reader, teachers are able to share ideas with a large number of other psychology teachers, and as a result they add to their knowledge, extend their repertoire of high-impact lessons for their classes, and grow their professional network. Along with knowledge and networking, teachers gather little "nuggets" that they like to utilize in their classroom, and the next section will share a few of the "greatest hits" for helping students remember content from the class.

Mnemonics

Mnemonic devices are handy ways for teachers to help students make strong memories out of the terms and concepts from class. While they come in many forms, the best of the best are simple, easy to use, and effective. The following is a quick list of memory helpers from a number of different AP Psychology teachers.

"So Peter Can Fly"—this phrase can help you remember the Piaget stages of cognitive development in the correct order: Sensory motor, Pre-operational, Concrete operations, and Formal operations.

"PONNOR"—this word can help you remember the difference between proactive and retroactive interference in memory: Pro-active Old interferes with New / New interferes with Old Retroactive.

"SAME"—this word can help you remember the direction of neuron communication: Sensory Afferent Motor Efferent.

"BATS–D"—this word can help you remember the different brain wave patterns associated with the stages of sleep: Beta, Alpha, Theta, Sleep Spindles, and Delta.

Punnett Square

Another helpful way of organizing information is the Punnett square. The Punnett square is used in a large number of psychology topics. Following is an illustration of a Punnett square as it applies to dominant and recessive genes followed by a list of other topics that can be mapped onto the square.

Punnett Square for Genetics	B	B
B	Bb	BB
b	Bb	bb

Other topics that map out on a Punnett square:
   James Marcia's identity states
   Balanced placebo study design
   Baumrind's parenting styles
   Reinforcement and punishment

Part Three

The final topic in this section is about do's and don'ts for exam day, and it includes tips for multiple-choice questions and FRQ responses. It is important to note that it is difficult to provide a comprehensive list that will address every student's needs, so the following are a few suggestions that are considered effective for most students.

Multiple-Choice Testing Tips

1. Read the entire question and all of the choices before selecting an answer.
2. Double check the bubble you penciled in to make sure it is the correct bubble.
3. If you don't know an answer, move on to the next question.
4. It is ok to skip a few questions and come back to them later. Just be very careful with your numbering and be sure to answer every question. One tendency in multiple-choice test questions is that the longest answer with the most detail is a good candidate for a guess. Also, to rule out choices on a multiple-choice question, you can look for absolutes like "always," "never," or "must" because there are not many absolutes in psychology research.
5. Take a few "mini" breaks during the test to relax and refocus.
6. Be judicious about second-guessing yourself. Research indicates that you are more likely to improve your score than hurt it by changing a dubious answer, so be ready to make a correction, especially if you misread part of the question or made an error marking an answer.
7. Do not think of the questions as "trick questions." While they may be difficult to answer, the test designers are not trying to be deceptive. Thinking of questions as being a "trick" can lead to imagining unlikely scenarios that are unclear because of "reading into" the question. Take the questions at face value, and if you are still unsure about an answer, go with the answer you have the best "feeling" about. There may be a reason that you have such a feeling for that answer.
8. Review your test for accuracy.
9. Keep working and don't dwell on a difficult question. You need to budget your time and stick to your budget.
10. Finally, choose to be optimistic about the exam. While there is conflicting research on the effects of optimism on test performance, few would question that being optimistic is a healthy approach to life's events, including taking an AP Psychology exam.

FRQ Testing Tips

1. Always attempt to answer all parts of the question.
2. Write down everything that you know about the topic including definitions, examples, and details that are relevant.
3. Be sure to write legibly. Poor handwriting can cost you points if your exam reader is unable to decipher what you wrote.
4. Budget your time and move on to the second question at the half-way point.
5. Do not spend time writing a lengthy introduction. Focus on the subparts of the question and start with the ones you know the best.
6. Do not spend time writing a lengthy conclusion. Move on to the next question and make good use of your time.
7. Use the language of the discipline. Example: Do not write, "He gave the dog a treat." It is better to write "He shaped the dog's behavior by using a treat as positive reinforcement."
8. Do not skip pages in your exam booklet. Start your second answer right after your first answer.
9. Do not waste time doodling, writing an apology, or writing anything else that is not relevant to your answer.
10. This next point is a more recent phenomenon, and it is with some reservation that it is mentioned. Through social networking Web sites, some students have popularized the idea of writing into AP written responses various coordinated quotes from movies, popular media, and songs. This is highly frowned upon and, in some cases, has led to severe consequences. The message here is, "Just don't do it!"

1. Preparing for the exam is a long-term process and needs to begin early. Do not wait for the last week of class and start cramming. Be in a constant state of reviewing and relearning.
2. Seek out and complete a large number of practice multiple-choice exams. The more ways you see a question posed, the better your chances are of recognizing the correct answer.
3. On exam day you should be sure to get a good night's rest the night before, get some light exercise in the morning, eat a nutritious meal that is moderate in the amount of carbohydrates, keep hydrated, avoid excessive amounts of caffeine, dress warmly, and bring a snack.
4. Consider preparing for the AP exam as a marathon and pace yourself accordingly. Be aware that a long and intense course can be fatiguing and you may need to give yourself a few breaks along the way.
5. Recognize that no person can know everything about psychology, and it is likely that some of the content that appears on the exam will be unfamiliar to you. Relax, be confident, and move on to the next question.
6. On test day follow all AP test-taking protocols carefully. Do not jeopardize your grade or the grade of any other student with a testing violation, such as bringing your cell phone into the exam area or sharing test information.

Conclusion

After reading through the introductory material to this test preparation guide, you now have a "big picture" view of the AP exam and testing process, you have learned some tips on how to prepare for the exam, and you have a list of strategies that you can use to improve your preparation. Along the path to exam day you will find that the unfamiliar language and terms of psychology start sinking in and connections between concepts, called schema, will begin to emerge in your thinking. The rest of this guide is designed to help you better understand the 14 AP Psychology topics and to keep your focus on the critical material you need to learn in order to maximize your performance on the exam. Enjoy your studies in AP Psychology and remember that no matter how distant, every journey begins with your first step.

YOU KNOW YOU HAVE MASTERED THE MAIN TOPICS IN THIS CHAPTER IF YOU ARE ABLE TO. . .

- Define psychology and describe the four goals that psychologists hope to achieve.
- Describe the history of psychology.
- Discuss the current state of psychology, including the most common perspectives and major professions in the field.
- Describe the scientific method and discuss its strengths and weaknesses.
- Describe and apply descriptive and inferential statistical analysis.
- Explain the basic guidelines and ethical concerns of psychological research.
- Introduce the criteria for critical thinking and its application in psychology.

RAPID REVIEW

Psychology is defined as the scientific study of behavior and mental processes. The goals of psychology are to describe, explain, predict, and control the behaviors and mental process of both humans and animals. The goals of psychology can be thought of in terms of what, why, when, and how behaviors and mental processes occur.

The field of psychology is relatively new (around 125 years old) but has its origins in the much older fields of physiology and philosophy. Wilhelm Wundt formed the first psychology laboratory in Germany in 1879. Wundt used the method of **objective introspection** in an attempt to objectively study human thought processes. Because of his innovative efforts, Wundt is often referred to as the father of psychology. The reality, however, is that multiple people in multiple locations began studying psychology and promoting their particular perspective around the same time. Five historical perspectives are discussed in the text.

Edward Titchener, a student of Wundt's, expanded on Wundt's ideas and brought the method of objective introspection to the United States. Titchener called his approach **structuralism** because his ultimate goal was to describe the precise structure of our mental processes. At the same time in the United States, William James was focused on discovering how our mental processes help us to function in our daily lives and began to promote his viewpoint known as **functionalism**. The terms structuralism and functionalism are no longer used to describe specific viewpoints in the field of psychology. Meanwhile, back in Germany, the Gestalt psychologists were studying how sensation and perception create a whole pattern that is greater than the sum of the individual components. Max Wertheimer was a major proponent of **Gestalt psychology**. In neighboring Austria, Sigmund Freud developed his theory of **psychoanalysis** based on the concept of the unconscious. Freud believed the unconscious played an important role in controlling our day-to-day behaviors and thoughts. Freud's theory is also referred to as the psychodynamic perspective. On the opposite end of the spectrum, and back in the United States, was John Watson. Watson expanded the findings of Russian physiologist Ivan Pavlov to promote the perspective of **behaviorism**. The behaviorists believed that psychology should focus on concepts that could be studied scientifically, and they felt that the only area of psychology that could be approached scientifically was observable behavior.

Today, there are eight major perspectives within the field of psychology. The **psychodynamic perspective** focuses on the role of the unconscious. **Behaviorism** attempts to study psychology by focusing on observable actions and events. The **humanistic perspective** emphasizes human potential and free will. The **biological perspective** focuses on the biology underlying our behavior and thoughts, while the **cognitive perspective** focuses on the thoughts or "cognitions" themselves. **Cognitive neuroscience** is a specific area of the cognitive perspective that focuses on the physical changes in the brain that occur when we think, remember, or engage in other mental processes. The **sociocultural perspective** explores the role of social and cultural factors on our behaviors and thoughts, while the **evolutionary perspective** attempts to explain behavior and thoughts in terms of their adaptive or "survival" qualities. The **biopsychosocial perspective** is holistic and focuses on the biology, psychology, and social interactions that shape human behavior.

There are many professional opportunities within the field of psychology. A **psychologist** attends graduate school to obtain a doctorate degree (either a Ph.D., Ed.D., or Psy.D.) and can select one of many career options from research to counseling to consulting for a business. **Psychiatrists** receive a medical degree (M.D.), treat serious psychological disorders, and can prescribe medication for their patients. A **psychiatric social worker** receives a Master of Social Work (M.S.W.) degree and provides counseling to patients or possibly conducts research. Two types of research to consider include **basic research,** for the sake of gaining scientific knowledge, and **applied research**, aimed at answering real-world problems.

Psychologists use the **scientific method** to reduce bias and error in their observations. The steps of the scientific method include asking a question, turning your question into a **hypothesis**—a statement about what you believe the actual answer is—testing your hypothesis, drawing a conclusion, and reporting your findings. Your findings can then be further strengthened if other researchers conduct a study and draw the same conclusions as you did, or in other words if other researchers **replicate** your findings. The method you use to test your hypothesis depends on which of the four goals of psychology you are attempting to achieve. If you would like to answer the question of "what" (goal = describe), you would use a descriptive method. **Naturalistic observation** provides a realistic picture of behavior but can become biased through the **observer effect** (subjects act differently when they know they are being watched) and **observer bias** (the researcher only sees what he or she wants to see). Laboratory observation is similar to naturalistic observation, but the participants are observed in a laboratory setting instead of "out in nature." Sometimes a researcher will disguise himself or herself as an actual participant in order to reduce the observer effect. This approach is called **participant observation**. A **case study** is a detailed investigation of one individual, or case, and can provide a great deal of information about that one person but is hard to generalize to a larger population. For a **survey**, researchers ask a group of subjects a series of questions. Surveys allow researchers to gather a lot of information quickly. However, with a survey there is no guarantee that the subjects will answer the questions truthfully. Also, researchers must be sure to take a **representative sample** of the **population** they are interested in. A researcher interested in discovering the relationship between two variables would use a method that mathematically measures the strength and nature of a potential **correlation**. A **correlation coefficient** tells the researcher the direction and strength of the relationship. The coefficient will always be a number between -1.00 and $+1.00$. A correlation shows that a relationship between two variables exists but cannot explain the cause of the relationship. In order to answer the question of "why," a researcher must conduct an experiment. Remember the example with the churches and the bars. The new churches did not cause the construction of the new bars. In an **experiment**, the researcher manipulates a variable (the **independent variable**) and measures some response from the participants (the **dependent variable**). In order to measure the dependent variable, the researcher must come up with an **operational definition** for the variable. An operational definition is a set of instructions that explains exactly how to measure the variable. For example, aggressive behavior could be operationally defined as the number of times a subject swings a toy sword in a five-minute observation period. The overall goal of the experiment is to keep everything the same except the independent variable. In order to accomplish this, the researcher usually observes two groups: an **experimental group** and a **control group**. The researcher will most likely use **random assignment** to determine which participants will go in which group. Often, the control group receives a fake treatment in order to control for the **placebo effect** in which the participant's expectations actually influence the results of the experiment. Normally, the subjects are not told which group they are in (**single-blind study**). In order to control for any expectations, the experimenter might have (the **experimenter effect**) the study is often designed so that neither the participants nor the experimenter know who is in what group (**double-blind study**). All psychological research must follow the ethical guidelines specified by the American Psychological Association.

Statistics are used by psychologists to summarize and make decisions about data gathered from research. **Descriptive statistics** are used to summarize data. The two types of descriptive statistics are measures of central tendency and measures of variability. To help visualize the data an illustration called a **frequency distribution,** in the form of a table or graph, is used to show how often different numbers appear in the data set. One form of a frequency distribution is a **histogram** and a second form is a **polygon**. The **normal curve** or "bell curve" is used as a model because it has specific relationships to measures of central tendency and **variability**. If a distribution isn't normal in shape it is described as a **skewed distribution**. A

positive skew contains extreme scores on the high end of a distribution and a **negative skew** contains extreme scores on the low end of a distribution. A **bimodal distribution** has two high points instead of just one high point in the curve. A **measure of central tendency** is used to summarize data and represents the central part of a frequency distribution. The three measures of central tendency are the **mean**, **median**, and **mode**. Extreme scores in a distribution are called **outliers** and can distort the accuracy of a measure of central tendency. **Measures of variability**, including **range** and **standard deviation**, determine how clustered or spread out scores are from the central scores. One way to compare different sets of data is to compute a **z score**, which indicates how the data sets deviate from a standard curve. **Inferential statistics** are used to determine if the results of an experiment have **statistical significance** and learn if the results occurred because of chance or because of the change in the independent variable. One method for determining if the results of an experiment are statistically significant is to calculate a **_t_-test** that would result in a single number (_t_) that evaluates the probability that the difference between the two groups of data resulting from an experiment is due to chance. The probability that the results are due to chance is symbolized by the letter _p_ and a less than 5 percent likely hood that the results of an experiment are due to chance is a commonly accepted standard in psychology research. A **significant difference** is reported when the results of a study have less than a 5 percent probability to be the product of chance.

To ensure the ethical treatment of people, internal review boards evaluate proposed research. Guidelines for doing research with people include, the well-being of participants, informed consent, deception must be justified, a participant's right to withdraw, participants must be protected and informed of possible risk, debriefing of participants, confidentiality, and correcting possible undesirable consequences for participants. Animals are used in research and ethical considerations are made especially to avoid exposing animals to any unnecessary pain or suffering.

Understanding the scientific method can help you in your daily life as you apply the four principles of **critical thinking** to problems you face day to day. The four criteria are that (1) most truths need to be tested, (2) all evidence is not equal, (3) authorities are not always right, and (4) an open mind is still important.

STUDY HINTS

1. Be careful not to confuse the independent variable (i.v.) with the dependent variable (d.v.). The independent variable is the variable the researcher manipulates her or himself. If you think about it as if you were the researcher conducting the experiment, the <u>i</u>ndependent variable is the one that **I** control. Another way to make sure you have correctly labeled the variables in an experiment is to insert the variable names into the following phrase and make sure it still makes sense. The test phrase is:

    How _____ affects _____ .
                   (i.v.)   (d.v.)

    Here is an example for you to practice using the test phrase.

    > _A researcher conducts a study looking at the color of different rooms and aggressiveness. She takes a group of 40 college students and randomly assigns 20 to the red room and 20 to the blue room. After the students have been in the rooms for 30 minutes, she measures each person's aggressiveness level on a scale of 1 to 10. In this experiment, which variable is the independent variable and which is the dependent? Try inserting the variable names into the phrase above._

    You can see that "How aggressiveness affects room color" does not make sense and is not what the researcher is interested in. However, "How room color affects aggressiveness" does correspond to the researchers' goals. So in this case, the room color is the independent variable and aggressiveness is the dependent variable.

Try one more example.

A researcher conducts an experiment to study memory skills and caffeine intake. The researcher has a total of 20 volunteer subjects. He gives 10 subjects a can of caffeinated soda and the other 10 subjects receive a can of decaffeinated soda. He then has all the subjects complete a memory task. What are his independent and dependent variables? Try inserting the variable names into the phrase above.

Again, you can see that "How memory skills affect caffeine intake" does not make sense and is not what the researcher is interested in. However, "How caffeine intake affects memory skills" does correspond to the researcher's goals. So in this case, the caffeine intake is the independent variable and memory skill is the dependent variable.

2. The concept of operational definitions is introduced in this chapter. An operational definition can be thought of as a recipe telling a researcher precisely how to make his or her observations. In other words, they define the operations or procedures the researcher should go through in order to record his or her data. Operational definitions are based on behaviors and actions that can be observed, and they are much different than the definitions given in a standard dictionary. For example, the dictionary might define fear as feeling anxious or apprehensive about a possible situation. However, that definition does not tell the researcher how to measure one individual's level of fear. On the other hand, the researcher might operationally define fear as the percent increase in heart rate from a baseline level during a two-minute observation period.

Try this example yourself.

Dictionary definition of anger: _____

Operational definition of anger: _____

The dictionary might define anger as a strong feeling of displeasure. However, an operational definition of anger might be something like the number of times an adult slams his or her fists on the table.

Now, try to figure out what variable is being operationally defined below.

The number of times a person laughs within a five-minute period.

Operational definition of _____:

The score an individual receives on an IQ test.

Operational definition of _____:

The first example is operationally defining the variable of happiness, and the second example gives an operational definition for intelligence.

3. Positive and negative skew is often difficult for students to understand. Skew occurs when the results of an experiment are graphed and they create a graph that differs from the standard curve, resulting in a graph that is somewhat "skewed" from the standard curve so that the shape is not like that of a "bell" curve. Instead the curve has a "tail" to the right or the left of the center that accounts for extreme outlier scores that are very distant from the more common scores in the center. The statistical description of a positive skew is that the mean of a distribution of numbers

is a number greater than the mode; therefore, if you were looking at the numbers on a number line, the mean would be to the right of the mode and the data would be skewed positively. A negative skew would be the reverse, and the mean would be a number less than the mode.

NEGATIVE SKEW

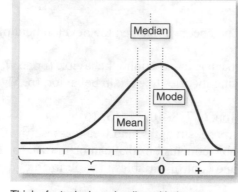

Think of a typical number line with the center at the mode. The mean is to the "Negative" side of the mode.

POSITIVE SKEW

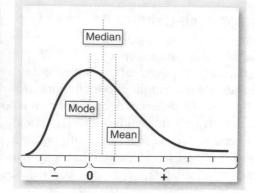

Think of a typical number line with the center at the mode. The mean is to the "Positive" side of the mode.

Examples of positively and negatively skewed curves

LEARNING OBJECTIVES

1.1 *What defines psychology as a field of study, and what are psychology's four primary goals?*

1.2 *Who were some of the early pioneers in psychology, and how did structuralism and functionalism differ?*

1.3 *What were the basic ideas and who were the important people behind the early approaches known as Gestalt, psychoanalysis, and behaviorism?*

1.4 *What are the basic ideas behind the eight modern perspectives, and what were the important contributions of Skinner, Maslow, and Rogers?*

1.5 *How does a psychologist differ from a psychiatrist, and what are the other types of professionals who work in the various areas of psychology?*

1.6 *Why is psychology considered a science, and what are the steps in using the scientific method?*

1.7 *How are naturalistic and laboratory settings used to describe behavior, and what are some of the advantages and disadvantages associated with these settings?*

1.8 *How are case studies and surveys used to describe behavior, and what are some drawbacks to each of these methods?*

1.9 *What is the correlational technique, and what does it tell researchers about relationships?*

1.10 *What are the steps involved in designing an experiment?*

1.11 *How do the placebo and experimenter effects cause problems in an experiment, and what are some ways to control for these effects?*

1.12 *What are some basic elements of a real-world experiment?*

1.13 *Why are statistics important to psychologists and psychology majors?*

1.14 *What types of tables and graphs represent patterns in data?*

1.15 *What types of statistics examine central tendencies in data?*

1.16 *What types of statistics examine variations in data?*

1.17 *How can statistics be used to determine if differences in sets of data are large enough to be due to something other than chance variation?*

| 1.18 | *What are some ethical concerns that can occur when conducting research with people and animals?* | 1.19 | *What are the basic principles of critical thinking, and how can critical thinking be useful in everyday life?* |

AP LEARNING OBJECTIVES

1. Recognize how philosophical and physiological perspectives shaped the development of psychological thought. (p. 6)
2. Describe and compare different theoretical approaches in explaining behavior. (pp. 6, 7, 9, 14)
3. Recognize the strengths and limitations of applying theories to explain behavior. (p. 5)
4. Distinguish the different domains of psychology. (p. 17)
5. Identify major historical figures in psychology. (pp. 6, 7, 8, 10, 11, 13, 16)
6. Differentiate types of research with regard to purpose, strengths, and weaknesses. (pp. 22, 27)
7. Describe how research design drives the reasonable conclusions that can be drawn. (p. 27)
8. Identify independent, dependent, confounding, and control variables in experimental designs. (p. 29)
9. Distinguish between random assignment of participants to conditions in experiments and random selection of participants, primarily in correlational studies and surveys. (p. 30)
10. Predict the validity of behavioral explanations based on the quality of research design. (p. 31)
11. Distinguish the purposes of descriptive statistics and inferential statistics. (pp. 22, 27, 34)
12. Apply basic descriptive statistical concepts, including interpreting and constructing graphs and calculating simple descriptive statistics. (p. 34)
13. Discuss the value of reliance on operational definitions and measurement in behavioral research. (p. 29)
14. Identify how ethical issues inform and constrain research practices. (p. 42)
15. Describe how ethical and legal guidelines protect research participants and promote sound ethical practice. (p. 43)
16. Discuss psychology's abiding interest in how heredity, environment, and evolution work together to shape behavior. (p. 16)
17. Predict how traits and behavior can be selected for their adaptive value. (p. 16)
18. Interpret the meaning of scores in terms of the normal curve. (pp. 35, 40)
19. Articulate the impact of social and cultural categories on self-concept and relations with others. (p. 15)

CHAPTER GLOSSARY

applied research	research conducted to answer real world problems.
basic research	research conducted for the sake of gaining scientific knowledge.
behaviorism	the science of behavior that focuses on observable behavior only.
bimodal distribution	occurs when there are two high points instead of just one high point in a curve which most likely indicates two groups in the data set.
biological perspective	perspective that attributes human and animal behavior to biological events occurring in the body, such as genetic influences, hormones, and the activity of the nervous system.
biopsychosocial perspective	perspective that combines three major facets of an individual—biology, psychology, and social interactions—in trying to help explain a person either medically or psychologically.
case study	study of one individual in great detail; modern perspective that focuses on memory, intelligence, perception, problem solving, and learning.
cognitive neuroscience	study of the physical changes in the brain and nervous system that occur during thinking or other mental processes.

cognitive perspective	modern perspective that focuses on memory, intelligence, perception, problem solving, and learning.
control group	subjects in an experiment that are not subjected to the independent variable and who may receive a placebo treatment.
correlation	a measure of the relationship between two variables.
correlation coefficient	a number for measuring a correlation that indicates the strength and the direction of the relationship between the two variables.
critical thinking	making reasoned judgments about claims.
dependent variable	variable in an experiment that represents the measurable response or behavior of the subjects in the experiment.
descriptive statistics	a way of organizing numbers and summarizing them so that they can be understood.
double-blind study	study in which neither the experimenter nor the subjects know if the subjects are in the experimental or control group.
evolutionary perspective	perspective that focuses on the biological bases of universal mental characteristics that all humans share.
experiment	a deliberate manipulation of a variable to see if corresponding changes in behavior result, allowing the determination of cause and effect relationships.
experimental group	subjects in an experiment that are subjected to the independent variable.
experimenter effect	tendency of the experimenter's expectations for a study to unintentionally influence the results of the study.
frequency distribution	scores represented in graph or pictorial form
functionalism	early perspective in psychology associated with William James, in which the focus of study is how the mind allows people to adapt, live, work, and play.
Gestalt psychology	early perspective in psychology focusing on perception and sensation, particularly the perception of patterns and whole figures.
histogram	a bar graph used as a visual way to look at data from frequency distributions.
humanistic perspective	perspective that emphasizes human potential and the idea that people have the freedom to choose their own destiny.
hypothesis	a statement about some event that can then be tested through observation.
independent variable	variable in an experiment that is manipulated by the experimenter.
inferential statistics	statistical techniques used to determine difference between meaningful vs. chance results
mean	the arithmetic average of a distribution of numbers.
measure of central tendency	a summation of data that best represents the central part of a frequency distribution.
measures of variability	used to discover how "spread out" the scores are from each other.
median	the score that falls in the middle of an ordered distribution of scores.
mode	the number that appears more times in a distribution of numbers than any other.
naturalistic observation	study in which the researcher observes people or animals in their normal environment.
negative skew	a distribution with a concentration of extreme scores on the low end.
normal curve	a common frequency distribution that is sometimes called the bell cureve.

objective introspection	the process of objectively examining and measuring one's own thoughts and mental activities.
observer bias	tendency of observers to see what they expect to see.
observer effect	tendency of people or animals to behave differently from normal when they know they are being observed.
operational definition	definition of a variable of interest that allows it to be directly measured.
outliers	extreme scores of very high or low values that can distort the accuracy of a measure of central tendency.
participant observation	approach to research in which the researcher actually becomes a participant in a group that is being observed.
placebo effect	the phenomenon in which the expectations of the participants in a study can influence their behavior.
polygon	a line graph that can represent the data in a frequency distribution and allows the shape of the data set to be easily viewed.
population	the entire group of people or animals that the researcher is interested in.
positive skew	a distribution of score with a concentration of extreme scores on the high end
psychiatric social worker	a social worker with some training in therapy methods who focuses on environmental conditions that can have an impact on mental disorders, such as poverty, overcrowding, stress, and drug abuse.
psychiatrist	a medical doctor who has specialized in the diagnosis and treatment of psychological disorders.
psychoanalysis	an insight therapy based on the theory of Freud, emphasizing the revealing of unconscious conflicts; Freud's term for both the theory of personality and the therapy based on it.
psychodynamic perspective	modern version of psychoanalysis that is more focused on the development of a sense of self and the discovery of other motivations behind a person's behavior than sexual motivations.
psychologist	a professional with an academic degree and specialized training in one or more areas of psychology.
psychology	the scientific study of behavior and mental processes.
random assignment	process of assigning subjects to the experimental or control groups randomly, so that each subject has an equal chance of being in either group.
range	the difference between the highest and lowest score in a set of scores.
replicate	in research, repeating a study or experiment to see if the same results will be obtained in an effort to demonstrate reliability of results.
representative sample	randomly selected sample of subjects from a larger population.
scientific method	system of gathering data so that bias and error in measurement are reduced.
significant difference	when the results of an experiment are found to produce a difference between the groups that is greater than results that could be the product of chance.
single-blind study	study in which the subjects do not know if they are in the experimental or the control group.
skewed distribution	when the distribution is not even on both sides of a central score with the highest frequency.
sociocultural perspective	perspective that focuses on the relationship between social behavior and culture.
standard deviation	a number that shows how each score in a data set deviates, on average, from the mean.

statistical significance	a way to test differences to see how likely it is that those differences are real and not just caused by the random variations in behavior.
structuralism	early perspective in psychology associated with Wilhelm Wundt and Edward Titchener, in which the focus of study is the structure or basic elements of the mind.
survey	study conducted by asking a series of questions to a group of people.
t-test	a calculation that determines the likelihood that the difference between the mean of two groups of scores from an experiment are due to chance.
variability	how spread out the numbers are in a set of data.
z score	used to compare different sets of data and indicates how a set of data varies from the distribution of scores in a standard curve.

CHAPTER PRACTICE TEST

For the following multiple-choice questions, select the answer you feel best answers the question.

1. How is psychology different from philosophy?
    a) Psychology uses the scientific method to answer questions.
    b) Psychology uses conjecture and rationalization to answer research questions.
    c) Psychology is interested in questions related to human behavior.
    d) There is no difference between philosophy and psychology.
    e) The field of psychology is much older than the field of philosophy.

2. A researcher is attempting to design a program to help people stop smoking. The goal he or she is attempting to achieve is to
    a) describe.
    b) predict.
    c) explain.
    d) control.
    e) summarize.

3. A researcher is interested in finding out the percentage of adolescents in the United States who have depression. The goal he or she is attempting to achieve is to
    a) describe.
    b) predict.
    c) explain.
    d) control.
    e) summarize.

4. Which of the following research questions would NOT fall within the field of psychology?
    a) How can you increase the amount of time a female bird stays with its mate after the birdlings hatch?
    b) What changes occur in the brain of a rat that has been deprived of sleep?
    c) Why do students perform better on exams when the exam is given in the same room in which they learned the material?
    d) How do environmental stimuli influence the development of the neural network?
    e) All of the questions above could be studied by a psychologist.

5. The first psychology laboratory was opened in _____ in order to study _____.
    a) 1065, psychological disorders
    b) 1946, learning
    c) 1879, objective introspection
    d) 1920, functionalism
    e) 1809, biopsychology

6. Which of these is the most accurate definition of the discipline of psychology?
    a) the science of behavior
    b) the science of mental processes
    c) the science of behavior and mental processes
    d) the science of human behavior
    e) the science of human behavior and mental processes

7. The psychological perspective of structuralism focused on
    a) how the whole structure is bigger than the individual parts.
    b) understanding each individual structure of human thought.
    c) how behavior was functional in our daily activities.
    d) how mental thought helps us structure our daily activities.
    e) the structure of society at large.

8. The school of psychology called *structuralism* used a technique called _____, which involved reporting the contents of consciousness to study a person's experiences.
    a) intervention
    b) objective introspection
    c) individuation
    d) insight inventory
    e) induction

9. William James believed that mental processes could not be studied as an isolated, static event but instead needed to be viewed in terms of how they helped people perform in their daily lives. James was a strong proponent for
    a) structuralism.
    b) functionalism.
    c) objective introspection.
    d) behaviorism.
    e) the humanistic perspective.

10. Gestalt psychologists are associated with which of the following sayings?
    a) The pineal gland is the seat of the human soul.
    b) Psychology should reach into the soul of mankind.
    c) Behavior should be broken down into its individual components.
    d) The whole is greater than the sum of its parts.
    e) Dreams are symbolic and should be interpreted.

11. Freud said phobias were _____, whereas Watson said phobias were _____.
    a) learned; inherited
    b) repressed conflicts; learned
    c) learned; inborn
    d) sexual; unconscious
    e) conditioned; unconditioned

12. Which of the following statements would Sigmund Freud have most likely been overheard saying?
    a) "Human behavior is largely determined by our own free will."
    b) "The only way to understand behavior is to study behavior."
    c) "We will never understand why people do the things they do."
    d) "The key to understanding behavior is in the unconscious."
    e) "The conscious mind is the largest and most influential component of the psyche."

13. What was John Watson's biggest complaint about the field of psychology?
   a) Psychologists were attempting to study nonobservable events using the scientific method.
   b) Psychologists were spending too much time studying the behavior of humans.
   c) Psychology was not focused enough on the free will of humans.
   d) Psychologists were ignoring the role of the unconscious in determining behavior.
   e) Psychologists were spending too much time doing research.

14. A researcher who studies the chemical changes in the brains of patients with depression would be approaching psychology from which perspective?
   a) behaviorist
   b) psychodynamic
   c) cognitive
   d) sociocultural
   e) biological

15. The biopsychosocial perspective is best described as:
   a) focused on the subconscious mind.
   b) clearly putting more emphasis on genetics than on environment in explaining human behavior.
   c) a holistic approach to explaining human behavior.
   d) the first major perspective in psychology.
   e) a perspective that is one-dimensional in its approach to explaining human behavior.

16. A humanistic psychologist would be interested in which of the following research studies?
   a) describing a group of people who claim to have reached their full potential
   b) using rewards to change a person's behavior
   c) understanding the role of the unconscious in a child's decision to disobey his or her parents
   d) investigating the role of hormones in the mating behavior of birds
   e) figuring out that visual illusions are possible

17. Cognitive psychologists are interested in
   a) social interactions.
   b) the adaptive value of particular behaviors.
   c) mental processes.
   d) the use of rewards and punishments.
   e) the unconscious.

18. Taylor received her degree from a medical school and now meets with patients on a daily basis. Most of her patients have a serious psychological disorder, and often Taylor will prescribe medication to treat the disorder. Taylor is a
   a) psychologist.
   b) psychiatrist.
   c) psychiatric social worker.
   d) human factors psychologist.
   e) school nurse.

19. Vido has an M.S.W. and is interested in working on the causes of poverty. What type of professional is Vido most likely to become?
    a) educational psychologist
    b) psychiatrist
    c) school psychologist
    d) psychiatric nurse
    e) psychiatric social worker

20. Why do psychologists use the scientific method?
    a) It is easier to use than other methods.
    b) All academic fields must use the scientific method.
    c) It is the only method available to answer questions.
    d) It prevents experiments from being replicated.
    e) It reduces bias and error in measurement.

21. The tendency to look for information that supports one's own belief is called _____.
    a) the principle of falsifiability
    b) confirmation bias
    c) criterion validity
    d) volunteer bias
    e) the null hypothesis

22. Deb spent the entire day at the park observing children with their parents to see whether fathers or mothers spent more time playing with their kids. Deb used the method of
    a) naturalistic observation.
    b) laboratory observation.
    c) survey.
    d) case study.
    e) participant observation.

23. Which of the following topics would be best studied using the case study method?
    a) the reaction times of adults in a stressful situation
    b) the sleep pattern of adolescents
    c) the impact of club sports involvement on female adolescent self-esteem
    d) the relationship between hyperactivity and sugar consumption
    e) the personality characteristics of a man accused of killing five people

24. What is an advantage of the survey method?
    a) nonrepresentative samples
    b) courtesy bias
    c) large amounts of information
    d) observer bias
    e) under reporting

25. A researcher stops people at the mall and asks them questions about their attitudes toward gun control. Which research technique is being used?
    a) survey
    b) experiment
    c) case study
    d) naturalistic observation
    e) placebo

26. A group of randomly selected subjects that matches the population on important characteristics such as age and sex is called _____.
    a) volunteer bias
    b) a representative sample
    c) the experimental group
    d) the control group
    e) the independent condition

27. The word *correlation* is often used as a synonym for _____.
    a) validity
    b) reliability
    c) variable
    d) unpredictable
    e) relationship

28. Which of the following correlation coefficients represents the strongest relationship between two variables?
    a) +0.62
    b) −0.98
    c) +0.01
    d) +1.24
    e) −0.50

29. A researcher finds that as the number of classes missed increases, the students' grades decrease. This is an example of a
    a) positive correlation.
    b) negative correlation.
    c) zero correlation.
    d) case study.
    e) monovariable correlation.

30. Marcy is trying to define *anxiety* in a way that can be empirically tested. She is attempting to find an appropriate _____.
    a) hypothesis
    b) operational definition
    c) double-blind study
    d) theory
    e) experimental bias

31. A researcher is investigating the effects of exercise on weight. What are the independent and dependent variables in this experiment?
    a) The dependent variable is weight; the independent variable is exercise.
    b) The independent variable is calories consumed; the dependent variable is diet.
    c) The independent variable is weight; the dependent variable is calories consumed.
    d) The dependent variable is amount of exercise; the independent variable is calories consumed.
    e) The dependent variable is exercise; the dependent variable is weight.

32. In a laboratory, smokers are asked to "drive" using a computerized driving simulator equipped with a stick shift and a gas pedal. The object is to maximize the distance covered by driving as fast as possible on a winding road while avoiding rear-end collisions. Some of the participants smoke a real cigarette immediately before climbing into the driver's seat. Others smoke a fake cigarette without nicotine. You are interested in comparing how many collisions the two groups have. In this study, the *cigarette without nicotine* is _____.
   a) the control group
   b) the driving simulator
   c) the experimental group
   d) the no-control group
   e) the socially biased group

33. A psychology professor feels that her students will do better on her exams if there is music playing while they take their exams. To test her hypothesis, she divides her class in half. One half takes the exam in a room with music playing, and the other half takes the exam in a similar room but without the music playing. In this case, the independent variable is
   a) the room the exam is taken in.
   b) the absence or presence of music playing.
   c) the exam.
   d) the students' scores on the exam.
   e) the students' random assignment.

34. For the experiment described in Question 33, the dependent variable is
   a) the room the exam is taken in.
   b) the absence or presence of music playing.
   c) the exam.
   d) the students' scores on the exam.
   e) the number of students in each group.

35. Twenty volunteers are brought into a sleep laboratory in the evening. Ten are allowed eight hours of sleep, while the other ten are only allowed two hours of sleep. In the morning, all 20 subjects are tested for their reaction time in a driving simulation program. For this experiment, the reaction time in the simulation program is the
   a) independent variable.
   b) illusory variable.
   c) confounding variable.
   d) random variable.
   e) dependent variable.

36. For the experiment described in Question 35, the amount of sleep allowed is the
   a) independent variable.
   b) dependent variable.
   c) confounding variable.
   d) random variable.
   e) disengaged variable.

37. Which of the following situations best illustrates the placebo effect?
    a) You sleep because you are tired.
    b) You throw up after eating bad meat.
    c) You have surgery to repair a defective heart valve.
    d) You drink a nonalcoholic drink and become "intoxicated" because you think it contains alcohol.
    e) You know you are in the experimental group and you behave the way you think the experimenter wants you to behave.

38. _____ is an experiment in which neither the participants nor the individuals running the experiment know if participants are in the experimental or the control group until after the results are tallied.
    a) A double-blind study
    b) Field research
    c) A single-blind study
    d) Correlational research
    e) The placebo design

39. Dr. Teresa Amabile conducted an actual experiment in which she had two groups of girls aged 7 to 10 years create artwork in the classroom. One group was told that the girl with the best artwork would receive a prize at the end of the session, and the other group was told that prizes would be raffled off when the session was over. Amabile then measured the level of creativity for the artwork in both groups and found that the second group had higher levels of creativity. In this experiment, the dependent variable is the
    a) prize.
    b) level of creativity.
    c) way the prize was distributed.
    d) group of girls.
    e) the length of the session.

40. Two ways psychologists use statistics with the data they collect are:
    a) summarizing the data and making judgments and decisions about the data.
    b) controlling the data and recording the data.
    c) skewing the data and deviating the data.
    d) analyzing the data and sampling the data.
    e) organizing the data and controlling the data.

41. The scores of students on a quiz are as follows: 9, 8, 9, 7, 2, 9, and 10. The mode for this list of scores is:
    a) 8.
    b) 9.
    c) 10.
    d) 2.
    e) 7.

42. The arithmetic average of a distribution of numbers is known as the:
    a) statistical significance.
    b) median score.
    c) mean score.
    d) correlation coefficient.
    e) mode score.

43. The median is a more accurate measure of central tendency in a set of scores that:
    a) clusters around the arithmetical average.
    b) contains scores that are bimodal.
    c) shows the differences between the experimental and control groups.
    d) is based on a very small sample of participants in an experiment.
    e) contains a few extreme scores that are outliers.

44. All inferential statistics have one thing in common.
    a) They are used to determine central tendency.
    b) They are used to find if the results of an experiment are statistically significant.
    c) They are used to find a positive or negative skew in a set of data.
    d) They are used to determine the variability in a set of data.
    e) They are used to compare the mean score to the median score in a set of data.

45. Each of the following is a common ethical guideline suggested by the American Psychological Association EXCEPT _____.
    a) participants must be informed of the nature of the research in clearly understandable language
    b) participants cannot be deceived or have information concealed from them at any time during an experiment
    c) risks, possible adverse effects, and limitations on confidentiality must be spelled out in advance
    d) informed consent must be documented
    e) experimenters must debrief participants

46. Which of the following is NOT one of the four principles of critical thinking?
    a) All truths need to be tested.
    b) An open mind is always important.
    c) Authorities cannot always be trusted.
    d) All evidence is not equal.
    e) It is better to use common sense and intuition to determine the truth.

47. Which of the following questions applies the concept of critical thinking to the real-world pseudo-psychology of astrology?
    a) What is my astrological sign?
    b) What does my astrological sign predict will happen to me today?
    c) How up to date are the charts used by astrologists today?
    d) Should I marry someone who is the same sign as I?
    e) Is today a good day to invest in the stock market?

CHAPTER PRACTICE TEST ANSWERS

1. a — Psychology bases its answers on observations, while philosophy answers its questions using logic and reasoning. Both fields are interested in human behavior. The field of psychology is only 125 years old, while philosophy is much older.

2. d — She is trying to change people's behaviors. This corresponds to the question of "how" (in other words, "How" do I help people to stop smoking?).

3. a — He would like to describe this particular group with regards to depression rates. He is trying to answer the question of "what." What is the current depression rate among U.S. teenagers?

4. e — All of the questions fall under the category of describing, predicting, explaining, or controlling behavior and/or mental processes of humans and animals.

5.   c   Wilhelm Wundt opened his laboratory in Germany in 1879 and used the method of objective introspection to study the basic elements of mental processes.

6.   c   Psychology deals with both behavior and mental processes and includes other animals besides humans.

7   b   Structuralists felt that mental processes had to be broken down into their most basic or elemental form in order to be understood.

8.   b   Objective introspection was used in an attempt to self-examine the structure of the mind. Although the word "intervention" looks similar, it has a completely different meaning.

9.   b   James believed we need to understand the *function* of mental processes.

10.   d   Gestalt psychologists believed that you had to look at the whole picture in order to understand the larger processes of perception and sensation and that it could not be broken down into its smaller components without losing its essence.

11.   b   Freud studied repressed (unconscious) conflict, and Watson studied observable behavior. Watson did not believe that the unconscious could be studied scientifically.

12.   d   Sigmund Freud was a major proponent of the perspective of psychoanalysis, which emphasizes the role of the unconscious on human behavior.

13.   a   John Watson started the idea of behaviorism that states the only subject matter that can be scientifically studied is observable behavior.

14.   e   The biological perspective focuses on studying the biological changes that underlie behavior and mental processes.

15.   c   The biopsychosocial perspective is a holistic approach to explaining human behavior because it includes biology, psychology, and social interaction.

16.   a   The humanistic perspective focuses on the uniqueness and potential of human beings and tries to suggest ways for humans to maximize their potential.

17.   c   Cognitive psychologists focus on "cognitions" or mental processes, including topics such as memory, decision making, problem solving, perception, language comprehension, creativity, and reasoning.

18.   b   Psychiatrists have M.D.s, counsel patients with serious disorders, and can prescribe medications.

19.   e   Psychiatric social workers typically have their Masters of Social Work (M.S.W.) and counsel patients with less severe disorders or focus on social issues such as poverty.

20.   e   The scientific method is based on observations so that the influence of the researcher's bias is minimized.

21.   b   The principle of falsifiability is not an actual principle in psychology.

22.   a   Naturalistic observation consists of recording behaviors as they occur in their normal settings.

23.   e   A case study focuses on one individual (or "case") and provides a detailed description of that individual.

24.   c   A survey allows the researcher to collect a large amount of information quickly. The other four options are all potential disadvantages of the survey method.

25.   a   A survey asks the same questions to many people, while naturalistic observation never involves asking questions.

26.   b   A representative sample is a randomly selected group that matches the population on important characteristics. An experimental group is not necessarily representative of the population.

27.   e   Correlation means relationship between two variables.

28.   b   The correlation coefficient must be between +1.00 and −1.00, so option D is automatically excluded. The sign of the coefficient indicates the direction of the relationship and the absolute value of the coefficient indicates the strength; therefore, 0.98 is the largest absolute value listed between 0 and 1.

29.   b   For a negative correlation, the variables move in the opposite direction. As one variable increases, the other one decreases. In this case, as the number of absences increase, the grade in class decreases.

30.   b   An operational definition defines responses in terms that allow them to be measured, while a hypothesis is an educated guess, not a definition.

31.   a   The exercise is controlled by the experimenter and is, therefore, *independent* of anything the participants do, while the participants' weight is expected to *depend* on the amount of exercise.

32.   a   A control group gets either no treatment or treatment that has no effect (in this case, experimenters are controlling for the possibility that the cigarette itself, and not the nicotine, might cause people to get into collisions).

33.   b   The independent variable is the variable the researcher manipulates. In this case, the instructor manipulated whether there was music playing or not.

34.   d   Recall the test phrase, "How _____ (*i.v.*) affects _____ (*d.v.*). The professor is testing "How music affects student test scores." The dependent variable is the subjects' responses. The room the test is taken in and the test itself should be the same for both groups.

35.   e   The reaction time is the response observed in the subject. It is not manipulated by the experimenter.

36.   a   Recall the test phrase, "How hours slept affects driving reaction time."

37.   d   The placebo effect is brought on by expectations, and in this case you felt drunk only because you believed you were drinking alcohol.

38.   a   The double-blind study is an experiment in which neither the participants nor the individuals running the experiment know if the participants are in the experimental or control group. In a single-blind study, only the participants are "blind."

39.   b   Dr. Amabile was looking at "how *method of reward* affects *creativity*," and creativity serves as the dependent variable.

40.   a   Summarizing the data and making judgments and decisions about the data is how psychologists use statistics to communicate their research findings.

41.   b   The mode is the most frequent number in a set of data.

42.   c   The arithmetic average of a distribution of numbers is the mean score.

43.   e   A list of scores that contains extreme or outlier scores will produce a positive or negative skew in the mean, and the median will be a more accurate measure to report.

44.   b   They are used to find if the results of an experiment are statistically significant beyond the possibility of chance.

45.   b   Participants may be deceived or have information concealed from them at any time during an experiment.

46.   e   Common sense and intuition are not reliable ways to understand human behavior.

47.   c   Critical thinking involves making reasoned judgments and questioning the basis that others are using to make judgments, such as in response c.

CHAPTER PRACTICE FREE RESPONSE QUESTION

You have 25 minutes to answer the following question. You must write in complete sentences and not just list facts. You should make your point clearly and use the language of psychology. Be sure to write legibly and respond to all parts of the question.

Mr. Smith, a high school psychology teacher, decided to study the effects of caffeine on achievement motivation in students at his school. Mr. Smith contacted his school's principal and gained permission from the principal to study the students in his classes. The next day Mr. Smith placed his first-period students in the control group and gave each student a noncaffeinated drink. Then he asked each student to complete a simple puzzle and timed how long it took the students to complete the puzzle. After lunch, he placed his eighth-period students into the experimental group and required his students to consume a caffeinated drink, and then he repeated the puzzle test with the experimental group. Mr. Smith found that the first-hour students' mean time to complete the puzzle was less than the eighth-hour students' mean time to complete the puzzle. A small number of first-hour students recorded extremely faster times to complete the puzzle than most of the other students. Mr. Smith concluded that caffeine has a negative effect on achievement motivation.

   A. Critique Mr. Smith's experimental design based on each of the following, and provide a suggestion on how to improve the research design:
- Random assignment
- Ethics
- Operational definition

   B. Critique Mr. Smith's conclusion based on each of the following, and provide a suggestion on how to improve the control of the experiment:
- Placebo effect
- Social factors
- Confounding variables

   C. Explain how the few very short times recorded for some of the first-period students could affect the analysis of the data.

SUGGESTED RUBRIC—Students should provide specific details and examples to support their assertions; definitions alone are not sufficient. Information about each topic should be discussed in the context of the question rather than abstractly. Successful essays may include the following arguments:

14 points

   A. Student must provide an evaluation of the experimental design on each of the points.
- Random assignment
  - Score—identifies that random assignment was not used to assign the students to the control or experimental groups.
  - Score—describes a method to randomly assign the students. Ex. Draw names, random number list, roll dice.
- Ethics
  - Score—identifies a relevant ethical issue. Ex. No parent permission slips, he required the students to participate, and he did not inform the students about the research or debrief the students after the study.
  - Score—describes a more ethical practice. Ex. Collects a signed parent permission slip from each student, make the experiment voluntary.
- Operational definition
  - Score—identifies the operational definition of "achievement motivation" as the time needed to complete the puzzle. Ex. Inferred that a lower time indicated a higher level of achievement motivation.
  - Score—explains why the operational definition may be inaccurate or incomplete. Ex. Other factors to achievement motivation such as persistence, accuracy, and difficulty of the task.

   B. Student must provide an evaluation of Mr. Smith's conclusion on each of the points.
- Placebo effect
  - Score—explains why the placebo effect needs to be controlled for in the experiment.
  - Score—explains how he could have controlled for placebo effect. Ex. Balanced placebo design.

- Social factors
  - Score—explains how social factors could influence the results.
  - Score—describes how to control for social factors. Ex. Blind or double-blind study.
- Confounding variables
  - Score—explains how uncontrolled variable could have skewed the results of the experiment. Ex. The first hour may have consumed caffeine just before school started.
  - Score—explains how to establish a better level of control in the experiment. Ex. Random assignment, sampling, standardization.

C.   Score—explains how a small number of extreme scores could affect the analysis of the data because of the potential for the extremely fast scores to skew the mean score for the first-period class.

YOU KNOW YOU HAVE MASTERED THE MAIN TOPICS IN THIS CHAPTER IF YOU ARE ABLE TO. . .

- Explain what neurons are and how they work to transfer and process information.
- Introduce the central and peripheral nervous systems and describe their roles in the body.
- Discuss the role of the endocrine system.
- Describe the methods used to observe the structure and activity of the brain.
- Identify the basic structures of the brain and explain their functions.

RAPID REVIEW

The **nervous system** is made up of a complex network of cells throughout your body. Since psychology is the study of behavior and mental processes, understanding how the nervous system works provides fundamental information about what is going on inside your body when you engage in a specific behavior, feel a particular emotion, or have an abstract thought. The field of study that deals with these types of questions is called **neuroscience**. The role of the nervous system is to carry information. Without your nervous system, you would not be able to think, feel, or act. The cells in the nervous system that carry information are called **neurons**. Information enters a neuron at the **dendrites**, then flows through the cell body (or **soma**) and down the **axon** in order to pass the information on to the next cell. Although neurons are the cells that carry the information, most of the nervous system consists of **glial cells**. Glial cells provide food, support, and insulation to the neuron cells. The insulation around the neuron is called **myelin** and works in a way very similar to the plastic coating of an electrical wire. Bundles of myelin-coated axons are wrapped together in cable-like structures called **nerves**.

Neurons use an electrical signal to send information from one end of its cell to the other. At rest, a neuron has a negative charge inside and a positive charge outside. When a signal arrives, gates in the cell wall next to the signal open and the positive charge moves inside. The positive charge inside the cell causes the next set of gates to open and those positive charges move inside. In this way, the electrical signal makes its way down the length of the cell. The movement of the electrical signal is called an **action potential**. After the action potential is over, the positive charges get pumped back out of the cell and the neuron returns to its negatively charged state. This condition is called the **resting potential**. A neuron acts in an **all-or-none** manner. This means the neuron either has an action potential or it does not. The neuron indicates the strength of the signal by how many action potentials are produced or "fired" within a certain amount of time.

Neurons pass information on to target cells using a chemical signal. When the electrical signal travels down the axon and reaches the other end of the neuron called the **axon terminal**, it enters the very tip of the terminal called the synaptic knob and causes the **neurotransmitters** in the **synaptic vesicles** to be released into the fluid-filled space between the two cells. This fluid-filled space is called the **synapse** or the **synaptic gap**. The neurotransmitters are the chemical signals the neuron uses to communicate with its target cell. The neurotransmitters fit into the **receptor sites** of the target cell and create a new electrical signal that then can be transmitted down the length of the target cell.

Excitatory neurotransmitters carry a signal that increases the likelihood of an action potential in the post synaptic neuron and **inhibitory neurotransmitters** carry a signal that decreases the likelihood of an action potential in the post synaptic neuron. Neurotransmitters can have two different effects on the target cell. If the neurotransmitter increases the likelihood of an action potential in the target cell, the connection is called an **excitatory synapse**. If the neurotransmitter decreases the likelihood of an action potential, the connection is called an **inhibitory synapse**. **Agonists** and **antagonists** are chemicals that are not naturally found in our body but that can fit into the receptor sites of target cells when they get into our nervous system. Agonists lead to a similar response in the target cell as the neurotransmitter itself, while antagonists block or reduce the action of the neurotransmitter on the target cell. There are at least 50 to100 different types of neurotransmitters in the human body. **Acetylcholine** was the first to be discovered; it is an excitatory neurotransmitter that causes your muscles to contract. Gamma aminobutyric acid (**GABA**) is an inhibitory neurotransmitter that decreases the activity level of neurons in your brain. **Serotonin** is both an excitatory and inhibitory neurotransmitter and has been linked with sleep, mood, and appetite. Low levels of the neurotransmitter **dopamine** have been found to cause Parkinson's disease, and increased levels of dopamine have been linked to the psychological disorder known as schizophrenia. **Endorphin** is a special neurotransmitter called a neural regulator that controls the release of other neurotransmitters. When endorphin is released in the body, the neurons transmitting information about pain are not able to fire action potentials. All the different types of neurotransmitters are cleared out of the synaptic gap through the process of **reuptake**, diffusion, or by being broken apart by an enzyme.

The **central nervous system (CNS)** is made up of the brain and the **spinal cord**. The spinal cord is a long bundle of neurons that transmits messages between the brain and the body. The cell bodies or somas of the neurons are located along the inside of the spinal cord, and the cell axons run along the outside of the spinal cord. **Afferent (sensory) neurons** send information from our senses to the spinal cord. For example, sensory neurons would relay information about a sharp pain in your finger. **Efferent (motor) neurons** send commands from the spinal cord to our muscles, such as a command to pull your finger back. **Interneurons** connect sensory and motor neurons and help to coordinate the signals. All three of these neurons act together in the spinal cord to form a **reflex arc**. The ability of the brain and spinal cord to change both in structure and function is referred to as **neuroplasticity**. One type of cell that facilitates these changes is **stem cells**.

There are a number of common misconceptions about the brain held by many people. Among these inaccurate notions are beliefs that older brains can't make new cells or that the Mozart effect is powerful and lasting. When considering a claim of this nature, it is important to ask critical questions about the source of the information. High-quality sources of information about psychology include peer-reviewed journals, professional organizations such as the APA and APS, and experts in the field of psychology.

The **peripheral nervous system (PNS)** is made up of all the nerves and neurons that are NOT in the brain or spinal cord. This includes all the nerves that connect to your eyes, ears, skin, mouth, and muscles. The PNS is divided into two parts, the **somatic nervous system** and the **autonomic nervous system**. The somatic nervous system consists of all the nerves coming from our sensory systems, called the **sensory pathway**, and all the nerves going to the skeletal muscles that control our voluntary movements, called the **motor pathway**. The autonomic nervous system is made up of the nerves going to and from our organs, glands, and involuntary muscles and is divided into two parts: the **sympathetic division** and the **parasympathetic division**. The sympathetic division turns on the body's fight-or-flight reactions, which include responses such as increased heart rate, increased breathing, and dilation of your pupils. The parasympathetic division controls your body when you are in a state of rest to keep the heart beating regularly, to control normal breathing, and to coordinate digestion. The parasympathetic division is active most of the time.

The **endocrine glands** represent a second communication system in the body. The endocrine glands secrete chemicals called **hormones** directly into the bloodstream. The **pituitary gland** is located in the brain and secretes the hormones that control milk production, salt levels, and the activity of other glands. The **pineal gland** is also located in the brain and regulates the sleep cycle through the secretion of melatonin. The **thyroid gland** is located in the neck and releases a hormone that regulates metabolism. The **pancreas** controls the level of blood sugar in the body, while the **gonad** sex glands—called the **ovaries** in females and the **testes** in males—regulate sexual behavior and reproduction. The **adrenal glands** play a critical role in regulating the body's response to stress.

Researchers have used animal models to learn a great deal about the human brain. Two of the most common techniques used in animals involve either destroying a specific area of the brain (deep **lesioning**) or stimulating a specific brain area (electrical stimulation of the brain, or ESB) to see the effect. In work with humans, researchers have developed several methods to observe the structure and activity of a living brain. If a researcher wants a picture of the structure of the brain, he or she might choose **computed tomography (CT)** or **magnetic resonance imaging (MRI)**. Computed tomography (CT) scans use x-rays to create images of the structures within the brain. Magnetic resonance images (MRIs) use a magnetic field to "take a picture" of the brain. MRIs provide much greater detail than CT scans. On the other hand, if a researcher wanted to record the activity of the brain, he or she might select **electroencephalograph (EEG)**, **functional magnetic resonance imaging (fMRI)**, or **positron emission tomography (PET)**. An electroencephalogram (EEG) provides a record of the electrical activity of groups of neurons just below the surface of the skull. A functional magnetic resonance image (fMRI) uses magnetic fields in the same way as an MRI but goes a step further and pieces the pictures together to show changes over a short period of time. A positron emission tomography (PET) scan involves injecting a person with a low dose of a radioactive substance and then recording the activity of that substance in the person's brain.

The brain can be roughly divided into three sections: the brainstem, the cortex, and the structures under the cortex. The **brainstem** is the lowest part of the brain that connects to the spinal cord. The outer wrinkled covering of the brain is the **cortex**, and the structures under the cortex are essentially everything between the brainstem and the cortex. The brainstem contains four important structures. The **medulla** controls life-sustaining functions such as heart beat, breathing, and swallowing. The **pons** influences sleep, dreaming, and coordination of movements. The **reticular formation** plays a crucial role in attention and arousal, and the **cerebellum** controls all of the movements we make without really "thinking" about it.

One main group of structures under the cortex is the **limbic system**. The limbic system includes the **thalamus**, **hypothalamus**, **hippocampus**, and **amygdala**. The thalamus receives input from your sensory systems, processes it, and then passes it on to the appropriate area of the cortex. The hypothalamus interacts with the endocrine system to regulate body temperature, thirst, hunger, sleeping, sexual activity, and mood. It appears that the hippocampus is critical for the formation of long-term memories and for memories of the locations of objects. The amygdala is a small almond-shaped structure that is involved in our response to fear.

The outer part of the brain, or cortex, is divided into right and left sections called **cerebral hemispheres**. The two hemispheres communicate with each other through a thick band of neurons called the **corpus callosum**. Each cerebral hemisphere can be roughly divided into four sections. These sections are called lobes. The **occipital lobes** are at the back of the brain and process visual information. The **parietal lobes** are located at the top and back half of the brain and deal with information regarding touch, temperature, body position, and possibly taste. The **temporal lobes** are just behind your temples and process auditory information. The **frontal lobes** are located at the front of your head and are responsible for higher mental functions such as planning, personality, and decision making, as well as language and motor movements. Motor movements are controlled by a band of neurons located at the back of the frontal lobe called the motor cortex.

Association areas are the areas within each of the lobes that are responsible for "making sense" of all the incoming information. **Broca's area** is located in the left frontal lobe in most people and is responsible for language production. A person with damage to this area would have trouble producing the words that he or she wants to speak. This condition is referred to as **Broca's aphasia**. The comprehension of language takes place in **Wernicke's area** located in the left temporal lobe. If this area of the brain is damaged, individuals are often still able to speak fluently, but their words do not make sense. This type of language disorder is referred to as **Wernicke's aphasia**. Damage to the right parietal and occipital lobes can cause a condition known as **spatial neglect** where the individual ignores objects in their left visual field.

The **cerebrum** is made up of the two cerebral hemispheres and the structures connecting them. The split-brain research studies of Roger Sperry helped scientists to figure out that the two cerebral hemispheres are not identical. The left hemisphere is typically more active when a person is using language, math, and other analytical skills, while the right hemisphere shows more activity during tasks of perception, recognition, and expression of emotions. This split in the tasks of the brain is referred to as lateralization.

Mirror neurons, neurons that fire when we perform an action and also when we see someone else perform that action, may explain a great deal of the social learning that takes place in humans from infancy on.

Attention-deficit/hyperactivity disorder (ADHD) is a developmental disorder involving behavioral and cognitive aspects of inattention, impulsivity, and hyperactivity. Although ADHD is most commonly diagnosed in children, the disorder tends to persist into adolescence and adulthood. Since ADHD involves a variety of behaviors and cognitive aspects, research has often looked for specific markers that may lead to the actual causes of the disorder. Much of the research over the past 10 years has focused on the cognitive markers for ADHD, such as attention problems. Aspects of attention that individuals with ADHD have problems with include vigilance and staying on task. Currently, researchers are reexamining the causes of ADHD and have highlighted the likelihood of more than one cause and more than one brain route to ADHD including genetics, environmental factors, family factors, and personality factors.

STUDY HINTS

1. You will need to know the different functions of the peripheral nervous system (PNS). Recall that the PNS is divided into two main sections: the somatic nervous system and the autonomic nervous system. The somatic nervous system deals with the senses and the skeletal muscles (all "S's") and is fairly straightforward to understand. The autonomic nervous system is slightly more complicated. First, understand that the *autonomic* nervous system deals with all the *automatic* functions of your body. What are some functions that are controlled automatically in your body? List them here:

   _____, _____, _____, _____

   You probably mentioned functions such as digestion, heart rate, pupil dilation, breathing, salivation, or perspiration, to name a few. These are the functions controlled by the autonomic system.

   There are two components of the autonomic system, and they serve to balance each other out. The two divisions are the sympathetic and parasympathetic divisions. Most of the time, the parasympathetic division is in control. Some people have called the parasympathetic division the *rest-and-digest system* because it controls the digestive processes, maintains a resting heart and breathing rate, and in general keeps your body in its normal relaxed state. The sympathetic division goes into action when your body needs to react to some type of threat. It might be helpful to associate **s**ympathetic with **s**urprise, since the sympathetic division is the part of your nervous system that responds when you are surprised. This system is often referred to as the *fight-or flight system*. What happens to your body when you are surprised? List some of the responses here:

   _____, _____, _____, _____

   You probably mentioned responses such as your heart rate increases, you breathe faster, your pupils dilate, you begin to sweat, to name a few. All of these responses are "turned on" by the sympathetic division of your autonomic nervous system and aid in your survival by allowing you to respond quickly to a threat.

2. Two of the brain structures most commonly confused with each other are the hippocampus and the hypothalamus. Both of the structures are located in the limbic system in the area of your brain above your brainstem and below the outer surface. The hippocampus has been found to be important in helping us form memories that last more than just a few seconds. Patients with damage to the hippocampus often cannot remember information for longer than a few seconds. Also, the hippocampus is very important in storing memories of where things are located, a spatial map. On the other hand, the hypothalamus is important in controlling many of our basic bodily functions such as sleeping, drinking, eating, and sexual activities. The structures are often confused because the two words sound so similar to each other. Can you think of any memory device or "trick" to help you keep these two brain structures separate? List your idea in the space below:

hippocampus: _____

hypothalamus: _____

One suggestion might be as follows. If you look at the word hippocampus *you can think of the last part of the word—*campus*. In order to get around on your college campus, you need to keep in mind where certain buildings and areas are located. This is exactly what your hippocampus is involved in. Without your hippo-*campus*, you would have a very hard time finding your way around your college* campus*.*

To remember the hypothalamus, first it might help to understand how the name came about. "Hypo" means under or below. For example, if someone has "hypothermia," their body temperature is under the normal amount and the person is probably feeling very cold. If someone has "hypoglycemia," they have under or lower than the normal amount of blood sugar (glycemia is referring to the sugar found in your blood). What do you think "hypothalamus" means?

_____

If you wrote "under the thalamus," then you are correct. The hypothalamus is located directly underneath the thalamus. You might also look at the name to try to remember some of the activities the hypothalamus regulates. Recall that we said the hypothalamus plays a role in hunger, sleep, thirst, and sex. If you look at the "hypo" of hypothalamus you might memorize "h"—hunger, "y"—yawning, "p"—parched (or very, very thirsty), and "o"—overly excited.

LEARNING OBJECTIVES

2.1 *What are the nervous system, neurons, and nerves, and how do they relate to one another?*

2.2 *How do neurons use neurotransmitters to communicate with each other and with the body?*

2.3 *How do the brain and spinal cord interact, what are some misconceptions about the brain, and what is neuroplasticity?*

2.4 *How do the somatic and autonomic nervous systems allow people and animals to interact with their surroundings and control the body's automatic functions?*

2.5 *How do the hormones released by glands interact with the nervous system and affect behavior?*

2.6 *How do psychologists study the brain and how it works?*

2.7 *What are the different structures of the hindbrain, and what do they do?*

2.8 *What are the structures of the brain that control emotion, learning, memory, and motivation?*

2.9 *What parts of the cortex control the different senses and the movement of the body?*

2.10 *What parts of the cortex are responsible for higher forms of thought, such as language?*

2.11 *How does the left side of the brain differ from the right side?*

2.12 *What are some potential causes of attention-deficit/hyperactivity disorder?*

AP LEARNING OBJECTIVES

1. Identify basic processes and systems in the biological bases of behavior including parts of the neuron and the process of transmission of a signal between neurons. (p. 54)
2. Discuss the influence of drugs on neurotransmitters (p. 60)
3. Discuss the effect of the endocrine system on behavior. (p. 71)
4. Describe the nervous system and its subdivisions and functions. (pp. 64, 67)
5. Discuss the role of neuroplasticity in traumatic brain injury. (p. 67)
6. Recount historic and contemporary research strategies and technologies that support research. (pp. 75, 89)
7. Discuss psychology's abiding interest in how heredity, environment, and evolution work together to shape behavior. (p. 94)
8. Identify key contributors to the study of the brain. (pp. 75, 88, 90, 92)

CHAPTER GLOSSARY

acetylcholine	the first neurotransmitter to be discovered. Found to regulate memories in the CNS and the action of skeletal and smooth muscles in the PNS.
action potential	the release of the neural impulse consisting of a reversal of the electrical charge within the axon.
adrenal glands	endocrine glands located on top of each kidney and which secrete over 30 different hormones to deal with stress, regulate salt intake, and provide a secondary source of sex hormones affecting the sexual changes that occur during adolescence.
afferent (sensory) neuron	a neuron that carries information from the senses to the central nervous system.
agonists	chemical substances that mimic or enhance the effects of a neurotransmitter on the receptor sites of the next cell, increasing or decreasing the activity of that cell.
all-or-none	referring to the fact that a neuron either fires completely or does not fire at all.
amygdala	brain structure located near the hippocampus, responsible for fear responses and memory of fear.
antagonists	chemical substances that block or reduce a cell's response to the action of other chemicals or neurotransmitters.
association areas	areas within each lobe of the cortex responsible for the coordination and interpretation of information, as well as higher mental processing.
attention-deficit/hyperactivity disorder (ADHD)	a developmental disorder involving behavioral and cognitive aspects of inattention, impulsivity, and hyperactivity.
autonomic nervous system	division of the PNS consisting of nerves that control all of the involuntary muscles, organs, and glands.
axon	long tube-like structure that carries the neural message to other cells.
axon terminals	branches at the end of the axon.
brainstem	section of the brain that connects directly to the spinal cord and regulates vital functions such as breathing, the heart, reflexes, and level of alertness.
Broca's aphasia	an inability to use or understand either written or spoken language,
Broca's area	association area of the brain located in the frontal lobe that is responsible for language production and language processing.

central nervous system (CNS)	part of the nervous system consisting of the brain and spinal cord.
cerebellum	part of the lower brain located behind the pons that controls and coordinates involuntary, rapid, fine motor movement.
cerebral hemispheres	the two sections of the cortex on the left and right sides of the brain.
cerebrum	the upper part of the brain consisting of the two hemispheres and the structures connecting them.
computed tomography (CT)	brain imaging method using computer-controlled x-rays of the brain.
corpus callosum	thick band of neurons that connects the right and left cerebral hemispheres.
cortex	outermost covering of the brain consisting of densely packed neurons, responsible for higher thought processes and interpretation of sensory input.
dendrites	branch-like structures that receive messages from other neurons.
dopamine	neurotransmitter that regulates movement, balance, and walking and is involved in the disorders of schizophrenia and Parkinson's disease.
efferent (motor) neuron	a neuron that carries messages from the central nervous system to the muscles of the body.
electroencephalograph (EEG)	machine designed to record the brain wave patterns produced by electrical activity of the surface of the brain.
endocrine glands	glands that secrete chemicals called hormones directly into the bloodstream.
endorphin	neurotransmitter that is found naturally in the body and works to block pain and elevate mood. It is chemically similar to morphine and its name is short for "endogenous morphine."
excitatory neurotransmitter	neurotransmitter that causes the receiving cell to fire.
excitatory synapse	a synapse that receives a neurotransmitter that makes the post synaptic cell more likely to reach an action potential.
frontal lobes	areas of the cortex located in the front and top of the brain, responsible for higher mental processes and decision making as well as the production of fluent speech.
functional magnetic resonance imaging (fMRI)	a method used to observe activity in the brain; it shows which structures are active during particular mental operations using the same basic procedure as MRI.
GABA	abbreviation for gamma aminobutyric acid, the major inhibitory neurotransmitter in the brain.
glial cells	grey fatty cells that provide support for the neurons to grow on and around, deliver nutrients to neurons, produce myelin to coat axons, and clean up waste products and dead neurons.
gonads	the sex glands.
hippocampus	curved structure located within each temporal lobe, responsible for the formation of long-term memories and the storage of memory for location of objects.
hormones	chemicals released into the bloodstream by endocrine glands.
hypothalamus	small structure in the brain located below the thalamus and directly above the pituitary gland, responsible for motivational behavior such as sleep, hunger, thirst, and sex.
inhibitory neurotransmitter	neurotransmitter that causes the receiving cell to stop firing.

inhibitory synapse	a synapse the receives a neurotransmitter that makes the post synaptic neuron less likely to reach an action potential.
interneuron	a neuron found in the center of the spinal cord which receives information from the sensory neurons and sends commands to the muscles through the motor neurons. Interneurons also make up the bulk of the neurons in the brain.
lesioning	destroying target areas of the brain with an electrical current to study the function of the brain.
limbic system	a group of several brain structures located under the cortex and involved in learning, emotion, memory, and motivation.
magnetic resonance imaging (MRI)	brain imaging method using radio waves and magnetic fields of the body to produce detailed images of the brain.
medulla	the first large swelling at the top of the spinal cord, forming the lowest part of the brain and responsible for life-sustaining functions such as breathing, swallowing, and heart rate.
mirror neurons	neurons that fire when an action is performed and also fire when an action is observed being performed by another person.
motor pathway	the nerves carrying messages from the central nervous system to the voluntary, or skeletal, muscles of the body.
myelin	fatty substances produced by certain glial cells that coat the axons of neurons to insulate, protect, and speed up the neural impulse.
nerves	bundles of axons in the peripheral nervous system.
nervous system	an extensive network of specialized cells that carry information to and from all parts of the body.
neurons	the basic cell that makes up the nervous system and which receives and sends messages within that system.
neuroplasticity	the ability to constantly change both the structure and function of many cells in the brain in response to experience and even trauma.
neuroscience	branch of the life sciences that deals with the structure and functioning of the brain and the neurons, nerves, and nervous tissue that form the nervous system.
neurotransmitter	chemical found in the synaptic vesicles which, when released, has an effect on the next cell.
occipital lobes	sections of the brain located at the rear and bottom of each cerebral hemisphere, containing the visual centers of the brain.
ovaries	female sex glands.
pancreas	endocrine gland that controls the levels of sugar in the blood.
parasympathetic division	part of the autonomic system that restores the body to normal functioning after arousal and is responsible for the day-to-day functioning of the organs and glands. Sometimes referred to as the rest-and-digest system.
parietal lobes	sections of the brain located at the top and back of each cerebral hemisphere, containing the centers for touch, taste, and temperature sensations.
peripheral nervous system (PNS)	all nerves and neurons that are not contained in the brain and spinal cord but which run through the body itself.
pineal gland	endocrine gland located near the base of the cerebrum which secretes melatonin.
pituitary gland	gland located in the brain that secretes human growth hormone and influences all other hormone-secreting glands. Also known as the master gland.

pons	the larger swelling above the medulla which connects the top of the brain to the bottom, and which plays a part in sleep, dreaming, left-right body coordination, and arousal.
positron emission tomography (PET)	brain imaging method in which a radioactive sugar is injected into the subject and a computer compiles a color-coded image of the activity of the brain, with lighter colors indicating more activity.
receptor sites	ion channels that allow only particular molecules of a certain shape to fit into them like a lock and key.
reflex arc	a signal sent from the spinal cord that causes a reflexive response.
resting potential	the state of the neuron when not firing a neural impulse.
reticular formation	an area of neurons running through the middle of the medulla and the pons and slightly beyond, responsible for selective attention.
reuptake	process by which neurotransmitters are taken back into the synaptic vesicles.
sensory pathway	all the nerves carrying messages from the senses to the central nervous system.
serotonin	neurotransmitter involved in pain disorders and emotional perceptions. Is also known as 5-hydroxytryptamine (5-HT).
soma	the cell body of the neuron, responsible for maintaining the life of the cell.
somatic nervous system	division of the PNS consisting of nerves that carry information from the senses to the CNS and from the CNS to the voluntary muscles of the body.
spatial neglect	condition in which a person with damage to the right parietal and occipital lobes of the cortex will ignore everything in the left visual field.
spinal cord	a long bundle of neurons that carries messages to and from the body to the brain and that is responsible for very fast, life-saving reflexes.
stem cells	cells that can become any cell in the body.
sympathetic division	part of the autonomic nervous system that is responsible for reacting to stressful events and bodily arousal. Also known as the fight-or-flight system.
synapse	a fluid filled space between an axon terminal of one neuron and the dendrite of another neuron.
synaptic gap	microscopic fluid-filled space between the rounded areas on the end of the axon terminals of one cell and the dendrites or surface of the next cell.
synaptic vesicles	sack-like structures found inside the synaptic knob containing chemicals.
temporal lobes	areas of the cortex located just behind the temples, containing the neurons responsible for the sense of hearing and meaningful speech.
testes	male sex glands.
thalamus	part of the limbic system located in the center of the brain; this structure relays sensory information from the lower part of the brain to the proper areas of the cortex, and processes some sensory information before sending it to its proper area.
thyroid gland	endocrine gland found in the neck that regulates metabolism.
Wernicke's aphasia	impairment in the ability to comprehend and produce speech.
Wernicke's area	association area of the brain in the temporal lobe that has been found to be involved in the comprehension of spoken language.

CHAPTER PRACTICE TEST

For the following multiple-choice questions, select the answer you feel best answers the question.

1. The function of the _____ is to carry information to and from all parts of the body.
    a) soma
    b) synapse
    c) nervous system
    d) endorphins
    e) medulla

2. The central nervous system is made of which two components?
    a) the somatic and autonomic systems
    b) both the left and right hemispheres of the brain
    c) the sympathetic and parasympathetic divisions
    d) neurotransmitters and hormones
    e) the brain and the spinal cord

3. A specialized cell that makes up the nervous system that receives and sends messages within that system is called a _____.
    a) glial cell
    b) neuron
    c) cell body
    d) myelin sheath
    e) agonist

4. What type of signal is used to relay a message from one end of a neuron to the other end?
    a) chemical
    b) hormonal
    c) biochemical
    d) electrical
    e) thermal

5. A chemical found in the synaptic vesicles which, when released, has an effect on the next cell is called a_____.
    a) glial cell
    b) neurotransmitter
    c) precursor cell
    d) synapse
    e) Schwann cells

6. What event causes the release of chemicals into the synaptic gap?
    a) an agonist binding to the dendrites
    b) an antagonist binding to the dendrites
    c) the reuptake of neurotransmitters
    d) excitation of the glial cells
    e) an action potential reaching the axon terminal

7. Sara has been experiencing a serious memory problem. An interdisciplinary team has ruled out a range of causes and believes that a neurotransmitter is involved. Which neurotransmitter is most likely involved in this problem?
    a) GABA
    b) dopamine
    c) serotonin
    d) acetylcholine
    e) oxytocin

8. A neuron releases neurotransmitters into the synaptic gap that reduce the frequency of action potentials in the neighboring cell. The neuron most likely released is _____.
    a) an inhibitory neurotransmitter
    b) an excitatory neurotransmitter
    c) Acetylcholine
    d) an agonist
    e) an uninhibitory neurotransmitter

9. Which part of the nervous system takes the information received from the senses, makes sense out of it, makes decisions, and sends commands out to the muscles and the rest of the body?
    a) spinal cord
    b) brain
    c) reflexes
    d) interneurons
    e) synaptic gap

10. Every deliberate action you make, such as pedaling a bike, walking, scratching, or smelling a flower, involves neurons in the _____ nervous system.
    a) sympathetic
    b) somatic
    c) parasympathetic
    d) autonomic
    e) limbic

11. Involuntary muscles are controlled by the _____ nervous system.
    a) somatic
    b) autonomic
    c) sympathetic
    d) limbic
    e) parasympathetic

12. Which of the following responses would occur if your sympathetic nervous system has been activated?
    a) increase blood flow to the brain
    b) pupil constriction
    c) slowed breathing
    d) increased digestion
    e) increased heart rate

13. Which of the following is a common misconception about the brain?
    a) The brain weighs more in adulthood than it does in infancy.
    b) The brain of humans has more corticalization than the brain of rats.
    The parts of the body that are more sensitive to touch have larger portions of the sensory
    c) strip.
    d) The motor strip on the left hemisphere controls the right side of the body.
    e) Older brains can't make new cells.

14. The brain's ability to modify its structure or function is known as _____.
    a) olfaction
    b) agonistic reaction
    c) afferent activity
    d) neuroplasticity
    e) corticalization

15. Small metal disks are pasted onto Miranda's scalp, and they are connected by wire to a machine that
    translates the electrical energy from her brain into wavy lines on a moving piece of paper. From this
    description, it is evident that Miranda's brain is being studied through the use of _____.
    a) a CT Scan
    b) functional magnetic resonance imaging (fMRI)
    c) a microelectrode
    d) an electroencephalograph
    e) a PET scan

16. Which method would a researcher select if he or she wanted to determine if his or her patient's right
    hemisphere was the same size as his or her left hemisphere?
    a) EEG
    b) deep lesioning
    c) CT scan
    d) PET scan
    e) transcranial magnetic stimulation

17. The hormone released by the pineal gland that reduces body temperature and prepares you for sleep
    is _____.
    a) melatonin
    b) DHEA
    c) parathormone
    d) thyroxin
    e) epinephrine

18. Which endocrine gland regulates your body's response to stress?
    a) pancreas
    b) thyroid gland
    c) pineal gland
    d) adrenal gland
    e) gonads

19. Which of the following is responsible for the ability to selectively attend to certain kinds of information in one's surroundings and become alert to changes in information?
    a) reticular formation
    b) pons
    c) medulla
    d) cerebellum
    e) sensory cortex

20. When a professional baseball player swings a bat and hits a homerun, he or she is relying on his or her _____ to coordinate the practiced movements of his or her body.
    a) pons
    b) medulla
    c) cerebellum
    d) reticular formation
    e) thalamus

21. Eating, drinking, sexual behavior, sleeping, and temperature control are most strongly influenced by the _____.
    a) hippocampus
    b) thalamus
    c) hypothalamus
    d) amygdala
    e) reticular formation

22. After a brain operation, a laboratory rat no longer displays any fear when placed into a cage with a snake. Which part of the rat's brain was most likely damaged during the operation?
    a) amygdala
    b) hypothalamus
    c) cerebellum
    d) hippocampus
    e) thalamus

23. Darla was in an automobile accident that resulted in an injury to her brain. Her sense of touch has been affected. Which part of the brain is the most likely site of the damage?
    a) frontal lobes
    b) temporal lobes
    c) occipital lobes
    d) parietal lobes
    e) prefrontal lobes

24. If a person damages his or her occipital lobes, which would be the most likely problem he or she would report to his or her doctor?
    a) trouble hearing
    b) problems with his or her vision
    c) decreased sense of taste
    d) numbness on the right side of his or her body
    e) problems with producing speech

25. Damage to what area of the brain would result in an inability to comprehend language?
   a) occipital lobes
   b) Broca's area
   c) Wernicke's area
   d) parietal lobe
   e) sensory strip

26. If Darren's brain is like that of most people, then language will be handled by his _____.
   a) corpus callosum
   b) occipital lobe
   c) right hemisphere
   d) left optic chiasm
   e) left hemisphere

27. The right hemisphere is most associated with _____.
   a) language
   b) nonverbal and perception-based tasks
   c) following step-by-step directions
   d) math problems
   e) names of objects

28. The aspect of attention individuals with ADHD do have problems with is _____.
   a) vigilance
   b) flow
   c) habituation
   d) hypnogogia
   e) deep structure processing

CHAPTER PRACTICE TEST ANSWERS

1. c   The nervous system is the correct answer because sending information to and from all parts of the body is the primary function of the nervous system. The soma and the synapse are both parts of an individual neuron, and endorphins are one type of neurotransmitter found in the body.

2. e   The central nervous system is composed of the nerves and neurons in the center of your body. Choices a and c are both components of the peripheral nervous system. Hormones are the chemical messengers for the endocrine system.

3. b   Choice b is the correct answer because neurons are specialized cells that make up the nervous system that receives and sends messages within that system. Choice a is incorrect because glial cells serve as a structure for neurons.

4. d   Neurons use electrical signals to communicate within their own cell. The electrical signal is called an action potential.

5. b   Neurotransmitters are stored in the synaptic vesicles. Choice d is incorrect because the synapse is the space between the synaptic knob of one cell and the dendrites.

6. e   When the electrical signal (called an action potential) reaches the axon terminal, the synaptic vesicles release their contents into the synaptic gap.

7. d   Acetylcholine is found in a part of the brain responsible for forming new memories.

8. a   Inhibitory neurotransmitters inhibit the electrical activity of the receptor cell.

9. b   The spinal cord carries messages to and/from the body to the brain, but it is the job of the brain to make sense of all the information.

10. b   The somatic nervous system controls voluntary muscle movement, whereas the autonomic nervous system consists of nerves that control all of the involuntary muscles, organs, and glands.

11.   b   The autonomic nervous system controls involuntary muscles such as the heart, stomach, and intestines.

12.   e   The sympathetic division is responsible for controlling your body's fight-or-flight response that prepares your body to deal with a potential threat. The responses include increased heart rate and breathing, pupil dilation, decreased digestion, among others.

13.   e   A common misconception about the brain is that older brains can't make new cells.

14.   d   Neuroplasticity refers to the brain's ability to modify its structure and function as the result of experience or injury.

15.   d   An electroencephalograph or EEG records brain wave patterns. CT scans take computer-controlled x-rays of the brain.

16.   c   Option c is the only selection that would allow the researcher to take a picture of the structure of the brain. All other options listed would provide information about the activity of the brain.

17.   a   The pineal gland secretes melatonin.

18.   d   The adrenal glands secrete several hormones in response to stress.

19   a   The reticular formation plays a role in selective attention.

20.   c   The cerebellum is responsible for controlling the movements that we have practiced repeatedly, the movements that we don't have to really "think about."

21.   c   The hypothalamus regulates sleep, hunger, thirst, and sex.

22.   a   The amygdala has been found to regulate the emotion of fear. The amygdala is found within the limbic system, a part of our brain responsible for regulating emotions and memories.

23.   d   The parietal lobes contain the centers for touch, taste, and temperature.

24.   b   The occipital lobes are responsible for processing visual information.

25.   c   Wernicke's area is located in the temporal lobe and is important in the comprehension of language. Broca's area is located in the frontal lobe and plays a role in the production of language.

26.   e   For most people, the left hemisphere specializes in language.

27.   b   The left hemisphere is more active during language and math problems, while the right hemisphere appears to play a larger role in nonverbal and perception-based tasks.

28.   a   According to recent research, people with ADHD have problems with vigilance.

CHAPTER PRACTICE FREE RESPONSE QUESTION

You have 25 minutes to answer the following question. You must write in complete sentences and not just list facts. You should make your point clearly and use the language of psychology. Be sure to write legibly, and respond to all parts of the question.

Describe the role the following parts of the brain would play if the parts were people who worked in a school. Be sure to link each part to a specific function in the school and provide a reason for the link.

- Cerebrum
- Thalamus
- Hippocampus
- Medulla
- Hypothalamus

SUGGESTED RUBRIC—Students should provide specific details and examples to support their assertions; definitions alone are not sufficient. Information about each topic should be discussed in the context of the question rather than abstractly. Successful essays may include the following arguments:

5 points

- Score—The cerebrum is the thinking part of the brain, so it could be the teachers or students because they have to do the thinking and learning in the school.
  - Other choices could be cited; however, the rationale must indicate the higher functions of the brain such as thinking or reasoning.
- Score—The thalamus is an organizer, so it could be linked to the secretaries because they organize student records and business files of the schools.
  - Other choices could be cited; however, the rationale must indicate the directing, routing, and organizing role in the brain.
- Score—The hippocampus plays an important role in memory of information, so it could be linked to the IT people in the school because they keep the school's computers working and are responsible for the storage of data.
- Other choices could be cited; however, the rationale must indicate a role related to the storage and maintenance of memories and information in the brain.
- Score—The medulla controls life support functions in the brain, so it could be the food service staff because they provide food that is needed for survival.
  - Other choices could be cited; however, the rationale must indicate a vital survival role.
- Score—The hypothalamus controls the homeostatic functions of the brain such as hunger, so it could be the custodians or maintenance staff in the school because they keep the air conditioning, lights, waste disposal, and other maintenance functions in order.
  - Other choices could be cited; however, the rationale must indicate a role of maintaining a level status.

YOU KNOW YOU HAVE MASTERED THE MAIN TOPICS IN THIS CHAPTER IF YOU ARE ABLE TO. . .

- Define sensation and introduce some of the key concepts developed by researchers in the study of sensation.
- Explain in detail how our sense of sight and our sense of hearing work and discuss some causes for impairments in these senses.
- Discuss the chemical senses of taste and smell and the lesser known somesthetic senses of touch, body position, and balance.
- Describe our experience of perception and illusion, especially in relation to visual stimuli.

RAPID REVIEW

Sensation allows us to receive information from the world around us. **Synesthesia** is the rare condition in which a person experiences more than one sensation from a single stimulus, for example the person who can hear and see a sound. Outside stimuli (such as the sound of your mother's voice) activate **sensory receptors** that convert the outside stimulus into a message that our nervous system can understand—electrical and chemical signals. Sensation is activated by **stimuli** in various forms that come from outside the body, can be picked up by the senses, and converted into neural signals. The process of converting the outside stimulus into the electrical-chemical signal of the nervous system is called sensory **transduction**. The sensory receptors are specialized forms of neurons and make up part of our somatic nervous system. Ernst Weber and Gustav Fechner were two pioneers in the study of sensory thresholds. Weber studied the smallest difference between two stimuli that a person could detect 50 percent of the time. He called this difference a **just noticeable difference (jnd)**, and he discovered that the jnd is always a constant. For instance, if a person needs to add 5 percent more weight to notice the difference in the heaviness of a package, then this person's jnd is 5 percent. If the initial weight of the package is 10 lbs, then 0.5 lbs would need to be added to detect a difference (5 percent of 10 lb = 0.5lb). If the initial weight is 100 lbs, then 5 lbs would need to be added in order for the person to detect a difference in weight (5 percent of 100 lbs = 5 lbs). The fact that the jnd is always a constant is known as **Weber's law**. Fechner investigated the lowest level of a stimulus that a person could detect 50 percent of the time. He called this level the **absolute threshold**. Stimuli that are below threshold are subliminal. While early research was overdramatized and claimed to produce strong subliminal responses, current research has found that subliminal stimuli in the form of fearful or threatening event-related potentials can elicit modest autonomic effects in research participants. **Habituation** and **sensory adaptation** are two methods our body uses to ignore unchanging information. Habituation takes place when the lower centers of the brain prevent conscious attention to a constant stimulus, such as the humming of a desktop computer. Sensory adaptation occurs in the sensory receptors themselves when the receptors stop responding to a constant stimulus, such as the feeling of your shirt on your skin.

The visual sensory system is activated by light waves. There are three psychological aspects to our experience of light. **Brightness** is determined by the height, or amplitude, of the wave. **Color**, or **hue**, is determined by the length of the light wave, and **saturation**, or purity, is determined by the mixture of wavelengths of varying heights and lengths. Light enters your eye through the cornea that protects your eye and helps to focus the light, and then travels through a hole in your iris, called pupil. The iris is a group of muscles that control the size of the pupil. The light then passes through the lens that focuses the light and allows you to focus on objects that are close or far away. This process is known as **visual accommodation**. The light then travels through the vitreous humor in the middle of your eyeball to reach the **retina** at the very back of your eye. The retina is the size of a postage stamp and contains the sensory receptor neurons that convert the incoming light waves in to an electrical-chemical signal that the nervous system can understand. Your eye contains two types of sensory receptors, **rods** and **cones**. About 70 percent of the sensory receptors in your eyes are rods. Rods detect the brightness of light and send information about the levels of black, white, and shades of gray. The rods are located over the entire retina except at the very center. Rods are extremely sensitive to light but produce images with low acuity, or sharpness. Our eyes' ability to adapt to a dark room and eventually see objects is mediated by the rods in our eyes and is called **dark adaptation**. Cones make up the remaining 30 percent of the sensory receptors in your eyes and are located mainly in the center of the retina. Cones transmit information about color and produce images with very high acuity. Our ability to quickly adapt when we enter a bright room is called **light adaptation** and is accomplished by the cones. The place where the information from the rods and cones leaves the eye is called the **blind spot** because there are no visual receptors there to receive information.

The exact method the cones use to transmit information about color is still unknown. Two theories are currently proposed. The **trichromatic theory** was originally proposed by Thomas Young and later modified by Hermann Helmholtz. The theory suggests that there are three types of cones, red, green, and blue, that combine to produce sensation of color much like three spotlights would combine to produce the full spectrum of colors. In more recent research, Brown and Wald (1964) found that the peak wavelength of light the different types of cones seem to be most sensitive to turns out to be just a little different from Young and von Helmholtz's original three corresponding colors. Short wavelength cones detect what we see as blue-violet, medium wavelength cones detect what we see as green, long wavelength cones detect what we see as green-yellow, and while none of the cones show a peak sensitivity to red, each cone responds to light across a range of wavelengths, so depending on the intensity of the light, both the medium and long wavelength cones respond to light that appears red. The trichromatic theory most likely is an accurate description of the cones but cannot explain certain visual phenomena such as the **afterimage**. The afterimage is the image you see after staring at something and then looking away. For example, stare at something red, then look away and you see a green afterimage. A different theory of color perception known as the **opponent-process theory** was developed to explain phenomena such as the afterimage. The theory states that cones are arranged in pairs with a red-green pair and a blue-yellow pair. If one member of the pair is firing, then the other member cannot. When you stare at something red, the red member sends information and the green member is inhibited. When you look away, the green member is no longer inhibited and sends information even though you are not looking at anything green. Both the trichromatic theory and the opponent-process theory are probably correct. The trichromatic theory most likely explains the actions of cones in the retina, while the opponent-process theory explains the actions higher up in the visual system in the thalamus of the brain.

After light is converted to an electrical-chemical signal by the rods and cones, the message travels out of the eye through the **optic nerve**, crosses over at the optic chiasm, enters the medulla and then the thalamus. From the thalamus the signal is sent to the occipital lobes, which if you recall from the previous chapter, are responsible for processing visual information. **Color blindness**, more common in men than women, is commonly caused by genetically defective cones in the retina and can be one of the three types.

Our sense of hearing, the auditory system, is activated by the vibrations of molecules in the air that surround us. These vibrations are called sound waves, and like light waves, we respond to three features of sound waves. **Pitch** corresponds to the frequency of the wave, **volume** is determined by the amplitude of the wave, and **timbre** relates to the purity of the wavelengths. Humans can only respond to wavelengths of a certain frequency. The average range for humans is between 20 and 20,000 **Hertz** (Hz) or waves per second. Sound waves enter our auditory system through the **pinna**, travel down the ear canal—also known as the **auditory canal,** and then vibrate the eardrum that causes the hammer, anvil, and stirrup to vibrate. The vibrations of the stirrup cause the oval window to move back and forth that causes the fluid in the **cochlea** to vibrate. The fluid causes the basilar membrane to vibrate that causes the organ of Corti to move up, and this causes the **hair cells** to bend. The hair cells are the sensory receptors of the auditory system, and the movement of the hair cells triggers an action potential in the axon. The axons travel to the brain in a bundle called the **auditory nerve**. A louder noise causes the hair cells to fire more action potentials. Sound localization is achieved by the brain's ability to detect the split-second difference in the time it takes for sound to travel to both ears. If the origin of a sound is directly to your right side, it will take approximately 66/10,000 of a second longer to reach your left ear. This very short time difference in sensation, along with other cues, helps you directionally locate the sound's origin.

There are three theories that explain how the brain receives information about pitch. **Place theory** states that pitch is determined by the place on the organ of Corti that is stimulated. The **frequency theory** suggests that the speed of vibrations of the basilar membrane determines the pitch heard by the person. The **volley principle** suggests that hair cells take turns firing in a process called volleying. All three theories are correct. Frequency theory holds true for wavelengths of 100 Hz or less, volley theory covers the wavelengths from 100 to 1000 Hz, and place theory seems to account for the wavelengths faster than 1000 Hz. Hearing impairment is the term used to describe difficulties in hearing. Conduction hearing impairment occurs from damage to the eardrum or the bones of the middle ear. Nerve hearing impairment is caused by problems in the inner ear or in the auditory pathways and cortical areas of the brain. Ordinary hearing aids are designed to assist with conduction hearing impairment, whereas **cochlear implants** can be used to restore some hearing for people with nerve hearing impairment.

The sense of taste, or **gustation**, is activated by chemicals that dissolve in the mouth. The sensory receptors are receptor cells found within the **taste buds** that are located on the little bumps on the tongue, cheek, and roof of your mouth. The little bumps that you can actually see with your eye are called papillae. Five basic tastes have been proposed; they are sweet, sour, salty, bitter, and umami. Umami is the newest taste and corresponds to a "brothy" taste like the taste from chicken soup and is a component of the seasoning ingredient monosodium glutamate.

The sense of smell, or **olfaction**, is also a chemical sense. Humans have about 10 million olfactory receptor cells located in a 1 square inch area at the top of the nasal passage. Olfactory receptor cells send their axons directly to the **olfactory bulbs** that are located right under the frontal lobes.

The sense of touch is actually composed of several sensations and is more accurately referred to as **somesthetic senses**. The three somesthetic senses are **skin**, **kinesthetic**, and **vestibular**. The skin contains at least six different types of sensory receptors and transmits information about touch, pressure, temperature, and pain. The currently accepted theory about pain is called **gate-control theory** and suggests that pain information is regulated by a number of factors in the brain and spinal cord. Two chemicals involved with pain messages are substance P and endorphins. Substance P transmits information about pain to the brain and spinal cord, while endorphins inhibit the transmission of signals of pain. The kinesthetic sense relays information about your body's sense of position in space. The information comes from sensory receptors called proprioceptive receptors located in your skin, joints, muscles, and tendons. Our sense of balance, or vestibular sense, is regulated by receptor cells in the otolith organs and the **semicircular canals**. Both structures are located near the cochlea of the inner ear. The otolith organs contain small crystals suspended in fluid. Movement causes the crystals to move and activates the sensory receptors. The semicircular canals are three fluid-filled cavities located in three different planes.

Perception is the interpretation of sensation and seems to follow some basic principles, although individual and cultural differences in perception have been recorded. Humans are continually exposed to a large number of stimuli at the same time. We are able to use our powers of attention to focus on certain stimuli in our environment and ignore the rest. Sometimes, we choose where to direct our attention; however, other times our attention is grabbed by a particularly unusual stimulus. The simple act of paying attention is the first step in the process of perception.

The phenomenon called the **cocktail party effect** is the ability to focus attention on a specific stimulus while filtering out a myriad of other stimuli. Despite the waffle of background noise, a person is able to pick out his or her name when it is spoken in a distant conversation. This is similar in fashion to the ability of a student sitting in a noisy lunchroom to hear his or her name being called across the cafeteria by the attendance supervisor, despite the numerous noises and conversations going on around him or her.

One principle is that of perceptual constancy. We tend to view objects as the same **size**, **shape**, and brightness even if the sensations we are receiving from our sensory systems are not constant in size, shape, or brightness. An example of perceptual constancy is our perception of the size and shape of a door as it is opened and closed. **Brightness constancy** is the tendency to perceive the apparent brightness of an object as the same even when the light conditions change. Gestalt psychologists believe that when people are presented with visual information, they interpret the information according to certain expected patterns or rules. The patterns are called the Gestalt principles of perception, and they include the following seven rules: **figure-ground relationships**, **closure**, **similarity**, **continuity**, **contiguity**, **proximity**, and common region. The principle of figure-ground relationships can be illustrated by looking at **reversible figures**, which are visual illusions in which the figure and ground seem to switch back and forth.

Visual perception of depth, called **depth perception**, appears to be present at a very early age. Researchers used the Visual Cliff Experiment to determine that between the ages of 6 and 14 months most infants were very reluctant to move beyond the edge of an apparent "drop off" suggesting they possessed a sense of depth perception. Visual cues for depth that require the use of one eye are referred to as **monocular cues** and include **linear perspective**, **relative size**, **overlap** or interposition, **aerial perspective**, **texture gradient**, **motion parallax**, and **accommodation**. Visual cues that use two eyes are called **binocular cues** and include **convergence** and **binocular disparity**. An **illusion** is a perception that does not correspond to reality. Some famous visual illusions include the **Müller-Lyer illusion**, the moon illusion, and illusions of motion. In addition to cultural and individual differences, perceptions can be influenced by **perceptual sets** or **perceptual expectancies**. One example of perceptual expectancy is **top-down processing** and occurs when a person uses preexisting knowledge to fit individual features into an organized whole. If there is no expectancy to help organize information, a person might use **bottom-up processing** to build a complete perception by making sense of the smaller features piece by piece. Perception is also influenced by a culture's level of technological development. The difference contributes to the ability of people to apply top-down processing or bottom-up processing when trying to reproduce a target image.

Parapsychology is the field of psychology that studies phenomenon that fall outside the normal realm of psychology such as extrasensory perception or ESP. Efforts at trying to verify the existence of extrasensory abilities have produced inconsistent results that have not been replicated. Consequently, it appears that claims suggesting a scientific basis for ESP may reflect the experimenter's expectations and biases toward the existence of ESP. By holding such biases, their ability to think critically on the topic they were studying was limited.

STUDY HINTS

1. Chapter 3 presented information about seven different sensory systems. A chart can be extremely helpful in organizing these various components. See how much of the information you can fill in below, and go to the textbook to find the remaining answers. The first row is filled in for you. A complete table can be found at the end of the Study Hints section.

Sensory System	External Stimulus	Sensory Organ	Sensory Receptor	Proposed Theories
visual system	*light waves*	*eyes*	*rods and cones*	*trichromatic theory opponent-process theory*

2.	Use one or more of the Gestalt principles to create a picture with at least two separate groups of objects.	Use one or more of the monocular depth cues to draw a picture of a tree, house, and a person. Make sure the tree is the farthest object and the person is the closest object.

Many students confuse the Gestalt principles of perception with the monocular cues for depth perception. The two are listed below. The principles of perception deal with the rules we use to decide which objects should be grouped together, while the monocular depth cues are used to determine how far away objects are.

Gestalt principles of perception	**Monocular depth cues**
closure	linear perspective
similarity	texture gradient
contiguity	aerial position
continuity	interposition
figure-ground relationship	motion parallax
proximity	relative size

In order to help clarify the difference, use these cues to draw two separate pictures.

Sensory System	External Stimulus	Sensory Organ	Sensory Receptor	Proposed Theories
visual system	light waves	eyes	rods and cones	trichromatic theory opponent-process theory
auditory system	sound waves	ears	hair cells in the organ of Corti	place theory frequency theory volley theory
gustatory system (taste)	soluble chemicals	tongue, cheeks, mouth	taste cells in the taste buds	
olfactory system (smell)	air-borne chemicals	nose	olfactory receptors	

skin senses	pressure, temperature, pain	skin	six different types including free nerve endings and Pacinian corpuscles	gate-control theory of pain
kinesthetic	body position	skin, joints, muscles, and tendons	propriocetive receptors	
vestibular	acceleration and tilt	semicircular canals and otolith organs	hair cells	

LEARNING OBJECTIVES

3.1 How does sensation travel through the central nervous system, and why are some sensations ignored?

3.2 What is light, and how does it travel through the various parts of the eye?

3.3 How do the eyes see, and how do the eyes see different colors?

3.4 What is sound, and how does it travel through the various parts of the ear?

3.5 Why are some people unable to hear, and how can their hearing be improved?

3.6 How do the senses of taste and smell work, and how are they alike?

3.7 What allows people to experience the sense of touch, pain, motion, and balance?

3.8 What are perception and perceptual constancies?

3.9 What are the Gestalt principles of perception?

3.10 What is depth perception, and what kind of cues are important for it to occur?

3.11 What are visual illusions, and how can they and other factors influence and alter perception?

AP LEARNING OBJECTIVES

1. Discuss basic principles of sensory transduction, including absolute threshold, difference threshold, signal detection, and sensory adaptation. (p. 100)
2. Describe sensory processes, including the specific nature of energy transduction, relevant anatomical structures, and specialized pathways in the brain for each of the senses. (p. 104)
3. Explain common sensory disorders. (pp. 110, 115, 122)
4. Describe general principles of organizing and integrating sensation to promote stable awareness of the external world. (p. 127)
5. Discuss how experience and culture can influence perceptual processes. (p. 134)
6. Explain the role of top-down processing in producing vulnerability to illusion. (p. 136)
7. Discuss the role of attention in behavior. (p. 126)
8. Challenge common beliefs in parapsychological phenomena. (p. 138)
9. Identify the major historical figures in the study of sensation and perception. (pp. 100, 101, 133)

CHAPTER GLOSSARY

absolute threshold	the smallest amount of energy needed for a person to consciously detect a stimulus 50 percent of the time it is present.
accommodation	as a monocular clue, the brain's use of information about the changing thickness of the lens of the eye in response to looking at objects that are close or far away.
aerial perspective	the haziness that surrounds objects that are farther away from the viewer, causing the distance to be perceived as greater.
afterimage	images that occur when a visual sensation persists for a brief time even after the original stimulus is removed.
auditory canal	short tunnel that runs from the pinna to the eardrum.
auditory nerve	bundle of axons from the hair cells in the inner ear.
binocular cues	cues for perceiving depth based on both eyes.
binocular disparity	the difference in images between the two eyes, which is greater for objects that are close and smaller for distant objects.
blind spot	area in the retina where visual information travels to the brain and thus no visual receptors are present.
bottom-up processing	the analysis of the smaller features to build up to a complete perception.
brightness	corresponds to the amplitude (or height) of a light wave.
brightness constancy	the tendency to perceive the apparent brightness of an object as the same even when the light conditions change.
closure	the tendency to complete figures that are incomplete.
cochlea	snail-like structure of the inner ear, filled with fluid.
cochlear implants	medical device surgically implanted to bypass damage in the inner ear and directly stimulate auditory nerve endings.
cocktail party effect	the ability to focus attention on a specific stimulus while filtering out a myriad of other stimuli.
color blindness	reduced ability to distinguish colors due to damage to the cones of the retina.
color or hue	determined by the frequency (or length) of a light wave.
cones	visual sensory receptor found at the back of the retina, responsible for color vision and sharpness of vision.
contiguity	the tendency to perceive two things that happen close together in time as being related.
continuity	the tendency to perceive things as simply as possible, with a continuous pattern rather than with a complex, broken-up pattern.
convergence	the rotation of the two eyes in their sockets to focus on a single object, resulting in greater convergence for closer objects and less convergence if objects are distant.
dark adaptation	the recovery of the eye's sensitivity to visual stimuli in darkness after exposure to bright lights.
depth perception	the ability to perceive the world in three dimensions.
figure-ground relationships	the tendency to perceive objects, or figures, as existing on a background.
frequency theory	states that the perceived pitch is caused by the frequency of the incoming sound wave and subsequently the frequency of firing in the auditory nerve.
gate-control theory	theory of pain that states the psychological experience of pain is controlled by a series of "gates" in the central and peripheral nervous system that can allow or block the flow of the pain information depending on a number of factors.

gustation	the sensation of taste.
habituation	tendency of the brain to stop attending to constant, unchanging information.
hair cells	sensory receptors of the auditory system. Specifically, specialized neurons that convert sound into an electrical-chemical signal.
Hertz (Hz)	cycles or waves per second, a measurement of frequency.
illusion	a perception that does not correspond to reality.
overlap	the assumption that an object that appears to be blocking part of another object is in front of the second object and closer to the viewer.
just noticeable difference (jnd)	the smallest difference between two stimuli that is detectable 50 percent of the time.
kinesthetic senses	sense of the location of body parts in relation to the ground and each other.
light adaptation	the recovery of the eye's sensitivity to visual stimuli in light after exposure to darkness.
linear perspective	the tendency for parallel lines to appear to converge on each other.
monocular cues	cues for perceiving depth based on one eye only.
motion parallax	the perception of motion of objects in which close objects appear to move more quickly than objects that are farther away.
Müller-Lyer illusion	illusion of line length that is distorted by inward-turning or outward-turning corners on the ends of the lines, causing lines of equal length to appear to be different.
olfaction	the sensation of smell.
olfactory bulbs	areas of the brain located just above the sinus cavity and just below the frontal lobes that receive information from the olfactory receptor cells.
opponent-process theory	theory of color vision that proposes four primary colors with cones arranged in pairs: red and green, blue and yellow.
optic nerve	bundle of axons carrying visual information from the retina to the brain.
parapsychology	the study of ESP, ghosts, and other subjects that do not normally fall in the realm of ordinary psychology.
perception	the method by which the sensations experienced at any given moment are interpreted and organized in some meaningful fashion.
perceptual expectancy	the tendency to perceive things a certain way because of pre-established expectations.
perceptual set	the tendency to perceive things a certain way because of previous experiences.
pinna	the outer ear that focuses sound waves for the middle and inner ears.
pitch	psychological experience of sound that corresponds to the frequency (or length) of the sound waves; higher frequencies are perceived as higher pitches.
place theory	theory of pitch that states that different pitches are experienced by the stimulation of hair cells in different locations on the organ of Corti.
proximity	the tendency to perceive objects that are close to each other as part of the same grouping.
relative size	perception that occurs when objects that a person expects to be of a certain size appear to be small and are therefore assumed to be much farther away.
retina	nerve tissue lining the inside of the back of the eye that contains sensory receptors that convert focused light into nerve impulses and transmits the information to the brain through the optic nerves.
reversible figures	visual illusions in which the figure and ground can be reversed.

rods	visual sensory receptor found at the back of the retina, responsible for noncolor sensitivity to low levels of light.
saturation	relates to the degree of mixture of light waves of varying frequency.
semicircular canals	three circular tubes filled with fluid and lined with hair-like receptors that fire when the body moves in any direction.
sensation	the activation of receptors in the various sense organs.
sensory adaptation	tendency of sensory receptor cells to become less responsive to a stimulus that is unchanging.
sensory receptors	specialized neurons designed to convey information regarding external stimuli to the nervous system.
shape constancy	the tendency to interpret the shape of an object as being constant, even when its shape changes on the retina.
similarity	the tendency to perceive things that look similar to each other as being part of the same group.
size constancy	the tendency to interpret an object as always being the same actual size, regardless of its actual distance.
somesthetic senses	the body senses consisting of the skin senses, the kinesthetic sense, and the vestibular senses.
stimuli	various forms of physical energy that the senses are prepared to detect and turn into neural activity.
synesthesia	a condition in which one sensory input is perceived by more than one sensory system. For example, the individual might eat something and experience the taste sensation along with a visual sensation.
taste buds	small structures located under the papillae in the mouth that contain the sensory receptors for the gustatory system.
texture gradient	the tendency for textured surfaces to appear to become smaller and finer as distance from the viewer increases.
timbre	(pronounced TAM-br) the quality of a sound that distinguishes it from other sounds with the same pitch and volume Also referred to as sound quality, for example, thin, thick, light, dark, sharp, dull, smooth, rough, warm, cold. It is this quality that allows you to distinguish between a flute and an oboe playing the same pitch at the same volume. Corresponds to the degree of mixture of varying wavelengths.
top-down processing	the use of pre-existing knowledge to organize individual features into a unified whole.
transduction	the process of converting outside stimuli into neural activity.
trichromatic theory	theory of color vision that proposes three types of cones: red, blue, and green.
vestibular senses	the sensations of movement, balance, and body position.
visual accommodation	changing shape of the lens from thick to thin to focus on objects that are close or far away
volley principle	theory of pitch that states that frequencies above 100 Hz cause the hair cells (auditory neurons) to fire in a volley pattern, or taking turns in firing.
volume	sensation of the loudness of sound determined by the amplitude (or height) of a sound wave.
Weber's law	states that the size of the just noticeable difference is a constant proportion.

CHAPTER PRACTICE TEST

For the following multiple-choice questions, select the answer you feel best answers the question.

1. The most important role of sensory receptors is to _____.
    a) coordinate communications within the body
    b) regulate the body's response to pain
    c) control skeletal muscle contractions
    d) convert an external stimulus into an electrical-chemical message the nervous system can use
    e) interpret electrical-chemical messages within the body

2. The point at which a person can detect a stimulus 50 percent of the time it is presented is called the _____.
    a) absolute threshold
    b) range threshold
    c) differential threshold
    d) noticeable threshold
    e) distributed threshold

3. An automobile manufacturer has decided to add a little bit of horsepower to its cars. They have a device that alters horsepower one unit at a time. Suppose drivers first notice the increase on a 200 horsepower car when it reaches 220 horsepower. How much horsepower must be added to a 150 horsepower car for drivers to notice the difference?
    a) 5
    b) 10
    c) 20
    d) 25
    e) 15

4. If you stared at a picture for a long period of time, you might think the image of the picture would fade due to sensory adaptation. This would be the case except for the tiny vibrations of your eye called _____.
    a) glissades
    b) saccades
    c) habituation movements
    d) light wave responses
    e) phosphenes

5. Light is said to have a dual nature, meaning it can be thought of in two different ways. These two ways are _____.
    a) particles and photons
    b) waves and frequencies
    c) photons and waves
    d) dark light and daylight
    e) ultra and infra

6. When light waves enter the eye, they first pass through the _____.
    a) iris
    b) lens
    c) pupil
    d) optic nerve
    e) cornea

7. Which of the following is true about cones?
   a) They are more sensitive to light than rods.
   b) They detect more color in low light.
   c) They operate mainly at night.
   d) They respond only to black and white.
   e) They are found mainly in the center of the eye.

8. The existence of afterimages in complementary colors best supports the _____ theory of color vision.
   a) opponent-process
   b) place
   c) vibrational
   d) Hering trichromatic
   e) photonic

9. Which of the following properties of sound would be the most similar to the color or hue of light?
   a) pitch
   b) loudness
   c) purity
   d) timbre
   e) amplitude

10. Vibrating molecules in the air are called _____.
    a) light waves
    b) sound waves
    c) odor molecules
    d) taste sensations
    e) photonic molecules

11. The membrane stretched over the opening to the middle ear is the _____.
    a) pinna
    b) oval window
    c) tympanic membrane
    d) cochlea
    e) malleus

12. Which is the correct order of the three bones of the middle ear, from the outside in?
    a) anvil, hammer, stirrup
    b) hammer, stirrup, anvil
    c) stirrup, anvil, hammer
    d) stirrup, hammer, anvil
    e) hammer, anvil, stirrup

13. Which theory proposes that above 400 Hz but below 4000 Hz, auditory neurons do not fire all at once but in rotation?
    a) place theory
    b) volley theory
    c) frequency theory
    d) rotational theory
    e) basilar theory

14. The _____ theory explains how we hear sounds above 1000 Hz.
   a) amplitude
   b) frequency
   c) volley
   d) adaptive
   e) place

15. Ringing or buzzing sensations in the ears may be a sign of _____.
   a) noise-produced hearing damage
   b) habituation of the hair cells
   c) rigidity of the ossicles
   d) volley theory morbidity
   e) adaptation to low-frequency sound

16. _____ is the term used to refer to difficulties in hearing.
   a) Hearing impairment
   b) Timbre blindness
   c) Acoustic stiffness
   d) Volley involution
   e) Subsonic perception

17. If a severe ear infection damages the bones of the middle ear, you may develop _____ hearing impairedness.
   a) nerve
   b) stimulation
   c) brain pathway
   d) conduction
   e) temporal

18. Cochlear implants bypass the _____.
   a) outer ear and inner ear
   b) outer and middle ear
   c) outer, middle, and inner ear
   d) middle and inner ear
   e) inner ear only

19. The "bumps" on the tongue that are visible to the eye are the _____.
   a) olfactory receptors
   b) taste buds
   c) papillae
   d) taste receptors
   e) supporting cells

20. An olfactory stimulus travels from receptor to _____.
   a) olfactory bulb
   b) thalamus
   c) amygdala
   d) pons
   e) medulla

21. In gate-control theory, Substance P _____.
    a) opens the spinal gates for pain
    b) closes the spinal gates for pain
    c) is unrelated to pain
    d) is similar in function to endorphins
    e) is similar in function to dopamine

22. Which is the best description of the vestibular senses?
    a) having to do with touch, pressure, temperature, and pain
    b) having to do with the location of body parts in relation to the ground and to each other
    c) having to do with movement and body position
    d) having to do with your location as compared to the position of the sun
    e) having to do with the combination of smell and taste

23. We know when we are moving up and down in an elevator because of the movement of tiny crystals in the _____.
    a) outer ear
    b) inner ear
    c) semicircular membrane
    d) middle ear
    e) otolith organs

24. Which might be the best explanation of motion sickness, according to your textbook?
    a) the conflict between vision and the vestibular organs
    b) fluid circulating in the semicircular canals
    c) human evolutionary history in that poisons make us dizzy, so when motion makes us dizzy we try to expel the poison
    d) the sensation of fullness in the digestive system
    e) sensory confusion between the olfactory bulb and the tympanic membrane

25. The cocktail party effect shows _____.
    a) how people have the ability to focus attention on a specific stimulus while filtering out a myriad of other stimuli
    b) how people react to social situations that include close friends
    c) how researchers explain the difference between the content of formal and casual conversations in social settings
    d) how those who attend a party are more attentive to others in attendance than a host or hostess
    e) how the ability to produce parapsychological phenomenon is enhanced by relaxing social experiences.

26. The tendency to interpret an object as always being the same size, regardless of its distance from the viewer, is known as _____.
    a) size constancy
    b) shape constancy
    c) brightness constancy
    d) color constancy
    e) depth constancy

27. Closure is the tendency to _____.
    a) perceive objects, or figures, on some background
    b) complete figures that are incomplete
    c) perceive objects that are close to each other as part of the same grouping
    d) perceive things with a continuous pattern rather than with a complex, broken-up pattern.
    e) perceive objects moving together as a single unit

28. Which Gestalt principle is at work in the old phrase, "birds of a feather flock together"?
    a) closure
    b) similarity
    c) expectancy
    d) continuity
    e) common fate

29. Visual distance and depth cues that require the use of both eyes are called _____.
    a) monocular cues
    b) diocular cues
    c) binocular cues
    d) dichromatic cues
    e) inocular cues

30. The Müller-Lyer illusion exists in cultures in which there are _____.
    a) more men than women
    b) more women than men
    c) few buildings
    d) buildings with a lot of corners
    e) buildings with a lot of curves

31. People's tendency to perceive things a certain way because their previous experiences or expectations influence them is called _____.
    a) a perceptual set
    b) binocular disparity
    c) motion parallax
    d) accommodation
    e) phi phenomenon

32. One cultural factor that influences perception is the _____.
    a) level of technological development
    b) nutritional value of available food
    c) level of attention to environmental issues
    d) need for improved medical care
    e) difference between use of monocular versus binocular cues

33. A recent review of studies on ESP using the ganzfeld procedure concluded that _____.
    a) no convincing evidence for psychic ability emerged from any of the studies
    b) no convincing evidence for psychic ability emerged from the majority of studies
    c) convincing evidence for psychic ability was found in the majority of studies
    d) convincing evidence for psychic ability was found in virtually all studies
    e) convincing evidence for psychic ability was found in unflawed studies

CHAPTER PRACTICE TEST ANSWERS

1.   d   Sensory receptors are the body's "antennae" to the outside world. Each sensory receptor type is specially designed to receive a specific external signal and convert it to an electrical-chemical signal.

2.   a   Gustav Fechner investigated the sensitivity of the human sensory systems and called the lowest level of a stimulus that a person could detect half of the time the absolute threshold.

3.   e   According to Weber's law, the just noticeable difference (jnd) is a constant proportion. A change from 200 to 220 represents an increase of 20 units and a jnd of 20/200 or 0.10, which is 10 percent. If the company starts with 150 horsepower, they will need to increase it by 10 percent in order for the driver to notice a difference. Ten percent of 150 is 15.

4.   b   Saccades are the small quick movements your eye makes in order to keep the visual stimuli changing. When our sensory receptors receive unchanging, constant stimuli, they eventually stop responding to the stimulus. This process is known as sensory adaptation.

5.   c   Light can be thought of as a wave and as particles. Photons are the specific type of particles that light is composed of.

6.   e   The cornea is the outermost coating of the eye. It is transparent and serves to protect the eye and to help focus the light coming in to the eye.

7.   e   Cones are the sensory receptors that respond to color and send visual information of high acuity or visual sharpness. The cones are located primarily in the center of the retina. Choices a and d more accurately describe the rods.

8.   a   The opponent-process theory of color vision was introduced, in part, to explain the phenomenon of the afterimage.

9.   a   Pitch is determined by the length of the wave just as color is determined by the length of the wave. Both brightness and loudness are determined by the height of the wave.

10.   b   The outer and middle ear are designed to funnel the vibrating air molecules to the inner ear where they are translated into an electrical signal and sent to the brain.

11.   c   The tympanic membrane is also known as the eardrum. Sound waves cause the tympanic membrane to vibrate when then causes the bones of the middle ear to move back and forth.

12.   e   The order of the bones is hammer, anvil, stirrup which spells "has."

13.   b   Volley theory describes the perception of pitch for the middle frequencies (400 to 4000 Hz). Frequency theory describes the low frequencies (100 Hz and less), and place theory describes the fastest frequencies (1000 Hz and higher).

14.   e   The idea is that at very high sound frequencies, the action potential frequency can't keep up, so pitch has to be coded by the place on the basilar membrane that is activated.

15.   a   Damage to the hair cells can cause the receptors to fire action potentials even when no stimulus is present. This can cause a sensation of ringing in the ears.

16.   a   Hearing impairments are usually divided into impairments of conduction and nerve.

17.   d   Conduction hearing impairment is caused by damage to the outer or middle ear.

18.   b   Cochlear implants use an electronic device instead of the movements of the bones in the middle ear to convert the sound wave into a signal that is then sent to the auditory nerve in the inner ear.

19.   c   The bumps you can see with your eye are the papillae. The taste buds are located along the sides of the papillae. Each taste bud contains 10 to 20 taste receptors.

20.   a   The olfactory system is the only system in which the receptors send their signal directly to the higher brain and bypass the filtering process of the lower brain.

21.   d   The gate-control theory of pain suggests that there are a number of factors in the central and peripheral nervous system that can inhibit or allow pain signals to be transmitted to the brain.

22.   c   The vestibular sense provides you with a sense of balance and sends your brain information about acceleration and tilt.

23.   e   Although the otolith organs are located in the inner ear, choice e is a more precise answer.

24. c   Although choice a is partially correct, the conflict between the visual and vestibular systems only explains the sense of dizziness, it does not explain the sense of nausea. Probably the best explanation for that is human evolutionary theory.

25. a   The ability to focus attention on a specific stimulus while filtering out a myriad of other stimuli is part of the perceptual process.

26. a   Size constancy refers to the fact that our perception of the size of an object tends to remain constant.

27. b   Closure is one of the Gestalt principles of perception and refers to our tendency to "close" objects to form a complete picture.

28. b   The saying is emphasizing that objects with similar characteristics ("birds of a feather") tend to be grouped together ("flock together"). This is the principle of similarity.

29. c   The phrase "ocular" means having to do with the eyes. "Mono" refers to one, and "bi" refers to two. Therefore, the term binocular means seeing depth with two eyes.

30. d   The carpentered-world theory states that the Müller-Lyer illusion does not exist in certain "primitive" cultures because they are not surrounded by straight lines and corners.

31. a   An individual's expectations, or perceptual set, often influence perception of objects.

32. a   A cultural factor that influences perception is level of technological development as it applies to the use of top-down and bottom-up processing when asked to reproduce a target image.

33. b   The majority of quality studies have found no evidence for ESP. The studies that reported positive results were flawed.

CHAPTER PRACTICE FREE RESPONSE QUESTION

You have 25 minutes to answer the following question. You must write in complete sentences and not just list facts. You should make your point clearly and use the language of psychology. Be sure to write legibly and respond to all parts of the question.

Pat is playing a favorite video game. Describe how the following could help and hinder Pat's ability to be successful at the game.
- Adaptation
- Figure-ground
- Place theory of hearing
- Perceptual set
- Weber's law

SUGGESTED RUBRIC—Students should provide specific details and examples to support their assertions; definitions alone are not sufficient. Information about each topic should be discussed in the context of the question rather than abstractly. Successful essays may include the following arguments:

10 points

- Adaptation
  - Score—help—adaptation could help as Pat might become used to distracting images that flash on the screen.
  - Score—hinder—adaptation could hinder Pat by causing him not to notice the presence of enemy figures in the game after seeing them quite often.
- Figure-ground
  - Score—help—figure-ground could help Pat by allowing Pat to hide his player in the game with camouflage.

- o Score—hinder—figure-ground could hinder Pat by making it difficult to see enemy targets in a game that are wearing camouflage.
- Place theory of hearing
  - o Score—help—the place theory of hearing explains how Pat can hear the differences in sounds above 1000 Hz, so he can hear the high-frequency sounds in the game.
  - o Score—hinder—place theory does not explain how Pat can hear the differences in sounds below 1000 Hz, so he would not be able to hear low-frequency sounds in the game.
- Perceptual set
  - o Score—help—perceptual set could help Pat recognize how to complete certain tasks in a game such as solving a maze.
  - o Score—hinder—perceptual set could hinder success in the game if Pat tries to use past skills to complete a new challenge or level in the game that requires a new approach.
- Weber's law
  - o Score—help—Weber's law could help Pat if there is a larger difference between friend and foe in the game as the intensity of the game increases.
  - o Score—hinder—Weber's law could hinder Pat if there is no change in the difference between friend and foe in the game as the intensity of the game increases, which would lead to more errors.

There are many variations on these themes that could score. The important factor that must be met is that the component of the game is linked to a relevant and accurate help or hindrance related to the concept in psychology.

YOU KNOW YOU HAVE MASTERED THE MAIN TOPICS IN THIS CHAPTER IF YOU ARE ABLE TO. . .

- Define consciousness and discuss the different levels of consciousness.
- Explain the factors that control sleep, theories on the purpose of sleep, the stages of sleep, and disorders of sleep.
- Talk about the effects of sleep deprivation.
- Discuss dreams and two theories that attempt to explain why we experience dreams.
- Introduce the phenomenon of hypnosis, outline two theories suggesting the underlying mechanisms of hypnosis, and describe historical and contemporary uses of hypnosis.
- Describe properties and potential dangers of psychoactive drugs including stimulants, depressants, narcotics, and hallucinogens.

RAPID REVIEW

Consciousness is defined as a person's awareness of the world around him or her. **Waking consciousness** is defined as the state of awareness where our thoughts and feelings are clear and organized. **Altered states of consciousness** describe a shift in the quality or pattern of a person's awareness. Examples of altered states of consciousness include using drugs, daydreaming, being hypnotized, or simply sleeping.

The sleep–wake cycle is a **circadian rhythm**, meaning one cycle takes about a day to complete. The cycle is regulated by the **suprachiasmatic nucleus (SCN)** located in the hypothalamus. The SCN responds to changes in daylight and regulates the release of **melatonin** from the pineal gland and body temperature accordingly. By the end of the day, higher melatonin levels and lower body temperature cause people to feel sleepy. In addition, high levels of serotonin are believed to produce feelings of sleepiness. The sleep–wake cycle tends to shift to a 25-hour cycle when subjects do not have access to the sun or clocks. **Sleep deprivation**, or loss of sleep, results in an increase in **microsleeps**, concentration problems, and an inability to perform simple tasks. Participants in a number of sleep deprivation studies reported that they were unaware of their impaired functioning. Two theories are currently proposed for why we sleep. The **adaptive theory** suggests that we sleep to avoid predators, while the **restorative theory** states that sleep is needed to replenish chemicals and repair cellular damage. Both theories are probably partially correct.

Based on brain wave activity recorded with the use of an EEG, sleep has been divided into two different types, **rapid eye movement (REM) sleep** and **non-REM sleep**. Non-REM sleep is a deep, restful sleep and consists of four stages. Stage 1 sleep is also called light sleep and occurs when brain activity begins to shift from **alpha** to **theta wave** activity. Many people experience a **hypnic jerk** in this stage when their body jerks suddenly and wakes them up. As body temperature continues to drop and heart rate slows, **sleep spindles** begin to appear on the EEG recording, signaling Stage 2 of non-REM sleep. Stage 3 occurs when the slow, large **delta waves** first appear; and when delta waves account for more than 50 percent of the total brain activity, the person is said to be in Stage 4, the deepest stage of sleep.

After a person cycles through Stages 1 to 4 and back, instead of entering Stage 1, people experience REM sleep. During this type of sleep, the brain is active and displays **beta wave** activity, the eye exhibits rapid movements, and the skeletal muscles of the body are temporarily paralyzed. This paralysis is referred to as **REM paralysis**. When a person is wakened from this type of sleep, they often report being in a dream state. Most likely, around 90 percent of dreams take place in REM sleep, although dreams also do occur in non-REM sleep. Contrary to popular belief, people do not go crazy when deprived of REM sleep; however, they do spend longer amounts of time in REM sleep when allowed to sleep normally again. This phenomenon is known as **REM rebound**. **Nightmares** are bad dreams and typically occur in REM sleep. **REM behavior disorder** is a rare disorder in which a person's muscles are not paralyzed during REM sleep, allowing them to thrash about and even get up and act out their dreams.

There are a large number of disorders associated with sleep. **Sleepwalking**, or somnambulism, occurs in Stage 4, as well as the rare disorder of **night terrors**. Most people state that they are not aware of the actions they committed during a sleepwalking episode. The explanation of "sleepwalking" has been used as a successful defense in several trials for murder, but in these cases, the term "sleepwalking" is more likely referring to the condition known as REM behavior disorder. **Insomnia** is the inability to get to sleep, stay asleep, or get a good night of quality sleep. **Sleep apnea** is a disorder in which a person actually stops breathing for brief periods throughout the night. **Narcolepsy** is a genetic disorder in which a person suddenly enters REM sleep during the day. The attack can occur many times throughout the day and without warning. The attacks often occur with cataplexy, or a sudden loss of muscle tone.

Several theories have been proposed to explain why dreams occur. Sigmund Freud believed that dreams represented our unconscious thoughts and desires. He called the actual content of our dream the **manifest content** and the real meaning of the dream the **latent content**. The **activation-synthesis hypothesis** was originally proposed by Hobson and McCarley and suggests that dreams are caused by lower brain areas activating the cortex and the cortex fitting together (or synthesizing) the random input from the lower brain. The **activation-information mode model (AIM)** expands on the activation-synthesis model in an attempt to explain the meaningful, realistic, and consistent nature of many dreams. AIM proposes that the cortex uses information from the previous days as it pieces together the input coming from the lower brain. A considerable amount of information is known about the content of dreams. Most dreams tend to reflect events in everyday life as well as the "personality" of the dreamer's culture. Men tend to dream about males, weapons, tools, cars, roads; and their dreams occur in outdoor or unfamiliar settings containing more physical aggression than women's dreams. Men also report more sexual dreams. Women tend to dream about men and women equally; they also are more likely to report dreams about people they know, family, home, concerns about their appearances, and dreams in which they are the victims of aggressive acts. Dreams of being naked in public appear to be common in many cultures.

Hypnosis is a state of consciousness in which a person is especially susceptive to suggestion. Hypnosis can reduce the sensation of pain, create temporary states of amnesia, and affect sensory perception; but it cannot increase physical strength, enhance memory, or regress a person back to his or her childhood. One theory of hypnosis proposed by Ernst Hilgard suggests that the hypnotized person is in a state of dissociation with one part of the brain unaware of the activities happening under hypnosis and another part aware and simply watching what is happening. Hilgard called the part of the conscious that was aware of the activities the hidden observer. The **social-cognitive explanation** of hypnosis states that people who are hypnotized are not in an altered state but are simply playing the role they feel is expected of them in the situation.

A **psychoactive drug** is any drug that alters a person's thinking, perception, or memory. **Physical dependence** on a drug occurs when the user's body does not function normally without the drug. Two signs of physical dependence are drug tolerance and symptoms of **withdrawal** when deprived of the drug. **Psychological dependence** occurs when a drug is needed to maintain a feeling of emotional or psychological well-being. Psychoactive drugs can be classified into major categories including stimulants, depressants, narcotics, and psychogenic drugs.

Stimulants are a class of drugs that increase the activity of the nervous system and the organs connected to it. Specifically, stimulants activate the fight-or-flight response of the sympathetic nervous system. **Amphetamines** are man-made stimulants and include drugs such as benzedrine, methedrine, and dexedrine. Large doses of amphetamines can lead to a severe mental disturbance and paranoia called amphetamine psychosis. **Cocaine** is a naturally occurring stimulant found in coca plant leaves. Cocaine produces feelings of happiness, energy, power, and pleasure and also reduces pain and suppresses appetite. Cocaine is highly addictive and can cause convulsions and death even in first-time users. Signs of cocaine abuse include compulsive use, loss of control, and disregard for the consequences of use. **Nicotine** is a mild yet toxic naturally occurring stimulant that raises blood pressure, accelerates the heart, and provides a rush of sugar into the bloodstream. Nicotine has been found to be more addictive than heroin or alcohol and is linked to nearly 430,000 deaths in the United States each year. **Caffeine** is a third naturally occurring stimulant that increases alertness and can enhance the effectiveness of certain pain relievers.

Depressants are drugs that slow down the central nervous system and include **barbiturates**, **benzodiazepines**, and **alcohol**. Barbiturates have a strong sedative, or sleep-inducing, effect and are known as the major tranquilizers. The minor tranquilizers, or benzodiazepines, have a relatively minor depressant effect and are used to lower anxiety and reduce stress. Some common benzodiazepines include Valium, Xanax, Halcion, Ativan, Librium, and Rohypnol (also known as the date rape drug). The most commonly used and abused depressant is alcohol.

Narcotics reduce the sensation of pain by binding to and activating the receptor sites for endorphins. All narcotics are derived from the plant-based substance of opium. **Opium** itself is made from the opium poppy and reduces pain as well as increases feelings of well-being. **Morphine** is made from opium and is used for the short-term relief of severe pain. Due to its highly addictive nature, the use of morphine is carefully controlled. **Heroin** is also made from opium but is not used as a medicine due to the fact that it is more addictive than morphine or opium. Narcotics are thought to be so addictive because they mimic the action of endorphins and subsequently cause the body to stop producing its own endorphins so that without the drug, there is no protection from pain. **Methadone** is made from opium but does not produce the feelings of euphoria produced by morphine and heroin. Methadone can be used to attempt to control heroin dependency. In addition to methadone treatment, heroin addiction is treated with behavioral therapies such as contingency management therapies and cognitive approaches such as cognitive-behavioral interventions.

Hallucinogens are psychogenic drugs that create false sensory perceptions, also known as hallucinations. **Lysergic acid diethylamide (LSD)** is synthesized from a grain fungus and is one of the most potent hallucinogens. Phenyl cyclohexyl piperdine or **PCP** is a synthesized drug that can act as a hallucinogen, stimulant, depressant, or analgesic depending on the dosage. PCP has also been shown to lead to acts of violence against others or suicide. **MDMA** or Ecstasy is an amphetamine that also produces hallucinations. Because of their stimulant and hallucinogenic properties, PCP and MDMA are now classified as stimulatory hallucinogenics. Naturally occurring hallucinogenics include **mescaline**, **psilocybin**, and **marijuana**. The effects of marijuana are milder than other hallucinogens, yet marijuana use can lead to a powerful psychological dependency.

Hypnogogic hallucinations can occur during Stage 1 sleep. Because Stage 1 is such a light sleep, if woken, you would likely not feel like you were sleeping. This combination of light sleep and hallucination can produce realistic images and sounds that may be mistaken for dramatic events such as alien abduction, ghostly visits, and other supernatural phenomena.

STUDY HINTS

1. Use the space below to create a visual summary of the brain wave and physiological changes that occur as your body moves from an awake state through the stages of sleep typical for one night of sleep. Use arrows to indicate the progression through the stages throughout the course of a night.

Stage	Brain wave activity	Other descriptions
Awake		
non-REM Stage 1		
non-REM Stage 2		
non-REM Stage 3		
non-REM Stage 4		
REM		

2. The textbook introduces six different sleep disorders. Pretend that you have each of the sleep disorders and write a brief description of a particular episode you experienced due to the disorder.

sleepwalking

I don't remember anything that happened but in the morning my mother told me that about 50 minutes after I had fallen asleep (right when I would be in the deepest stage of sleep, Stage 4) I walked past her in the kitchen and I was carrying a bath towel. I put the towel in the refrigerator, looked right at her, and then went back to bed in my bedroom. Supposedly I do this type of thing quite often.

night terrors

_____
_____
_____

REM behavior
disorder

_____
_____
_____

insomnia

_____
_____
_____

apnea

_____
_____
_____

narcolepsy

_____
_____
_____

Suggested solutions for Question 1

Awake	beta	
non-REM Stage 1	alpha	hypnic jerk occurs here
non-REM Stage 2	theta	sleep spindles are seen in this stage
non-REM Stage 3	delta waves	initial appearance of delta waves, they make up minority of brain wave activity
non-REM Stage 4	more than 50 percent delta waves	deepest stage of sleep, hardest to wake the person up, sleepwalking and night terrors occur in this stage
REM	beta	skeletal muscles are paralyzed (except for people with REM behavior disorder), eyes dart back and forth rapidly below the eyelids

LEARNING OBJECTIVES

4.1   *What does it mean to be conscious, and are there different levels of consciousness?*

4.2   *Why do people need to sleep, and how does sleep work?*

4.3   *What are the different stages of sleep, including the stage of dreaming and its importance?*

4.4   *How do sleep disorders interfere with normal sleep?*

4.5   *Why do people dream, and what do they dream about?*

4.6   *How does hypnosis affect consciousness?*

4.7   *What is the difference between a physical dependence and a psychological dependence on a drug?*

4.8   *How do stimulants and depressants affect consciousness, and what are the dangers associated with taking them, particularly alcohol?*

4.9   *What are some of the effects and dangers of using hallucinogens, including marijuana?*

4.10   *How can the workings of our consciousness explain "supernatural" visitations?*

AP LEARNING OBJECTIVES

1. Describe various states of consciousness and their impact on behavior. (pp. 144, 154, 162)
2. Discuss aspects of sleep and dreaming. (p. 145)
3. Explain historic and contemporary uses of hypnosis. (p. 162)
4. Explain hypnotic phenomena. (p. 163)
5. Identify the major psychoactive drug categories and classify specific drugs, including their psychological and physiological effects. (p. 166)
6. Discuss drug dependence, addiction, tolerance, and withdrawal. (p. 166)
7. Identify the major figures in consciousness research. (pp. 144, 158, 164)

CHAPTER GLOSSARY

activation-information mode model (AIM)	revised version of the activation-synthesis explanation of dreams in which information that is accessed during waking hours can have an influence on the synthesis of dreams.
activation-synthesis hypothesis	explanation of dreaming that states that dreams are created by the higher centers of the cortex to explain the activation by the brainstem of cortical cells during REM sleep periods.
adaptive theory	theory of sleep proposing that animals and humans evolved sleep patterns to avoid predators, sleeping when predators are most active.
alcohol	depressant drug resulting from fermentation or distillation of various kinds of vegetable matter.
alpha waves	brain waves that indicate a state of relaxation or light sleep.
altered states of consciousness	state in which there is a shift in the quality or pattern of mental activity as compared to waking consciousness.
amphetamines	stimulants that are synthesized (made) in laboratories rather than being found in nature.
barbiturates	depressant drugs that have a sedative effect.
benzodiazepines	depressant drugs that lower anxiety and reduce stress.
beta waves	brain waves that indicate a state of being awake and alert.
caffeine	a mild stimulant found in coffee, tea, and several other plant-based substances.
circadian rhythm	a cycle of bodily rhythm that occurs over a 24-hour period.
cocaine	a natural stimulant derived from the leaves of the coca plant.
consciousness	a person's awareness of everything that is going on around him or her at any given moment.

delta waves	long, slow waves that indicate the deepest stage of sleep.
depressants	drugs that decrease the functioning of the nervous system.
hallucinogens	drugs that cause false sensory messages, altering the perception of reality.
Heroin	narcotic drug derived from opium that is extremely addictive.
hypnic jerk	an involuntary muscle twitch that often occurs during the transition from wakefulness to sleep.
hypnosis	state of consciousness in which the person is especially susceptible to suggestion.
insomnia	the inability to get to sleep, stay asleep, or get a good quality of sleep.
latent content	term coined by Sigmund Freud to identify the real or "hidden" meaning of a dream.
lysergic acid diethylamide (LSD)	powerful synthetic hallucinogen.
manifest content	term coined by Sigmund Freud to identify the actual or "apparent" content of a dream.
marijuana	mild hallucinogen derived from the leaves and flowers of a particular type of hemp plant.
MDMA	designer drug that can have both stimulant and hallucinatory effects.
melatonin	hormone released from the pineal gland that is associated with the sleep–wake cycle.
mescaline	natural hallucinogen derived from the peyote cactus buttons.
methadone	narcotic drug derived from opium used to treat heroin addiction.
microsleeps	brief episodes of sleep lasting only a few seconds.
morphine	narcotic drug derived from opium, used to treat severe pain.
narcolepsy	sleep disorder in which a person falls immediately into REM sleep during the day, without warning.
narcotics	a class of opium-related drugs that suppress the sensation of pain by binding to and stimulating the nervous system's natural receptor sites for endorphins.
nicotine	a natural stimulant and the active ingredient in tobacco.
night terrors	relatively rare disorder in which the person experiences extreme fear and screams or runs around during deep sleep, without waking fully.
nightmares	bad dreams occurring during REM sleep.
non-REM sleep	any of the stages of sleep that do not include REM.
opium	substance derived from the opium poppy from which all narcotic drugs are derived.
PCP	synthesized drug now used as an animal tranquilizer and which can cause stimulant, depressant, narcotic, or hallucinogenic effects.
physical dependence	a physical state in which rapid discontinuation of consumption of a particular drug leads to a condition of withdrawal.
psilocybin	natural hallucinogen found in certain mushrooms.
psychoactive drug	drugs that alter thinking, perception, and memory.
psychological dependence	the feeling that a drug is needed to continue a feeling of emotional or psychological well-being.
rapid eye movement (REM) sleep	stage of sleep in which the eyes move rapidly under the eyelids and the person is typically experiencing a dream.
REM behavior disorder	a rare disorder in which the mechanism that blocks the movement of the voluntary muscles fails to function, allowing the person to thrash around and even get up and act out nightmares.
REM paralysis	the inability to move the voluntary muscles during REM sleep.

REM rebound	increased amounts of REM sleep after being deprived of REM sleep on earlier nights.
restorative theory	theory of sleep proposing that sleep is necessary to the physical health of the body and serves to replenish chemicals and repair cellular damage.
sleep apnea	disorder in which the person stops breathing for nearly half a minute or more during sleep.
sleep deprivation	any significant loss of sleep, resulting in problems in concentration and irritability.
sleep spindles	bursts of brain wave activity seen on the EEG during Stage 2 sleep.
sleepwalking	occurring during the deep sleep of Stage 4 non-REM sleep, an episode of moving around or walking around in one's sleep.
social-cognitive explanation	theory that assumes that people who are hypnotized are not in an altered state but are merely playing the role expected of them in the situation.
stimulants	drugs that increase the functioning of the nervous system.
suprachiasmatic nucleus (SCN)	area in the hypothalamus that is sensitive to daylight and controls the body's sleep–wake cycle.
theta waves	brain waves indicating the early stages of sleep.
waking consciousness	state in which thoughts, feelings, and sensations are clear, organized, and the person feels alert.
withdrawal	physical symptoms that can include nausea, pain, tremors, crankiness, and high blood pressure, resulting from a lack of an addictive drug in the body systems.

CHAPTER PRACTICE TEST

For the following multiple-choice questions, select the answer you feel best answers the question.

1. What term do psychologists use to designate our personal awareness of feelings, sensations, and thoughts?
   a) thinking
   b) cognition
   c) conscience
   d) consciousness
   e) attention

2. A biological cycle, or rhythm, that is approximately 24 hours long is a(n) _____ cycle.
   a) infradian
   b) circadian
   c) diurnal
   d) ultradian
   e) zeitgebian

3. The hormone melatonin reaches peak levels in the body during the _____.
   a) morning
   b) early evening
   c) afternoon
   d) night
   e) early afternoon

4. Sid is taking part in research on the effects of sleep deprivation; he has been without sleep for 75 hours. Right now researchers have asked him to sit in front of a computer screen and hit a button each time he sees the letter "S" on the screen. A few days ago, Sid was a whiz at this task; however, he is doing very poorly today. How are sleep researchers likely to explain Sid's poor performance?
    a) Due to the sleep deprivation, Sid does not understand the task.
    b) Microsleeps are occurring due to the sleep deprivation, and he is asleep for brief periods of time.
    c) He is determined to ruin the research because of the suffering he is enduring at the hands of the researchers.
    d) He is probably dreaming that he is somewhere else and has no interest in responding to the "here and now."
    e) The researchers have changed the speed of the testing and Sid is unable to keep up.

5. According to this theory, sleep is a product of evolution.
    a) restorative theory
    b) adaptive theory
    c) psychoanalytic theory
    d) dream theory
    e) integration theory

6. If the EEG record reveals evidence of very small and very fast waves, you are likely to conclude that the sleeping person is _____.
    a) really not sleeping and is awake
    b) in Stage 2
    c) in Stage 3
    d) in Stage 4
    e) really not sleeping and is in a coma

7. Each of the following is true of sleepwalking EXCEPT _____.
    a) more boys than girls sleepwalk
    b) sleepwalking is more common among children than adults
    c) waking a sleepwalker is difficult
    d) sleepwalking occurs in about 20 percent of the population
    e) waking a sleepwalker is dangerous

8. For several months, Ted has been taking increasingly larger doses of barbiturate sleeping pills to treat insomnia. He just decided to quit taking any barbiturate sleeping pills. What is likely to happen to Ted when he stops taking the barbiturate sleeping pills?
    a) He will become depressed.
    b) He will experience the REM rebound.
    c) He will increase his intake of caffeine.
    d) He will suffer the symptoms of narcolepsy.
    e) He will suffer from apnea.

9. REM paralysis _____.
    a) is a myth
    b) only occurs in the elderly
    c) prevents the acting out of dreams
    d) may become permanent
    e) is the result of neural activity in the motor strip

10. REM behavior disorder results from _____.
    a) too much sleep
    b) not enough sleep
    c) failure of the pons to block brain signals to the muscles
    d) deterioration of the medial hypothalamus
    e) REM deprivation

11. What is the rationale for the use of "sleepwalking" as a defense for committing a crime?
    a) It was too dangerous to awaken the sleepwalking criminal.
    b) The suspect actually suffers from REM behavior disorder and was unknowingly acting out a dream.
    c) High levels of anxiety and stress were created by the sleep deprivation caused by the sleepwalking episodes.
    d) The suspect was highly susceptible to suggestion at the time of the crime.
    e) Dreams are unconscious drives and uncontrollable.

12. Mary is having insomnia. Which piece of advice would you give to help her deal with it?
    a) Take sleeping pills.
    b) Go to bed every night at a different time.
    c) Study in bed and then go immediately to sleep.
    d) Don't do anything but sleep in your bed.
    e) Eat large meals before going to bed.

13. Sleep apnea is a disorder characterized by _____.
    a) difficulty falling or remaining asleep
    b) nodding off without warning in the middle of the day
    c) difficulty breathing while asleep
    d) experiencing temporary paralysis immediately after waking up from sleep
    e) waking up with vivid and unpleasant content in dreams

14. What two categories of dream content did Sigmund Freud describe?
    a) poetic and realistic
    b) literal and symbolic
    c) latent and manifest
    d) delusional and hallucinatory
    e) REM and non-REM

15. The activation-information mode model suggests _____.
    a) events that occur during waking hours may influence dreams
    b) nothing influences dreams
    c) activation-synthesis is all wrong
    d) dreams have more latent content than once thought
    e) the manifest content of dreams makes them difficult to interpret

16. According to the text, girls and women tend to dream about _____.
    a) animals
    b) cars
    c) people they know
    d) strangers
    e) conflict

17. A social interaction in which one person responds to suggestions offered by another person for experiences involving alterations in perception, memory, and voluntary action defines _____.
    a) biofeedback
    b) meditation
    c) truth induction
    d) extrasensory perception
    e) hypnosis

18. Tests of "hypnotic susceptibility" have been found to _____.
    a) be similar for almost everyone
    b) make use of a series of suggestions
    c) be almost completely inherited
    d) use deception
    e) reveal changes in reaction time

19. Hypnosis can _____.
    a) give people superhuman strength
    b) reliably enhance accuracy of memory
    c) regress people back to childhood
    d) induce amnesia
    e) increase intelligence

20. The idea of "hidden observer" was suggested by _____.
    a) Freud
    b) Watson
    c) Hilgard
    d) Kirsch
    e) Loftus

21. Psychoactive drugs are _____.
    a) drugs that speed up activity in the central nervous system
    b) drugs capable of influencing perception, mood, cognition, or behavior
    c) drugs that slow down activity in the central nervous system
    d) drugs derived from the opium poppy that relieve pain and produce euphoria
    e) drugs that cause hallucinations

22. Psychological dependence is best described as _____.
    a) a desire to take a drug
    b) drug tolerance and signs of withdrawal when deprived of the drug
    c) needing a drug to maintain a feeling of emotional or psychological well-being
    d) feelings of euphoria following the ingestion of a drug
    e) growing dependence on a therapist for emotional support

23. Drugs that speed up the functioning of the nervous system are called _____.
    a) opiates
    b) depressants
    c) narcotics
    d) psychogenics
    e) stimulants

24. The most addictive and dangerous (as defined by the number of deaths caused by the drug) stimulant in use today is _____.
    a) alcohol
    b) amphetamine
    c) nicotine
    d) cocaine
    e) opium

25. Cathy has just taken a drug that has caused her heart rate and breathing to slow down considerably. Most likely, Cathy has taken a(n) _____.
    a) amphetamine
    b) barbiturate
    c) cocaine
    d) hallucinogen
    e) caffeine

26. Your doctor has decided to give you a prescription for a drug to reduce your anxiety levels. Most likely, your doctor will prescribe a _____.
    a) narcotic
    b) hallucinogen
    c) cannabinoids
    d) stimulant
    e) depressant

27. Which of the following is classified as a depressant?
    a) cocaine
    b) LSD
    c) heroin
    d) marijuana
    e) alcohol

28. Jane has a loss of equilibrium, decreased sensory and motor capabilities, and double vision. According to the table in the text, how many drinks has Jane had?
    a) 1–2
    b) 3–5
    c) 6–7
    d) 8–10
    e) 11–15

29. Morphine, heroin, and methadone _____.
    a) are stimulants
    b) all known to be nonaddictive substances
    c) are often used with ADHD
    d) increase the action of the central nervous system
    e) are derived from opium

30. LSD is similar to which of the following drugs?
    a) cocaine
    b) methadone
    c) PCP
    d) CHT
    e) opium

31. Bill is taken to the emergency room of the hospital after he reports hearing dogs screaming and seeing fire shooting across his shirt and pants. Assuming his condition is due to a drug overdose, which type of drug did Bill most likely consume?
    a) a depressant
    b) a stimulant
    c) a narcotic
    d) a hallucinogen
    e) a barbiturate

32. One of the greatest risks of using marijuana is _____.
    a) physical dependency
    b) psychological dependency
    c) weight gain
    d) heart attack
    e) memory loss

33. Hypnogogic hallucinations can explain experiencing images associated with _____.
    a) sleep apnea
    b) somambulism
    c) alien or ghost visitations
    d) night terrors
    e) age regression

CHAPTER PRACTICE TEST ANSWERS

1.   d   Consciousness is defined as personal awareness of feelings, sensation, and thoughts. Your conscience is your sense of morality or right and wrong.

2.   b   If you break down the word, "circa" means about or around (such as circa 1960) and "dia" means day. So circa-dia means about one day long.

3.   d   High melatonin levels is one of the signals for our body that it is time to sleep. The release of melatonin is controlled by signals coming from the suprachiasmatic nucleus, which is light sensitive. In this way, the release of melatonin follows the light–dark patterns of the day.

4.   b   Microsleeps are brief episodes of sleep that we enter and exit rapidly. Sleep deprivation often leads to decreased performance in simple tasks.

5.   b   Adaptive theory states that a species sleeps during the time when its predators are most likely to be out hunting, thus increasing the likelihood of survival for that species.

6.   a   The faster the brain wave activity, the more alert and awake the person is. Another option would have been that the person was in REM sleep where fast small brain wave activity is also seen.

7.   e   Waking the sleepwalker is not dangerous, it just might be hard to do since they are in Stage 4 deep sleep.

8.   b   Barbiturate sleeping pills interfere with REM sleep, so since Ted has been deprived of REM he is likely to spend a longer than usual amount of time in REM for the next few nights. This phenomenon is known as REM rebound.

9.   c   During REM sleep the pons sends messages to the spinal cord that inhibits the movements of skeletal muscles.

10.   c   REM behavior disorder occurs when REM paralysis does not work and a person acts out his or her dreams. The paralysis is mediated by the pons in the brainstem.

11.   b   The sleepwalking defense is actually referring to a suspect thought to have REM behavior disorder.

12.   d   The idea is that the only association you should have with your bed is sleeping and this will make it easier for you to fall asleep when you get in bed.

13.   c   Sleep apnea is a sleeping disorder in which a person actually stops breathing for brief periods throughout the night.

14.   c   Freud thought dreams had two levels—the actual content that he called the manifest content and then the real meaning that he called the latent content.

15.   a   Activation-information mode recognizes that recent events in memory may influence the synthesis of dreams.

16.   c   Women tend to dream about both men and women as well as people they know, while men tend to dream about men.

17.   e   This is simply another way of describing a state of consciousness in which the person is especially susceptible to suggestion.

18.   b   The tests used to determine how likely it is for a person to be hypnotized generally include a list of suggestions.

19.   d   Hypnosis has only been found to induce temporary amnesia, reduce pain, and alter sensory perceptions.

20.   c   Ernst Hilgard suggested that hypnosis was possible because the subject dissociates himself into a part that is aware of what is going on (the hidden observer) and a part that is unaware.

21.   b   The rest of the choices describe a specific category of psychoactive drug.

22.   c   Choice c is the definition for psychological dependence.

23.   e   Stimulants speed up heart rate, blood pressure, and breathing, among other activities.

24.   c   Nicotine has been linked to nearly 430,000 deaths per year in the United States alone.

25.   b   Barbiturate is the only drug listed that is a depressant.

26.   e   The depressants known as the mild tranquilizers, or benzodiazepines, are often prescribed to lower anxiety levels.

27.   e   Alcohol slows down the activity of the central nervous system.

28.   d   See the table in the textbook.

29.   e   All narcotics are derived from the opium poppy. All three of the drugs listed are classified as narcotics.

30.   c   LSD and PCP are both hallucinogens.

31.   d   Hallucinogens produce false sensory perceptions.

32.   b   The effect of psychological dependence can be very powerful.

33.   c   Hypnogogic hallucinations are experienced during Stage 1 sleep and are very real to the person experiencing them.

CHAPTER PRACTICE FREE RESPONSE QUESTION

You have 25 minutes to answer the following question. You must write in complete sentences and not just list facts. You should make your point clearly and use the language of psychology. Be sure to write legibly and respond to all parts of the question.

Define social roles and explain how social roles could bias a person's experiences with each of the following:

- Hypnosis
- Withdrawal
- Sleep deprivation
- Circadian rhythm

SUGGESTED RUBRIC—Students should provide specific details and examples to support their assertions; definitions alone are not sufficient. Information about each topic should be discussed in the context of the question rather than abstractly. Successful essays may include the following arguments:

5   Points

- Do not score simply "people are acting" or simply "people are faking."
  - Score—social roles—socially defined expectations that individuals in a given situation are expected to fulfill.
  - Score—hypnosis—people under hypnosis could be playing roles that they base on dramatic depictions of hypnotized people demonstrating various "powers" of suggestion.
  - Score—withdrawal—people going through withdrawal can experience uncomfortable physical symptoms; however, depictions of people in detox often include dramatic and traumatic psychological reactions.
  - Score—sleep deprivation—people suffering from sleep deprivation are often depicted as becoming irrational and violent because of the lack of sleep and dreaming; however, the research indicates that people deprived of sleep lose some functioning on simple tasks, show irritability, get very tired, and eventually fall asleep.
  - Score—circadian rhythm—disruption of daily cycles can have effects that require a person to make adjustments in their schedules; however, people that have no indications of time do not suffer psychologically and usually slip into a 25-hour cycle.

YOU KNOW YOU HAVE MASTERED THE MAIN TOPICS IN THIS CHAPTER IF YOU ARE ABLE TO. . .

- Define learning.
- Explain what classical conditioning is, how it works, and how it was discovered.
- Describe the mechanisms of operant conditioning.
- Cite examples of biological constraints and how they contribute to learning predispositions.
- Introduce the characteristics of insight, latent, and observational/social learning..
- Identify the researchers who contributed to our understanding of the learning process and explain various ways that their ideas can be applied in the real world.

RAPID REVIEW

Learning is the process that allows us to adapt to the changing conditions of the environment around us and is defined as any relatively permanent change in behavior brought about by experience or practice (as opposed to changes brought about by maturation). **Ivan Pavlov**, a Russian physiologist, discovered one of the simplest forms of learning, called **classical conditioning**. In classical conditioning, an organism learns to make a reflex response to a stimulus other than the original stimulus that produced the response in the first place. The original stimulus is called the **unconditioned (or "unlearned") stimulus (UCS)**, and the reflex response is the **unconditioned response (UCR)**. If a **neutral stimulus (NS)** is repeatedly paired with the UCS, it will eventually produce the same kind of reflexive response. At this point, the NS is called a **conditioned stimulus (CS)** and the response is called a **conditioned, or learned, response (CR)**. The repeated pairing of the NS and UCS is known as **acquisition**. In order for classical conditioning to occur, the CS must occur before the UCS, the CS and UCS must occur close together in time, the CS and UCS must be paired together repeatedly, and the CS should be distinctive. Two other principles of classical conditioning are **stimulus generalization**, the ability of a stimulus that resembles the CS to produce a CR, and **stimulus discrimination**, learning to respond to different stimuli in different ways. In classical conditioning, **extinction** occurs after the CS is repeatedly presented without the UCS and no longer produces a CR. **Spontaneous recovery** occurs when the CS is presented after being absent for a period of time and produces a mild CR. When a powerful conditioned stimulus is paired with a neutral stimulus, the conditioned stimulus itself can function as a UCS and turn the neutral stimulus into a second conditioned stimulus. This process is called **higher-order conditioning**.

John Watson demonstrated a particular type of classical conditioning called **conditional emotional response** with Little Albert and his learned phobia of white rats. **Vicarious conditioning** occurs when a person becomes classically conditioned simply by watching someone else respond to a stimulus. **Conditioned taste aversions** are a unique form of classical conditioning that can occur with only one neutral stimulus–unconditioned stimulus pairing. Superstitions are established in a person's behavior when an event pairs the behavior with a coincidental reinforcement or punishment. For example, "knocking on wood" is paired with preventing something inevitable and bad from happening after making a favorable or boastful statement. The knocking-on-wood behavior is negatively reinforced by the assumption that something negative was taken away when nothing bad happens, and as a result of the perceived reinforcement the behavior becomes more frequent. Conditioning is believed to occur so rapidly due to the **biological preparedness** of most mammals. Pavlov suggested that classical conditioning works through the process of **stimulus substitution**, in that the close pairing in time of the CS with the UCS eventually leads to the CS serving as a substitute stimulus for the UCS and activating the same brain area as the UCS. Psychologists who agree with the **cognitive perspective**, such as Robert Rescorla, suggested that the CS must provide some information about the upcoming UCS and that it is this expectancy that causes the association to occur.

Operant conditioning is a type of learning more strongly associated with voluntary behavior and is based on **Edward Thorndike**'s work with cats and the puzzle box. Based on his research, Thorndike formulated the **Law of Effect** which states that if a response is followed by a pleasurable consequence it will tend to be repeated and if a response is followed by an unpleasant consequence it will tend not to be repeated. **B.F. Skinner** expanded on Thorndike's Law of Effect and coined the term "operant conditioning" for this type of learning, since the term **operant** refers to any voluntary behavior. While classical conditioning focuses on what happens *before* the response, the key to operant conditioning is what happens *after* the response, or in other words, the consequence. **Reinforcement** or a **reinforcer** is a consequence that is pleasurable and strengthens the response that came before it. There are two types of reinforcers. **Primary reinforcers** satisfy basic needs and don't need to be learned. **Secondary reinforcers** get their reinforcing power through prior associations with a primary reinforcer and thus are learned. Reinforcement works by adding a pleasurable consequence after a response occurs (**positive reinforcement**) or removing something unpleasant after a response occurs (**negative reinforcement**). Both positive and negative reinforcement increase the likelihood that the response will occur again.

An important principle that Skinner discovered is that the timing of reinforcement can make a significant difference on how fast a response is learned. **Continuous reinforcement** occurs when a reinforcer is presented after every response. **Partial reinforcement** occurs when a reinforcer is given after some, but not all, of the correct responses. Partial reinforcement takes longer to go through extinction, or in other words, is more resistant to extinction. This is known as the **partial reinforcement effect**. The timing of partial reinforcement is referred to as the **schedule of reinforcement**. There are four different schedules of reinforcement: **fixed ratio**, **variable ratio**, **fixed interval**, and **variable interval**. A ratio schedule occurs when a reinforcer depends on the number of responses that are made. In an interval schedule, reinforcers are presented after a certain period of time has passed. If the reinforcers are always given after a set period of time or number of responses, the schedule is said to be fixed. If the reinforcer is given after varying periods of time or numbers of responses, the schedule is labeled as variable.

Punishment, on the other hand, always decreases the likelihood of a response. Punishment is any consequence of a response that causes that response to be less likely to happen again. While reinforcement strengthens a response that already exists, the goal of punishment is often to eliminate the response, which is usually a much harder task. Typically punishment only temporarily suppresses the response. **Positive punishment** describes the situation in which a response is followed by the addition of something unpleasant. Positive punishment is not the most effective way to modify behavior and has a number of serious drawbacks. **Negative punishment** occurs when a response is followed by the removal of something pleasant. Punishment can be made more effective if it is administered immediately after the undesired behavior, is administered consistently, and is paired with reinforcement for the right behavior.

Shaping involves the use of operant conditioning to reward **successive approximations** until the desired response is obtained. Operant conditioning has several parallels with classical conditioning, such as that **extinction** involves the removal of the reinforcement and **spontaneous recovery** occurs when an organism attempts a previously learned response in order to receive a reward. In addition, a **discriminative stimulus** is defined as any stimulus that provides an organism with a signal or cue for making a certain response in order to get reinforcement. In the lab, researchers found that even though animals could be operantly conditioned to perform certain tasks, they possessed biological constraints to learning other tasks and often had a tendency to go back to their genetic, or natural, way of doing things. This tendency to revert to genetically controlled patterns is called **instinctive drift**.

The term **behavior modification** is used to describe the process of using operant conditioning to change behavior. A **token economy** involves the use of tokens to modify behavior. **Time-outs** are an example of negative punishment where the child is removed from a situation where he or she could get attention from others. **Applied behavior analysis (ABA)** uses shaping techniques to obtain a desired behavior and is particularly successful with children with disorders such as autism. The technique called **biofeedback** uses operant conditioning to modify involuntary behaviors such as blood pressure and heart rate. When this technique is used to try to change brain wave activity, it is referred to as **neurofeedback**.

Cognitive learning theorists focus on the mental processes (or cognitions) that occur during learning. **Edward Tolman** studied the phenomenon of **latent learning** in rats placed in a maze but not reinforced for finding their way out. He found that when the rats were subsequently reinforced, learning occurred much faster than for rats that had never been in the maze. **Martin Seligman** studied a phenomenon he called **learned helplessness** in dogs. He found that dogs classically conditioned to a tone followed by a painful shock would not later try to escape the shock when provided the opportunity. Seligman extended the concept of learned helplessness to humans in an attempt to explain depression. A third cognitive psychologist, **Wolfgang Köhler**, studied the phenomenon of **insight learning** in animals. Köhler believed insight learning involved a sudden perception of relationships that could not be gained through trial and error learning. All three theories of learning are related in that they focus on what's going on inside the learner's mind during the learning process as opposed to the external stimuli and rewards of classical and operant conditioning.

A third category of learning is that of **observational learning**, or the learning of a new behavior by observing someone else who is performing that behavior. The term **learning/performance distinction** describes the fact that learning can take place without actual performance. **Albert Bandura** has been a major contributor to the study of observational learning and conducted a series of classic studies observing children's learned behaviors with a blow-up "Bobo" doll. Bandura concluded that four elements were needed for observational learning to occur; the four elements are attention, memory, imitation, and desire/motivation.

STUDY HINTS

1. Many students get confused with the terms of classical conditioning. There are four major components to this type of learning: unconditioned stimulus (UCS), conditioned stimulus (CS), unconditioned response (UCR), and conditioned response (CR). The best way to keep these terms straight is to ask yourself two questions.

    1. Is the event I am interested in a stimulus or a response?
    2. Is the stimulus/response something that was learned or something that occurs naturally by instinct?

    The first question is the easiest way to break down the information. If an event is a stimulus, it will cause something else to happen. List some examples of stimuli here.

    _____

    You might have mentioned any number of stimuli including events such as a bright light, a puff of air, a loud siren, a soft whisper, a touch on your arm, the smell of cookies, or a written word. The list is quite large. A stimulus is any event that causes a response.

    Now that you have a good feeling for what stimuli are, try listing some examples of some possible responses.

    _____

    You might have mentioned events such as blinking your eyes, laughing, crying, jumping up, heart rate increasing, feeling scared, raising your hand, driving faster. A response is any behavior (inside or outside of your body) that can be observed.

    Once you determine if your event is a stimulus or response, the second question is fairly easy. Is the stimulus something the subject had to learn how to respond to? If so, then it would be a learned or conditioned stimulus. If the stimulus is something that causes the response automatically, then it is an unlearned or unconditioned stimulus. The same rule applies for the responses. If this is a response that does not occur by instinct but instead has been learned through experience, then this is a learned or conditioned response. If the response happens the first time you encounter the stimulus, as an instinct, then it is an unlearned or unconditioned response. Now try some examples and see how you do.

A puff of air is aimed at your eye and you blink.

The event we are interested in is: *the blink*

Question 1: Is this a stimulus or a response?

_____

If you wrote response, then you are correct.
Blinking is a behavior that we can observe.

Question 2: Is this response learned or unlearned?

_____

If you wrote unlearned, then you are correct.
Blinking to a puff of air is an instinct.

Now you can fill in the blanks.
   The first answer tells you this is a response, so it is either a CR or a UCR.

The second answer tells you this is unlearned or unconditioned, so it must be a UCR.

Now circle the right term:

	Stimulus	Response
Learned	CS	CR
Unlearned	UCS	UCR

Try some more on your own.

A picture of a piece of chocolate cake causes your mouth to water.
   The event we are interested in is: *the picture of the cake*

Question 1: Is this a stimulus or a response?

_____

Question 2: Is this response learned or unlearned?

_____

Now circle the right term:

	Stimulus	Response
Learned	CS	CR
Unlearned	UCS	UCR

Your heart speeds up as you see a police car pull up behind you.
The event we are interested in is: *your heart speeding up*

   Question 1: Is this a stimulus or a response?

   _____

   Question 2: Is this response learned or unlearned?

   _____

Now select the right term:

	Stimulus	Response
Learned	CS	CR
Unlearned	UCS	UCR

A loud noise causes someone to jump.
The event we are interested in is: *the loud noise*

   Question 1: Is this a stimulus or a response?

   _____

   Question 2: Is this response learned or unlearned?

   _____

Now select the right term:

	Stimulus	Response
Learned	CS	CR
Unlearned	UCS	UCR

You should have selected the following
blinking your eyes is a UCR
the piece of cake is a CS
your heart speeding up is a CR
the loud noise is a UCS

2. Negative reinforcement and negative punishment are often confused. In negative reinforcement, something bad is taken away. In negative punishment, something good or desirable is taken away. Most people would enjoy being negatively reinforced but would be upset about being negatively punished. Work through the following scenarios to determine whether the person is being negatively reinforced or negatively punished. The first one has been completed for you.

Behavior	Consequence	Is something good or bad taken away?	Is this negative reinforcement or negative punishment?	Will the behavior increase or decrease?
Taking an aspirin for a headache.	Headache goes away.	bad	negative reinforcement	increase
Running a red light.	Driver's license is taken away.			
Cleaning your room so that you are no longer grounded.	You are no longer grounded.			
Drinking coffee in the morning when you are very tired.	You no longer feel tired.			
Staying out past your curfew.	Your parents ground you.			
Getting in a fight with a friend.	Your friend will not talk to you anymore.			
Fastening your seatbelt when the buzzer is making a noise.	The buzzer stops.			
Driving your car until it runs out of gas.	You can't drive your car anymore.			
Your boyfriend nags you until you take him out to dinner.	The nagging stops.			

Suggested answers

Behavior	Consequence	Is something good or bad taken away?	Is this negative reinforcement or punishment?	Will the behavior increase or decrease?
Taking an aspirin for a headache.	Headache goes away	bad	negative reinforcement	increase
Running a red light.	Driver's license is taken away.	good	negative punishment	decrease
Cleaning your room so that you are no longer grounded.	You are no longer grounded.	bad	negative reinforcement	increase

Drinking coffee in the morning when you are very tired.	You no longer feel tired.	*bad*	*negative reinforcement*	*increase*
Staying out past your curfew.	Your parents ground you.	*good*	*negative punishment*	*decrease*
Getting in a fight with a friend.	Your friend will not talk to you anymore.	*good*	*negative punishment*	*decrease*
Fastening your seatbelt when the buzzer is making a noise.	The buzzer stops.	*bad*	*negative reinforcement*	*increase*
Driving your car until it runs out of gas.	You can't drive your car anymore.	*good*	*negative punishment*	*decrease*
Your boyfriend nags you until you take him out to dinner.	The nagging stops.	*bad*	*negative reinforcement*	*increase*

LEARNING OBJECTIVES

5.1 *What does the term learning really mean?*

5.2 *How was classical conditioning first studied, and what are the important elements and characteristics of classical conditioning?*

5.3 *What is a conditioned emotional response, and how do cognitive psychologists explain classical conditioning?*

5.4 *How does operant conditioning occur, and what were the contributions of Thorndike and Skinner?*

5.5 *What are the important concepts in operant conditioning?*

5.6 *What are the schedules of reinforcement?*

5.7 *What is punishment, and how does it differ from reinforcement?*

5.8 *What are some of the problems with using punishment?*

5.9 *How do operant stimuli control behavior, and what are some other concepts that can enhance or limit operant conditioning?*

5.10 *What is behavior modification, and how can behavioral techniques be used to modify involuntary biological responses?*

5.11 *How do latent learning, insight, and learned helplessness relate to cognitive learning theory?*

5.12 *What is observational learning, and what are the four elements of modeling?*

5.13 *What is a real-world example of the use of conditioning?*

AP LEARNING OBJECTIVES

1. Distinguish general differences between principles of classical conditioning, operant conditioning, and observational learning. (p. 182)
2. Describe basic classical conditioning phenomena such as acquisition, extinction, spontaneous recovery, generalization, discrimination, and higher-order learning. (p. 183)
3. Predict the effects of operant conditioning. (p. 192)
4. Predict how practice, schedules of reinforcement, and motivation will influence quality of learning. (p. 192)
5. Interpret graphs that exhibit the results of learning experiments. (pp. 187, 193, 198, 213)
6. Provide examples of how biological constraints create learning predispositions. (p. 206)
7. Describe the essential characteristics of insight learning, latent learning, and social learning. (pp. 209, 211)
8. Apply learning principles to explain emotional learning, taste aversion, superstitious behavior, and learned helplessness. (pp. 189, 194, 213)
9. Suggest how behavior modification, biofeedback, coping strategies, and self-control can be used to address behavioral problems. (p. 207)
10. Identify key contributors in the psychology of learning. (pp. 183, 189, 190, 191, 192, 211, 215)

CHAPTER GLOSSARY

acquisition	in classical conditioning, the repeated pairing of a neutral stimulus with an unconditioned stimulus in order to produce a conditioned response.
Albert Bandura	1925–present. conducted a series of classic studies on how children model aggressive behavior toward an inflatable Bobo doll and developed the concept of observational learning.
applied behavior analysis (ABA)	modern term for a form of behavior modification that uses shaping techniques to mold a desired behavior or response.
B.F. Skinner	1904–1990. proponent of behaviorist perspective and pioneer in the field of operant conditioning.
behavior modification	the use of operant conditioning techniques to bring about desired changes in behavior.
biofeedback	the use of feedback about biological conditions to bring involuntary responses, such as blood pressure and relaxation, under voluntary control.
biological preparedness	referring to the tendency of animals to learn certain associations, such as taste and nausea, with only one or few pairings due to the survival value of the learning.
classical conditioning	learning to make a reflex response to a stimulus other than the original, natural stimulus that normally produces the reflex.
cognitive learning	learning model that focuses on the mental processes required for the acquisition of new behaviors.
cognitive perspective	modern theory in psychology that focuses on mental processes and the study of conscious experiences.
conditional emotional response	emotional response that has become classically conditioned to occur to learned stimuli, such as a fear of dogs or the emotional reaction that occurs when seeing an attractive person.
conditioned, or learned response (CR)	learned reflex response to a conditioned stimulus.
conditioned stimulus (CS)	stimulus that becomes able to produce a learned reflex response by being paired with the original unconditioned stimulus.
conditioned taste aversions	development of a nausea or aversive response to a particular taste because that taste was followed by a nausea reaction, occurring after only one association.

continuous reinforcement	the reinforcement of each and every correct response.
discriminative stimulus	any stimulus, such as a stop sign or a doorknob, that provides the organism with a cue for making a certain response in order to obtain reinforcement.
Edward Thorndike	1874–1949. discovered the law of effect and laid the groundwork for operant conditioning through his work with puzzle boxes.
Edward Tolman	1886–1959. developed several theories of cognitive learning including the concept of latent learning.
extinction	in operant conditioning, the disappearance or weakening of a learned response following the removal of a reinforcer.
fixed interval	schedule of reinforcement in which the interval of time that must pass before reinforcement becomes possible is always the same.
fixed ratio	schedule of reinforcement in which the number of responses required for reinforcement is always the same.
higher-order conditioning	occurs when a strong conditioned stimulus is paired with a neutral stimulus, causing the neutral stimulus to become a second conditioned stimulus.
insight learning	the sudden perception of relationships among various parts of a problem, such as an "aha!" experience, allowing the solution to the problem to come quickly.
instinctive drift	tendency for an animal's behavior to revert to genetically controlled patterns.
Ivan Pavlov	1849–1936. a Russian physiologist who first described the phenomenon now known as classical conditioning.
latent learning	learning that remains hidden until its application becomes useful.
Law of Effect	law stating that if a response is followed by a pleasurable consequence, it will tend to be repeated, and if followed by an unpleasant consequence, it will tend to not be repeated.
learned helplessness	the tendency to fail to act to escape from a situation because of a history of repeated failures in the past.
learning	relatively permanent change in behavior due to experience or practice.
learning/performance distinction	referring to the observation that learning can take place without actual performance of the learned behavior.
Martin Seligman	1942–present. cognitive learning theorist who conducted a series of studies on learned helplessness in dogs.
negative punishment	the punishment of a response by the removal of a pleasurable stimulus.
negative reinforcement	the reinforcement of a response by the removal, escape from, or avoidance of an unpleasant stimulus.
neurofeedback	a form of biofeedback using brain-scanning devices to provide feedback about brain activity in an effort to modify behavior.
neutral stimulus (NS)	stimulus that has no effect on the desired response.
observational learning	learning new behavior by watching a model perform that behavior.
operant	any behavior that is voluntary.
operant conditioning	the learning of voluntary behavior through the effects of pleasant and unpleasant consequences to responses.
partial reinforcement	the reinforcement of some, but not all, of the correct responses.
partial reinforcement effect	the tendency for a response that is reinforced after some, but not all, correct responses to be very resistant to extinction.
positive punishment	the punishment of a response by the addition or experiencing of an unpleasant stimulus.

positive reinforcement	the reinforcement of a response by the addition or experiencing of a pleasure stimulus.
primary reinforcers	any reinforcer that is naturally reinforcing by meeting a basic biological need, such as hunger, thirst, or touch.
punishment	any event or object that, when following a response, makes that response less likely to happen again.
reinforcement	the strengthening of a response that occurs when that response is followed by a pleasurable consequence.
reinforcer	any event or object that, when following a response, increases the likelihood of that response occurring again.
schedule of reinforcement	timing of reinforcement for correct responses.
secondary reinforcers	any reinforcer that becomes reinforcing after being paired with a primary reinforcer, such as praise, tokens, or gold stars.
shaping	the reinforcement of simple steps in behavior that lead to a desired, more complex behavior.
spontaneous recovery	the reappearance of a learned response after extinction has occurred.
stimulus discrimination	the tendency to stop making a generalized response to a stimulus that is similar to the original conditioned stimulus because the similar stimulus is never paired with the unconditioned stimulus.
stimulus generalization	the tendency to respond to a stimulus that is similar to the original conditioned stimulus with the conditioned response.
stimulus substitution	original theory in which Pavlov stated that classical conditioning occurred because the conditioned stimulus became a substitute for the unconditioned stimulus by being paired closely together.
successive approximations	small steps in behavior, one after the other, that lead to a particular goal behavior.
time-out	behavior modification technique where subject is removed from all sources of attention. An example of negative punishment.
token economy	type of behavior modification in which desired behavior is rewarded with tokens that can then be used to acquire items of value.
unconditioned response (UCR)	an involuntary response to a naturally occurring or unconditioned stimulus.
unconditioned stimulus (UCS)	a naturally occurring stimulus that leads to an involuntary response.
variable interval	schedule of reinforcement in which the interval of time that must pass before reinforcement becomes possible is different for each trial or event.
variable ratio	schedule of reinforcement in which the number of responses required for reinforcement is different for each trial or event.
vicarious conditioning	classical conditioning of a reflex response or emotion by watching the reaction of another person.
Wolfgang Köhler	1887–1967. co-founder of Gestalt psychology, studied problem-solving in animals and promoted the concept of insight learning.

CHAPTER PRACTICE TEST

For the following multiple-choice questions, select the answer you feel best answers the questions.

1. _____ is any relatively permanent change in behavior brought about by experience or practice.
   a) Learning
   b) Adaptation
   c) Memory enhancement
   d) Muscle memory
   e) Reinforcement

2. The researcher responsible for discovering classical conditioning was _____.
   a) Skinner
   b) Tolman
   c) Kohler
   d) Pavlov
   e) Watson

3. Which of the following correctly describes the process of classical conditioning?
   a) pairing a stimulus that naturally causes a certain response with a second stimulus that naturally causes the same response
   b) pairing a stimulus that naturally causes a certain response with a second stimulus that does not naturally cause that response
   c) presenting a pleasurable stimulus after the occurrence of a specific response
   d) presenting an unpleasant stimulus after the occurrence of a specific response
   e) presenting an unpleasant stimulus after the performance of a naturally occurring response

4. When Pavlov placed meat powder or other food in the mouths of canine subjects, they began to salivate. The salivation was a(n) _____.
   a) unconditioned response
   b) unconditioned stimulus
   c) conditioned response
   d) conditioned stimulus
   e) neutral stimulus

5. Judy would sometimes discipline her puppy by swatting its nose with a rolled-up newspaper. One day she brought the newspaper into the house still rolled up, and her puppy ran from her in fear. By pairing the rolled paper with the swat, Judy's puppy had developed a(n) _____ response to the rolled-up paper.
   a) generalized
   b) scheduled
   c) unconditioned
   d) discriminative
   e) conditioned

6. You decide you want to try to classically condition your pet dog. What is the correct order that you should use to present the stimuli to your dog?
   a) unconditioned stimulus–neutral stimulus
   b) neutral stimulus–neutral stimulus
   c) neutral stimulus–unconditioned stimulus
   d) present the unconditioned stimulus only
   e) present the neutral stimulus only

7. After you successfully classically conditioned your pet dog, you repeatedly presented the conditioned stimulus without ever pairing it with the unconditioned stimulus. Over time, your dog stops performing the conditioned response. What has happened?
    a) extinction
    b) spontaneous recovery
    c) generalization
    d) stimulus discrimination
    e) higher-order conditioning

8. John Watson and his colleague, Rosalie Rayner, offered a live white rat to Little Albert and then made a loud noise behind his head by striking a steel bar with a hammer. The white rat served as the _____ in their study.
    a) discriminative stimulus
    b) counterconditioning stimulus
    c) conditioned stimulus
    d) unconditioned stimulus
    e) extinguished stimulus

9. Pavlov discovered classical conditioning through his study of _____.
    a) cats escaping from a puzzle box
    b) primate research into problem solving
    c) digestive secretions in dogs
    d) lever-pressing responses of rats
    e) dogs experiencing electric shocks

10. Television advertisers have taken advantage of the fact that most people experience positive emotions when they see an attractive, smiling person. This association is an example of _____.
    a) operant conditioning
    b) learned helplessness
    c) negative reinforcement
    d) punishment
    e) a conditioned emotional response

11. The current view of why classical conditioning works the way it does, by cognitive theorists such as Rescorla, adds the concept of _____ to the conditioning process.
    a) generalization
    b) habituation
    c) memory loss
    d) expectancy
    e) extinction

12. "If a response is followed by a pleasurable consequence, it will tend to be repeated. If a response is followed by an unpleasant consequence, it will tend not to be repeated." This is a statement of _____.
    a) the law of positive reinforcement
    b) Rescorla's cognitive perspective
    c) reward paradox effect
    d) Garcia's conditional emotional response
    e) Thorndike's Law of Effect

13. Kenra has a new pet cat and decides to modify her cat's behavior by administering pleasant and unpleasant consequences after her cat's behaviors. Kenra is using the principles of _____.
    a) observational learning
    b) operant conditioning
    c) classical conditioning
    d) insight learning
    e) latent learning

14. A box used in operant conditioning of animals, which limits the available responses and thus increases the likelihood that the desired response will occur, is called a _____.
    a) trial box
    b) response box
    c) Watson box
    d) Skinner box
    e) insight box

15. A negative reinforcer is a stimulus that is _____ and thus _____ the probability of a response.
    a) removed; does not change
    b) removed; decreases
    c) presented; increases
    d) presented; decreases
    e) removed; increases

16. The partial reinforcement effect refers to the fact that a response that is reinforced after some, but not all, correct responses will be _____.
    a) more resistant to extinction than a response that receives continuous reinforcement (a reinforcer for each and every correct response)
    b) less resistant to extinction than a response that receives continuous reinforcement (a reinforcer for each and every correct response)
    c) more variable in its resistance to extinction than a response that receives continuous reinforcement (a reinforcer for each and every correct response)
    d) totally resistant to extinction unlike a response that receives continuous reinforcement (a reinforcer for each and every correct response)
    e) Partial reinforcement does not influence the resistance to extinction.

17. Which example best describes the fixed interval schedule of reinforcement?
    a) receiving a paycheck after two weeks of work
    b) receiving a bonus after selling 20 cell phones
    c) giving your dog a treat every time it comes when you call it
    d) giving your dog a treat every third time it comes when you call it
    e) giving your dog a treat only on that times that it comes when you call it after you make a noise with its favorite squeak toy

18. Which schedule of reinforcement should you select if you would like to produce the highest number of responses with the least number of pauses between the responses?
    a) fixed ratio
    b) variable ratio
    c) fixed interval
    d) variable interval
    e) discriminative interval

19. When a stimulus is removed from a person or animal and it decreases the probability of response, that is known as _____.
    a) positive punishment
    b) negative punishment
    c) negative reinforcement
    d) positive reinforcement
    e) token punishment

20. Your child has begun drawing on the walls of your house, and you would like this activity to stop. Which of the following actions would, at least temporarily, decrease the occurrence of the behavior in your child?
    a) use insight learning to get your child to stop drawing on the wall
    b) use classical conditioning to create a positive association with drawing on the wall
    c) negatively reinforce your child after he or she draws on the wall
    d) punish your child after he or she draws on the wall
    e) apply only a variable interval schedule of reinforcement when the child writes on the wall

21. An example of a discriminative stimulus might be a/the _____.
    a) stop sign
    b) stimulus that acts as a UCS in classical conditioning
    c) white rat in Watson's Little Albert study of producing phobias
    d) pay off from a slot machine
    e) star on your paper from teacher

22. In their 1961 paper on instinctive drift, the Brelands determined that three assumptions most Skinnerian behaviorists believed in were not actually true. Which is one of the assumptions that were NOT true?
    a) The animal comes to the laboratory a tabula rasa, or "blank slate," and can therefore be taught anything with the right conditioning.
    b) Differences between species of animals are significant.
    c) All responses are not equally able to be conditioned to any stimulus.
    d) Only humans can learn.
    e) All responses must be classically conditioned.

23. Applied behavior analysis or ABA has been used with autistic children. The basic principle of this form of behavior modification is _____.
    a) partial reinforcement
    b) classical conditioning
    c) negative punishment
    d) shaping
    e) positive punishment

24. Biofeedback is an application of _____.
    a) classical conditioning
    b) vicarious punishment
    c) social learning
    d) preparedness
    e) operant conditioning

25. Cognition refers to _____.
    a) behavior that is observable and external
    b) behavior that is directly measurable
    c) the mental events that take place while a person is behaving
    d) memories
    e) neural activity that takes place in the peripheral nervous system

26. The idea that learning occurs, and is stored up, even when behaviors are not reinforced is called _____.
    a) insight
    b) latent learning
    c) placebo learning
    d) innate learning
    e) participant learning

27. A researcher places dogs in a cage with metal bars on the floor. The dogs are randomly given electric shocks and can do nothing to prevent them or stop them. Later, the same dogs are placed in a cage where they can escape the shocks by jumping over a low hurdle. When the shocks are given, the dogs do not even try to escape. They just sit and cower. This is an example of _____.
    a) learned helplessness
    b) stimulus discrimination
    c) aversive conditioning
    d) vicarious learning
    e) instinctive drift

28. The "aha!" experience is known as _____.
    a) latent learning
    b) insight learning
    c) thoughtful learning
    d) serial enumeration
    e) observational learning

29. If you learn how to fix your car by watching someone on TV demonstrate the technique, you are acquiring that knowledge through _____.
    a) latent learning
    b) operant conditioning
    c) classical conditioning
    d) variable schedule learning
    e) observational learning

30. In Bandura's study with the Bobo doll, the children in the group who saw the model punished did not imitate the model at first. They would only imitate the model if given a reward for doing so. The fact that these children had obviously learned the behavior without actually performing it is an example of _____.
    a) latent learning
    b) operant conditioning
    c) classical conditioning
    d) insight learning
    e) reverse learning

31. In Bandura's study of observational learning, the abbreviation AMIM stands for _____.
    a) attention, memory, imitation, motivation
    b) alertness, motivation, intent, monetary reward
    c) achievement, momentum, initiative, memory
    d) achievement, motivation, intellectual capacity, memory
    e) activation, motivation, illustration, memory
32. Which of the following real-world situations is using the principles of classical conditioning?
    a) giving a child a star for completing his or her homework assignment
    b) sending a child to time-out for stealing his or her friend's toy truck
    c) grounding a child until he or she gets his or her room cleaned
    d) a hungry child smiling at the sight of the spoon his or her dad always uses to feed him or her lunch
    e) picking up a crying baby because he or she stops crying when you do

CHAPTER PRACTICE TEST ANSWERS

1. a   This is the definition of learning given in the textbook and restated in the summary.
2. d   Skinner developed the theory of operant conditioning, and both Kohler and Tolman focused on cognitive learning.
3. b   Classical conditioning occurs when you pair a neutral stimulus (NS) with an unconditioned stimulus (UCS). After repeated pairings, the NS now causes a response similar to the naturally occurring response. The stimulus is now called a conditioned stimulus, and the response is the conditioned response.
4. a   An unconditioned response is a response that occurs naturally and does not have to be learned. When food is placed in a dog's mouth, the dog will naturally begin to salivate.
5. e   A conditioned response is a response that has been learned through association. Originally, the rolled-up newspaper did not cause a response of fear in the puppy, but after repeated pairings with a swat, it now causes the fear response.
6. c   For classical conditioning to occur, the neutral stimulus must be repeatedly paired with an unconditioned stimulus. In addition, the neutral stimulus must be presented before the unconditioned stimulus.
7. a   Extinction occurs when the CS is continuously presented without the UCS.
8. c   First, decide if the rat is a stimulus or a response. Obviously, the rat is a stimulus. Then figure out if the rat naturally, or instinctively, will cause the response of fear or if the response needs to be learned. If it needs to be learned, then the stimulus is a conditioned stimulus.
9. c   Pavlov was a Russian physiologist who won a Nobel prize for his study of the digestive system in dogs. It was during this research that he observed the phenomenon of classical conditioning and devoted the rest of his years in research to the study of classical conditioning.
10. e   The association between attractive people and feelings of happiness is learned through classical conditioning and is specifically referred to as a conditioned emotional response since it deals with a response of emotion. Notice that all the other choices were related to operant conditioning.
11. d   Expectancy is the idea that the conditioned stimulus has to provide some information about the upcoming unconditioned stimulus so that we are expecting the UCS to occur.
12. e   Thorndike developed this principle through his study of animals escaping from puzzle boxes.
13. b   This is a modified form of the definition of operant conditioning.
14. d   The Skinner box was designed by B.F. Skinner and typically included an apparatus for the animal to move (such as a lever to press) and a mechanism for delivering a reward to the animal.

15. e   Always start with the fact that reinforcement always increases the response. This immediately eliminates options b and d. Negative reinforcement occurs when an unpleasant stimulus is removed, making e the correct choice.

16. a   If a response is resistant to extinction, that means that the person will continue making that response even when it is not followed by a reinforcer.

17. a   Fixed means that the reinforcement will always be presented after the same period of time or number of responses. Interval means that you are dealing with the passage of time.

18. b   The ratio schedule produces the most rapid responses since the reward depends on making a certain number of responses. The variable schedule reduces the pauses after receiving the reinforcer because the next reward could be given at any time.

19. b   Remember that punishment decreases behavior and reinforcement increases behavior. Since the question is asking about a behavior decrease, it must be talking about punishment. Removing a stimulus is described as negative punishment.

20. d   Once again, you would like the behavior to decrease so you should select punishment.

21. a   A discriminative stimulus is defined as a stimulus that provides a cue that a response might lead to reinforcement. It is a term used with operant conditioning.

22. a   The Brelands questioned the idea of tabula rasa, or blank slate, because of instinctive drift.

23. d   ABA rewards closer and closer approximations to the desired behavior, which is the definition of shaping.

24. e   The change in physiological state is the response and the light or tone serves as the reinforcement.

25. c   Cognitive psychologists focus on our thought process and mental activities.

26. b   The word "latent" means something that is present but not visible.

27. a   Learned helplessness was studied by Seligman as a potential animal model of depression.

28. b   With this type of learning, you have a sudden realization or "insight."

29. e   Observational learning occurs when you learn a new behavior or new knowledge through the observation of a model.

30. a   Latent learning occurs when a new behavior has been acquired but the behavior is not performed, as the children in Bandura's experiment did not imitate the model until they were encouraged and rewarded to do so.

31. a   Since all the selections match the abbreviation, try to think about what skills would be needed to learn by observation. First of all, you need to watch the person you are trying to learn from. Choices c and d can be eliminated because they don't list any skill that would assist with the observation. Choice b can be eliminated if you realize that observational learning can occur without any rewards being offered. Choice e is eliminated because it does not include attention and imitation.

32. d   Choices a, b, c, and e are all examples of operant conditioning.

CHAPTER PRACTICE FREE RESPONSE QUESTION

You have 25 minutes to answer the following question. You must write in complete sentences and not just list facts. You should make your point clearly and use the language of psychology. Be sure to write legibly and respond to all parts of the question.

Renee is interested in trying out for a sport. Explain how the following could influence Renee's participation in tryouts for the team.

- Positive reinforcement
- Negative reinforcement
- Observational learning
- Vicarious punishment
- Classical conditioning

SUGGESTED RUBRIC—Students should provide specific details and examples to support their assertions; definitions alone are not sufficient. Information about each topic should be discussed in the context of the question rather than abstractly. Successful essays may include the following arguments:

5 Points

- Score—positive reinforcement—Renee receives a reinforcer for trying out. Ex. Renee makes the team and receives a varsity letter.
- Score—negative reinforcement—Renee experiences reinforcement by having something removed. Ex. Renee tries out for the sport and makes the team. Now other students stop teasing Renee.
- Score—observational learning—Renee learns from watching a model. Ex. The student ahead of Renee complements the coach and is selected for the team. Renee witnesses this during the tryouts, complements the coach, and then is selected for the team.
- Score—vicarious punishment—Renee watches a model experience punishment, learns from the observation of punishment, and a similar behavior by Renee decreases. Ex. Renee is argumentative and always argues with coaches. The student ahead of Renee at the tryouts argues with the coach and is ejected from the team. Renee witnesses this, does not argue with the coach, and is selected for the team.
- Score—classical conditioning—Renee learns to associate an unconditional response to a new stimulus and now the conditioned stimulus elicits a conditioned response. Ex. Every time the ball is passed to Renee the coach blows a whistle and Renee flinches. After several pairings of the ball being passed and the whistle blowing, Renee now flinches at the sight of the ball being passed and doesn't catch the pass.

YOU KNOW YOU HAVE MASTERED THE MAIN TOPICS IN THIS CHAPTER IF YOU ARE ABLE TO. . .

- Introduce the study of memory including the basic processes of encoding, storage, and retrieval as well as current theories of how memory works.
- Discuss the information-processing theory of memory in detail including the concepts of sensory, short-term memory, long-term memory, and attention.
- Identify the basic mechanisms and limitations in the retrieval of information including false memories.
- Describe Ebbinghaus's work on forgetting and proposed explanations for forgetting.
- Explain the biological processes thought to underlie memory and the deterioration of memory including sleep, diet, and exercise.

RAPID REVIEW

Memory can be thought of as an active system that receives information from the senses, organizes and alters it as it stores it, and then retrieves information from storage. All the current models of memory involve the three processes of **encoding**, **storage**, and **retrieval**.

Three models or theories about memory are discussed in the text. One is the **levels-of-processing model**, which proposes that how long a memory will be remembered depends on the depth to which it was processed. A second model is the **parallel distributed processing model**, which proposes that memories are created and stored across a network of neural circuits simultaneously, or in other words, in a parallel fashion. The third and currently most accepted model of memory is the **information-processing model**, which proposes that memory is divided into three components—**sensory**, **short term**, and **long term**. Sensory memory is the first stage of memory and involves information from our sensory systems. Visual sensory memory is called **iconic memory** and was studied extensively by **George Sperling** through the use of the partial report method. The capacity of iconic memory is everything that can be seen at one time, and the duration is around half a second. Short-term memory is limited in size and temporary. **Eidetic imagery**, also known as photographic memory, is the ability to access visual sensory memory over a long period of time. Iconic memory is useful for allowing the visual system to view the surroundings as continuous and stable. **Echoic memory** is the memory of auditory information and has the capacity of what can be heard at any one moment and has a duration of about two seconds.

The information-processing model proposes that information moves from sensory memory to short-term memory through the process of **selective attention**. This process explains the phenomenon of the **cocktail party effect**, when you are at a party and hear your name in a conversation across the room. **Divided attention**, the processing of multiple cognitive tasks simultaneously, tends to result in diminishing the ability to successfully process one task at the same level as another due the limited size of working memory and the scope of the tasks the mind is attempting to process. For example, trying to read and reply to a text message from a friend while listening to a lecture will reduce the ability of a student to recall the content of the lecture. In the case of two very different tasks, the competition between the tasks can be minimized. For example, humming a familiar tune while washing the dishes places a cognitive task against a manual task and results in minimal competition for space in working memory. Another name for short-term memory is **working memory**, and some researchers propose that short-term memory consists of a central control process along with a visual "sketch pad" and auditory "recorder." **George Miller** studied the capacity of short-term memory using the digit-span memory test and discovered that people can store an average of seven chunks of information (plus or minus two) in their short-term memory. **Chunking** is the process of reorganizing the information into meaningful units. The duration of short-term memory is between 10 and 30 seconds without rehearsal. **Maintenance rehearsal** describes the process of continuing to pay attention to a piece of information, such as reciting a name over and over again in your head.

Long-term memory is the third stage of memory proposed by the information-processing theory and has an essentially unlimited capacity and duration. Information may by encoded into long-term memory through **elaborative rehearsal**, a way of transferring information by making it meaningful. Long-term memories can be divided into two types, procedural and declarative. **Procedural, or nondeclarative memories** are memories for skill and habits, in other words, memories for things people can *do*. **Declarative memories** are memories of facts, or things people can *know*. There are two types of declarative memories, semantic and episodic. **Semantic memory** is memory for the meanings of words and concepts, while **episodic memory** is the memory of events or "episodes." Procedural memories appear to be stored in the cerebellum and amygdala, while declarative memories most likely involve the frontal and temporal lobes. Procedural memory is sometimes referred to as **implicit memory**, and declarative memory can be thought of as **explicit memory**. Explicit memories are easily verbalized, while implicit memories are nearly impossible to state in words. It is not entirely clear how the brain organizes information in long-term memory. The **semantic network model** suggests that information is stored in the brain in a connected fashion with related concepts physically close to each other.

Retrieval describes the process of pulling memories out of long-term memory. A **retrieval cue** is a stimulus that aids in the process of remembering. When the environment in which you learned an item serves as a retrieval cue, it is referred to as **encoding specificity**. If an emotional state serves as a retrieval cue, it is called **state-dependent learning**. Information can be retrieved through the process of **recall**, such as filling in the blanks, or **recognition**, such as multiple-choice questions in which the correct answer only needs to be "recognized." Not all information can be recalled equally well. The **serial position effect** describes the finding that information at the beginning and end of a list is more likely to be remembered than the information in the middle. The **primacy effect** proposes that the information at the beginning of the list is remembered due to rehearsal, while the **recency effect** proposes that the information at the end of the list is remembered due to the fact that it is still in short-term memory. Recognition is usually a much easier task than recall since the retrieval cue is the actual piece of information you are trying to remember, yet retrieval errors are still made when using recognition. A **false positive** occurs when someone recognizes a piece of information as a memory even though it did not happen. For example, a witness says he or she saw broken glass at the scene of an accident, when there was no glass broken in the accident. **Elizabeth Loftus** has spent over 30 years investigating the reliability of eyewitness memories and has found that what people see and hear about an event after the fact can affect the accuracy of their memories for that event. **Automatic encoding** is a term used to describe the memory process when we aren't actively paying attention to the information. A **flashbulb memory** is a specific type of automatic encoding that occurs when an unexpected and often emotional event occurs. Flashbulb memories typically contain a great deal of information including many details but might not be as accurate as they appear.

The retrieval of memories is a much more **constructive process** than most people assume. Several factors affect the accuracy of information retrieval. One factor is the **misinformation effect** in which false information presented after an event influences the memory of that event. When suggestions from others create inaccurate or false memories, this is referred to as the **false memory syndrome**. The false memory syndrome has frequently been observed while people are under hypnosis. Research by Loftus has suggested that in order for an individual to interpret a false event as a true memory, the event must seem plausible and the individual should be given information that supports the belief that the event could have happened to them personally. **Hindsight bias** is the tendency of people to falsely believe that they would have been able to accurately predict a result.

Herman Ebbinghaus was one of the first scientists to systematically study the process of forgetting. Using lists of **nonsense syllables**, he discovered that most forgetting occurs in the initial hour after the material is learned. He presented his findings in a visual graph called the **curve of forgetting**. There are at least four different causes for forgetting. **Encoding failure** occurs when the information does not make it past the initial encoding process and never really becomes a memory. Another possible cause of forgetting is the **decay** (or **disuse**) of the **memory trace** in short-term memory or the disuse of the information in long-term memory. The final two causes of forgetting discussed in the textbook have to do with interference. **Proactive interference** occurs when information from the past disrupts newly learned information. **Retroactive interference** occurs when the newly learned information interferes with the memories of the information from the past. Ebbinghaus found he could greatly improve memory if he spaced out his study sessions, a technique called **distributed practice**, as opposed to "cramming" or trying to learn all the information the night before the exam.

It is still unclear exactly how memories are physically stored in the brain. The concept of the physical change that takes place in the brain when memories are formed is called the **engram**, and scientists continue their search for the engram. In general, there is strong evidence to suggest that long-term procedural memories are stored in the cerebellum, while long-term declarative memories are stored in the frontal and temporal lobes. Storage of short-term memories has been associated with the prefrontal cortex and the temporal lobe. The process of physically storing a memory in your brain is called **consolidation** and could consist of a number of changes including an increase in receptor sties, increased sensitivity at the synapse, changes on the dendrites, or changes in proteins in the neuron. The hippocampus has been found to play an important role in the formation of new memories. This fact was mainly discovered by observing patients with damage to the hippocampus and noting their inability to form any new memories. A man named **H.M.** is the most famous of these patients. H.M.'s hippocampi were removed during a surgical procedure to reduce the severity of his epileptic seizures. After the surgery, H.M. could not form any new declarative memories. H.M. could, however, still form new procedural memories. **Amnesia** is a disorder that is characterized by severe memory loss, such as that of H.M., and can take one of two forms. **Retrograde amnesia** is an inability to retrieve memories from the past, while **anterograde amnesia** is an inability to form any new memories. **Alzheimer's disease**, at least in the beginning, is a form of anterograde amnesia and is one type of dementia that is associated with severe memory loss. Currently, there is no cure for Alzheimer's disease, but researchers are working hard to find one. An inability to remember events from the first few years of life has been described as **infantile amnesia** and may be due to the implicit, or nonverbal, nature of those memories.

Sleep facilitates the consolidation of memories, and sleep deprivation can reduce the ability to acquire new memories. Brief exercise after learning new information can improve memory consolidation. A diet high in an omega-3 fatty acid called DHA showed in animal research an improvement in memory function.

STUDY HINTS

1. Two of the most important concepts presented in this chapter consist of a three-part model. One concept is the basic processes involved in memory—encoding, storage, and retrieval. The other concept is the information-processing model of memory that consists of sensory, short-term, and long-term memory. Students often get these ideas confused. To help you clarify the concepts, correctly identify the components of the information-processing model in the diagram below. Remember that encoding, storage, and retrieval can happen at each of these stages. List an example of encoding, storage, and retrieval for each stage.

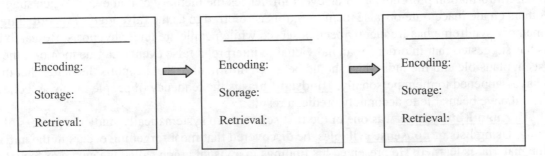

2. Long-term memory can be divided into two basic types of memory—procedural and declarative. Declarative memories can be further broken down into episodic and semantic. To help you understand the difference between these types of memories, come up with a specific memory from your own life and write it in the appropriate box.

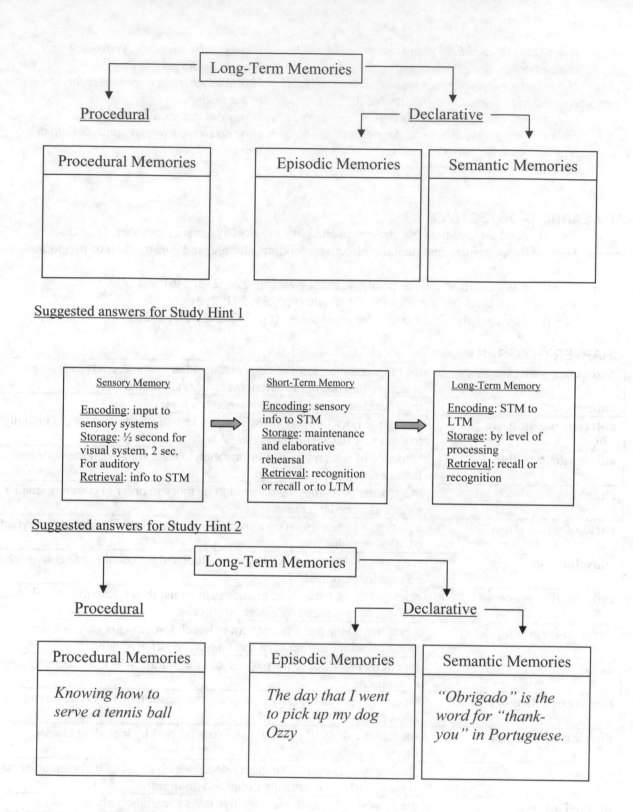

Long-Term Memories

Procedural

Procedural Memories

Declarative

Episodic Memories

Semantic Memories

Suggested answers for Study Hint 1

Sensory Memory	Short-Term Memory	Long-Term Memory
Encoding: input to sensory systems Storage: ½ second for visual system, 2 sec. For auditory Retrieval: info to STM	Encoding: sensory info to STM Storage: maintenance and elaborative rehearsal Retrieval: recognition or recall or to LTM	Encoding: STM to LTM Storage: by level of processing Retrieval: recall or recognition

Suggested answers for Study Hint 2

Long-Term Memories

Procedural

Procedural Memories
Knowing how to serve a tennis ball

Declarative

Episodic Memories
The day that I went to pick up my dog Ozzy

Semantic Memories
"Obrigado" is the word for "thank-you" in Portuguese.

LEARNING OBJECTIVES

6.1 *What are the three processes of memory and the different models of how memory works?*

6.2 *How does sensory memory work?*

6.3 *What is short-term memory, and how does it differ from working memory?*

6.4 *How is long-term memory different from other types of memory?*

6.5 *What are the various types of long-term memory, and how is information stored in long-term memory organized?*

AP LEARNING OBJECTIVES

1. Describe and differentiate psychological and physiological systems of memory. (p. 228)
2. Outline the principles that underlie effective encoding, storage, and construction of memories. (pp. 226, 228)
3. Compare and contrast various cognitive processes. (pp. 226, 236, 246)
4. Describe strategies for memory improvement. (pp. 235, 241, 260)
5. Identify key contributors in cognitive psychology. (pp. 232, 245, 248, 252)

CHAPTER GLOSSARY

Alzheimer's disease	the most common form of dementia in elderly people, leads to severe cognitive loss due to the deterioration of brain tissue.
amnesia	disorder characterized by severe memory loss.
anterograde amnesia	loss of memory from the point of injury or trauma forward, or the inability to form new long-term memories.
automatic encoding	tendency of certain kinds of information to enter long-term memory with little or no effortful encoding.
chunking	the process of regrouping material in memory in order to combine smaller pieces into one larger unit.
cocktail party effect	ability to focus attention on a specific stimulus while filtering out a myriad of other stimuli.
consolidation	the changes that take place in the structure and functioning of neurons when an engram is formed.
constructive process	referring to the retrieval of memories in which those memories are altered, revised, or influenced by newer information.
curve of forgetting	a graph showing a distinct pattern in which forgetting is very fast within the first hour after learning a list and then tapers off gradually.
decay	loss of memory due to the passage of time, during which the memory trace is not used.
declarative memory	type of long-term memory containing information that is conscious and known.
distributed practice	spacing the study of material to be remembered by including breaks between study periods.
disuse	another term to describe memory decay which suggests that memories that are not used will eventually decay and disappear.
divided attention	the processing of multiple cognitive tasks simultaneously
echoic memory	the brief memory of something a person has just heard.
eidetic imagery	the ability to access a visual memory for 30 seconds or more.
elaborative rehearsal	a method of transferring information from STM into LTM by making that information meaningful in some way.
Elizabeth Loftus	psychologist working on memory and how it can be influenced, she is known for her work with false memories.

encoding	the set of mental operations that people perform on sensory information to convert that information into a form that is usable in the brain's storage systems.
encoding failure	failure to process information into memory.
encoding specificity	the tendency for memory of information to be improved if related information (such as surroundings or physiological state) available when the memory is first formed is also available when the memory is being retrieved.
episodic memory	type of declarative memory containing personal information not readily available to others, such as daily activities and events.
explicit memory	memory that is consciously known, such as declarative memory.
false memory syndrome	a condition in which a person has a memory that is objectively false but strongly believed to be true.
false positive	error of recognition in which people think that they recognize some stimulus that is not actually in memory.
flashbulb memory	type of automatic encoding that occurs because an unexpected event has strong emotional associations for the person remembering it.
George Miller	1920–present. Published a paper in 1956 called "The magical number seven plus or minus two" which described the capacity of short-term memory without rehearsal.
George Sperling	psychologist who first studied iconic memory and discovered the duration of iconic memory is around half a second.
H.M.	famous patient who lost the ability to form new memories after surgical removal of his hippocampi.
Herman Ebbinghaus	German psychologist who was a pioneer in the study of human memory. Made extensive use of nonsense syllables in his studies.
hindsight bias	the tendency to falsely believe, through revision of older memories to include newer information, that one could have correctly predicted the outcome of an event.
iconic memory	visual sensory memory, lasting only a fraction of a second.
implicit memory	memory that is not easily brought into conscious awareness, such as procedural memory.
infantile amnesia	the inability to retrieve memories from much before the age of 3.
information-processing model	model of memory that assumes the processing of information for memory storage is similar to the way a computer processes memory, in a series of three stages.
levels-of-processing model	model of memory that assumes information that is more "deeply processed," or processed according to its meaning rather than just the sound or physical characteristics of the word or words, will be remembered more efficiently and for a longer period of time.
long-term memory	the system of memory into which all the information is placed to be kept more or less permanently.
maintenance rehearsal	practice of saying some information to be remembered over and over in one's head in order to maintain it in short-term memory.
memory	an active system that receives information from the senses, organizes and alters it as it stores it away, and then retrieves the information from storage.
memory trace or engram	physical change in the brain that occurs when a memory is formed.
misinformation effect	the tendency of misleading information presented after an event to alter the memories of the event itself.
nonsense syllables	consonant–vowel–consonant combinations that can be pronounced but have no semantic meaning.

parallel distributed processing model	a model of memory in which memory processes are proposed to take place at the same time, over a large network of neural connections.
primacy effect	tendency to remember information at the beginning of a body of information better than the information that follows.
proactive interference	memory retrieval problem that occurs when older information prevents or interferes with the retrieval of newer information.
procedural (nondeclarative) memory	type of long-term memory including memory for skills, procedures, habits, and conditioned responses. These memories are not conscious but are implied to exist because they affect conscious behavior.
recall	type of memory retrieval in which the information to be retrieved must be "pulled" from memory with very few external cues.
recency effect	tendency to remember information at the end of a body of information better than the information ahead of it.
recognition	the ability to match a piece of information or a stimulus to a stored image or fact.
retrieval	getting information that is in storage into a form that can be used.
retrieval cue	a stimulus for remembering.
retroactive interference	memory retrieval problem that occurs when newer information prevents or interferes with the retrieval of older information.
retrograde amnesia	loss of memory from the point of some injury or trauma backwards, or loss of memory for the past.
selective attention	the ability to focus on only one stimulus from among all sensory input.
semantic memory	type of declarative memory containing general knowledge, such as knowledge of language and information learned in formal education.
semantic network model	model of memory organization which assumes that information is stored in the brain in an connected fashion, with concepts that are related to each other stored physically closer to each other than concepts that are not highly related.
sensory memory	the very first stage of memory, the point at which information enters the nervous system through the sensory systems.
serial position effect	tendency of information at the beginning and end of a body of information to be remembered more accurately than information in the middle of the body of information.
short-term memory	the memory system in which information is held for brief periods of time while being used.
state-dependent learning	the ability to retrieve information more readily when a person is in the same emotional state they were in when the information was learned.
storage	holding onto information for some period of time.
working memory	an active system that processes the information present in short-term memory

CHAPTER PRACTICE TEST

For the following multiple-choice questions, select the answer you feel best answers the question.

1. _____ is defined as an active system that receives information from the senses, organizes and alters it as it stores it away, and then retrieves the information from storage.
   a)   Classical conditioning
   b)   Operant conditioning
   c)   Learning
   d)   Memory
   e)   Aquisition

2. _____ is retention of memory for some period of time.
   a) Encoding
   b) Maintenance
   c) Retrieval
   d) Evaluation
   e) Storage

3. Janie is taking an exam in her history class. On the exam, there is a question that asks her to state and discuss the five major causes of the Trans-Caspian War (whatever that was!). Janie remembers four of them. She knows there is a fifth, but time is up. As Janie is walking down the stairs, all of a sudden, she remembers that fifth point, but it is too late. Janie had a problem with _____.
   a) encoding
   b) storage
   c) consolidation
   d) evaluation
   e) retrieval

4. The processes of encoding, storage, and retrieval are seen as part of the _____ model of memory.
   a) enhanced precoding
   b) processing of meaning
   c) distributed practice
   d) information-processing
   e) direct integration

5. The "levels-of-processing" concept of Craik and Lockhart would suggest that which of the following questions would lead to better memory of the word "frog"?
   a) "Does it rhyme with blog?"
   b) "Is it in capital letters?"
   c) "Is it written in cursive?"
   d) "Would it be found in a pond?"
   e) "Does it have four letters?"

6. In the parallel distributed processing model of memory, _____.
   a) information is simultaneously stored across a network that stretches across the brain
   b) information is stored simultaneously in unconnected regions of the brain
   c) information is associated in sets of classically conditioned neurons across the neocortex
   d) information is temporarily stored in the temporal lobe
   e) information is connected to afferent neurons to create memory pathways in the neocortex

7. The three parts of the information-processing model of memory are _____.
   a) sensory memory, short-term memory, and long-term memory
   b) CS, UCS, and UR
   c) encoding, storage, and retrieval
   d) shallow, medium, and deep processing
   e) elaboration, peg word, and method of loci

8. Which memory system provides us with a very brief representation of all the stimuli present at a particular moment?
   a) primary memory
   b) sensory memory
   c) long-term memory
   d) short-term memory
   e) semantic memory

9. Your friend asks you a question, and just as you say "What?" you realize what the person said. Which part of your memory was maintaining your friend's words?
   a) iconic sensory memory
   b) echoic sensory memory
   c) short-term memory
   d) long-term memory
   e) rehearsal memory

10. Ronnie nearly failed the memory quiz in psychology class. Before the quiz, Ronnie was texting a friend during the lecture on memory. The poor performance on the memory quiz is likely the result of Ronnie trying to use _____ while performing two high-level cognitive tasks at the same time.
    a) Broadbent's process of selective memory
    b) the Phi phenomenon
    c) divided attention
    d) cue-controlled inhibition
    e) dichotic retention

11. _____ is synonymous with short-term memory.
    a) Shadow memory
    b) Working memory
    c) Secondary memory
    d) Sensory registers
    e) Echoic memory

12. Your professor asks you to get up in front of the class and repeat a long list of numbers that he or she reads to you. If you are not given a chance to repeat the numbers to yourself as he or she reads them, what is the longest list of numbers you will most likely to be able to remember?
    a) 2
    b) 7
    c) 12
    d) 25
    e) 27

13. You try to remember a phone number by repeating it over and over to yourself. What type of rehearsal are you using?
    a) condensed
    b) permanent
    c) elaborative
    d) maintenance rehearsal
    e) iconic

14. Of the following, which is the most similar to the concept of long-term memory?
    a) a revolving door
    b) a filing cabinet
    c) a desk top
    d) a computer keyboard
    e) a light bulb

15. Long-term memories are encoded in terms of _____.
    a) only sounds and visual images
    b) only visual images and meanings of words and concepts
    c) concepts and images but not words or sounds
    d) sounds, visual images, and meanings of words and concepts
    e) visual images, but not sounds and words

16. Procedural memories are to _____ memories as declarative memories are to _____ memories.
    a) implicit; explicit
    b) explicit; implicit
    c) general knowledge; personal facts
    d) personal facts; general knowledge
    e) short-term; sensory

17. Which of the following types of LTM are forms of explicit memory?
    a) procedural
    b) conditional
    c) persistent
    d) residual
    e) episodic

18. As a young child, you spent hours on your skateboard. After several years of not skating, you jump on your board as if you never missed a day. The long-term memory of how to skate is an example of what type of memory?
    a) explicit
    b) episodic
    c) semantic
    d) procedural
    e) repressed

19. As you are skating down the street on your skateboard, you think back to the day you accidentally skated into a parked car and had to go the hospital to get stitches. The memory of this event would be described as a(n) _____ memory.
    a) procedural
    b) implicit
    c) episodic
    d) semantic
    e) phonological

20. According to the semantic network model, it would take more time to answer "true" to which sentence?
    a)   "A salmon is an animal."
    b)   "A salmon is a fish."
    c)   "A canary is a bird."
    d)   All of these would take the same time.
    e)   The time it takes to answer cannot be measured precisely enough to determine if one takes more time than another.

21. If memory was like the sea, we could say that _____ is long-term memory, _____ are the memories, and _____ are retrieval cues.
    a)   the sea, fish, hooks
    b)   a boat, worms, fish
    c)   a boat, hooks, worms
    d)   an island, worms, fishing poles
    e)   the fish, hooks, the worms

22. Which of the following concepts describes why it is best to take a test in the same room in which you learned the material?
    a)   state-dependent learning
    b)   encoding specificity
    c)   tip-of-the-tongue phenomenon
    d)   cocktail party effect
    e)   semantic encoding

23. While you were studying for your history final, you were very angry at your roommate for playing her music too loud. If you wanted to maximize your ability to remember the information on the final, what mood should you be in while you are taking the final?
    a)   happy
    b)   sad
    c)   angry
    d)   surprised
    e)   disgusted

24. Under most circumstances, when you are intentionally trying to remember an item of information, _____ is an easier task than _____.
    a)   dual encoding; dual processing
    b)   recall; recognition
    c)   priming; the savings method
    d)   the savings method; priming
    e)   recognition; recall

25. When the sound of the word is the aspect that cannot be retrieved, leaving only the feeling of knowing the word without the ability to pronounce it, this is known as _____.
    a)   encoding failure
    b)   extinction of acoustic storage
    c)   auditory decay
    d)   the tip-of-the-tongue effect
    e)   semantic decay

26. The test you are taking right now requires which type of memory retrieval process?
    a) recall
    b) recognition
    c) encoding
    d) echoic
    e) priming

27. False positives occur when a person incorrectly "matches" a stimulus that is merely similar to a real memory. One major problem with eyewitness testimony is that _____.
    a) extinction of auditory memories causes the witness to forget what was said
    b) witnesses are prone to habituate to the courtroom and forget what happened
    c) false positives can cause eyewitness testimony to be quite inaccurate
    d) false positives can cause dissociative retrieval
    e) false positives can lead to memory fixation and transference

28. Is eyewitness testimony usually accurate?
    a) Yes, because seeing is believing.
    b) No, because eyewitnesses are not usually honest.
    c) Yes, because eyewitnesses are very confident about their testimony.
    d) No, because there is a great possibility of a "false positive" identification.
    e) Yes, because eyewitnesses prefer to be helpful when questioned.

29. For more than 30 years, the most influential researcher into eyewitness memory has been _____.
    a) Broadbent
    b) Sperling
    c) Baddeley
    d) Treisman
    e) Loftus

30. Flashbulb memories _____.

    a) are not subject to periodic revision
    b) usually concern events that are emotionally charged
    c) are almost always highly accurate
    d) usually concern events from early childhood
    e) are memories associated with bursts of light

31. In this view, memories are literally "built" from the pieces stored away at encoding. This view is called _____.
    a) constructive processing
    b) hindsight bias
    c) adaptation of memory traces
    d) flashbulb integration
    e) the integrated memory model

32. Which of the following phenomena provides support for the concept that memories are reconstructed as they are retrieved or remembered?
   a) tip-of-the-tongue
   b) hindsight bias
   c) cocktail party effect
   d) retrograde amnesia
   e) constructive adaptation

33. Which of the following is an example of the misinformation effect?
   a) forgetting where you left your keys
   b) falsely remembering that a friend was wearing a jacket after being asked what color your friend's jacket was
   c) remembering a traumatic event from childhood
   d) telling someone a lie
   e) an old memory interfering with a new memory

34. Which of the following statements about hypnosis is NOT true?
   a) Subjects cannot always distinguish between memories which they have always had and new "memories" recently recovered under hypnosis.
   b) Hypnotic age regression appears to increase the accuracy of childhood recall.
   c) The impact of hypnosis on the reliability of later memory depends on the type of question asked. Open-ended questions cause less memory "contamination" than closed-ended, leading questions.
   d) Some pseudomemories (false memories) suggested by hypnosis do not persist after the hypnosis.
   e) Memories obtained through hypnosis should not be considered accurate without solid evidence from other sources.

35. Which of the following techniques are used by therapists to implant a false memory?
   a) hypnosis, drugs, and suggestion
   b) partial reinforcement, rewards, and punishments
   c) presentations of images of the person's problems, presented in a subliminal fashion
   d) coercion, stress, and sleep deprivation
   e) misinformation, flashbulb induction, and rewards

36. Which of these is viewed as the major problem in the repressed-memory controversy?
   a) guaranteeing the right to sue alleged abusers
   b) therapists' unwillingness to help recover memories
   c) deliberate deception on the part of those who claim abuse
   d) distinguishing true repressed memories from false memories
   e) many repressed memories go unreported to authorities

37. Ebbinghaus found that information is forgotten _____.
   a) more rapidly as time goes by
   b) gradually at first, then increasing in speed of forgetting
   c) quickly at first, then tapering off gradually
   d) most quickly one day after learning
   e) most quickly when deep encoding is not used

38. Retroactive interference as used in the study of memory refers to when _____.
    a) older information already in memory interferes with the retrieval of newer information
    b) newer information interferes with the retrieval of older information
    c) the information is not attended to and fails to be encoded
    d) information that is not accessed decays from the storage system over time
    e) hypnosis is used to take a person back to childhood memories

39. Shalissa has two exams today. One is in French and the other is in history. Last night she studied French before history. When she gets to her history test, all she can remember is French! Shalissa's memory is suffering from _____.
    a) cue-dependent forgetting
    b) proactive interference
    c) decay
    d) retroactive interference
    e) reactive memory tapering

40. In the famous case of H.M., after having part of his brain removed, he could no longer _____.
    a) pay attention to specific stimuli
    b) retrieve memories
    c) remember faces but he could remember names
    d) make sense of memories
    e) form new memories

41. The physical processes that occur when a memory is formed are called _____.
    a) consolidation
    b) actuation
    c) potentiation
    d) depolarization
    e) serialization

42. When a person's _____ is damaged or removed, anterograde amnesia results.
    a) hippocampus
    b) prefrontal lobe
    c) amygdala
    d) cerebellum
    e) lateral hypothalamus

43. Which of the following best describes a strategy for memory improvement?
    a) After studying for a test, perform a strenuous exercise routine, maintain a high level of fat in your diet, and avoid sleeping soon after studying.
    b) After studying for a test, perform brief exercise, maintain a high level of the omega-3 fatty acid DHA in your diet, and avoid sleep deprivation.
    c) Avoid exercise after studying, and increase the amount of time between sleep and studying.
    d) Use multitasking to combine the processing of two high-level cognitive tasks in order to engage more of the mind in the consolidation of memories.
    e) Link the new information you are trying to remember to irrelevant information that you already remember to form neural bonds that will consolidate memories of the new information.

CHAPTER PRACTICE TEST ANSWERS

1. d   Memory involves the three processes of encoding, storage, and retrieval. All four other choices deal with the process of learning.

2. e   When you store something, you keep it (or retain it) for a certain period of time. In the study of memory, the term "storage" involves keeping or retaining information for a certain period of time.

3. e   Retrieval is the process of pulling information back out of memory.

4. d   Encoding, storage, and retrieval are the basic processes for memory and part of the information-processing model. The rest of the choices are inaccurate names of memory theories.

5. d   The levels-of-processing model proposes that the "deeper" the level of processing, the more likely it is to be remembered. This means that the more meaning or significance you can give to a piece of information, the better you remember it. Associating a frog with the place it lives is the most meaningful association of all the four choices.

6. a   The name of the model describes the theory. The parallel distributed model proposes a series of networks that work in parallel in the brain.

7. a   As mentioned in Question 4, all models of memory include the concepts of encoding, storage, and retrieval. The aspects of the information-processing model that make it unique are the concepts of sensory, short-term, and long-term memory.

8. b   Sensory memory is the briefest of all the memory stages proposed by the information-processing model. Visual sensory memory lasts only about one-half a second.

9. b   Echoic memory is the memory of sounds. It should be easy to remember if you just think of an "echo" for echoic.

10. c   The likely effect of divided attention is a reduction in the ability to effectively conduct one cognitive task as successfully as another when multitasking.

11. b   Short-term memory is thought to be the place where memories either enter long-term memory or disappear. The idea is that if we work with the information, using memory techniques or rehearsal strategies, then the information will be retained in long-term memory.

12. b   The amount of information we can retain in short-term memory was studied by George Miller and presented in a paper called "The magic number 7 plus or minus two."

13. d   Maintenance rehearsal is one of the most basic methods to remember something and involves simply repeating the information over and over. Elaborative rehearsal is more complex and involves forming an association with the information.

14. b   Long-term memory is where information is stored for an indefinite amount of time. If you look at the choices for this question, the only item that accommodates the storage of anything for a long period of time is a filing cabinet.

15. d   Memories are encoded in terms of sounds, visual images, and meanings of words and concepts. The rest of the answers are incomplete or exclude one of the components.

16. a   Procedural memories (such as how to ride a bike) are hard to verbalize just as implicit memories are hard to verbalize. If something is explicit, that means it is very clear and obvious, just as declarative memories (like the memory of your first kiss) are very easy to identify.

17. e   Episodic memories are explicit and are memories of episodes, such as your last birthday celebration.

18. d   Procedural memories are memories for procedures (or habits and skills).

19. c   This is a memory of a specific episode.

20. a   In selection a, you have to move across two categories—salmon to fish to animal—whereas in selections b and c, you are only moving across one category—salmon to fish and canary to bird. Research has determined that moving across two categories takes a measurably greater amount of time to complete.

21.　a　Try to consider the most important aspects of long-term memory, memories, and retrieval cues. Long-term memory can hold a large amount of information like the sea, a boat, or an island. The memories are what are found in long-term memory. We find fish in the sea but we don't typically store a large number of worms or hooks in a boat or worms in an island. Just to make sure you are correct, retrieval cues are used to pull out the memories, hooks can pull out worms. None of the other options make sense (fish don't pull out worms, worms don't pull out hooks, and fishing poles don't pull out worms). So the correct choice is a.

22.　b　Encoding specificity refers to your physical surroundings and how they can act as retrieval cues for information.

23.　c　State-dependent learning refers to your emotional state and how being in the same mood during retrieval as you were during the encoding process can help you remember more information.

24.　e　Recognition simply requires "recognizing" the right answer. This means you are given all the options and you simply select the correct choice.

25.　d　The tip-of-the-tongue phenomenon gives us one clue as to how retrieval works.

26.　b　You are given the right answer and you simply have to select it from choices a to e.

27.　c　The work of Elizabeth Loftus has demonstrated that false positives among eyewitnesses are more frequent than we used to believe.

28.　d　Although eyewitness testimony can be accurate, there is always the possibility of false positives.

29.　e　Elizabeth Loftus is one of the most influential researchers into false memories.

30.　b　Flashbulb memories can be altered over time.

31.　a　Constructive processing assumes that all the pieces of a memory are stored in different locations and "re-assembled" every time the memory is retrieved.

32.　b　In hindsight bias, our memory of a past event is influenced by new information.

33.　b　The misinformation effect occurs when a leading question or statement actually alters your memory of an event.

34.　b　Studies on memories retrieved under hypnosis have failed to find an increase in accuracy for recalling childhood events.

35.　a　Therapists have mainly used hypnosis, drugs, or suggestion to implant false memories.

36.　d　Often an individual cannot distinguish between his or her own true memories and false memories.

37.　c　Most forgetting occurs within the first hour after the material is learned.

38.　b　Retroactive interference occurs when the new information gets in the way or "interferes" with the already learned material.

39.　b　Proactive interference occurs with the already learned material interferes with the new information.

40.　e　After H.M's hippocampus was removed, he lost the ability to move memories from short-term to long-term memory.

41.　a　The term "consolidation" refers to the physical basis of memories. Researchers are still working to determine the precise details of consolidation.

42.　a　Anterograde amnesia is described as the inability to form any new memories. Just like the case of H.M., when a person's hippocampus is removed or damaged, anterograde amnesia is often the result.

43.　b　Avoiding sleep deprivation, brief exercise after studying, and a diet high in DHA have been shown to improve memory in humans and animals.

CHAPTER PRACTICE FREE RESPONSE QUESTION

You have 25 minutes to answer the following question. You must write in complete sentences and not just list facts. You should make your point clearly and use the language of psychology. Be sure to write legibly and respond to all parts of the question.

Val, a junior in high school, and a classmate are having lunch in the cafeteria of their former elementary school after giving a presentation to the third-grade class on what it is like to be in high school. They start discussing their early years at elementary school. The classmates each give an account of their first day in kindergarten. Explain how the following may influence the memories the friends share about their first day of school.

- Memory reconstruction
- Encoding specificity
- Retroactive interference
- Flashbulb memories
- Ebbinghaus forgetting curve

SUGGESTED RUBRIC—Students should provide specific details and examples to support their assertions; definitions alone are not sufficient. Information about each topic should be discussed in the context of the question rather than abstractly. Successful essays may include the following arguments:

- Score—memory reconstruction—memories may be inaccurate because in the process of reconstructing the memories they fill in lost details with details that could be accurate. Ex. Val shares a memory of a large clock in the classroom; however, in this case, there was no clock in the kindergarten classroom.
- Score—encoding specificity—their memories are more accurate because they are recounting the memories in the cafeteria of their former elementary school. Ex. When telling a story about what happened one day during lunch in the elementary school cafeteria, Val remembers more details because the memories are now being accessed while having lunch in the same cafeteria.
- Score—retroactive interference—the memories are inaccurate because newer memories interfere with old memories. Ex. While telling about the first day of kindergarten Val actually includes details from the first day of fifth grade like substituting the name of the fifth-grade teacher for the name of the kindergarten teacher.
- Score—flashbulb memories—memories of kindergarten are enhanced because of a strong emotional experience. Ex. Val was very frightened by another student and remembers with great detail what the other student was wearing that day.
- Score—Ebbinghaus forgetting curve—the majority of their memories of the first day were lost within a short time; however, a few details are still in their memory. Ex. they cannot remember the names of all their classmates in kindergarten but they can remember the name of their teacher.

YOU KNOW YOU HAVE MASTERED THE MAIN TOPICS IN THIS CHAPTER IF YOU ARE ABLE TO. . .

- Introduce cognition, as it relates to mental images, concepts and problem solving.
- Describe factors that limit the ability to solve problems and the characteristics of creativity and creative thinking.
- Define intelligence, and describe several prominent theories of intelligence.
- Describe approaches to measuring intelligence.
- Outline intelligence test construction issues including reliability, validity, standardization, and how culture influences intelligence.
- Discuss the concepts of intellectual disability, giftedness, and emotional intelligence and the influences of heredity and environment on their origins.
- Explain the basis of language and the relationship between language and thought processes.

RAPID REVIEW

Thinking, or **cognition**, can be defined as mental activity that goes on in the brain when a person is processing information. Cognition includes both verbal and nonverbal processes. Two examples of cognition are **mental images**, which are picture-like representations that stand in for objects or events, and **concepts**, or ideas that represent a class of objects. Concepts can be ranked from general to specific by applying the terms **superordinate**, **basic level type**, and **subordinate**. **Formal concepts** are defined by specific rules, while **natural concepts** are formed as a result of experience. A **prototype** is a specific example of a concept that closely resembles the defining features of a concept. Concepts are formed through experience and culture and have an impact on our thinking.

Problem solving involves using our thoughts or cognitions to reach a goal and consists of at least four different techniques. **Trial-and-error** problem solving makes use of mechanical solutions. When someone uses **algorithms** to problem-solve they are following step-by-step procedures to solve the problem. **Heuristics** are general "rules of thumb" that can be applied to many situations. **Means-end analysis** is an example of one type of heuristic where the difference between where you are and where you want to be is determined and then steps are taken to reduce that difference. **Insight** consists of solving the problem by having a sudden moment of inspiration or "aha!" moment. **Artificial intelligence** is the creation of a machine that can think like a human and is represented today through computer program such as Deep Blue.

Some factors that interfere with problem solving include **functional fixedness**, which is when a person thinks about objects only in terms of their typical uses; **mental sets**, which are tendencies to use the same problem-solving strategies that worked in the past; and **confirmation bias**, which consists of the search for evidence that fits your beliefs while ignoring any contradictory information. **Creativity** occurs when a person solves a problem by combining ideas and behaviors in a new way. Many methods of problem solving utilize **convergent thinking**, which assumes that one single answer exists for the problem. **Divergent thinking** is the opposite process of convergent thinking. When an individual uses divergent thinking, he or she starts from one point and comes up with many possibilities or ideas based on that point.

Intelligence can be defined as the ability to learn from one's experiences, acquire knowledge, and use resources effectively in adapting to new situations or solving problems. Currently, there is still much disagreement on exactly what is meant by the term "intelligence" In 1904, **Charles Spearman** proposed that intelligence was split between two abilities. The first ability was a general intelligence, labeled the **g factor**, and the other was a specific intelligence referred to as the **s factor**. Spearman believed that both the g and s factors could be measured using standardized intelligence tests. **Howard Gardner**, on the other hand, proposed that at least nine different kinds of intelligence exist. **Robert Sternberg** proposed the **triarchic theory of intelligence**, which states that intelligence can be divided into three types: **analytical**, **creative**, and **practical intelligence**.

In France in 1916, **Alfred Binet** and Theodore Simon developed the first formal test for intelligence in order to determine a child's mental age. The Stanford–Binet test used a ratio of mental age to chronological age to determine an individual's **intelligence quotient** or **IQ**. In the United States, the Wechsler intelligence tests are now used more frequently than the Stanford–Binet, and IQ scores are now based on individual **deviation IQ scores** rather than a ratio. The Wechsler tests are designed for specific age groups and can be administered individually. To determine the quality of a psychological test, you need to look at the test's **validity**, **reliability**, and procedure used to obtain the **norms**. Validity refers to how well the test measures what it claims to measure, while reliability indicates the test's ability to produce the same result when given to the same person under similar conditions. Norms are determined by the **standardization group** selected by the researchers and should be a representative sample of the population who will be taking the test. All psychological tests should also be examined for the cultural biases. Adrian Dove created an intelligence test call the Dove Counterbalance General Intelligence Test (also known as the Chitling Test) to demonstrate the cultural biases present in many of the intelligence tests currently in use.

Intellectual disability, formerly known as mental retardation, occurs in about 1 percent of the U.S. population and is defined by an IQ score of 70 (two standard deviations below the mean) or lower along with adaptive behaviors significantly below the expected level for the person's age group. Diagnosis of intellectual disability is determined by assessing levels of deficit in the conceptual, social, and practical domains. Intellectual disability is classified from mild to profound in each of the domains. Common biological causes of intellectual disability are Down syndrome, fetal alcohol syndrome, and fragile X syndrome.

Individuals who receive scores of 130 or above on intelligence tests are referred to as **gifted**. **Lewis Terman** conducted a longitudinal study of the traits and behaviors of over 1,500 gifted children. The children were known as Terman's Termites, and his findings showed that many of the common myths about the "nutty genius" were unfounded.

More recently, the concept of **emotional intelligence**, the accurate awareness of and ability to manage one's own emotions to facilitate thinking and attain specific goals, and the ability to understand what others feel, has been suggested as an important factor for success in life. Research is emerging that shows emotional intelligence is a valid and measurable concept and that a relationship exists between emotional intelligence and general intelligence. The role of a person's environment, or **nurture**, and heredity, also referred to as **nature**, on the development of intelligence continues to be debated. Studies of identical and fraternal twins raised together and apart have provided one method for investigating the roles of nature and nurture. While claims have been made linking race and intelligence, it is clear that there is no real scientific evidence to support the notion of genetic differences in intelligence between races. IQ tests are not free of cultural or socioeconomic bias. That being the case, just being aware of negative stereotypes can result in an individual scoring poorly on intelligence tests, a response called **stereotype threat.**

Language is defined as a system for combining symbols (such as words) so that an unlimited number of meaningful statements can be made for the purpose of communicating with others and can be analyzed at many levels. **Semantics** is the rules for determining the meaning of words and sentences. **Phonemes** are the most basic units of sounds used in a specific language, **morphemes** combine the units of sound into the smallest units that have meaning, **grammar** includes all the rules for combining morphemes into words, and **syntax** is the rules for combining words into sentences. **Pragmatics** deals with the practical aspects of communicating with others. The relationship between language and thought has been studied extensively. The **Sapir–Whorf hypothesis**, also known as the **linguistic relativity hypothesis**, proposes that the words people use determine how they think about themselves and the world. An opposing theory, known as **cognitive universalism**, proposes that certain ways of thinking are shared among all groups of people and influence the development of language in similar ways. Animals other than humans demonstrate a diverse ability to communicate, but it is unclear whether or not they have the capability for language as demonstrated by the ability to use abstract symbols to communicate. Kanzi, a bonobo chimpanzee, has demonstrated an ability to understand about 150 spoken English words. However, none of the animals studied to date appear to have been able to use and comprehend syntax.

Researchers have found that "exercising" the brain with mental exercises can produce gains in specific cognitive areas like language; moreover, physical exercise is strongly linked to improvements in executive control and memory processes.

STUDY HINTS

1. In this chapter, you were presented with four different approaches to problem solving. In order to better understand how these approaches differ from each other, take the following problem and come up with an example of how you could solve the problem using each of the four different approaches.

    Problem: You are packing up to move to college and you have one more box to fit in the trunk of your car, but it looks like there is simply no room left. You don't want to leave the box behind. How will you solve this problem?

Approach	Solution
trial and error	
algorithm	
heuristics	
insight	

The two most commonly used methods to assess any psychological test are to determine the validity and reliability of the test. Examine the following test descriptions and determine whether the test has a potential problem with its reliability or validity.

Example	Validity or Reliability Issue?
A personality test gives a very different score for the same person when they retake it six months later.	
An individual takes an online IQ test that measures how long she can hold her breath.	
A 5-year-old child is diagnosed as intellectually disabled based on his IQ scores, but when he is brought back and given the same test, his scores fall in the above average range.	

Suggested Answers to Question 1

Approach	Solution
trial and error	*Keep placing the box in various places and positions in your car until you find one that works.*
algorithm	*Go online and find a website that deal with physics. Enter in the dimensions of your car and the exact dimensions of every box and item that you are trying to fit in your car. Get a printout of the optimal placement for each box and follow it step by step to fit everything in.*
heuristics	*Think back to how your mom always told you to pack the big things first and then squeeze the little ones in. Take your boxes out and pack them again using this general rule of thumb to guide you.*
insight	*Sit back with your friends for a few minutes and relax. As you are talking with your friends, all of a sudden you remember that your family has a "Big Mac" container that will attach to the top of the car. Strap the container on, place your box in the container, and take off for school.*

Suggested Answers to Question 2

Example	Validity or Reliability Issue?
A personality test gives a very different score for the same person when they retake it six months later.	*reliability—the scores are not consistent over time for the same person*
An individual takes an online IQ test that measures how long she can hold her breath.	*validity—does holding your breath give a very accurate assessment of your IQ?*
A 5-year-old child is diagnosed as intellectually disabled based on his IQ scores, but when he is brought back and given the same test, his scores fall in the above average range.	*This question illustrates that without reliability a test will also lack validity. The test scores are inconsistent over time, which indicates that the test is not really measuring what it claims to measure since we assume that intelligence is a fairly constant factor.*

LEARNING OBJECTIVES

7.1 *How are mental images and concepts involved in the process of thinking?*

7.2 *What are the methods people use to solve problems and make decisions?*

7.3 *Why does problem solving sometimes fail, and what is meant by creative thinking?*

7.4 *How do psychologists define intelligence, and how do various theories of intelligence differ?*

7.5 *How is intelligence measured, and how are intelligence tests constructed, and what role do these tests play in neuropsychology?*

7.6 *What is intellectual disability, and what are its causes?*

7.7 *What defines giftedness, and how are giftedness and emotional intelligence related to success in life?*

7.8 *What is the influence of heredity and environment on the development of intelligence?*

7.9 *How is language defined, and what are its different elements and structure?*

7.10 *Does language influence the way people think, and are animals capable of learning language?*

7.11 *What are some ways to improve thinking?*

AP LEARNING OBJECTIVES

1. Identify major historical figures in psychology. (p. 299)
2. Identify problem-solving strategies as well as factors that influence their effectiveness. (p. 270)
3. List the characteristics of creative thought and creative thinkers. (p. 275)
4. Compare and contrast historic and contemporary theories of intelligence. (p. 278)
5. Define intelligence and list characteristics of how psychologists measure intelligence. (p. 278)
6. Explain how psychologists design tests including standardization strategies and other techniques to establish reliability and validity. (p. 282)
7. Discuss how culture influences the definition of intelligence. (pp 269, 276, 284)
8. Debate the appropriate testing practices, particularly in relation to culture-fair test uses. (pp. 285, 296)
9. Interpret the meaning of scores in terms of the normal curve. (p. 283)
10. Describe relevant labels related to intelligence testing. (p. 289)
11. Identify key contributors in intelligence research and testing. (pp. 278, 279, 280, 281, 282, 291)
12. Synthesize how biological, cognitive, and cultural factors converge to facilitate acquisition, development, and use of language. (p. 298)
13. Identify key contributors in cognitive psychology. (pp. 272, 298, 300)
14. Identify key contributors in developmental psychology. (p. 300)

CHAPTER GLOSSARY

Alfred Binet	1857–1911. French psychologist who developed the first formal test for intelligence.
algorithms	very specific, step-by-step procedures for solving certain types of problems.
analytical intelligence	the ability to break problems down into component parts, or analysis, for problem solving.
basic level type	an example of a type of concept around which other, similar concepts are organized, such as "dog," "cat," or "pear."
Charles Spearman	1863–1945. English psychologist who proposed the two-factor theory of intelligence consisting of the g factor and the s factor.
cognition (thinking)	mental activity that goes on in the brain when a person is organizing and attempting to understand information, and communicating information to others.
cognitive universalism	theory that concepts are universal and influence the development of language.
concepts	ideas that represent a class or category of objects, events, or activities.
confirmation bias	the tendency to search for evidence that fits one's beliefs while ignoring any evidence that does not fit those beliefs.
convergent thinking	type of thinking in which a problem is seen as having only one answer, and all lines of thinking will eventually lead to that single answer, using previous knowledge and logic
creative intelligence	the ability to deal with new and different concepts and to come up with new ways of solving problems.
creativity	the process of solving problems by combining ideas or behavior in new ways.
deviation IQ score	a type of intelligence measure which assumes that IQ is normally distributed around a mean of 100 with a standard deviation of about 15.
divergent thinking	type of thinking in which a person starts from one point and comes up with many different ideas or possibilities based on that point.
emotional intelligence	the awareness of and ability to manage one's own emotions as well as the ability to be self-motivated, able to feel what others feel, and socially skilled.
formal concepts	concepts that are defined by specific rules or features.
functional fixedness	a block to problem solving that comes from thinking about objects in terms of only their typical functions.
g factor	the ability to reason and solve problems, or general intelligence.

gifted	the two percent of the population falling on the upper end of the normal curve and typically possessing an IQ of 130 or above.
grammar	the system of rules by which the symbols of language are arranged.
heuristics	a general strategy that may help narrow down the possible solutions for a problem. Also known as a "rule of thumb."
Howard Gardner	1943–present. cognitive psychologist who has acted as a major proponent on the concept of multiple intelligences. Current theory suggests that nine types of intelligence exist.
insight	when the solution to a problem comes suddenly, also referred to as a "aha!" moment.
intellectual disability	an IQ score of 70 (two standard deviations below the mean) or lower along with adaptive behaviors significantly below the expected level for the person's age group.
intelligence	the ability to learn from one's experiences, acquire knowledge, and use resources effectively in adapting to new situations or solving problems.
intelligence quotient (IQ)	a number representing a measure of intelligence, resulting from the division of one's mental age by one's chronological age and then multiplying that quotient by 100.
language	a system for combining symbols (such as words) so that an unlimited number of meaningful statements can be made for the purpose of communicating with others.
Lewis Terman	1877–1956. cognitive psychologist well known for his longitudinal study of gifted children, affectionately referred to as Terman's Termites.
linguistic relativity hypothesis (Sapir–Whorf hypothesis)	the theory that thought processes and concepts are controlled by language.
means-end analysis	heuristic in which the difference between the starting situation and the goal is determined and then steps are taken to reduce that difference.
mental images	mental representations that stand in for objects or events and have a picture-like quality.
mental set	the tendency for people to persist in using problem-solving patterns that have worked for them in the past.
morphemes	the smallest units of meaning within a language.
natural concepts	concepts people form as a result of their experiences in the real world.
nature	the role a person's heredity plays in his or her development.
norms	the standards used to assess the score of any individual who completes a standardized test.
nurture	the role a person's environment plays in his or her development.
phonemes	the basic units of sound in language.
practical intelligence	the ability to use information to get along in life and become successful.
pragmatics	aspects of language involving the practical aspects of communicating with others, or the social "niceties" of language.
problem solving	process of cognition that occurs when a goal must be reached by thinking and behaving in certain ways.
prototype	an example of a concept that closely matches the defining characteristics of a concept.

reliability	the tendency of a test to produce the same scores again and again each time it is given to the same people.
Robert Sternberg	1949–present. proposed the triarchic theory of intelligence which states that intelligence is composed of three different abilities.
s factor	the ability to excel in certain areas, or specific intelligence.
semantics	the rules for determining the meaning of words and sentences.
standardization group	a randomly selected group chosen to represent the population for whom a psychological test is intended. Norms are calculated based off on the scores of the standardization group.
stereotype threat	the effect that just being aware of negative stereotypes can result in an individual scoring poorly on intelligence tests.
subordinate	the most specific category of a concept, such as one's pet dog or a pear in one's hand.
superordinate	the most general form of a type of concept, such as "animal" or "fruit."
syntax	the system of rules for combining words and phrases to form grammatically correct sentences.
trial and error	problem-solving method in which one possible solution after another is tried until a successful one is found.
triarchic theory of intelligence	Sternberg's theory that there are three kinds of intelligences: analytical, creative, and practical.
validity	the degree to which a test actually measures what it's supposed to measure.

CHAPTER PRACTICE TEST

For the following multiple-choice questions, select the answer you feel best answers the question.

1. Mental images _____.
   a) represent abstract ideas
   b) have a picture-like quality
   c) consist entirely of unconscious information
   d) are always prototypes
   e) are constructed in the temporal lobe

2. If three people used mental images to tell you how many windows they each had in their individual houses, which person would take the longest to answer?
   a) the person with 2 windows in his or her house
   b) the person with 8 windows in his or her house
   c) the person with 10 windows in his or her house
   d) the person with 12 windows in his or her house
   e) They would all take the same amount of time to answer.

3. Concepts are ideas that represent _____.
   a) a class or category of objects, events, or activities
   b) thoughts, images, and muscle patterns of behavior
   c) higher-order conditioning and secondary reinforcers
   d) lower-order conditioning and primary reinforcers
   e) muscle patterns of behavior, objects, and reinforcers

4. A very general form of a concept, such as "vegetable," represents which concept level?
   a) subordinate
   b) superordinate
   c) basic level
   d) hyperordinate
   e) prototypical

5. The trial-and-error method of solving problems is also known as _____.
   a) the use of a heuristic device
   b) the use of algorithms
   c) the mechanical solution
   d) the A.I. solution
   e) means-end analysis

6. Zach could not remember the four-digit combination needed to open the lock on his bicycle. After struggling to figure out what to do, he turned to start the long walk home, and all of a sudden he remembered the combination to the lock. The problem-solving strategy Zach used would be best described as _____.
   a) trial-and-error
   b) algorithm
   c) a heuristic
   d) insight
   e) the A.I. solution

7. Not being able to notice that pliers could be used as a weight when tied to a string and used to swing the string toward you like a pendulum is an example of: _____.
   a) insight
   b) hindsight
   c) algorithmic thinking
   d) functional fixedness
   e) the unavailability heuristic

8. The tendency for people to persist in using problem-solving patterns that have worked for them in the past is known as _____.
   a) top-down processing
   b) confirmation bias
   c) creativity
   d) divergent thinking
   e) mental set

9. Luann needs to hammer a nail into the wall, but the only tool she can find in the house is a screwdriver. Luann's inability to see how the handle of the screwdriver could be used as a hammer best represents the concept of _____.
   a) functional fixedness
   b) confirmation bias
   c) creativity
   d) artificial bias
   e) heuristic failure

10. The ability to produce solutions to problems that are unusual, inventive, novel, and appropriate is called _____.
    a) creativity
    b) insight
    c) heuristics
    d) latent learning
    e) algorithmic processing

11. Which of the following activities would NOT increase your creativity?
    a) keeping a journal
    b) brainstorming
    c) subject mapping
    d) divergent thinking
    e) convergent thinking

12. The ability to understand the world, think rationally or logically, and use resources effectively when faced with challenges or problems, or the characteristics needed to succeed in one's culture, is the psychologist's working definition of _____.
    a) divergent problem solving
    b) creative thinking
    c) heuristic usage
    d) intelligence
    e) convergent thinking

13. The "g" in Spearman's g factor of intelligence stands for _____.
    a) gifted intelligence
    b) general intelligence
    c) graded intelligence
    d) gradual intelligence
    e) The g does not stand for anything.

14. Which of the following is not included in Gardner's multiple intelligence theory?
    a) logical
    b) correlational
    c) mathematical
    d) interpersonal
    e) intrapersonal

15. Sternberg has found that _____ intelligence is a good predictor of success in life but has a low relationship to _____ intelligence.
    a) practical; analytical
    b) practical; creative
    c) analytical; practical
    d) academic; creative
    e) emotional; academic

16. What three types of intelligence constitute Sternberg's triarchic theory of intelligence?
    a) global, intuitive, and special
    b) general, global, and specific
    c) analytical, creative, and practical
    d) mathematical, reasoning, and verbal
    e) intuitive, emotional, and general

17. An 8-year-old child who scored like an average 10-year-old on an intelligence test would have a mental age of _____ and an IQ of _____.
   a) 8; 80
   b) 8; 125
   c) 10; 100
   d) 10; 80
   e) 10; 125

18. Because of the need to measure the IQ of people of varying ages, newer IQ tests base their evaluation of IQ on _____.
   a) mental age alone
   b) deviation scores from the mean of the normal distribution
   c) giving extra points for older folks to compensate for their slower processing times
   d) chronological age alone
   e) subjective measures alone

19. If a test consistently produces the same score when administered to the same person under identical conditions, that test can be said to be high in _____.
   a) reliability
   b) validity
   c) accuracy
   d) norms
   e) reusability

20. Denny has a defect in a gene on the X chromosome of the 23rd pair, leading to a deficiency in a protein needed for brain development. Denny would most likely be diagnosed with _____.
   a) Down syndrome
   b) Wilson's syndrome
   c) fetal alcohol syndrome
   d) cretinism
   e) fragile X syndrome.

21. Which two of the following aspects are included in the definition of intellectual disability?
   a) IQ scores and adaptive behavior
   b) age and socioeconomic status
   c) race and country of origin
   d) only IQ scores are considered
   e) socioeconomic status and country of origin

22. Which of the following statements about the gifted is true?
   a) They are more likely to suffer from mental illnesses.
   b) They are physically weaker than nongifted persons.
   c) They are often skilled leaders.
   d) They are socially unskilled.
   e) They are below average in height.

23. Which was NOT a finding of the Terman and Oden (1974) study of gifted kids?
   a) They were socially well adjusted.
   b) They were more resistant to mental illness.
   c) They were clearly much more likely to be females.
   d) They were above average in weight and height.
   e) They were above average in physical attractiveness.

24. If intelligence is determined primarily by heredity, which pair should show the highest correlation between IQ scores?
   a) fraternal twins
   b) identical twins
   c) brothers and sisters
   d) parents and children
   e) fraternal twins separated at birth

25. If a researcher believed that *nature* was the most important factor in determining an individual's intelligence level, she would most closely agree with which of the following statements?
   a) Intelligence is largely inherited from your parents.
   b) Intelligence has no relationship to your biological family.
   c) The environment is the most important factor in determining a child's intelligence level.
   d) A child's intelligence can be greatly increased by providing stimulating toys throughout infancy.
   e) Eating certain foods helps increase intelligence.

25. Just being aware of negative stereotypes can result in an individual scoring poorly on intelligence tests, a response called _____.
   a) stereotype threat
   b) bell curve enhancement
   c) cultural bias
   d) cognitive reconstruction
   e) statistical misinterpretation

27. Language, by definition, _____.
   a) is not symbolic
   b) is capable of only a finite set of meaningful utterances
   c) begins at a later age in eastern cultures
   d) can be written, spoken, or signed
   e) can only be learned before a critical age

28. The basic units of sound are called _____.
   a) morphemes
   b) phonemes
   c) semantics
   d) syntax
   e) geons

29. Syntax is _____.
    a) a system of rules for combining words and phrases to form sentences
    b) the smallest units of meaning within a language
    c) the basic units of sound
    d) the rules to determine the meaning of words
    e) the small gestures used to enhance the meaning of words

30. The linguistic relativity hypothesis suggests that _____.
    a) one's language determines the pattern of one's thinking and view of the world
    b) one's thinking and view of the world determines the structure of one's language
    c) we decide which objects belong to a concept according to what is most probable or sensible, given the facts at hand
    d) perception of surface structure precedes deep structure in understanding a sentence
    e) perception of deep structure precedes surface structure in understanding a sentence

31. Which theory would support the idea that certain concepts are shared by all people regardless of the language spoken?
    a) Sapir–Whorf hypothesis
    b) linguistic relativity hypothesis
    c) cognitive universalism
    d) heuristic theory
    e) whole language theory

32. Dolphins, according to TV and movies, are very intelligent and have strong language abilities. They might even be able to talk! However, which statement is true from the research?
    a) Dolphins have been shown to master syntax.
    b) Dolphins have the language abilities of a 3-year-old.
    c) Dolphin communication with parrots has been firmly established.
    d) Dolphins can teach other dolphins symbolic language.
    e) Dolphin language studies have met with limited success.

33. You are worried about your aging parents. You would like them to make good choices toward maintaining their cognitive abilities. Thus you suggest _____.
    a) they stop reading as it will tire their brains out faster
    b) they start a program of aerobic fitness for increased oxygen and blood flow to the brain
    c) they seek activities that require mental engagement but minimal physical activity
    d) Nothing will help—don't bother to suggest anything
    e) they reduce their challenging mental activities to an age appropriate level

CHAPTER PRACTICE TEST ANSWERS

1. b   Mental images are mental representations of objects that have a picture-like quality.
2. d   Research has found that if the individuals used mental images to answer the question, they would actually visualize the house and have to count the windows, so the person with the most windows would take the longest time to answer.
3. a   The definition for concepts is that they are ideas that represent a class or category of objects or events.
4. b   Superordinate is the highest or most general level of a concept. Basic level is the level most commonly used (such as potato or lettuce); subordinate is the most specific, such as a russet potato or romaine lettuce.
5. c   Again, this is asking for the straight definition of trial-and-error problem solving.

6.   d   Insight problem solving occurs when you get a sudden inspiration that leads you to the solution to your problem.

7.   d   Functional fixedness is seeing objects only in terms of their typical uses.

8.   e   A mental set exists when someone continues to use the same approaches that worked in the past. Confirmation bias occurs when someone pays attention to information that confirms his ideas and ignores any contradictory input.

9.   a   Functional fixedness occurs when an individual is *fixed* on only one *function* of a particular object.

10.   a   This is the definition of creativity.

11.   e   Convergent thinking occurs when you assume there is only one single answer or solution to a problem. Typically, convergent thinking decreases creative ability.

12.   d   As can be seen, intelligence is a broad idea that can be difficult to define.

13.   b   Spearman proposed a two-factor theory of intelligence. The g factor was for general intelligence, and the s factor was for specific intelligence.

14.   b   Correlational is not an intelligence identified by Gardner.

15.   a   Sternberg has found that practical intelligence is a good predictor of success in life but has a low relationship to analytical intelligence.

16.   c   Sternberg proposed that intelligence should actually be broken down into three components that can be thought of as book smarts, street smarts, and creativity.

17.   e   The IQ is based on a mental age of 10 divided by a chronological age of 8 and multiplied by 100. This gives an IQ = 125.

18.   b   Deviation IQ scores are based on the norms of a representative sample of the population (also known as the standardization group).

19.   a   Reliability indicates a test consistency, while validity indicates accuracy, or how well the test measures what it says it measures.

20.   e   Denny most likely suffers from fragile X syndrome..

21.   a   The diagnosis of intellectual disability is based on IQ scores as well as how well the individual is able to function in day-to-day life.

22.   c   C is the only true statement; the other four statements are myths that have not been supported by research.

23.   c   There were actually slightly more males than females in the sample of subjects selected for the Terman study.

24.   b   Identical twins should show the strongest correlation since they share 100 percent of the same genes.

25.   a   Nature refers to the influence of heredity on behaviors and traits. A is the only selection that focuses on inheritance of genes.

26.   a   Stereotype threat has been shown to reduce performance on intelligence tests.

27.   d   The definition of language includes all three of these attributes.

28.   b   Phonemes are the basic units of sound.

29.   a   Syntax refers to the rules we use to form meaningful sentences.

30.   a   *Linguistic relativity* hypothesis (also referred to as the Sapir–Whorf hypothesis) states that our thought processes are *relative* to the *language* (or linguistic setting) in which we grew up.

31.   c   Cognitive universalism proposes that our basic thought processes, or cognitions, are universally shared by all people.

32.   e   Dolphins, parrots, and chimpanzees have demonstrated some language skills, but no animal to date has demonstrated the ability to use and comprehend syntax.

33.   b   Increased oxygen and blood flow have been shown to improve cognitive functioning in the elderly.

CHAPTER PRACTICE FREE RESPONSE QUESTION

You have 25 minutes to answer the following question. You must write in complete sentences and not just list facts. You should make your point clearly and use the language of psychology. Be sure to write legibly and respond to all parts of the question.

Casey, who is a notorious gum chewer and always has a pack of gum handy, went on an end-of-the-year school trip to an amusement park with classmates from psychology class. A popular attraction at the amusement park was a giant maze with high walls. On a dare, Casey was blindfolded, taken to the center of the maze, and turned in circles until all sense of direction was lost. A friend then removed Casey's blindfold and Casey began to search for a way out of the maze. Explain how the following could assist or impede Casey's efforts to exit the maze.

- Top-down processing
- Functional fixedness
- Means-end analysis
- Confirmation bias
- Bottom-up processing

SUGGESTED RUBRIC—Students should provide specific details and examples to support their assertions; definitions alone are not sufficient. Information about each topic should be discussed in the context of the question rather than abstractly. Successful essays may include the following arguments:

5 points

- Score—Top-down processing—Casey knows general rules about most mazes. For example, Casey knows that mazes have dead ends, left or right turns, an entrance and an exit, and markings on the walls can be used to help keep track of areas in the maze.
- Score—Functional fixedness—Casey may need to use something in a non-conventional way to solve the maze. For example, Casey needs something to mark the walls of the maze. Casey has a pack of gum; however, Casey does not think to chew the gum and use it as a marker by sticking it to the wall.
- Score—Means-end analysis—Casey needs to work closer to the solution by steps. For example, Casey's friends can see into the maze from above. When Casey is moving in the correct direction they say "warmer," and when Casey turns in the wrong direction they say "colder." This helps Casey move closer to the solution in increments and eventually solve the maze.
- Score—Confirmation bias—Casey only pays attention to evidence that confirms a belief and ignores evidence that challenges it. For example, Casey believes that left turns are luckier than right turns. A friend gave Casey a hint on how to solve the maze by turning left and then right alternatively. Casey ignores the information in the clue and continues to believe that left turns are "luckier" than right turns. After making a long series of left turns Casey exits the maze, and the belief that left turns are "luckier" is confirmed, even though the hint would lead to a more efficient solution.
- Score—Bottom-up processing—Casey pieces together bits of information and develops a larger mental picture of the maze. For example, Casey tries different solutions to the maze. The different attempts add information into Casey's mental map of the maze. Eventually Casey will develop a complete mental picture of the maze and find the exit.

YOU KNOW YOU HAVE MASTERED THE MAIN TOPICS IN THIS CHAPTER IF YOU ARE ABLE TO. . .

- Introduce the research methods and major issues in developmental psychology, including the nature versus nurture controversy.
- Describe the stages of prenatal development and potential hazards.
- Describe the physical and cognitive development in infancy and childhood including language development, and describe autism spectrum disorder.
- Explain the concept of personality including the idea of temperament, attachment theory, and Erikson's psychosocial model.
- Describe how men and women differ in thinking, social behavior, and personality.
- Identify the major stages of development in adolescence and adulthood.
- Discuss theories of aging and Kübler-Ross's stages of dying.
- Outline cross-cultural differences in views of death and dying.

RAPID REVIEW

Human development is the scientific study of the changes that occur in people as they age from conception to death. Since age cannot be directly manipulated by a researcher, developmental psychologists have had to develop alternative methods to investigate the effects of aging on psychological processes. Three common methods used are **longitudinal**, **cross-sectional**, and **cross-sequential** studies. Longitudinal studies have the advantage of following the same subject across time but are limited due to the amount of time and money required to complete the study and the problem of attrition. Cross-sectional studies are cheaper, faster, and easier to conduct since they gather information from different age groups at one particular period of time; however, results from these studies may be confounded due to individual and history differences. Cross-sequential studies are a combination of longitudinal and cross-sectional techniques and often represent an ideal compromise. One of the biggest debates among developmental psychologists is the question of **nature** versus **nurture**. Nature refers to the influence of everything you inherited genetically from your biological parents, and nurture refers to the influence your environment has had on your development. More recently, the question of interest has switched from nature *versus* nurture to the interaction of nature *and* nurture. Behavioral genetics is the field of science that studies the interactions of nature, or genes, and nurture, or the environment.

Genetics is the science of heredity and involves the study of DNA, genes, and chromosomes. **DNA (deoxyribonucleic acid)** is the smallest unit of the three and consists of strands of molecules linked together like a twisted ladder. The links are made up of amines, and their names are abbreviated with the letters A, T, G, and C. The next largest unit is the **genes**, which are sections of the ladder containing instructions on how to make a specific protein. One way to think of genes is as individual recipes for proteins. The biggest unit is the **chromosomes**, which are long strands of DNA twisted together and wound up in coils. The chromosomes are found in the nucleus of all the cells of your body except red blood cells. Humans have a total of 46 chromosomes, 23 from the mother's egg and 23 from the father's sperm. Each chromosome from the mother matches a chromosome from the father to form 23 pairs. Both chromosomes in the pair have the same genes (for example, each chromosome contains a gene for hair color). Even though they contain the same gene, the instructions on that gene might be slightly different; for example, one of the genes has the instructions for blonde hair while the other gene contains the instructions for brown hair. The first 22 pairs of chromosomes are called *autosomes,* and the last pair (the 23rd) contains the instructions for determining sex and is called the *sex chromosomes.* **Dominant genes** are the genes that are more likely to influence the trait. **Recessive genes** are not as strong and will only get their instructions carried out if the other chromosome in the pair also contains a recessive gene. In reality, almost all traits are determined by multiple gene pairs. This is called **polygenic inheritance**. Some diseases result from problems with recessive genes and are only expressed when both parents have the recessive gene, while some disorders result from the fact that there are the wrong number of chromosomes in the fertilizing egg or sperm.

Many people believe that **conception** represents the beginning of life. **Fertilization** occurs when the sperm penetrates the egg (or **ovum**). The result is a single cell with 46 chromosomes (23 from the sperm and 23 from the egg). This cell is called a **zygote**. **Monozygotic (or identical) twins** result from the zygote splitting into two separate masses early in the division process. **Dizygotic (or fraternal) twins** result from two eggs being fertilized by two separate sperm. Siamese twins are more properly referred to as **conjoined twins** and result from an incomplete separation of the zygotic mass. Brittany and Abby Hensel are an example of conjoined twins. The **germinal period** of pregnancy is the first two weeks after fertilization during which the zygote migrates down to the uterus and attaches to the uterine wall. The placenta and umbilical cord both begin to develop during this period. The **embryonic period** lasts from about Week 2 to Week 8, after which the **embryo** is about one inch long with primitive eyes, nose, lips, teeth, arms, and legs. **Critical periods** are times in development during which an environmental influence can impact the development of the fetus. Different organs and structures have different critical periods. The environmental influences that can impact the development of the fetus are called **teratogens**. The **fetal period** lasts from the eighth week after conception to the end of the pregnancy. Tremendous growth of the **fetus** occurs during this time. A baby born before the 38th week of pregnancy is considered preterm and is at risk for survival, especially if he or she weighs less than five and a half pounds. Most miscarriages, also called spontaneous abortions, occur in the first three months of a pregnancy.

Infants have a large number of capabilities even immediately after birth. Most infants are able to perform five innate reflexes. Touch is the most well developed sense followed by smell and taste. Vision is the least functional of the senses. The rods are developed at birth, but cones must develop over a six-month time period. At birth, an infant's vision is most clear seven to ten inches from his or her face. Also, infants appear to show a preference for the human voice and human faces. Due to a recent trend of many parents choosing not to give immunization shots to their children, there is a growing concern over the possibility of widespread epidemics. Most immunizations are made from the dead virus and cannot cause an infection in the recipient. No link has been found between autism and immunization.

The brain triples in weight during the first two years of life with the increase being caused by the expansion of existing cells, not the growth of new ones. **Jean Piaget** believed that the primary factor in the development of a child's cognitive abilities was the child's interactions with objects in the environment. Piaget believed that children form mental concepts or **schemes** as they experience new situations and events. He proposed four stages of **cognitive development** from infancy to adolescence. The **sensorimotor stage**, lasting from infancy to age 2, involves the use of the senses and muscles to learn about the environment and includes the development of **object permanence** and symbolic thought. The **preoperational stage** lasts from age 2 to 7 and involves language and concept development through the process of asking questions. Children in this stage display the ability of symbolic thought through make-believe play and also display characteristics of **egocentrism**, **centration**, and **irreversibility**. The **concrete operational stage** lasts from age 7 to 12 and includes the development of concepts such as **conservation** and reversible thinking. However, children in this stage are still unable to deal with abstract concepts such as freedom or love. The **formal operational stage** is the final stage of cognitive development, according to Piaget, and lasts from the age of 12 on. During this stage abstract, hypothetical thinking develops. Research suggests that about one-half of the adults in the United States reach this stage of cognitive development. Piaget's concepts have been successfully applied in schools but have also been criticized for their emphasis on distinct stages of development, overemphasis on egocentrism, and failure to mention the role of the family or social environment in the child's development.

Lev Vygotsky was a Russian psychologist who felt the primary factor in development was the social environment. He proposed a concept called **scaffolding** in which a more highly skilled person gives the learner help and then stops as the learner develops on his own. Vygotsky believed that each child has a **zone of proximal development** or **ZPD**, which is the difference between what a child can do alone and what he or she can do with the help of a teacher. Vygotsky's principles have been applied in the classroom through the use of cooperative learning and reciprocal teaching.

Psychologists interested in information-processing theory have investigated the memory capabilities of the developing infant and have found that infants demonstrate memory from birth; 4- to 5-year-olds appear to be able to store about three items in their short-term memory and have both episodic and procedural memories in long-term memory. Language development appears to be an important step in cognitive development and facilitates the development of symbolic thinking. The stages of language development experienced by all speakers include **cooing** around two months of age, **babbling** at six months of age, one-word speech or **holophrases** around 1 year of age, **telegraphic speech** at around a year and a half, and then whole sentences. **Autism spectrum disorder (ASD)** is a neurodevelopmental disorder that actually encompasses a whole range of previous disorders which cause problems in thinking, feeling, language, and social skills in relating to others.

Temperament refers to the behavioral and emotional characteristics observed in infancy. Several researchers have suggested the existence of three types of temperaments: easy, difficult, and slow to warm up. **Attachment** is the emotional bond between an infant and caregiver. Mary Ainsworth and others studied attachment using the Strange Situation and observed four attachment styles: secure, avoidant, ambivalent, and disorganized/disoriented. Konrad Lorenz studied ducklings and coined the term **imprinting**, which describes how infant animals attach themselves to or follow the first animal/person that they see immediately after birth. Harry Harlow studied the nature of attachment behaviors by observing rhesus monkeys interact with two different "surrogate" mothers. He found that **contact comfort** was an important factor in attachment.

Erik Erikson, who originally trained as a Freudian psychoanalyst, proposed an eight-stage theory of development that occurred over the entire life span. Each stage involved an emotional crisis in the individual's social interactions. The first four stages occurred during infancy and childhood and consisted of the crises of **trust versus mistrust**, **autonomy versus shame and doubt**, **initiation versus guilt**, and **industry versus inferiority**. Most children begin to understand **gender** differences around the age of 2 and begin to develop their own **gender identity**.

Adolescence is the period of time from around age 14 to the early 20s and is most clearly identified by the physical changes that occur in **puberty**. Mentally, many adolescents are moving into Piaget's formal operational stage of development, which includes the ability to think in the abstract and to consider hypothetical situations. At the same time, adolescents still demonstrate a considerable amount of egocentric thinking as can be seen in the thought processes of the **personal fable**, in which the adolescent feels they are different from all others, and the **imaginary audience**, where the adolescent is convinced that everyone is looking at him or her.

Lawrence Kohlberg proposed a theory about the development of moral thinking and divided the development into three levels, **pre-conventional**, during which the individual conforms to social norms; **conventional**, during which time the consequences determine morality; and **post-conventional**, during which a person's individual moral principles determine right and wrong. The social crisis proposed by Erikson for the period of adolescence is that of **identity versus role confusion**. Gender differences in cognition include stronger language skills in females and stronger math skills in males. These differences are likely caused by psychological and social factors rather than biological factors. Personality differences are difficult to separate from socialization forces that promote holding in emotions for boys and building emotional attachments for girls. Social differences include conversation styles where men engage in "report" style communication and women engage in "relate" style communication. Erickson's psychosocial stage faced during adolescence is identity versus role confusion. A teenager must choose from among many options for values and beliefs, and from these options a consistent sense of self must be found. Conflict between parents and adolescents tends to center over trivial issues like clothing and hair style choices, while agreement is more consistent in important moral issues.

Adulthood can be roughly identified as the time period from the early 20s until death. Middle age is often associated with an increase in health problems and includes the events of **menopause** for women and **andropause** for men. Cognitive abilities do not decline overall, but the speed of processing does appear to slow down and people tend to have a harder time retrieving specific information from their memory. Erikson proposed three psycho-social developmental stages for adulthood. The stages are **intimacy versus isolation**, **generativity versus stagnation**, and **ego integrity versus despair**. Parenting is a significant part of many people's adulthood. Diana Baumrind proposed three basic parenting styles, **authoritarian**, **permissive**, and **authoritative**. Permissive parents can either be **permissive neglectful** or **permissive indulgent**.

There are a number of theories as to why our bodies physically age. The cellular clock theory suggests that cells are limited in the number of times they can reproduce. The wear-and-tear theory proposes that aging is a result of outside stressors such as physical exertion and bodily damage. The free radical theory states that as people get older, more and more free radicals accumulate in their bodies. Socially, the **activity theory** suggests that elderly people adjust more positively to aging when they remain active in some way.

Elizabeth Kübler-Ross proposed a well-known theory of the dying process. Based on her work with dying patients, Kübler-Ross felt that people experienced a series of five different emotions including denial, anger, bargaining, depression, and acceptance. Others see dying as more of a process rather than a series of stages.

STUDY HINTS

1. Perhaps the most influential theory on cognitive development is Jean Piaget's theory. He proposed four stages of cognitive development. To enhance your learning of these stages, fill in the chart below. Try to fill it in as much as possible without going back to your notes and/or the textbook. The first stage has been filled in as an example.

Stage	Age	Characteristics	How would you test to see if someone is in this stage?
Sensorimotor	*0–2 years*	• Children explore using their sensory and motor systems. • Develop object permanence.	*Hide a toy under a blanket and see if the child looks under the blanket for the toy.*

2. Another major theory of development is the theory proposed by Erik Erikson. Erikson's theory focuses more on the development of personality, with each stage marked by a crisis that needs to be resolved. The crisis typically involves the social interactions of the individual and is represented by the two extremes of the possible outcomes (for example, industry versus inferiority). One way to keep track of these stages is to realize that the labels follow a pattern of "desirable outcome versus undesirable outcome." Also, they reflect the social activities that are typically going on at that age. Fill in the chart below to help you understand Erikson's theory of development.

Age	Social Activities	Desirable Outcome	Undesirable Outcome
0–1 years	Being fed, taken care of by someone else	Sense of trust	Sense of mistrust

Suggested Answers for Question 1

Stage	Age	Characteristics	How would you test to see if someone is in this stage?
Sensorimotor	0–2 years	• Children explore using their sensory and motor systems. • Develop object permanence.	Hide a toy under a blanket and see if the child looks under the blanket for the toy.
Preoperational	2–7 years	• A lot of egocentric thinking. • Children can represent objects mentally. • Engage in make-believe play. • Do not understand concepts of conservation. • Tend to focus on one aspect of an object.	Ask the child if she would rather have two quarters or five pennies (she will probably want the five pennies). See if the child can play a make-believe game.
Concrete Operational	7–12 years	• Show an understanding for the principles of conservation. • Demonstrate logical thinking and can solve analogies. • Focus mostly on concrete objects and ideas.	Divide a string of clay into five pieces and see if the child thinks there is as much clay in the five pieces as there was in the one string.
Formal Operational	12 years and on	• Can use abstract reasoning to solve problems. • Able to consider hypothetical situations.	Ask the child an abstract question and see how she responds. An example of a question could be "What if snow were black?"

Suggested Answers for Question 2

Age	Social Activities	Desirable Outcome	Undesirable Outcome
0–1 years	Being fed, taken care of by someone else	Sense of <u>trust</u>	Sense of <u>mistrust</u>
1–3 years	Learning to walk, talk, dress yourself, etc.	Sense of <u>autonomy</u> (feeling that you are in control of your own body)	Sense of <u>shame</u> and doubt
3–5 years	Going to preschool, being responsible to obey family rules, learning your role as a member of a family	Sense of <u>initiative</u>	Sense of <u>guilt</u> or irresponsibility
5–12 years	Going to school, completing school assignments, participating in social activities with peers	Sense of <u>industry</u> (feeling capable of completing your work)	Sense of <u>inferiority</u> or incompetence
12–18 years	Deciding "what you want to be when you grow up" choosing a career path, selecting your own group of friends	Sense of <u>identity</u>	Feeling of <u>role confusion</u>, unsure of who you are
18–40 years	Finding a partner to form a life-long commitment, succeeding in a career	Sense of <u>intimacy</u>, feel comfortable forming close relationships	Sense of <u>isolation</u>, not able to form close ties with others
40–60 years	Focus on career and family. Perhaps grandchildren begin to enter the picture. Begin thinking of the legacy that you will leave for your children and/or the future generation	Sense of <u>generativity</u>, or succeeding in creating something that will benefit others in the future	Sense of <u>stagnation</u>, or feeling that you have done nothing for the next generation
60 years and on	Dealing with retirement from your career, family might be more involved in their own lives, facing the fact of death among those in your social group	Sense of <u>ego integrity</u>, or a sense of acceptance of your life and acceptance of death.	Sense of <u>despair</u> about your life and a fear of your inevitable death.

LEARNING OBJECTIVES

8.1 *What are some of the special research methods used to study development?*

8.2 *What is the relationship between heredity and environmental factors in determining development?*

8.3 *How do chromosomes, genes, and DNA determine a person's characteristics or disorders?*

8.4 *What happens during conception and prenatal development, and what are some prenatal hazards?*

8.5 *What kind of physical changes take place in infancy and childhood?*

8.6 *What are two ways of looking at cognitive development, how does language develop, and what is autism spectrum disorder?*

8.7 *How do infants and children develop personalities and form relationships with others, and what are Erikson's stages of psychosocial development for children?*

8.8 *What are the physical, cognitive, and personality changes that occur in adolescence, including concepts of morality and Erikson's search for identity?*

8.9 *How do men and women differ in thinking, social behavior, and personality?*

8.10 *What are the physical, cognitive, and personality changes that occur during adulthood and aging, including Erikson's last three psychosocial stages, and patterns of parenting?*

8.11 *How do psychologists explain why aging occurs, and what are the stages of death and dying?*

8.12 *What are some cross-cultural differences in views of death and dying?*

AP LEARNING OBJECTIVES

1. Discuss the interaction of nature and nurture in the determination of behavior. (p. 310)
2. Explain the process of conception and gestation, including factors that influence successful fetal development. (p. 316)
3. Discuss maturation of motor skills. (p. 321)
4. Describe the influence of temperament and other social factors on attachment and appropriate socialization. (p. 331)
5. Explain the maturation of cognitive abilities. (p. 323)
6. Compare and contrast models of moral development. (p. 339)
7. Discuss maturational challenges in adolescence including related family conflicts. (p. 337)
8. Explain how parenting styles influence development. (pp. 342, 345)
9. Characterize the development of decisions related to intimacy as people mature. (p. 345)
10. Predict the physical and cognitive changes that emerge as people age including steps that can be taken to maximize function. (pp. 344, 348)
11. Describe how sex and gender influence socialization and other aspects of development. (p. 340)
12. Identify key contributors in developmental psychology. (pp. 323, 327, 332, 334, 335, 339, 340, 345)
13. Synthesize how biologic, cognitive, and cultural factors converge to facilitate acquisition, development, and use of language. (p. 328) (This objective is repeated here from the unit on cognition.)
14. Identify key contributors in the psychology of motivation and emotion. (p. 338) (This objective is repeated here from the unit on motivation and emotion.)
15. Articulate the impact of social and learning categories on self-concept and relations with others. (p. 335)

CHAPTER GLOSSARY

activity theory	theory of adjustment to aging that suggests older people are happier if they remain active in some way.
adolescence	the period of life from about age 13 to the early 20s, during which a young person is no longer physically a child but is not yet an independent, self-supporting adult.
andropause	gradual changes in the sexual hormones and reproductive system of males.
attachment	the emotional bond between an infant and the primary caregiver.

authoritarian	parenting style that is rigid, demanding, controlling, uncompromising, and overly concerned with rules.
authoritative	parenting style that involves combining firm limits on behavior combined with love, warmth, affection, respect, and a willingness to listen.
autism spectrum disorder (ASD)	a neurodevelopmental disorder that actually encompasses a whole range of previous disorders which cause problems in thinking, feeling, language, and social skills in relating to others
autonomy versus shame and doubt	second stage of personality development in which the toddler strives for physical independence.
babbling	consonant and vowel sounds representing the second stage of language development, usually occurring around six months of age
centration	in Piaget's theory, the tendency of a young child to focus on only one feature of an object while ignoring other, relevant features.
chromosome	tightly wound strand of genetic material (or DNA).
cognitive development	the development of thinking, problem solving, and memory.
conception	the moment at which a female becomes pregnant.
concrete operational stage	third stage of cognitive development in which the school-age child becomes capable of logical thought processes but is not yet capable of abstract thinking.
conjoined twins	often called Siamese twins, occurring from an incomplete separation of the zygotic cells.
conservation	in Piaget's theory, the ability to understand that simply changing the appearance of an object does not change the object's nature.
contact comfort	variable of tactile sensation that was proposed by Harry Harlow to be an important component in the formation of attachment.
conventional morality	second level of Kohlberg's stages of moral development in which the child's behavior is governed by conforming to the society's norms of behavior.
cooing	vowel-like sounds made by babies around two months of age representing the first stage of language development.
critical periods	times during which some environmental influence can have an impact on the development of the infant.
cross-sectional design	research design in which several different age groups of participants are studied at one particular point in time.
cross-sequential design	research design in which participants are first studied by means of a cross-sectional design but also followed and assessed for a period of no more than six years.
dizygotic(or fraternal) twins	often called fraternal twins, occurring when two eggs each get fertilized by two different sperm, resulting in two zygotes in the uterus at the same time.
DNA (deoxyribonucleic acid)	special molecule that contains the genetic material of the organism.
dominant gene	referring to a gene that actively controls the expression of a trait.
ego integrity versus despair	eighth and final stage of Erikson's model of development in which the goal is to develop a sense of wholeness that comes from having lived a full life and the ability to let go of regrets, the final completion of the ego.
egocentrism	the inability to see the world through anyone else's eyes.
Elizabeth Kübler-Ross	1926–2004. Swiss psychiatrist known for her work with dying patients and her proposed theory of five stages of dying.

embryo	name for the developing organism from two weeks to eight weeks after fertilization.
embryonic period	the period from two to eight weeks after fertilization, during which the major organs and structures of the organism develop.
Erik Erikson	1902–1994. developmental psychologist trained in the methods of psychoanalysis who proposed a theory of personality development based on a series of emotional crises.
fertilization	the union of the ovum and sperm.
fetal period	the time from about eight weeks until the birth of the child.
fetus	name for the developing organism from eight weeks after fertilization to the birth of the baby.
formal operational stage	Piaget's last stage of cognitive development in which the adolescent becomes capable of abstract thinking.
gender	the behavior associated with being male or female.
gender identity	perception of one's gender and the behavior that is associated with that gender.
gene	section of DNA having the same arrangement of chemical elements.
generativity versus stagnation	seventh stage of Erikson's model of personality development in which the crisis involves providing guidance to one's children or the next generation, contributing to the well-being of the next generation through career or volunteer work or developing a sense of stagnation.
genetics	the science of inherited traits.
germinal period	first two weeks after fertilization, during which the zygote moves down to the uterus and begins to implant in the lining.
holophrases	single-word utterances seen universally in the stages of language development.
human development	the scientific study of the changes that occur in people as they age, from conception until death.
identity versus role confusion	fifth stage of personality development in which the adolescent must find a consistent sense of self.
imaginary audience	type of thought common to adolescents in which young people believe that other people are just as concerned about the adolescent's thoughts and characteristics as they themselves are.
imprinting	how infant animals attach themselves to or follow the first animal or person that they see immediately after birth
industry versus inferiority	fourth stage of personality development in which the adolescent strives for a sense of competence and self-esteem.
initiation versus guilt	third stage of personality development in which the preschool-aged child strives for emotional and psychological independence and attempts to satisfy curiosity about the world.
intimacy versus isolation	sixth stage of Erikson's model of personality development in which an emotional and psychological closeness that is based on the ability to trust, share, and care, while still maintaining one's sense of self is developed.
irreversibility	in Piaget's theory, the inability of the young child to mentally reverse an action.
Jean Piaget	1896–1980. Swiss developmental psychologist who proposed a four-stage theory of cognitive development based on the concept of mental operations.
Lawrence Kohlberg	1927–1987. developmental psychologist known for his theory on the development of moral reasoning.

Lev Vygotsky	1896–1934. Russian developmental psychologist who emphasized the role of the social environment on cognitive development and proposed the idea of zones of proximal development.
longitudinal design	research design in which one participant or group of participants is studied over a long period of time.
menopause	the cessation of ovulation and menstrual cycles and the end of a woman's reproductive capability.
monozygotic (or identical) twins	identical twins formed when one zygote splits into two separate masses of cells, each of which develops into a separate embryo.
nature	the influence of our inherited characteristics on our personality, physical growth, intellectual growth, and social interactions.
nurture	the influence of the environment on personality, physical growth, intellectual growth, and social interactions.
object permanence	the knowledge that an object exists even when it is not in sight.
ovum	the female sex cell or egg.
permissive	parenting style in which the parent puts very few demands on the child for behavior.
permissive indulgent	permissive parenting style in which the parents seem to be too involved with their children, allowing them to act any way they wish.
permissive neglectful	permissive parenting style in which the parents are not involved with their children.
personal fable	type of thought common to adolescents in which young people believe themselves to be unique and protected from harm.
polygenic inheritance	a trait or characteristic that is determined by more than one gene pair.
post-conventional morality	third level of Kohlberg's stages of moral development in which the person's behavior is governed by moral principles that have been decided upon by the individual and which may be in disagreement with accepted social norms.
pre-conventional morality	first level of Kohlberg's stages of moral development in which the child's behavior is governed by the consequences of the behavior.
preoperational stage	Piaget's second stage of cognitive development in which the preschool child learns to use language as a means of exploring the world.
puberty	the physical changes that occur in the body as sexual development reaches its peak.
recessive gene	referring to a gene that only influences the expression of a trait when paired with an identical gene.
scaffolding	process in which a more skilled learner gives help to a less skilled learner, reducing the amount of help as the less skilled learner becomes more capable.
scheme	a mental concept formed through experiences with objects and events.
sensorimotor stage	Piaget's first stage of cognitive development in which the infant uses its senses and motor abilities to interact with objects in the environment.
telegraphic speech	type of speech in words are left out of a sentence but the meaning of the sentence remains, such as "want cookie" to mean "I would like a cookie."
temperament	the behavioral characteristics that are fairly well established at birth, such as easy, difficult, and slow to warm up.
teratogen	any factor that can cause a birth defect.
trust versus mistrust	first stage of personality development in which the infant's basic sense of trust or mistrust develops as a result of consistent or inconsistent care.

zone of proximal development (ZPD)	Vygotsky's concept of the difference between what a child can do alone and what that child can do with the help of a more skilled teacher.
zygote	cell resulting from the uniting of the ovum and sperm.

CHAPTER PRACTICE TEST

For the following multiple choice questions, select the answer you feel best answers the question.

1. A researcher who selects a sample of people of varying ages and studies them at one point in time is, by definition, using the _____ method.
    a) cohort design
    b) longitudinal design
    c) behavior genetics design
    d) cross-sectional design
    e) balanced placebo design

2. Which of the following is an example of a longitudinal study?
    a) observing three groups of children (ages 2, 6, and 12) for a two-hour period
    b) observing three groups of children (ages 2, 6, and 12) for a two-week period
    c) observing a group of 30 children at age 2 and again at age 6 and once more when the children turn 12 years of age
    d) surveying a group of middle-aged adults, half male and half female
    e) using an experimental group and introducing a change in the independent variable

3. What relatively new field investigates the influence of genes and heredity on behavior?
    a) psychobiology
    b) neuropsychology
    c) behavioral genetics
    d) psychoanalysis
    e) genetic behaviorism

4. When a researcher discusses the contributions of "nature" on development, she is referring to the effects of your _____.
    a) environment
    b) heredity
    c) social interactions
    d) teratogens
    e) birth order

5. Which of the following is a special molecule that contains the genetic material of the organism?
    a) DNA
    b) gene
    c) chromosomes
    d) amines
    e) astrocyte

6. Which of the following is essentially a "recipe" or set of instructions for making a protein?
    a) DNA
    b) a chromosome
    c) an electrolyte
    d) an enzyme
    e) a gene

7. Why are males more likely than females to exhibit sex-linked traits?
   a) Males' X chromosome may not have a necessary dominant gene.
   b) Females are actually the stronger sex.
   c) Females have a protective enzyme in their sex hormones.
   d) Males are not more likely than females to exhibit sex-linked traits.
   e) Males' Y chromosome may not have a necessary dominant gene.

8. Dizygotic twins are formed from _____.
   a) two eggs and one sperm
   b) two eggs and two sperm
   c) one egg and one sperm
   d) one egg and two sperm
   e) Zygotes can only form triplets.

9. Monozygotic twins _____.
   a) are genetically identical
   b) are genetically different
   c) will be of a different sex
   d) are more likely to occur when a woman is taking fertility drugs
   e) can only be male and dizygotic twins can only be female

10. Brittany and Abby Hensel are a type of twin produced when a zygote does not completely separate and they are commonly referred to as _____.
    a) nonidentical
    b) dizygotic
    c) fraternal
    d) rejoined
    e) conjoined

11. The specialized organ that provides nourishment and filters away waste products from the developing baby is called the _____.
    a) placenta
    b) uterus
    c) umbilical cord
    d) embryo
    e) amniotic sac

12. What are some of the common consequences to a child if the mother smoked while pregnant?
    a) increased birth weight and lethargy
    b) lower birth weight and short stature
    c) severe hearing loss and heart defects
    d) severely deformed limbs and muscle spasms
    e) flattened lip and widely spaced eyes

13. The longest prenatal period during which tremendous growth occurs and the organs continue to develop and become functional is called _____.
    a) germinal
    b) embryonic
    c) fetal
    d) gestational
    e) zygotic

14. In the _____ reflex, the baby moves its head toward any light touch to its face.
    a) sucking
    b) startle
    c) rooting
    d) grasping
    e) Babinski

15. Which sense is the most well developed at birth?
    a) taste
    b) touch
    c) sight
    d) hearing
    e) smell

16. Which of the following statements about immunizations is true?
    a) Children who are given an immunization are fairly likely to get the disease itself.
    b) Immunizations almost always cause bad reactions.
    c) Immunizations are needed even if the disease has been eliminated.
    d) Some immunizations cause autism in children.
    e) Immunization should only be giving if a disease has been detected in an area or country.

17. Your little sister picks up objects, feels every part of them, and then puts them in her mouth. What stage of Jean Piaget's model of cognitive development does this behavior suggest?
    a) concrete operations
    b) sensorimotor
    c) preoperational
    d) formal operations
    e) post-formal operations

18. A theory that looks at the way people deal with the information that comes in through the senses is called _____.
    a) information-processing theory
    b) sensorimotor intelligence
    c) habituation
    d) metamemory
    e) long-term potentiation theory

19. Which of the following would a child in Piaget's preoperational stage of cognitive development NOT be able to do?
    a) mentally represent an object
    b) play make-believe
    c) see the world from someone else's perspective
    d) use symbolic thought
    e) understand object permanence

20. Vygotsky's idea that children develop cognitively when someone else helps them by asking leading questions and providing examples is called _____.
    a) scaffolding
    b) centration
    c) conservation
    d) metamemory
    e) accommodation

21. The first noticeable signs of language development in infants is _____.
    a) babbling
    b) cooing
    c) telegraphic speech
    d) holophrases
    e) telephonic speech

22. By about 12 months, most infants _____.
    a) begin to use intonation in their language
    b) have passed the critical period for language acquisition
    c) begin to distinguish, in their language, between themselves and others
    d) begin to form two- and three-word sentences
    e) build a vocabulary of one-word phrases, or holophrases

23. Infants in different cultures and of different languages _____.
    a) experience different stages of language development.
    b) experience the same stages of language development.
    c) start cooing at the same time, but infants from Western cultures start babbling earlier.
    d) start babbling at the same time, but infants from Eastern cultures use whole sentences earlier.
    e) will utter the same holophrases from birth to two months of age.

24. If an infant in Mary Ainsworth's Strange Situation was unwilling to explore, became very upset by the stranger, and demanded to be picked up by his mother but then kicked to get away, he would most likely be classified as _____.
    a) secure
    b) avoidant
    c) ambivalent
    d) disorganized/disoriented
    e) post traumatic

25. Chester is irritable, loud, and negative most of the time. He really doesn't like when new people pick him up and hold him and has irregular sleeping, eating, and waking schedules. What temperament does he exhibit?
    a) active
    b) slow to warm up
    c) difficult
    d) easy
    e) sanguine

26. Erikson's theory of social development viewed the ages of 3 to 6, his third stage, as being characterized by the major challenge of _____.
    a) identity versus role diffusion
    b) industry versus inferiority
    c) initiative versus guilt
    d) autonomy versus shame and doubt
    e) trust versus mistrust

27. According to Erikson, when children between the ages of 5 and 12 succeed at learning new skills, they develop a sense of _____, and if they fail to develop new abilities, they feel _____.
    a) shame; doubt
    b) trust; guilty
    c) industry; inferior
    d) identity; despair
    e) intimacy; isolation

28. _____ theorists believe that gender identity is learned through direct reinforcement and observational learning.
    a) Social learning
    b) Cognitive
    c) Psychoanalytic
    d) Humanistic
    e) Evolutionary

29. The growth spurt for boys typically begins at age _____.
    a) 9
    b) 12
    c) 10
    d) 15
    e) 17

30. Fifteen-year-old Todd is writing an impassioned novel about growing up in America. In his novel he describes his experiences in a way that portrays himself as unique and special, such that no one has ever thought such deep thoughts or experienced such ecstasy before. Todd's writings most clearly reflect _____.
    a) his sense of autonomy
    b) the personal fable
    c) the period of rebellion common to all adolescents
    d) his developing sense of conscience
    e) an overdeveloped super-ego

31. Which of the following questions would an adolescent who has NOT reached Piaget's stage of formal operations have trouble thinking about?
    a) What date did Columbus arrive in America?
    b) How many 2-inch pieces can a 10-inch rope be cut into?
    c) What if you had been born to different parents?
    d) What is the definition of democracy?
    e) Where is the source of the Nile?

32. Jeremy is 17 years old. According to Erikson, his chief task will be acquiring a sense of _____.
    a) identity
    b) intimacy
    c) generativity
    d) autonomy
    e) trust

33. The cessation of menstruation and ovulation is called _____.
    a) climacteric
    b) perimenopause
    c) menopause
    d) andropause
    e) menarche

34. All of the following are reasons why middle adults experience changes in memory EXCEPT _____.
    a) stress
    b) more information to remember
    c) more information stored in memory
    d) desensitization to information
    e) hardening of the arteries

35. A young adult who is having difficulty trusting others is most likely still trying to resolve Erikson's stage of _____.
    a) autonomy versus shame and doubt
    b) ego integrity versus despair
    c) industry versus inferiority
    d) intimacy versus isolation
    e) generativity versus isolation

36. Which of the following is an example of generativity?
    a) completing a crossword puzzle
    b) starting a new hobby
    c) getting married
    d) finding your own identity
    e) becoming a mentor

37. The _____ theory of aging suggests that unstable oxygen molecules cause damage to the structure of cells, increasing with age.
    a) wear-and-tear
    b) cellular clock
    c) disengagement
    d) free radical
    e) social damages

38. Which theory correctly explains why the aging process occurs?
    a) cellular clock theory
    b) free radical theory
    c) wear-and-tear theory
    d) the Hayflick limit
    e) No theory to date has thoroughly explained the aging process.

39. Several weeks of diagnostic tests have revealed the cancer has spread throughout Barry's body. His physician suggested that he "take care of important matters." Barry realizes his family's home needs repairs, so he arranges to have that done right away. To relieve his family of the agony of planning his funeral, he has made all the arrangements. Barry told his minister he has a good life and just wants to make sure he provides for his family after his death. This description fits the stage Kübler-Ross called _____.
   a) denial
   b) acceptance
   c) bargaining
   d) depression
   e) anger

CHAPTER PRACTICE TEST ANSWERS

1. d   D is correct. Cross-sectional design studies several different age groups at the same time.

2. c   C is correct because a longitudinal study involves the study of a group of individuals at two or more time points in their lives. It may be helpful to remember that a *longi*tudinal study takes a *long* time to complete

3. c   Genetics is a field that investigates the effects of genes and environmental influences on behavior, whereas psychobiology is the study of the biological bases of behavior.

4. b   Nature refers to everything you inherit biologically. Nurture refers to the effects of your surroundings, or environment.

5. a   DNA, genes, and chromosomes all contain the genetic material of an organism, but DNA is the only molecule listed.

6. e   A gene is a section of DNA that contains instructions for making proteins. Chromosomes are large strands of DNA that contain many genes.

7. e   In the 23rd pair of chromosomes, females have an XX pair and males have an XY pair. The Y chromosome is smaller than the X chromosome and so some genes on the X chromosome don't have a "match" on the Y chromosome. Because there is no competition, a recessive gene on the X chromosome is more likely to be expressed in males than in females.

8. b   "Di" means two, and "zygotic" is referring to the zygote which is formed when the egg and sperm unite. Dizygotic (or fraternal) twins are formed from two eggs and two sperm.

9. a   Monozygotic twins are formed from one egg and one sperm ("mono" means one). After the egg and sperm unite they split to form two zygotes. Because all the DNA comes from the same egg and sperm, monozygotic twins are genetically identical.

10. e   Conjoined twins (commonly referred to as Siamese twins) are physically joined due to the fact that the zygotes do not completely separate from each other.

11. a   The placenta provides protection and nourishment to the fetus.

12. b   Multiple studies have found that babies of mothers who smoked are smaller in weight and height than babies from mothers who didn't smoke.

13. c   The fetal period is the longest and last stage of prenatal development and is when the most growth occurs in the fetus.

14. c   The rooting reflex is thought to help the baby with breast-feeding.

15. b   Touch and taste are fairly well developed at birth, with touch being the most highly developed. The sense of sight takes the longest to fully develop after birth.

16. c   Even if the disease has been eliminated in a specific area or country, there are possibilities of infection from other countries.

17. b   The sensorimotor stage involves exploring the world through the use of the sensory and motor systems. During the sensorimotor stage infants interact deliberately with objects by chewing, grasping, and tasting them. It is the first of Piaget's four stages of cognitive development.

18.   a   Information-processing theory looks at the way in which people deal with the information that comes in through the senses. Metamemory is one's knowledge about the workings of memory and memory strategies.

19.   c   In the preoperational stage of development, children are still very egocentric and have a very hard time seeing the world from someone else's viewpoint.

20.   a   Scaffolding is the process of helping a child develop by providing the framework for learning.

21.   b   Cooing is the first visible sign of language development in infants, followed by babbling, holophrases, and then telegraphic speech.

22.   e   By about one year of age, children are communicating one-word "phrases." Telegraphic speech, which consists of two- or three-word sentences, usually develops around one-and-a-half to two years of age.

23.   b   It appears that all infants experience the same stages of language development.

24.   c   The ambivalent child exhibits ambivalent behaviors towards his or her mother. An example is begging to be picked up by the mother and then struggling to get away from the mother once he or she is picked up.

25.   c   Difficult babies tend to be irritable, are not comfortable with change, and have irregular schedules.

26.   c   Initiative versus guilt is Erikson's third stage of development. Autonomy versus shame and doubt is the second stage, and industry versus inferiority is the fourth stage. Trust versus mistrust is the first stage.

27.   c   Industry versus inferiority is Erikson's fourth stage of development and corresponds closely with the primary school years.

28.   a   Social learning theorists focus on how personality is learned.

29.   b   Boys show a growth spurt around age 12, whereas girls typically show a growth spurt earlier, around age 10.

30.   b   The personal fable describes a phenomenon commonly seen in adolescents in which they feel that no one else has experienced the emotions or thoughts that they are currently experiencing.

31.   c   The key to Piaget's fourth and final stage of cognitive development is the ability to consider hypothetical and abstract situations. The question in choice c is the only question requiring abstract thought.

32.   a   Erikson believed most of the adolescent years involved the crisis of identity versus role confusion.

33.   c   Menopause is the correct answer. Perimenopause is the term used to describe the period of five to ten years during which a woman's reproductive system begins to decline.

34.   e   Memory changes during middle age have not been found to be associated with physical decline.

35.   d   Erikson proposed the stage of intimacy versus isolation for young adults as they try to form intimate relations with others and learn to trust in someone other than themselves.

36.   e   Generativity involves helping a younger generation and engaging in activities that will leave a legacy.

37.   d   Radicals are oxygen molecules in the cells that are thought to cause damage.

38.   e   None of the theories to date have thoroughly explained the aging process.

39.   b   Kübler-Ross described the stage of acceptance as an emotional state of acknowledging one's impending death and being at peace with the idea.

CHAPTER PRACTICE FREE RESPONSE QUESTION

You have 25 minutes to answer the following question. You must write in complete sentences and not just list facts. You should make your point clearly and use the language of psychology. Be sure to write legibly and respond to all parts of the question.

Kris just started a new job at a toy store. The store carries toys for all age groups. Kris is approached by a customer who is looking for an appropriate toy to buy for a baby that is having a first birthday. Kris must help the customer pick out an age appropriate toy. Explain how each of the following may influence the toy they decide upon.

- Sensorimotor
- Object permanence
- Temperament
- Gender roles
- Motor milestones

SUGGESTED RUBRIC—Students should provide specific details and examples to support their assertions; definitions alone are not sufficient. Information about each topic should be discussed in the context of the question rather than abstractly. Successful essays may include the following arguments:

5 Points
- Score—sensorimotor—the toy that they pick out might have features that stimulate the senses. Ex. blinking lights, noises, textures.
- Score—Object permanence—they might look for a toy that will not roll away and out of the child's sight because if the toy rolled away the child would forget about it.
- Score—Temperament—the toy should be a good match for the child's temperament. Ex. An easy temperament child might like a noisy or surprising toy more than a difficult temperament child.
- Score—Gender roles—many toys have associations with gender identity, and the age of the child or parental views on gender roles may influence the final choice. Ex. A toy that follows traditional gender roles versus a toy that would break from traditional gender roles.
- Score—Motor milestones—the toy selected should be appropriate for a child that is around walking age. Ex. A toy that helps develop the pincer grasp might not be as good a choice as a toy that requires pushing.

YOU KNOW YOU HAVE MASTERED THE MAIN TOPICS IN THIS CHAPTER IF YOU ARE ABLE TO . . .

- Introduce the concept of motivation and discuss the major theories proposed to explain motivated behavior.
- Discuss the specific motivation of hunger and examine the physiological and social components in addition to common eating disorders.
- Describe the three elements of emotion, and present six theories on how emotions are processed.
- Explain what the positive psychology movement is.

RAPID REVIEW

Motivation is the process by which activities are started, directed, and continued so that physical or psychological needs or wants are met. When motivation comes from outside the self it is called **extrinsic motivation**; on the other hand, if a person does something because it is satisfying in some internal manner, the motivation is called **intrinsic motivation**. Several theories have been proposed to explain the process of motivation including the theories of instinct, drive reduction, needs, arousal, incentive, humanism, and self-determination. The **instinct approach** suggests that people are motivated by **instincts**, biologically determined and innate patterns of behavior. Unfortunately, instinct theory only describes behavior and is unable to explain why people do what they do. The drive-reduction approach proposes that a **need**, or requirement, produces a **drive** and that people act in order to reduce these drives. The drives can be **primary drives** such as hunger and thirst or **acquired (secondary) drives** such as the need for money. The rationale for drive reduction includes the idea that the body has a tendency to try to maintain a steady state referred to as **homeostasis**. When the body is out of balance, a need develops and the tension provides the drive to reduce the need and return the body to a state of balance. **Drive-reduction theory**, however, cannot explain why people would increase their internal tension by doing things like parachuting out of an airplane. **Need theory** attempts to explain motivation by understanding three specific needs, the **need for achievement (nAch)**, **need for affiliation (nAff)**, and **need for power (nPow)**. Dweck's self theory of motivation suggests the need for achievement is closely linked to personality factors, including a person's view of how *self* can affect the individual's perception of the success or failure of his or her actions. Those who believe intelligence is fixed and unchangeable often demonstrate an external locus of control when faced with difficulty, leading them to give up easily or avoid situations in which they might fail. The other type of person believes that intelligence is changeable and can be shaped by experiences and effort in small increases, or increments. These people also tend to show an internal locus of control, both in believing that their own actions and efforts will improve their intelligence and in taking control or increasing their efforts when faced with challenges. **Arousal theory** suggests that people are motivated to maintain an optimal level of arousal or tension. The level of arousal is achieved by increasing or decreasing stimulation and is driven by a proposed **stimulus motive**. The **Yerkes–Dodson law** demonstrates that for an easy task, performance is best when arousal is a little higher than average, whereas for a difficult task, performance is best when arousal is a little below average. Individuals who consistently seek out high levels of arousal have been labeled as **sensation seekers**. According to **incentive approaches** of motivation, people's actions are determined by the rewards or **incentives** for their behaviors. **Expectancy-value theories** are a subset of incentive theories that assume a person's expectancies, or beliefs, about what will happen in the future need to be taken into account in order to understand his or her motivation.

Abraham Maslow was a major proponent of the **humanistic approach** to motivation and proposed a **hierarchy of needs** that individuals must fulfill before they can reach the highest need of **self-actualization**, where a person reaches his or her fullest potential. According to Maslow, basic needs such as hunger and thirst must be satisfied before the higher level needs can be achieved. Also, Maslow referred to the times in which self-actualization is attained as **peak experiences**. Another theory of motivation similar to Maslow's is the **self-determination theory** that proposes that there are three inborn and universal needs that humans work to satisfy. These needs are the need for autonomy, competence, and relatedness.

One specific area of motivation that has been studied extensively is the motivation to eat, also known as hunger. The hunger drive can be divided into physiological and social components. Physiologically, **insulin** and **glucagons** are hormones that regulate the level of glucose in the bloodstream. Insulin increases blood sugar levels, which leads to feelings of hunger. A hormone called **leptin** may play a role in controlling how hungry an individual feels. Several areas in the **hypothalamus** also play an important role in regulating eating behavior, perhaps by influencing the specific weight that our bodies try to maintain, or our **weight set point**. Another factor that influences the weight set point is the **basal metabolic rate**, which decreases as we age, causing a corresponding increase in the weight set point. The social factors that influence hunger include the times of day when a person typically eats, using food to reduce stress or provide comfort, and the appeal of a tempting dessert item. Cultural factors and gender also play a part in determining hunger and eating habits. Women in the United States were found to be much more likely to start eating for emotional reasons. Japanese women were more likely to eat because of hunger signals or social demands. Some problems associated with eating behaviors are **obesity**, in which a person weighs 20 to 30 percent over his or her ideal weight. Factors contributing to obesity include genetics, overeating, and slowing of metabolism as people age. Eating disorders include **anorexia nervosa**, in which a person weighs 15 percent less than his or her ideal weight; **bulimia**, in which a person develops a cycle of overeating, followed by deliberate vomiting; and **binge-eating disorder**, where a person binge eats but does not purge or use other inappropriate methods for avoiding weight gain. Causes of eating disorders are not clear, but an increased sensitivity to food and its reward value may play a role in bulimia and binge-eating disorder, while fear and anxiety may become associated with food in anorexia nervosa. Eating disorders are found in non-Western cultures. Chinese and Chinese American women are far less likely to suffer from eating disorders than non-Hispanic white women, and the rate of eating disorders is increasing among young African American women.

Emotions can be defined as the "feeling" aspect of consciousness, characterized by a certain physical arousal, a certain behavior, and an inner awareness of feelings. As can be seen in the definition, emotions can be divided into three components: physiology, behaviors, and subjective experience. Different emotions have been found to be associated with different physiological reactions. The **amygdala** has been found to play a role in the regulation of emotions in humans as well as other animals. The behaviors of emotions include facial expressions, body movements, and other actions. Research has supported the idea that at least seven basic facial expressions are recognized and mimicked in cultures around the world. However, the **display rules**, or exactly when, where, and how these emotions can be expressed, appear to differ across cultures. The subjective experience of emotions involves the cognitive process of assigning a label, such as "happy," to your feelings. Several theories have been developed in an attempt to explain the process humans use to label our emotions. **Common sense theory** suggests that a stimulus causes a particular emotion to occur, which then leads to the behavioral and physiological response. The **James–Lange theory** of emotion proposes that a stimulus leads to a particular physiological response, which then leads to the subjective experience of an emotion. The **Cannon–Bard theory** suggests that the physical and subjective experience of emotions occur at the same time. A stimulus leads to activation of the thalamus, which then simultaneously activates the sympathetic nervous system and higher cortical areas, which interpret the signal as a particular emotion. **Schachter and Singer** proposed the **cognitive arousal theory**, which proposes that after a stimulus occurs our body has a physical reaction, and we make a cognitive appraisal of the situation. Based on feedback from both these sources, we then come up with a subjective label for the emotion we are experiencing. The **facial feedback hypothesis** assumes that facial expressions provide feedback to the brain regarding the emotion being expressed and can then intensify or even cause the emotion. Lazarus's **cognitive–mediational theory** of emotion suggests that following a stimulus, we engage in a cognitive appraisal of the situation, which then triggers a subjective experience of an emotion followed by a physiological response.

The Getting Things Done (GTD) method can be applied to help manage time and tasks. The five stages of the method help organize and process tasks by focusing on outcomes and "next actions."

STUDY HINTS

1. By far, the most confusing concept of this chapter is keeping track of the theories of emotion. The following hints are designed to help you work through this process. To start with, try filling in the following table correctly. Remember when we are discussing emotions there are several components we are interested in. The theories vary according to which component comes first. The components are

   • physiological experience of emotion (increased heart rate, sweating, etc.)
   • subjective experience of emotion (the "feeling" of happiness, sadness, or anger)
   • cognitive appraisal (using your thought process to assess the situation)
   • subcortical brain activity (not considered cognitive types of action)

   Using these key components, fill in the following table. The first row has already been filled in for you.

Theory	Event	1st response	2nd response	3rd response
Common Sense	*Stimulus (dog barking)*	*Subjective experience (fear)*	*Physiological experience (increased heart rate)*	
James–Lange Theory				
Cannon–Bard Theory				
Schachter–Singer Theory				
Facial Feedback Hypothesis				
Cognitive–Mediational Theory				

Now look over the chart you just completed. Which of the theories are similar and which are different? Can you come up with a way to group the theories together based on similarity?
As you learned in the chapter on memory, processing the information in this manner will help you better retain the material and make retrieval for the exam an easier process. Try grouping the theories into the following three categories:

Category 1: Physiological experience occurs after you "feel" the emotion.

_____

_____

Category 2: "Feeling" the emotion occurs after the physiological changes.

_____

_____

_____

Category 3: "Feeling" the emotion and the physiological changes occur at the same time.

_____

Suggested Answers for Question 1

Theory	Event	1st response	2nd response	3rd response
Common Sense	*Stimulus (dog barking)*	*Subjective experience (fear)*	*Physiological experience (increased heart rate)*	
James–Lange Theory	*Stimulus (dog barking)*	*Physiological (increased heart rate)*	*Subjective (fear)*	
Cannon–Bard Theory	*Stimulus (dog barking)*	*Subcortical brain activity*	*Physiological and subjective at the same time*	
Schachter–Singer Theory	*Stimulus (dog barking)*	*Physiological response (increased heart rate)*	*Cognitive appraisal (there is a scary-looking dog barking at me)*	*Subjective experience (fear)*
Facial Feedback Hypothesis	*Stimulus (dog barking)*	*Facial expression of fear*	*Subcortical brain activity*	*Subjective experience (fear)*
Cognitive–Mediational Theory	*Stimulus (dog barking)*	*Cognitive appraisal (there is a scary-looking dog barking at me)*	*Subjective experience (fear)*	*Physiological experience (increased heart rate)*

Suggested Answers for Question 2

Category 1: Physiological experience occurs after you "feel" the emotion.

    Common sense theory

    Cognitive–mediational theory

Category 2: "Feeling" the emotion occurs after the physiological changes.

    James–Lange theory

    Schachter–Singer theory of cognitive arousal

    Facial feedback hypothesis

Category 3: "Feeling" the emotion and the physiological changes occur at the same time.
_____Cannon–Bard theory_____

LEARNING OBJECTIVES

9.1   How do psychologists define motivation, and what are the key elements of the early instinct and drive-reduction approaches to motivation?

9.2   What are the characteristics of the three types of needs?

9.3   What are the key elements of the arousal and incentive approaches to motivation?

9.4   How do Maslow's humanistic approach and self-determination theory explain motivation?

9.5   What happens in the body to cause hunger, and how do social factors influence a person's experience of hunger?

9.6   What are some biological, social, and cultural factors that contribute to obesity?

9.7   What are different types of eating disorders, how do they differ, and who are they most likely to affect?

9.8   What are the three elements of emotion?

9.9   How do the James–Lange and Cannon–Bard theories of emotion differ?

9.10 What are the key elements in cognitive arousal theory, the facial feedback hypothesis, and the cognitive–mediational theory of emotion?

9.11 What are the stages of the GTD method?

AP LEARNING OBJECTIVES

1. Identify and apply basic motivational concepts to understand the behavior of humans and other animals. (pp. 356, 363)
2. Discuss the biological underpinnings of motivation, including needs, drives, and homeostasis. (p. 357)
3. Compare and contrast motivational theories, including the strengths and weaknesses of each. (p. 357)
4. Describe classic research findings in specific motivation systems. (p. 367)
5. Compare and contrast major theories of emotion. (p. 380)
6. Describe how cultural influences shape emotional expression, including variations in body language. (p. 379)
7. Identify key contributors in the psychology of motivation and emotion. (pp. 363, 381, 382)

CHAPTER GLOSSARY

Abraham Maslow	1908–1970. American psychologist who was a major proponent of the humanistic movement in psychology.
acquired (secondary) drives	those drives that are learned through experience or conditioning, such as the need for money or social approval.
amygdala	brain structure located near the hippocampus, responsible for fear responses and memory of fear.
anorexia nervosa	a condition in which a person reduces eating to the point that a weight loss of 15 percent below the ideal body weight or more occurs.
arousal theory of motivation	theory of motivation in which people are said to have an optimal (best or ideal) level of tension that they seek to maintain by increasing or decreasing stimulation.
basal metabolic rate	the rate at which the body burns energy when the organism is resting.
binge-eating disorder	involves uncontrolled binge eating but differs from bulimia because individuals with binge-eating disorder do not purge or use other inappropriate methods for avoiding weight gain.
bulimia	a condition in which a person develops a cycle of "binging," or overeating enormous amounts of food at one sitting, and "purging," or deliberately vomiting after eating.
Cannon–Bard theory of emotion	theory in which the physiological reaction and the emotion are assumed to occur at the same time.

cognitive arousal theory	theory of emotion in which both the physical arousal and the labeling of that arousal based on cues from the environment must occur before the emotion is experienced.
cognitive–mediational theory	theory of emotion in which a stimulus must be interpreted (appraised) by a person in order to result in a physical response and an emotional reaction.
common sense theory	idea held by most people that a stimulus leads to the subjective experience of an emotion which then triggers a physiological response.
display rules	learned ways of controlling displays of emotion in social settings.
drive	a psychological tension and physical arousal arising when there is a need that motivates the organism to act in order to fulfill the need and reduce the tension.
drive-reduction theory	approach to motivation that assumes behavior arises from physiological needs which cause internal drives to push the organism to satisfy the need and reduce tension and arousal.
emotion	the "feeling" aspect of consciousness, characterized by a certain physical arousal, a certain behavior that reveals the emotion to the outside world, and an inner awareness of feelings.
expectancy-value theories	a type of incentive theory that assumes the actions of humans cannot be predicted without understanding the beliefs, values, and the importance that a person attaches to those beliefs and values at any given moment.
extrinsic motivation	type of motivation in which a person performs an action because it leads to an outcome that is separate from or external to the person.
facial feedback hypothesis	theory of emotion which assumes that facial expressions provide feedback to the brain concerning the emotion being expressed, which in turn causes and intensifies the emotion.
glucagons	hormones that are secreted by the pancreas to control the levels of fats, proteins, and carbohydrates in the body by increasing the level of glucose in the bloodstream.
hierarchy of needs	a theory of motivation proposed by Maslow which suggests that as people meet their basic needs they seek to satisfy successively higher needs as laid out in the hierarchy.
homeostasis	The tendency of the body to maintain a steady state.
humanistic approach of motivation	theories of motivation which focus on human potential and the drive to be the best a person can be.
hypothalamus	small structure in the brain located below the thalamus and directly above the pituitary gland, responsible for motivational behavior such as sleep, hunger, thirst, and sex.
incentive approach of motivation	theories of motivation in which behavior is explained as a response to the external stimulus and its rewarding properties.
incentives	things that attract or lure people into action.
instinct approach of motivation	approach to motivation that assumes people are governed by instincts similar to those of other animals.
instincts	the biologically determined and innate patterns of behavior that exist in both people and animals.
insulin	a hormone secreted by the pancreas to control the levels of fats, proteins, and carbohydrates in the body by reducing the level of glucose in the bloodstream.
intrinsic motivation	type of motivation in which a person performs an action because the act itself is rewarding or satisfying in some internal manner.
James–Lange theory of	theory in which a physiological reaction leads to the labeling of an

emotion	emotion.
leptin	a hormone that, when released into the bloodstream, signals the hypothalamus that the body has had enough food and reduces the appetite while increasing the feeling of being full.
motivation	the process by which activities are started, directed, and continued so that physical or psychological needs or wants are met.
need	a lack of some material (such as food or water) that is required for survival of the organism.
need for achievement (nAch)	a need which involves a strong desire to succeed in attaining goals, not only realistic ones but also challenging ones.
need for affiliation (nAff)	the need for friendly social interactions and relationships with others.
need for power (nPow)	the need to have control or influence over others.
needs theory of motivation	theory of motivation that examines the three specific needs for achievement, affiliation, and power.
obesity	condition in which a person weighs 20 percent or more over his or her ideal weight.
peak experiences	according to Maslow, times in a person's life during which self-actualization is temporarily achieved.
primary drives	those drives that involve needs of the body such as hunger and thirst.
Schachter and Singer	two psychologists responsible for proposing the cognitive arousal theory of emotions.
self-actualization	according to Maslow, the seldom-reached point at which people have sufficiently satisfied the lower needs and achieved their full human potential.
self-determination theory (SDT)	theory of human motivation in which the social context of an action has an effect on the type of motivation existing for the action.
sensation seeker	someone who needs more arousal than the average person.
stimulus motive	a motive that appears to be unlearned but causes an increase in stimulation. An example of this motive is curiosity.
weight set point	the particular level of weight that the body tries to maintain.
Yerkes–Dodson law	predicts that a certain level of arousal will be motivating, but too much arousal or too little arousal will decrease motivation. The optimal level of arousal appears to depend on the individual and the difficulty of the task.

CHAPTER PRACTICE TEST

For the following multiple-choice questions, select the answer you feel best answers the question.

1. The process by which activities are started, directed, and continued so that physical or psychological needs or wants are met is called _____.
    a) motivation
    b) emotion
    c) achievement
    d) synergy
    e) initiative

2. Which statement about motivation is true?

     a)   Motives only originate from biological needs.
     b)   We are always aware of motivational processes.
     c)   Different motives always lead to different behaviors.
     d)   Two people motivated by the same factor will satisfy that motive through similar means.
     e)   A motive energizes and directs behavior.

3. In the early 20th century, psychologists were inclined to explain motivated behavior by attributing it to _____.

     a)   emotions
     b)   incentives
     c)   learned responses
     d)   instincts
     e)   genetics

4. William McDougal proposed _____ instincts for humans early in the 20th century.

     a)   5
     b)   9
     c)   18
     d)   24
     e)   36

5. Each of the following is a valid criticism of instinct theories of motivation EXCEPT _____.

     a)   human behavior is rarely rigid, inflexible, and found throughout the species
     b)   instinct theories name behaviors without pinpointing their origins
     c)   they were the dominant explanation for human behavior early in the 20th century
     d)   instinct theories only describe behaviors
     e)   instinct theories do not explain behaviors

6. Salmon swimming upstream to spawn are an example of _____.

     a)   incentives
     b)   motives
     c)   instinct
     d)   needs
     e)   shaping

7. Drives serve to activate responses that are aimed at reducing the drive, thereby returning the body to a more normal state called _____.

     a)   stability
     b)   equilibrium
     c)   homeostasis
     d)   physiological balance
     e)   automaticity

8. Some psychologists believe that behavior is motivated by the body's attempts to achieve a state of balance in which the body functions effectively, or in _____.

     a)   reciprocity
     b)   acquiescence
     c)   propinquity
     d)   circadian rhythm
     e)   homeostasis

9. Primary drives _____.
   a) are exceptions to the drive-reduction principle
   b) are learned
   c) are influenced by stimuli within the body
   d) are influenced by stimuli outside the body
   e) vary from culture to culture

10. Monica put all her time and energy into getting into the acting club because her main goal in life "was to be a famous star!" Monica's drive to be famous was a _____ drive.
    a) primary
    b) reflexive
    c) tertiary
    d) secondary
    e) instinctual

11. Homeostasis is like a _____.
    a) TV remote control
    b) scale
    c) carburetor
    d) bicycle
    e) thermostat

12. Your text discusses all of the following needs EXCEPT _____.
    a) achievement
    b) affiliation
    c) power
    d) sex
    e) survival

13. Which of the following is correct for people high in need for achievement?
    a) They look for careers which make a lot of money.
    b) They look for careers which require a high degree of social interaction.
    c) They look for careers which require little education.
    d) They look for careers which will make them famous.
    e) They look for careers and hobbies that allow others to evaluate them.

14. According to Carol Dweck, need for achievement is closely related to _____.
    a) genetics
    b) geography
    c) luck
    d) personal factors
    e) education

15. In arousal theory, people are said to have a(n) _____ level of tension.
    a) ultimate
    b) lower
    c) unmeasurable
    d) high
    e) optimal

16. Indiana Jones goes off to foreign lands in search of artifacts hidden in dangerous places and guarded by fierce protectors. Dr. Jones would be described as _____ in arousal theory.
    a) a sensation seeker
    b) nAff
    c) fool-hardy
    d) high nPow
    e) desensitized

17. As a class assignment you are required to collect advertising slogans and describe how they may be relevant to concepts in psychology. You select the Jell-O slogan, "There's always room for Jell-O," and describe in class that it is relevant to one of the theories of motivation. Which theory?
    a) instinctive
    b) affiliation
    c) drive-reduction
    d) optimum-level
    e) incentive

18. One interesting thing about incentive approaches is that incentives _____.
    a) exist inside a narrow collection of internal stimuli
    b) exist independently of any need or level of arousal
    c) exist inside a narrow collection of external stimuli
    d) only work for adults
    e) can only work if they are based on money

19. Jill is motivated by money and the things money will bring her. Jack is motivated by doing good things, and his incentives are based on that idea and belief. What theory incorporates both these types of motivational causes?
    a) sensation seeking theory
    b) entity theory
    c) increment theory
    d) expectancy-value theory
    e) survival need theory

20. According to Abraham Maslow, developing one's potential to its fullest extent results in _____.
    a) safety
    b) self-esteem
    c) belongingness
    d) self-actualization
    e) valley moments

21. Which of the following does NOT show the motivating power of self-actualization?
    a) Joan wants to live in a house with all the modern conveniences so that she may have more time to seek fulfillment from her career and family.
    b) Frank feels that he is a good salesman because he likes what he does and knows how to do it well.
    c) Barbara knows that, as a teacher, she is a good person because she realizes the importance of imparting knowledge to society.
    d) Mark works hard as an attorney only so that he can attract more clients, earn more money, and be secure in the knowledge that his family can survive.
    e) Alan is partially retired from his career as a plumber and now plays music on the weekends with his band "The Wrenches" to raise money for needy groups.

22. Self-determination theory (SDT) best fits which type of motivation?
    a) the need for affiliation
    b) intrinsic motivation
    c) extrinsic motivation
    d) a mastery goal
    e) instinctual

23. Intrinsic motivation is defined as _____.
    a) the pursuit of an activity for external rewards
    b) the pursuit of an activity for its own sake
    c) the pursuit of an activity to relieve the state of tension caused by deprivation
    d) the pursuit of an activity in order to be judged favorably by others
    e) the pursuit of an activity for possible fame

24. One factor in hunger seems to be the increase in _____ that occurs after we begin to eat.
    a) cholesterol
    b) lipoproteins
    c) insulin
    d) glucose
    e) glucagon

25. The ventromedial hypothalamus (VMH) may be involved in _____.
    a) increasing hunger
    b) decreasing hunger
    c) processing low fats
    d) food allergies
    e) a desire for unappealing foods

26. The lateral hypothalamus (LH) may be involved in _____.
    a) stoppage of eating
    b) the onset of cating
    c) processing low fats
    d) food allergies
    e) the visual appeal of foods

27. Anna Nicole weighed about 125lbs most of her adult life. However, it seemed like whenever Anna Nicole gained weight it was easy to lose it and get back to 125. But when she wanted to go below 125 it took forever, and even the slightest deviation from her diet got her back to 125. What explanation would you give Anna Nicole?
    a) Use better diet products.
    b) Start a reality TV show.
    c) Her weight, 125, is her set point.
    d) Her BMR is causing all the problems.
    e) She needs to switch to high carbohydrate and high fat foods.

28. The concept of "comfort food" suggests that food _____.
    a) may be influenced by social factors
    b) has genetic ways to comfort
    c) may release hormones and neurotransmitters that are comforting
    d) is reflexive
    e) creates lower levels of desire for comfort

29. Which component of hunger is most likely contributing to the fact that sometimes a person who has just had a late breakfast will still feel hungry at noon?
    a) social
    b) behavioral
    c) physiological
    d) intrinsic
    e) metabolic

30. Obesity is defined as someone who is at least _____ percent or more over the ideal body weight.
    a) 10
    b) 20
    c) 30
    d) 40
    e) 50

31. Which individual has the highest risk for developing anorexia nervosa?
    a) a lower-class 26-year-old European man
    b) an upper-class 16-year-old American boy
    c) a lower-class 26-year-old European woman
    d) an upper-class 16-year-old American girl
    e) a lower-class 26-year-old American man

32. An eating disorder characterized by binges of eating followed by self-induced vomiting is called _____.
    a) anorexia nervosa
    b) bulimia
    c) Karposi's anemia
    d) Huntington's chorea
    e) Hawthorne's effect

33. All of the following statements are correct about bulimia EXCEPT _____.
    a) individuals with bulimia have a distorted view of how much food is too much food
    b) bulimics typically gorge on sugary, fattening foods
    c) binge eating and vomiting are common symptoms
    d) individuals with bulimia have a distorted body image
    e) bulimia is not as damaging as anorexia nervosa

34. You are a hormone. You are secreted into the bloodstream by fatty tissue, and your job is to signal the hypothalamus that the body has enough food, reducing appetite and increasing the feeling of being full. Who are you?
    a) adrenalin
    b) peptic acid
    c) leptin
    d) lippotor
    e) melamine

35. What Latin word connects both motive and emotion?
    a) The Latin word for "to emote."
    b) The Latin word for "to move."
    c) The Latin word for "to mote."
    d) The Latin word for "to mate."
    e) The Latin word for "to make."

36. Paul Ekman and his colleagues gathered abundant evidence supporting the universality of _____ basic facial expressions of emotion.
    a) 3
    b) 5
    c) 7
    d) 9
    e) 11

37. According to Ekman, which of the following is NOT one of the universal facial expressions?
    a) disgust
    b) fear
    c) contempt
    d) anger
    e) shame

38. To explain the human universality and variability of emotions, Ekman and his associates _____.
    a) developed a concept of "display rules," which are rules for emotional expression
    b) developed an inter-observer system to make sure that observers defined expressions reliably
    c) interviewed all participants in order to assess unexpressed feelings and motivations
    d) monitored the brain waves of participants to determine which hemisphere had higher activation
    e) studied only Western cultures for patterns of emotional responses

39. Which one of the following is NOT one of the elements of emotion discussed in the text?
    a) physiology
    b) labeling
    c) behavior
    d) labeling
    e) attractiveness

40. Which theory states that a stimulus triggers physiological changes that produce emotion?
    a) Cannon–Bard theory
    b) James–Lange theory
    c) Schachter–Singer theory
    d) common sense view of emotions
    e) Lazarus's theory

41. Which statement is most consistent with the James–Lange theory of emotion?
    a) "I run because I'm afraid."
    b) "I'm laughing because I am happy."
    c) "I'm crying because I'm sad."
    d) "I'm anxious because I perspire."
    e) "I'm smiling because I am nervous."

42. What is the correct sequence of events in emotional response according to the Cannon–Bard theory?
    a) stimulus → emotion → physiological changes
    b) stimulus → physiological changes → emotion
    c) physiological changes → stimulus → emotion
    d) stimulus → subcortical activity → emotion AND physiological changes (simultaneous)
    e) physiological changes → emotion → stimulus

43. "I think I'm afraid, therefore I am afraid" is a statement that is most consistent with which of the following theories?
    a) the James–Lange theory
    b) activation theory
    c) cognitive arousal theory
    d) the Cannon–Bard theory
    e) the activation–synthesis theory

44. You just finished a cup of very strong coffee, which causes your body to have a general feeling of arousal. That afternoon you attend the funeral of a friend. According to Schachter and Singer, which of the following would most likely occur?
    a) Your emotion would be happy in spite of the funeral because of the arousal.
    b) You would work very hard to control your emotion.
    c) Your emotion would be sad since the context would affect your labeling.
    d) Your emotional state would be impossible to predict.
    e) Your physical state would be controlled by your emotional state of arousal.

45. According to the theory of emotion proposed by Schachter and Singer, what is the most important determinant of your subjective experience of emotion?
    a) physiological reactions
    b) cognitive appraisal of the situation
    c) facial expressions
    d) intensity of the stimulus
    e) autonomic responses

46. In the classic study of emotion conducted by Schachter and Singer, after receiving the epinephrine, the subjects placed in the room with the angry man reported feeling _____.
    a) angry
    b) happy
    c) both angry and happy
    d) no emotions
    e) fear

47. Which recent study below casts doubt on the facial feedback hypothesis?
    a) a woman with a paralyzed face still responded emotionally to slides meant to stimulate emotions
    b) a blind woman still responded emotionally to slides meant to stimulate emotions
    c) a woman paralyzed from the waist down still responded emotionally to slides meant to stimulate emotions
    d) a woman with Down syndrome still responded emotionally to slides meant to stimulate emotions
    e) a woman with emotional paralysis was found to produce facial feedback

48. According to the facial feedback hypothesis, if you would like to make yourself feel more happy you should _____.
    a) spend time with friends
    b) talk to a counselor
    c) think about all the positive aspects of your life
    d) smile
    e) listen to happy music

49. According to the cognitive–mediational theory, which factor would be most important in determining whether you feel nervous when asked to speak in front of the class?
    a) your physiological reaction to the request
    b) activation of subcortical brain activity
    c) your cognitive appraisal of the situation
    d) your change in blood pressure
    e) your perspiration and heart rate

50. Which of the following is not a stage of the Getting Things Done (GTD) method?
    a) capturing
    b) processing
    c) procrastinating
    d) organizing
    e) reviewing

CHAPTER PRACTICE TEST ANSWERS

1. a   This is the definition in the text. If you answered b, then you are confusing emotion with motivation.
2. e   This is simply the definition of motive.
3. d   Instinct theory was one of the first proposed theories of motivation in psychology. Be careful not to confuse incentive with instincts!
4. c   McDougal proposed a total of 18 basic instincts.
5. c   This is not a criticism but simply a statement.
6. c   Instincts are innate, biologically determined behaviors.
7. c   Homeostasis is the term psychologists and physiologists use to refer to the body's state of balance. Equilibrium means the same thing but is not the term used by psychologists.
8. e   Homeostasis is a sense of balance.
9. c   These internal stimuli would include things such as hunger or thirst.
10. d   Secondary drives are drives that we acquire through learning. The drive to be famous is learned.
11. e   A scale is not correct because it only has one direction.
12. d   The four needs discussed with regard to motivation were the needs for achievement, affiliation, power, and survival.
13. e   High achievers need feedback from others.
14. d   There was no mention of genetics in her theory, but there was considerable discussion about an individual's sense of self and views on intelligence.
15. e   Arousal theory argues that arousal should be neither too high nor too low.
16. a   His actions indicate that he needs a higher level of arousal than most people.
17. e   Incentive theory suggests that we often eat food items because of their reward value and not simply because we are hungry.
18. b   Incentives motivate behavior whether or not we have a specific need and regardless of our arousal level.
19. d   Expectancy value theory states that the values of a person determine his or her motivation levels.
20. d   Self-actualization is at the top of Maslow's hierarchy of needs.

21.   d   This is the only situation in which the person is focusing on basic needs for himself and his family. In all the other examples, the individuals were focused on growth needs.

22.   b   Self-determination theory is characterized by intrinsic motivations.

23.   b   All the other motivations are based on external factors. Intrinsic motivation deals with forces within the individual.

24.   c   Insulin is associated with feelings of hunger and is related to blood sugar levels.

25.   b   When the ventromedial hypothalamus was removed in experimental animals, the animals no longer controlled their eating and became extremely obese.

26.   b   When the lateral hypothalamus was removed in experimental animals, the animals stopped eating and had to be force-fed.

27.   c   The set point is the level of weight the body tends to maintain.

28.   a   Social factors in hunger include the social cues associated with food.

29.   a   Social factors can have a strong impact on feelings of hunger.

30.   b   This percentage was discussed in your textbook and arrived at by health professionals.

31.   d   According to government statistics, white upper-class females in the United States show the highest prevalence rates for anorexia.

32.   b   This is the definition given in the textbook. Note that the vomiting distinguishes bulimia from anorexia.

33.   e   Although the damage from bulimia is different than that from anorexia, it is still a very dangerous disorder.

34.   c   Leptin appears to be the hormone that causes you to feel full.

35.   b   This is the definition given in your textbook.

36.   c   The research found seven facial expressions that appear to be universal.

37.   e   Shame was not found in all cultures. The seven facial expressions he did find were anger, fear, disgust, happiness, surprise, sadness, and contempt.

38.   a   Ekman found that display rules tend to vary across cultures, whereas the recognition of basic emotions tends to be universal.

39.   e   Emotion was broken down into its physical, behavioral, and subjective (or labeling) components.

40.   b   The James–Lange theory states that the changes in our body come first, followed by our subjective experience of an emotion.

41.   d   The physiological change comes before the experience of the emotion.

42.   d   Cannon and Bard believed the subjective and physiological experience occurred simultaneously.

43.   c   The cognitive aspect (or thinking component) is the factor that determines your emotions according to the cognitive arousal theory.

44.   c   According to Schachter and Singer, the coffee causes an arousal, and then you seek environmental cues to come up with a label for your arousal.

45.   b   See the answer to number 44.

46.   a   In accordance with Schachter and Singer's theory, the participants use the environmental cues of an angry co-subject to determine that their own arousal was due to anger as well.

47.   a   If her face is paralyzed, she would not be able to send feedback to her brain regarding her facial expression and thus her emotions would be significantly reduced according to the facial feedback hypothesis.

48.   d   The facial feedback hypothesis proposes that our brain receives feedback on our facial expressions which then serves to enhance whatever emotion we are expressing.

49.   c   The cognitive–mediational theory believes that we first assess the situation before we have a subjective experience of emotion or a physiological reaction.

50.   c   Procrastinating is not one of the stages of the GTD method.

CHAPTER PRACTICE FREE RESPONSE QUESTION
You have 25 minutes to answer the following question. You must write in complete sentences and not just list facts. You should make your point clearly and use the language of psychology. Be sure to write legibly and respond to all parts of the question.

Domino is at the movie theater watching the latest blockbuster psycho-thriller. At the midpoint of the movie, the theater holds an intermission. Apply the following to explain the behavior Domino might exhibit during the intermission:

- Drive theory
- Display rules
- Intrinsic motivation
- Extrinsic motivation
- Schachter-Singer two-factor model

SUGGESTED RUBRIC—Students should provide specific details and examples to support their assertions; definitions alone are not sufficient. Information about each topic should be discussed in the context of the question rather than abstractly. Successful essays may include the following arguments:

5 points

- Score—Drive theory—during the course of the first part of the movie Domino may experience an increase of an internal drive and will be motivated to meet that need. Ex. Domino now feels hungry and goes to the lobby to buy some popcorn to eat and end the hunger pangs.
- Score—Display rules are cultural rules about appropriate display of emotion in public. If Domino is from an Eastern culture, it would be inappropriate to make dramatic displays of emotion in the presence of others.
- Score—Intrinsic motivation—Domino's behavior must be for the act itself and not an external reward. Ex. Domino sees a young child drop a wallet. Domino picks up the wallet and returns it to the child for the internal feeling of satisfaction from doing a good deed.
- Score—Domino's behavior must be for an external reward and not just for the act itself. Ex. In exchange for $20, Domino gives up a centrally located seat in the theater to another person for a bad seat in the back.
- Score—Schachter–Singer two factor model—Domino is feeling an elevated heart rate and respiration. Domino references the physiological indicators with the content of the movie. The cues from the movie indicate that the emotion Jamie is experiencing is fear.

YOU KNOW YOU HAVE MASTERED THE MAIN TOPICS IN THIS CHAPTER IF YOU ARE ABLE TO . . .

- Define stress and identify the external and psychological factors that influence an individual's experience of stress.
- Discuss the causes of stress.
- Describe the physical reaction to stress and the relation of this reaction to cognitive, personality, and social factors.
- Explain the methods used to cope with stress including those influenced by culture and religion.

RAPID REVIEW

Stress is the physical, emotional, cognitive, and behavioral responses to events that are perceived as threatening or challenging. When a person's stress response is unpleasant or undesirable it is called **distress**, and when it is an optimal amount that helps a person function it is called **eustress**. The events that cause stress are called **stressors** and can be either internal or external events. Stressors can include external events such as catastrophes, major life changes, and hassles, along with internal experiences such as pressure, uncontrollability, and frustration. A **catastrophe** is an unpredictable event that happens on a large scale such as a tornado or flood. The terrorist-driven destruction of the World Trade Center in New York City on September 11, 2001, is a prime example of a catastrophe, and nearly 8 percent of the people living in the area near the attacks developed a severe stress disorder. A number of researchers have suggested that any major life change, such as moving, getting married, or getting a new job, would result in stress. Holmes and Rahe developed the **Social Readjustment Rating Scale (SRRS)** to measure the amount of change and thus stress in a person's life. Researchers have found a moderate correlation between scores on the SRRS and physical health. A majority of the stressors that people have to deal with are the little daily annoyances, or **hassles**. Surveys that measure the number of hassles an individual has to deal with are actually a better predictor of short-term illnesses than the SRRS. The internal experience of **pressure** is also considered a stressor. Pressure is the psychological experience produced by demands and expectations from outside sources. Two additional internal causes of stress are **uncontrollability**, or a lack of control in a situation, and **frustration**, or being blocked from achieving a desired goal. Typical reactions to frustration include persistence and **aggression**, or actions meant to harm or destroy. **Displaced aggression** occurs when a person takes out his or her frustrations on less threatening, more available targets and is a form of displacement. Another possible reaction to frustration is **escape or withdrawal**. An extreme reaction to stress in the way of a final escape is suicide, or intentionally taking one's own life.

Conflict is another source of stress and occurs when a person feels pulled toward two or more goals but can only achieve one of them. **Approach–approach conflict** occurs when an individual is attempting to choose between two desirable goals. **Avoidance–avoidance conflict** occurs when someone must choose between two undesirable goals. **Approach–avoidance conflict** describes a single goal that has both desirable and undesirable outcomes. An individual faced with two options in which each option has positive and negative aspects is dealing with a **double approach–avoidance conflict**. If there are more than two options, the conflict is called a **multiple approach–avoidance conflict**.

Endocrinologist **Hans Selye** was a pioneer in the study of the physical consequences of exposure to stressors. He proposed that the body goes through a sequence of three stages he called the **general adaptation syndrome (GAS)**. The initial stage is called **alarm** and represents the immediate reaction to stress mediated by our **sympathetic nervous system**. Typical alarm reactions include increased heart rate and blood pressure and release of sugar into the blood stream. As the stress continues, the body enters the **resistance** stage, during which time the sympathetic nervous system works overtime to give the body more energy. When the body's resources have been exhausted, the **parasympathetic nervous system** is activated and the body enters the **exhaustion** stage. Selye believed that it was the prolonged release of stress hormones during the resistance stage that led to the breakdown of the body's **immune system** and the onset of the stress-related physical conditions. Researchers in the field of **psychoneuroimmunology** who study the effects of psychological factors on the immune system have found that stress actually causes an increase in the activity of the immune system. High levels of stress have been linked to increased risk of heart disease. Also, stress has been shown to decrease the amount of **natural killer cells**, which are the cells responsible for fighting cancerous growths. **Health psychology** is a new area of psychology focusing on how physical activities, psychological traits, and social relationships affect overall health.

The **cognitive–mediational theory** of emotions proposed by Richard Lazarus states that the way people think about and appraise a stressor is a major factor in their stress response. The first step in appraising a stressor is called **primary appraisal** and involves estimating the severity of the stressor and classifying it as a threat, challenge, or loss. In **secondary appraisal**, an individual determines what resources he or she has available for dealing with the threat or loss. Personality has also been linked to stress-related health risks. In 1974, Meyer Freidman and Ray Rosenman published a book describing the **Type A** and **Type B personalities** and their link to heart disease. Based on studies of their own patients, Freidman and Rosenman proposed that individuals with Type A personality (a person who is competitive, ambitious, workaholic, with a constant sense of pressure) were more likely to develop heart disease than someone with a Type B personality. Several studies found that the specific trait of hostility in Type A individuals was the best predictor of future heart problems. A third personality type called **Type C** (in which a person holds in their emotions and tends to be pleasant) was later identified and is currently being investigated as to its possible link with cancer rates. Finally, research has suggested a fourth personality type, the **hardy personality**, which is associated with decreased illness due to stress. An individual with a hardy personality shows commitment, displays a sense of control, and sees stresses as challenges to be met and answered. In addition to personality, links have been found between an individual's attitude and his or her physical reactions to stress. Specifically, **pessimists** have been found to have significantly more stress-related health problems than **optimists**. One way to become an optimist is to recognize any negative thoughts you are having and work to get rid of them.

Social factors also play a key role in the amount of stress an individual experiences. Living in poverty and job stress are two major sources of stress. A serious consequence of job stress is **burnout**, or negative changes in thoughts, emotions, and behaviors as a result of prolonged stress or frustration. **Acculturative stress** describes the stress an individual experiences when having to adapt to a new culture. The method of adaptation can affect the stress level. Some of the methods of adapting to a new culture include integration, assimilation, separation, and marginalization. The effects of negative social factors on health can be minimized by a strong **social support system**, or network of family and friends who can offer help when a person is in need.

Coping strategies are actions that people take to master, tolerate, reduce, or minimize the effects of stressors and include both behavioral and psychological strategies. **Problem-focused coping** occurs when a person tries to eliminate the source of stress or reduce its impact by taking some action, while **emotion-focused coping** involves changing the way you feel or react to a stressor. **Meditation** is a series of mental exercises meant to refocus attention. **Concentrative meditation**, the form of meditation best known to the general public, has been found to be an effective coping strategy. Culture and religion have also been found to affect an individual's level of stress as well as the strategies used to cope with that stress.

Martin Seligman and others have shown that optimistic thinking is a good thing. The way to become an optimist is to monitor one's own thinking. Recognition of negative thoughts is the first step, followed by disputing those same negative thoughts.

STUDY HINTS

1. One important component to understanding this chapter is to understand the difference between a stressor and stress. The stressor is the event that causes us to experience stress. The event can be external, such as getting stuck in traffic, or internal, such as worrying about an upcoming exam. Our reaction to the event is called stress and can be physical, emotional, mental, and behavioral. Try coming up with some examples of events that could be considered stressors along with possible stress reactions. The first example has already been completed for you.

Stressor	Stress Reaction
Having to take an exam	*Increased heart rate*

2. Many students find the different types of conflicts confusing. Look over the Key Concepts area to refresh yourself on the meaning of each type of conflict and then try to come up with an example from your own life that illustrates each type of conflict. List your examples in the space below.

Approach–Approach Conflict: _____

_____

Approach–Avoidance Conflict: _____

_____

Avoidance–Avoidance Conflict: _____

_____

LEARNING OBJECTIVES

10.1 *How do psychologists define stress?*

10.2 *What kinds of external events can cause stress?*

10.3 *What are some psychological factors in stress?*

10.4 *How does stress affect the physical functioning of the body and its immune system?*

10.5 *How do cognitive factors and personality differences affect the experience of stress?*

10.6 *What social factors influence stress reactions?*

10.7 *What are some ways in which people cope with stress reactions?*

10.8 *How is coping with stress affected by culture and religion?*

10.9 *What are some ways to become a more optimistic thinker?*

AP LEARNING OBJECTIVES

1. Describe classic research findings in specific motivation systems. (p. 415)
2. Discuss theories of stress and the effects of stress on psychological and physical well-being. (pp. 399, 401, 404)
3. Identify key contributors in the psychology of motivation and emotion. (pp. 395, 404) (This LO is from the unit on motivation and emotion and is repeated here.)

CHAPTER GLOSSARY

acculturative stress	stress resulting from the need to change and adapt one's ways to the majority culture.
aggression	actions meant to harm or destroy.
alarm	the first stage of Hans Selye's general adaptation syndrome during which the sympathetic nervous system prepares the body for action.
approach–approach conflict	conflict occurring when a person must choose between two desirable goals.
approach–avoidance conflict	conflict occurring when a person must choose or not choose a goal that has both positive and negative aspects.
avoidance–avoidance conflict	conflict occurring when a person must choose between two undesirable goals.
burnout	negative changes in thoughts, emotions, and behavior as a result of prolonged stress or frustration.
catastrophe	an unpredictable, large-scale event that creates a tremendous need to adapt and adjust as well as overwhelming feelings of threat.
cognitive–mediational theory	theory of emotions proposed by Richard Lazarus that states the way people think about and appraise a stressor is a major factor in their stress response.
concentrative meditation	form of meditation in which a person focuses the mind on some repetitive or unchanging stimulus so that the mind can be cleared of disturbing thoughts and the body can experience relaxation.
conflict	psychological experience of being pulled toward or drawn to two or more desires or goals, only one of which may be attained.
coping strategies	actions that people can take to master, tolerate, reduce, or minimize the effects of stressors.
displaced aggression	taking out one's frustrations on some less threatening or more available target, a form of displacement.
distress	the effect of unpleasant and undesirable stressors.
double approach–avoidance conflict	conflict in which the person must decide between two goals, with each goal possessing both positive and negative aspects.
emotion-focused coping	coping strategies that change the impact of a stressor by changing the emotional reaction to the stressor.
escape or withdrawal	leaving the presence of a stressor, either literally or by a psychological withdrawal into fantasy, drug abuse, or apathy.
eustress	the effect of positive events, or the optimal amount of stress that people need to promote health and well-being.
exhaustion	the third stage of Hans Selye's general adaptation syndrome during which the parasympathetic nervous system takes over and the body experiences any number of physical illnesses.
frustration	the psychological experience produced by the blocking of a desired goal or fulfillment of a perceived need.
general adaptation syndrome (GAS)	the three stages of the body's physiological reaction to stress, including alarm, resistance, and exhaustion.
Hans Selye	1907–1982. Canadian endocrinologist who studied the physical response to stress and developed the concept of the general adaptation syndrome.
hardy personality	a person who seems to thrive on stress but lacks the anger and hostility of the Type A personality.
hassles	the daily annoyances of everyday life.

health psychology	area of psychology focusing on how physical activities, psychological traits, and social relationships affect overall health and rate of illness.
immune system	the system of cells, organs, and chemicals of the body that respond to attacks from diseases, infections, and injuries.
meditation	a series of mental exercises meant to refocus attention.
multiple approach–avoidance conflict	conflict in which the person must decide between more than two goals, with each goal possessing both positive and negative aspects.
natural killer cells	immune system cell responsible for suppressing viruses and destroying tumor cells.
optimists	people who expect positive outcomes.
parasympathetic nervous system	the division of the autonomic nervous system responsible for regulating the routine functions of the body, such as heartbeat, digestion, sleeping.
pessimists	people who expect negative outcomes.
pressure	the psychological experience produced by urgent demands or expectations for a person's behavior that come from an outside source.
primary appraisal	the first step in assessing a stress; involves estimating the severity of a stressor and classifying it as either a threat or a challenge.
problem-focused coping	coping strategies that try to eliminate the source of a stress or reduce its impact through direct actions.
psychoneuroimmunology	the study of the effects of psychological factors such as stress, emotions, thoughts, and behavior on the immune system.
resistance	the second stage of Hans Selye's general adaptation syndrome during which the sympathetic nervous system recruits resources to maintain an elevated level of activity and energy.
secondary appraisal	the second step in assessing a threat, involves estimating the resources available to the person for coping with the stressor.
Social Readjustment Rating Scale (SRRS)	assessment that measures the amount of stress in a person's life over a one-year period resulting from major life events.
social support system	the network of family, friends, neighbors, coworkers, and others who can offer support, comfort, or aid to a person in need.
stress	the term used to describe the physical, emotional, cognitive, and behavioral responses to events that are appraised as threatening or challenging.
stressors	events that cause a stress reaction.
sympathetic nervous system	the division of the autonomic nervous system responsible for mobilizing the body's energy and resources during times of stress and arousal.
Type A personality	person who is ambitious, time-conscious, extremely hard-working, and tends to have high levels of hostility and anger as well as being easily annoyed.
Type B personality	person who is relaxed and laid-back, less driven and competitive than Type A and slow to anger.
Type C personality	pleasant but repressed person, who tends to internalize his or her anger and anxiety and who finds expressing emotions difficult.
uncontrollability	the psychological experience caused by having no ability to change your particular set of circumstances.

CHAPTER PRACTICE TEST
For the following multiple-choice questions, select the answer you feel best answers the question.

1. The term used to describe the physical, emotional, cognitive, and behavioral responses to events that are viewed as threatening or challenging is _____.
   a) stress
   b) stressors
   c) uncontrollability
   d) pressures
   e) adaptation

2. The response an individual might have to an unpleasant stressor, such as losing his job, would be called _____.
   a) eustress
   b) anxiety
   c) stress appraisal
   d) negative stressors
   e) distress

3. After we have decided that a certain event is a stressor, we must decide how we will deal with it and what resources are available for coping with the stressor. This process is called _____.
   a) primary appraisal
   b) a fight or flight response
   c) stress-related decision
   d) hassle-related decision
   e) secondary appraisal

4. The area of psychology focusing on how physical activities, psychological traits, and social relationships affect overall health and rate of illness in known as _____.
   a) optimistic psychology
   b) coping psychology
   c) cognitive appraisal psychology
   d) health psychology
   e) biosocial psychology

5. Which of the following is an example of a stressor that would be classified as a hassle according to Richard Lazarus?
   a) getting married
   b) going through a divorce
   c) losing your house due to a flood
   d) the death of a family member
   e) locking your keys in the car

6. The Social Readjustment Rating Scale (SRRS) measures stress related to _____.
   a) positive and negative life events
   b) only negative life events
   c) only positive life events
   d) internal stressors
   e) positive or negative coping strategies

7. Gloria is a tax accountant, who is very busy from January to April 15, which is the tax return filing deadline. She feels that she must work very long hours during this time to meet the April 15 deadline for all of her clients. Gloria is experiencing _____.
    a) anxiety
    b) pressure
    c) overload
    d) cognitive dissonance
    e) disassociation

8. A woman who had an unpleasant confrontation with her boss and then goes home and yells at the dog would be displaying _____.
    a) uncontrollability
    b) pressure
    c) projection
    d) catastrophe
    e) displaced aggression

9. Which of the following is an example of an avoidance–avoidance conflict?
    a) A person who enjoys the ocean has to choose between retiring in the Bahamas or in Tahiti.
    b) You want to drive to a friend's house but the roads are icy.
    c) Someone wants to eat some cake but does not want the calories.
    d) A person who loves chocolate must choose between chocolate cake or chocolate ice cream.
    e) A student has to decide whether to turn in an unfinished paper and receive a failing grade or hand it in late and lose many points.

10. Trying to decide on taking a trip to the Bahamas, which would be very enjoyable but would severely limit the amount of money you would have to spend on other items is an example of a(n) _____.
    a) approach–approach conflict
    b) approach–avoidance conflict
    c) avoidance–avoidance conflict
    d) multiple approach–avoidance conflict
    e) challenge–ignore conflict

11. The general adaptation syndrome proposed by Hans Selye describes how we respond to stress with regard to our _____.
    a) psychological reactions
    b) emotional reactions
    c) social reactions
    d) physical reactions
    e) emotional and social reactions

12. According to Selye, some people may develop illnesses such as high blood pressure or weakened immune system during the _____ stage of the GAS.
    a) alarm
    b) collapse
    c) exhaustion
    d) resistance
    e) latent

13. Stress has been shown to be related to _____.
    a) increased resistance to environmental threats
    b) decreased efficiency of the reticular formation
    c) increased galvanic skin response
    d) decreased efficiency of the body's immune system
    e) decreased activity in the sympathetic system

14. When stress levels are elevated, the amount of natural killer cells in the body tends to
    _____.
    a) increase
    b) decrease
    c) stay the same
    d) There is not enough data to say at this point.
    e) increase and unnatural killer cells decrease.

15. The Type A behavior pattern is a significant predictor of _____.
    a) mental illness
    b) coronary heart disease
    c) cancer
    d) respiratory illnesses
    e) aneurysms

16. Someone who would be classified as having a Type C personality would be likely to
    _____.
    a) openly express his or her anger at someone
    b) try to always look on the bright side of a situation
    c) display a great deal of hostility when things don't go his or her way
    d) internalize his or her anger so that no one can see his or her true emotion
    e) share their feelings of sadness with others

17. _____ is the term used to describe the excessive anger exhibited by drivers in response to
    ordinary traffic frustration.
    a) Road rage
    b) Conflict
    c) Driving stress
    d) Frustration
    e) High anxiety

18. Pepe moved from Argentina to France. He chose not to learn to speak and write French, continues to
    maintain his old culture's styles of dress and customs, and lives in a neighborhood where only
    people from Argentina live. Pepe has used which method of entering the majority culture?
    a) integration
    b) assimilation
    c) separation
    d) marginalization
    e) dissemination

19. Which method of acculturation would tend to lead to the greatest degree of stress?
    a) integration
    b) assimilation
    c) separation
    d) marginalization
    e) dissemination

20. Her mother is ill and Vanna is feeling overwhelmed and sad. To cope with this stress of her mother's illness, Vanna has been writing her feelings down in a journal. Vanna is using _____.
   a) problem-focused coping
   b) emotion-focused coping
   c) distraction
   d) reappraisal
   e) reaction formation

21. Research shows that _____ lowers blood pressure in adolescents and adults.
   a) sensory deprivation
   b) concentrative meditation
   c) sublimation
   d) implosive meditation
   e) projection

22. You are a psychologist working with a new client, an immigrant from China, who is experiencing adjustment problems due to stress. Which of the following are you first going to consider when assessing your client's ability to cope?
   a) use of meditative strategies
   b) use of psychological defense mechanisms
   c) ability to use biofeedback equipment
   d) cultural background
   e) the education background of the client

23. Several studies have found a positive correlation between _____.
   a) level of religious commitment and life expectancies
   b) level of religious commitment and a decreased sense of meaning to life and death
   c) level of religious commitment and feeling alone in life
   d) level of religious commitment and unhealthy lifestyle choices
   e) level of religious commitment and negative feelings about personal weaknesses

24. Eating a healthy breakfast _____.
   a) has been shown to increase the risk of obesity
   b) has been shown to decrease the ability to concentrate
   c) has been shown to decrease the risk of obesity
   d) has been shown to increase the need for a morning nap
   e) has been shown to have no relationship to obesity

CHAPTER PRACTICE TEST ANSWERS

1. a   The response itself is called stress, and the event that causes the response is called a stressor.
2. e   The response to negative stressors is called distress, and the response to positive stressors or the optimal level of stressors is referred to as eustress.
3. e   Secondary appraisal involves deciding how to deal with a stressor and estimating the resources available for coping with it, while primary appraisal is the first step we take when facing a potential threat; it involves estimating its severity and determining whether it is a challenge or a threat.
4. d   Health psychology is a relatively new area of psychology that focuses on how physical activities, psychological traits, and social relationships affect overall health.
5. e   Lazarus focused on the minor daily annoyances, such as losing your car keys, as a significant source of stress in our lives.

6.   a   The SRRS assumes that any change (either positive or negative) will serve as a stressor in an individual's life.

7.   b   Although anxiety may be a result of pressure, Gloria is experiencing pressure as a result of her need to work longer hours to meet a deadline.

8.   e   Displaced aggression often occurs when the person or object that a person is really angry at is not an accessible target.

9.   e   Avoidance–avoidance conflicts involve having to choose between two undesirable outcomes.

10.   b   Approach–avoidance conflicts focus on one decision that has both positive and negative aspects to it.

11.   d   The general adaptation syndrome describes our body's physical reactions to stress.

12.   d   During the resistance stage, the body uses its resources to fight off the stressor. It is not until the next stage, exhaustion, that bodily resources are so depleted that stress-related diseases can develop.

13.   d   Stress is related to decreased efficiency of the immune system.

14.   b   Natural killer cells are important cells in the body that serve to limit the growth of cancerous cells. During times of stress, the level of natural killer cells tends to decrease, thus increasing the chances of tumor growth.

15.   b   The original development of the idea of Type A personality was in order to describe and predict the individuals who were at high risk for heart disease.

16.   d   Type C personalities tend to internalize their emotions.

17.   a   Driving stress may be what a person with road rage feels, but road rage is the term for excessive anger exhibited by some drivers over ordinary traffic frustration.

18.   c   Separation occurs when a person tries to maintain his or her original cultural identity. Assimilation occurs when a person completely gives up his or her old cultural identity and completely adopts the majority culture's ways.

19.   d   Marginalization occurs when an individual is not a part of his original culture, nor is he a part of the new culture. This method of acculturation has been found to create the greatest amount of acculturative stress.

20.   b   Vanna is coping with her stress by focusing on and thinking about her emotions.

21.   b   Concentrative meditation places one in a state of relaxation and lowers blood pressure. There is no such term as implosive meditation.

22.   d   Psychological defense mechanisms are significant but would not be as important in your initial assessment as would cultural background, especially since the client is from a country with a very different culture.

23.   a   Although these studies do not prove a cause-and-effect relationship, they have shown a correlation between religious affiliation and longevity.

24.   c   Eating a healthy breakfast has been shown to decrease the risk of obesity.

CHAPTER PRACTICE FREE RESPONSE QUESTION

You have 25 minutes to answer the following question. You must write in complete sentences and not just list facts. You should make your point clearly and use the language of psychology. Be sure to write legibly and respond to all parts of the question.

Jamie just won first-class tickets to a destination of choice aboard No Chance Airlines. Jamie enjoys traveling; however, the thought of air travel is stressful because Jamie fears flying. Explain how the following will apply to the stress that Jamie is experiencing over the decision to take the trip and how the stress may affect Jamie's health:

- Approach–avoidance conflict
- General adaptation syndrome
- Type A personality
- Optimism

- Problem-focused coping
- Displaced aggression

SUGGESTED RUBRIC—Students should provide specific details and examples to support their assertions; definitions alone are not sufficient. Information about each topic should be discussed in the context of the question rather than abstractly. Successful essays may include the following arguments:

6 Points

- Score—Approach–avoidance conflict—Jamie is experiencing stress because the approach–avoidance conflict can induce stress when struggling to make a difficult decision. Jamie wants to travel (approach), but the trip involves air travel (avoid). Jamie will have to decide if the fear of flying will prohibit Jamie from going on the trip. Jamie may face health risks like an illness if the stress over the decision is prolonged.
- Score—General adaptation syndrome—Jamie is faced with a frightening decision and initially will be in the alarm stage. Jamie will resist the stress, but if the stress continues any ability to resist will be drained. In the stage of exhaustion, Jamie will succumb to a stress-related disease or even coronary heart disease.
- Score—Type A personality—Jamie is a Type A personality, and the stress of the decision to travel may cause Jamie to be hostile and overeat, leading to coronary heart disease.
- Score—Optimism—Jamie may be optimistic about the trip, and optimism is related to lower stress, longer life, and better health. Jamie will be less likely to get sick and enjoy the trip.
- Score—Problem-focused coping—Jamie decides to focus on the problem and try to reduce the stress by eliminating the problem. Ex. Jamie trades the plane tickets for train tickets and is still able to have a trip. As a result of focusing on the problem Jamie is less susceptible to a stress- related illness.
- Score—Displaced aggression—Jamie cannot attack the source of the stress. However, because Jamie's cat is a safe target, Jamie displaces the stress and yells at the pet animal instead. While not especially good for the cat, Jamie is releasing the stress and may feel better.

YOU KNOW YOU HAVE MASTERED THE MAIN TOPICS IN THIS CHAPTER IF YOU ARE ABLE TO . . .

- Describe the role social influence plays on conformity, compliance, and obedience.
- Discuss the issues of social cognition including the formation and development of attitudes, impressions, and attributions.
- Introduce concepts of social interaction including prejudice, discrimination, interpersonal attraction, aggression, and altruism.
- Outline advancements in the study of social neuroscience.

RAPID REVIEW

<u>Social psychology</u> is the scientific study of how a person's behavior, thoughts, and feelings are influenced by the real, imagined, or implied presence of others. Social psychology can be broadly divided into the areas of social influence, social cognition, and social interaction.

<u>Social influence</u> is the process in which the presence of other people influences the behavior, feelings, and thoughts of an individual. <u>Conformity</u> involves changing one's own behavior to more closely match the actions of others. In 1951 <u>Solomon Asch</u> conducted a classic experiment on conformity by having subjects judge the length of a line after hearing a group of confederates all report an obviously incorrect answer. Asch found that the subjects conformed to the group answer around one-third of the time and that conformity increased as the group size increased, up to a group of four confederates. In a later study, Asch found that conformity greatly decreased when at least one confederate gave the right answer. <u>Groupthink</u> is a type of conformity in which people feel it is more important to maintain the group's cohesiveness than to consider the facts more realistically. <u>Group polarization</u> is the tendency for members involved in a group discussion to take more extreme positions when compared to individuals who have not participated in a group discussion. The presence of others can also influence how well an individual performs a specific task in a process. The positive influence of others on performance is called <u>social facilitation</u>, while the negative influence is sometimes called <u>social impairment</u>. If the task is easy, the presence of others seems to improve performance, but if the task is difficult, the presence of others actually has a negative impact on performance. <u>Social loafing</u> describes the tendency for people to put less effort into a simple task when working in a group as opposed to working alone. <u>Deindividuation</u> occurs when people in a group experience the lessening of their sense of personal identity and personal responsibility, increasing the likelihood of a sense of anonymity and impulsivity as a result.

Social influence can also be used to describe the phenomenon of <u>compliance</u>, which occurs when people change their behavior as a result of another person or the group asking or directing them to change. <u>Consumer psychology</u> is an area of psychology that studies how people get other people to buy things. There are a number of techniques that people use to obtain the compliance of others including the <u>foot-in-the-door technique</u>, in which compliance with a small request is followed by a larger request, and the <u>door-in-the-face technique</u>, which is the process of making a large request which is almost always refused and then a smaller request that is often agreed to. One additional compliance technique includes the <u>lowball technique</u> in which the cost of the commitment is increased *after* the commitment is already made. Cultural differences exist in people's susceptibility to these techniques. For the foot-in-the-door technique in particular, research has shown that people in individualist cultures (such as the United States) are more likely to comply with the second request than are people in collectivist cultures (such as Japan). Technically, a <u>cult</u> refers to any group of people with a particular religious or philosophical set of beliefs and identities; however, most people associate the term *cult* with a group of people whose beliefs are so different from the mainstream that they are viewed with suspicion. In compliance, an individual changes his or her behavior because someone asks him or her; in <u>obedience</u>, an individual changes his or her behavior because an authority figure gives him or her an order. <u>Stanley Milgram</u> conducted one of the most famous experiments on obedience in which he measured the number of volts a participant would administer to another participant simply because the experimenter instructed him or her to do so. In reality, no electrical shocks were being administered. Milgram found that about two-thirds of the subjects (65 percent) administered electrical shocks up to a lethal level of 450 volts when instructed to do so.

Social cognition deals with the ways people think about other people and includes attitudes, impressions, and attributions. An **attitude** can be defined as a tendency to respond positively or negatively toward a certain idea, person, object, or situation. Attitudes are composed of the way people feel, act, and think. The affective component describes the feelings associated with attitudes, the behavior component describes the actions, and the cognitive component describes the thoughts. Attitudes have been found to be only weak predictors of actual behavior. Attitude formation occurs in or as a learning process that occurs through direct contact, direct instruction, interaction with others, and vicarious (or observational) learning. **Persuasion** is the process by which one person tries to change the belief, opinion, position, or course of action of another person through argument, pleading, or explanation. Factors that influence the effectiveness of persuasion include the source, the message, the target audience, and the medium. The **elaboration likelihood model** examines how likely it is that an individual will elaborate on a persuasive message and what the outcome of the elaboration will most likely be. When people attend to the content of the message, the model describes it as **central-route processing**, and when people pay attention to information outside of the message content itself, it is referred to as **peripheral-route processing**. **Cognitive dissonance** is a sense of discomfort that occurs when a person's behavior does not match up with that person's attitudes. When a person experiences cognitive dissonance, he or she typically changes the conflicting behavior to match the attitude, changes the attitude to match his or her behavior, or forms new cognitions to justify his or her behavior. **Impression formation** involves the process of forming the first knowledge that a person has concerning another person—in other words, the "first impression." One component of impression formation involves **social categorization**, which is the assignment of a person to a category based on characteristics the person has in common with other people with whom one has had experience in the past. Social categorization can often result in **stereotypes**, or a set of characteristics that people believe are shared by all members of a particular social category. People often form their own categories based on **implicit personality theories**, or sets of assumptions about how different types of people, personality traits, and actions are all related. Most implicit personality theories are formed in childhood. The final aspect of social cognition discussed in the textbook is **attribution**, or the process of explaining one's own behavior and the behavior of others. **Fritz Heider** originally described **attribution theory** and divided attributions into two categories: **situational causes** were explanations that relied on external causes, and **dispositional causes** assume behavior is the result of some internal factor. The **fundamental attribution error** is the most well-known bias of attribution and is the tendency for some people to almost exclusively use dispositional attributes to explain other people's behavior. Cross-cultural research strongly suggests that in more interdependent, collectivist cultures found in China, Hong Kong, Japan, and Korea, people tend to assume that external situational factors are more responsible for the behavior of other people than are internal dispositional factors.

Social interaction, or the relationship between people, is the third main area of study in the field of social psychology. When a person holds an unsupported and often negative attitude about the members of a particular group it is called a **prejudice**, and when a person acts differently towards a person based on that attitude it is called **discrimination**. Prejudice toward those from different ethnic groups because of the belief that your culture reigns supreme over all other cultures is called **ethnocentrism**. The creation of **in-groups** and **out-groups** can often intensify discrimination. The **realistic conflict theory** states that prejudice and discrimination will be increased between groups that are in conflict. Jane Elliot used her second-grade classroom to demonstrate the power of prejudice and discrimination by dividing her class based on the color of the students' eyes and observing the effects. Conflicts between groups tend to increase as pressures and stresses increase. Often the prejudice exists because of the need for a **scapegoat**, a person or group who serves as the target for the frustrations and negative emotions of the group with the prejudiced attitude. Several theories have been proposed to explain the formation and persistence of prejudice. **Social identity theory** suggests that the three processes of social categorization, **social identification**, and **social comparison** are involved in the formation of prejudice attitudes. **Stereotype vulnerability** refers to the effect that a person's knowledge of someone else's stereotyped opinion can have on that person's behavior. The resulting feeling of anxiety is referred to as **stereotype threat**. The negative impact of stereotype threat on an individual's performance can actually cause a person to act in the way that the stereotype predicts, thus confirming an outside observer's prejudice attitude. **Self-fulfilling prophecy** occurs when a person acts according to his or her existing beliefs and his or her actions make it more likely that his or her beliefs are confirmed. The best defense against prejudice is becoming informed about people who are different from you. **Equal status contact**, in which all individuals involved have the same amount of power in the situation, is crucial for reducing prejudice. Educators have attempted to create situations of equal status in the classroom by setting up **jigsaw classrooms**, in which students have to work together to reach a specific goal. Another area of social interaction discussed in your textbook is **interpersonal attraction**, or liking or having the desire for a relationship with someone else. Several factors are involved in the attraction of one person to another including physical attractiveness, **proximity** (or how close a person is to you physically), similarity, and **reciprocity of liking** (or liking someone who likes you). Robert Sternberg proposed a theory of love that contains three components: intimacy, passion, and commitment. He felt that seven types of love could be described by various combinations of these three components. Two of Sternberg's proposed types of love are **romantic love** and **companionate love**. In many non-Western cultures, companionate love is seen as more sensible. A very different type of social interaction is that of violence. **Aggression** is defined as any behavior intended to hurt or destroy another person. Social psychologists have examined the role of both biology and the environment on aggression. Twin studies have shown a higher correlation of aggression levels in identical twins than in fraternal twins. Certain areas of the brain have been found to control aggressive responses, and testosterone levels are related to aggression. However, a large portion of human aggression is influenced by learning. Several studies, including **Philip Zimbardo's** "prisoners" and "guards" experiment at Stanford University, have suggested that taking on a particular **social role** can lead to an increase in aggressive behavior. A number of studies have also supported the link between exposure to violent media and aggression. The final area of social interaction discussed in your textbook is **prosocial behavior**, or socially desirable behavior that benefits others rather than bringing them harm. **Altruism** is a specific type of prosocial behavior in which an individual helps someone else with no expectation of reward. Sometimes the presence of other people can decrease the likelihood of prosocial behavior as can be seen in the **bystander effect** and **diffusion of responsibility**. Bibb Latané and John Darley conducted a series of experiments that found that participants were less likely to respond to an emergency situation where other people were present than when they were alone. Some of the decisions an individual must make when deciding whether to offer help or not include noticing the situation, defining the situation as an emergency, taking responsibility, planning a course of action, and taking action.

Social neuroscience is the study of how our bodies and brains work during social behavior. Research suggests that the temporoparietal junction (TPJ) and the prefrontal cortex are part of the structures in our brains for social interactions and decisions.

STUDY HINTS

1. The text introduces four common methods that are used to gain the compliance of another person. In order to better understand the differences among these methods, assume that you are trying to get your friend to come pick you up and then go shopping at the mall with you. In the space below, come up with an example of how you might get your friend to comply with your request using each of the techniques listed.

Technique	Example
Foot-in-the-door	

Door-in-the-face	
Lowball	
That's-not-all	

2. Social psychology contains a large number of well-known researchers along with the famous studies they carried out. It is important to be able to remember which researcher goes with which study. Next to the researchers listed below, briefly describe the experiment they carried out along with the topic they studied. In the final column, come up with a mnemonic to help you remember the information.

Researcher	Experiment	Topic	Mnemonic
Solomon Asch			
Stanley Milgram			
Jane Elliot			
Latané and Darley			
Philip Zimbardo			

LEARNING OBJECTIVES

11.1 What factors influence people to conform to the actions of others, and how does the presence of others affect individual task performance?

11.2 How is compliance defined, and what are four common ways to gain the compliance of another?

11.3 What factors make obedience more likely?

11.4 What are the three components of an attitude, how are attitudes formed, and how can attitudes be changed?

11.5 How do people react when attitudes and behavior are not the same?

11.6 How are social categorization and implicit personality theories used in impression formation?

11.7 How do people try to explain the actions of others?

11.8 How are prejudice and discrimination different?

11.9 Why are people prejudiced, and how can prejudice be stopped?

11.10 What factors govern attraction and love, and what are some different kinds of love?

11.11 How is aggressive behavior determined by biology and learning?

11.12 What is altruism, and how is deciding to help someone related to the presence of others?

11.13 What is social neuroscience?

AP LEARNING OBJECTIVES

1. Apply attribution theory to explain motives. (p. 447)
2. Describe the structure and function of different kinds of group behavior. (p. 431)
3. Explain how individuals respond to expectations of others, including groupthink, conformity, and obedience to authority. (p. 428)
4. Discuss attitudes and how they change. (p. 439)
5. Predict the impact of the presence of others on individual behavior. (pp. 432, 465)
6. Describe processes that contribute to differential treatment of group members. (p. 450)
7. Articulate the impact of social and cultural categories on self-concept and relations with others. (p. 452) (This objective is repeated here from the unit on development across the life span.)
8. Anticipate the impact of behavior on a self-fulfilling prophecy. (p. 453)
9. Describe the variables that contribute to altruism, aggression, and attraction. (p. 456)
10. Discuss attitude formation and change, including persuasion strategies and cognitive dissonance. (p. 441)
11. Identify important figures in social psychology. (pp. 428, 435, 443, 462)
12. Discuss psychology's abiding interest in how heredity, environment, and evolution work together to shape behavior. (p. 461)

CHAPTER GLOSSARY

aggression	behavior intended to hurt or destroy another person.
altruism	prosocial behavior that is done with no expectation of reward and may involve the risk of harm to oneself.
attitude	a tendency to respond positively or negatively toward a certain person, object, idea, or situation.
attribution	the process of explaining one's own behavior and the behavior of others.
attribution theory	the theory of how people explain behavior.
bystander effect	referring to the effect that the presence of other people has on the decision to help or not help, with help becoming less likely as the number of bystanders increases.
central-route processing	type of information processing that involves attending to the content of the message itself.

cognitive dissonance	sense of discomfort or distress that occurs when a person's behavior does not correspond to that person's attitudes.
companionate love	type of love proposed by Robert Sternberg consisting of intimacy and commitment.
compliance	changing one's behavior as a result of other people directing or asking for the change.
conformity	changing one's own behavior to match that of other people.
consumer psychology	branch of psychology that studies people's buying habits in the marketplace.
cult	any group of people with a particular religious or philosophical set of beliefs and identity.
deindividuation	the lessening of group members' sense of personal identity and personal responsibility.
diffusion of responsibility	occurs when a person fails to take responsibility for actions or for inaction because of the presence of other people who are seen to share the responsibility.
discrimination	treating people differently because of prejudice toward the social group to which they belong.
dispositional cause	cause of behavior attributed to internal factors such as personality or character.
door-in-the-face technique	asking for a large commitment and being refused, and then asking for a smaller commitment.
elaboration likelihood model	model of persuasion stating that people will either elaborate on the persuasive message or fail to elaborate on it, and that the future actions of those who do elaborate are more predictable than those who do not.
equal status contact	contact between groups in which the groups have equal status, with neither group having power over the other.
ethnocentrism	the belief that your culture reigns supreme over all other cultures.
foot-in-the-door technique	asking for a small commitment and, after gaining compliance, asking for a bigger commitment.
Fritz Heider	1896–1988. German social psychologist known for the development of attribution theory.
fundamental attribution error	the tendency to overestimate the influence of internal factors in determining behavior while underestimating situational factors.
groupthink	kind of thinking that occurs when people place more importance on maintaining group cohesiveness than on assessing the facts of the problem with which the group is concerned.
group polarization	the tendency for members involved in a group discussion to take somewhat more extreme positions and suggest riskier actions when compared to individuals who have not participated in a group discussion.
implicit personality theories	sets of assumptions about how different types of people, personality traits, and actions are related to each other.
impression formation	the forming of the first knowledge that a person has concerning another person.
in-groups	social groups with whom a person identifies; "us."
interpersonal attraction	liking or having the desire for a relationship with another person.
jigsaw classroom	educational technique in which each individual is given only part of the information needed to solve a problem, causing the separate individuals to be forced to work together to find the solution.
lowball technique	getting a commitment from a person and then raising the cost of that commitment.
obedience	changing one's behavior at the command of an authority figure.

out-groups	social groups with whom a person does not identify; "them."
peripheral-route processing	type of information processing that involves attending to factors not involved in the message, such as the appearance of the source of the message, the length of the message, and other noncontent factors.
persuasion	the process by which one person tries to change the belief, opinion, position, or course of action of another person through argument, pleading, or explanation.
Philip Zimbardo	social psychologist at Stanford University known for the "prisoners" and "guards" experiment on social roles.
prejudice	negative attitude held by a person about the members of a particular social group.
prosocial behavior	socially desirable behavior that benefits others.
proximity	physical or geographical nearness. Greater proximity increases the likelihood of forming a relationship.
realistic conflict theory	theory stating that prejudice and discrimination will be increased between groups that are in conflict.
reciprocity of liking	tendency of people to like other people who like them in return.
romantic love	type of love proposed by Robert Sternberg consisting of intimacy and passion.
scapegoat	an individual who is punished for the mistakes of someone else.
self-fulfilling prophecy	the tendency of one's expectations to affect one's behavior in such a way as to make the expectation more likely to occur.
situational cause	cause of behavior attributed to external factors, such as delays, the action of others, or some other aspect of the situation.
social categorization	the assignment of a newly met person to a category based on characteristics the new person has in common with other people with whom the person doing the assigning has had experience in the past.
social cognition	deals with the ways people think about other people and includes attitudes, impressions, and attributions.
social comparison	the comparison of oneself to others in ways that raise one's self-esteem.
social facilitation	the tendency for the presence of other people to have a positive impact on the performance of an easy task.
social identification	the part of the self-concept including one's view of self as a member of a particular social category.
social identity theory	theory in which the formation of a person's identity within a particular social group is explained by social categorization, social identity, and social comparison.
social impairment	the negative influence of others on performance.
social influence	the process through which the real or implied presence of others can directly or indirectly influence the thoughts, feelings, and behavior of an individual.
social interaction	the relationship between people.
social loafing	the tendency for people to put less effort into a simple task when working with others on that task.
social neuroscience	the study of how our bodies and brains work during social behavior.
social psychology	the scientific study of how a person's thoughts, feelings, and behavior are influenced by the real, imagined, or implied presence of others.
social role	the pattern of behavior that is expected of a person who is in a particular social position.
Solomon Asch	1907–1996. pioneer in the field of social psychology well-known for his experiments on conformity.

Stanley Milgram	1933–1984. social psychologist at Yale University famous for his experiments on obedience to authority.
stereotype threat	the feeling of anxiety that a person's knowledge of someone else's stereotyped opinion can have on that person's behavior.
stereotype vulnerability	the effect that people's awareness of the stereotypes associated with their social group affect their behavior.
stereotypes	a set of characteristics that people believe are shared by all members of a particular social category.
that's-not-all technique	the persuader makes an offer and then adds something extra to make the offer look better before the target person can make a decision.

CHAPTER PRACTICE TEST

For the following multiple-choice questions, select the answer you feel best answers the question.

1. Vince has always believed children deserve the best prenatal care available. During a class discussion, he hears the first of several speakers express very negative attitudes toward spending tax money on prenatal care for the poor. When it is his turn to speak, he voices an opinion more in keeping with the previous speakers. Vince's behavior is an example of _____.
   a) compliance
   b) persuasion
   c) conformity
   d) obedience
   e) avoidance

2. _____ conducted a series of studies on conformity that involved having a subject judge the length of three lines after a group of confederates all reported an obviously incorrect answer.
   a) Jane Elliot
   b) Stanley Milgram
   c) Philip Zimbardo
   d) Jane Goodall
   e) Solomon Asch

3. All of the following are causes for groupthink EXCEPT _____.
   a) the belief that the group can do no wrong
   b) the belief that the group is invulnerable
   c) the belief that opposition to the group is unsound
   d) openness to differing opinions
   e) the belief that the group is morally correct

4. _____ occurs when people begin to think in more extreme terms after exposure to a group that expresses more extreme view points.
   a) Group polarization
   b) The lowball technique
   c) Groupthink
   d) Social loafing
   e) The foot-in-the-door technique

5. At a local supermarket, a group of senior citizens is gathered to protest a change in the store's policy that ends the practice of double coupon days for seniors. Shortly after gathering peacefully, the group becomes agitated, and one of the group members throws a brick through the store window. This lessening of the protestors' personal identity and personal responsibility to remain peaceful is best explained by the concept of _____.
   a) norm of reciprocity
   b) deindividuation
   c) group polarization
   d) social facilitation
   e) bystander effect

6. Selena is trying to get her boyfriend to wash the dishes for her. To start with, she asks her boyfriend to cook dinner for her. When her boyfriend refuses, she asks, "Well, will you at least wash the dishes then?" to which he readily agrees. Selena has just used the _____.
   a) foot-in-the-door technique
   b) door-in-the-face technique
   c) lowball technique
   d) that's-not-all technique
   e) norm of reciprocity technique

7. Changing one's behavior due to a direct order of an authority figure is referred to as _____.
   a) compliance
   b) obedience
   c) conformity
   d) persuasion
   e) invulnerability

8. Imagine 100 individuals are asked to take part in a replication of Milgram's famous study on obedience. How are these 100 people likely to respond?
   a) The majority would administer 450 volts as instructed.
   b) The majority would immediately realize the use of deception and leave.
   c) Most of the women would refuse to obey, whereas almost all of the men would obey.
   d) Most of the participants would work together to force the experimenter to end the experiment.
   e) Most of the women would obey, whereas most of the men would not obey.

9. A teacher decides against assigning group projects in which all group members get the same grade. What social psychological phenomenon might the teacher be concerned about?
   a) conformity
   b) social loafing
   c) social influence
   d) social facilitation
   e) compliance

10. Ashley has practiced her drum routine over and over. When she gets up to play it at the recital in front of 100 people, she performs it better than she ever has. Her improved performance is an example of _____.
    a) social compliance
    b) persuasion
    c) social cooperation
    d) social impairment
    e) social facilitation

11. Which of the following is the best example of the behavioral component of an attitude?
    a) Bea feels recycling is a great concept.
    b) Bob is upset when he hears a corporation plans to build a polluting plant near his home.
    c) Bill struggles to understand the arguments both sides present in a debate over a new manufacturing plant.
    d) Betty writes a letter to her senator asking for support of a law making corporations responsible for the pollution they cause.
    e) Barney feels upset about news of the plan for a polluting plant to be built near his house, but later he feels good about news of the plan to build a recycling center near his house.

12. Which of the following is NOT a factor that influences attitude formation?
    a) direct contact with an individual
    b) reading information about both sides of a controversial issue
    c) instructions from your parents
    d) observing someone else's actions
    e) DNA inherited from your parents

13. Kerry's positive attitude toward China, even though she has never been there, seems to be related to the fact that her mother is Chinese and talks about China all the time with Kerry. Which method of attitude formation is involved in this example?
    a) direct contact
    b) direct instruction
    c) cognitive dissonance
    d) classical conditioning
    e) interaction with others

14. Which communicator would likely be most persuasive?
    a) an attractive person who is an expert
    b) a moderately attractive person who is an expert
    c) an attractive person who has moderate expertise
    d) a moderately attractive person who has moderate expertise
    e) a moderately attractive who is an expert in an unrelated area

15. _____ describes the situation in which people attend to the content of a message.
    a) Peripheral dissonance
    b) Cognitive dissonance
    c) Social facilitation
    d) Peripheral-route processing
    e) Central-route processing

16. Which of the following was a finding in the classic study by Festinger and Carlsmith (1959)?
    a) There was no difference between the reports of the groups.
    b) Those who got $20 to perform a boring task said the task was more interesting than did those who got $1.
    c) Paid groups said the task was less boring than did nonpaid groups.
    d) Women performed the tasks for less money than men.
    e) Those who got $1 to perform a boring task said the task was more interesting than did those who got $20.

17. Which of the following represents an example of cognitive dissonance?
    a) A boy learns how to ride a bicycle without the training wheels.
    b) A father tells his daughter that he will really only be proud of her if she gets all A's like she did last semester.
    c) A student stays up all night to study for an upcoming exam.
    d) A woman who is arguing that it is morally wrong to kill animals for food becomes upset when she is asked to explain why she is wearing a leather belt and leather shoes.
    e) A group of environmental activists participate in a protest against herbicide treatments for lawns.

18. What is the term for the process of developing an opinion about another person?
    a) social interaction
    b) stereotyping
    c) impression formation
    d) interpersonal judgment
    e) categorization

19. Toni sees a picture of the new international exchange student and notices that the student looks happy, so Toni automatically assumes that he is also friendly. This automatic assumption about the student's personality is an example of _____.
    a) central-route processing
    b) implicit personality theory
    c) cognitive dissonance
    d) discrimination
    e) heuristic personality theory

20. The process of explaining one's own behavior and the behavior of other people is called

    _____.
    a) stereotyping
    b) attribution
    c) central-route processing
    d) cognitive dissonance
    e) implicit personality theory

21. "Look, Officer, I didn't see the stop sign back there because the sun was in my eyes." The police officer responds, "You were not paying attention." How would a social psychologist describe this situation?
    a) Both individuals were making fundamental attribution errors.
    b) Both individuals were making situational attributions.
    c) The driver was making a dispositional attribution; the officer was making a situational attribution.
    d) The driver was making a situational attribution; the officer was making a dispositional attribution.
    e) The driver was making a fundamental attribution error; the officer was making a situational attribution.

22. While watching the TV game show *Jeopardy*, your roommate says, "The game show host, Alex Trebek, knows all the answers. He must be a genius." You tell your roommate she probably would not have said that if she had attended class the day the instructor discussed the topic of

_____.
    a) social facilitation
    b) stereotyping illusions
    c) internal attribution biases
    d) fundamental attribution errors
    e) distributive attribution errors

23. A bank loan officer thinks people who speak with an accent are lazy; consequently, he refuses to grant them loans. The loan officer's belief is an example of _____. His refusal to grant them loans is an example of _____.
    a) discrimination; prejudice
    b) stereotyping; attribution
    c) attribution; stereotyping
    d) prejudice; discrimination
    e) attribution; prejudice

24. The part of a person's self-concept that is based on his or her identification with a nation, culture, or ethnic group or with gender or other roles in society is called _____.
    a) the fundamental attribution error
    b) self-serving bias
    c) ethnocentrism
    d) social identity
    e) internal social facilitation

25. Which of the following does NOT represent an effective method for reducing prejudice?
    a) establishing a jigsaw classroom
    b) bringing diverse groups of people into contact with each other
    c) learning about people who are different from you
    d) establishing equal status contact between different groups of people
    e) seeing members of other groups as people rather than "as outsiders"

26. We tend to _____ attractive people more than we do less attractive people.
    a) Attractiveness does not influence the way be feel about people.
    b) dislike
    c) ignore
    d) hate
    e) like

27. When opposites attract it is said that they have _____ characteristics.
    a) proximal
    b) complementary
    c) rewarding
    d) reciprocal
    e) superficial

28. Which of the following was NOT a component of Robert Sternberg's theory of love?
    a) intimacy
    b) lust
    c) passion
    d) commitment
    e) triangular love theory

29. Behavior that is intended to hurt or destroy another person is referred to as _____.
    a) empty love
    b) prejudice
    c) aggression
    d) dissonance
    e) empathy

30. The fact that a social role can lead to an increase in aggressive behavior points to _____ as a major contributor to aggression.
    a) biology
    b) the environment
    c) DNA
    d) chemical influences
    e) heredity

31. What term refers to helping behavior that is performed voluntarily for the benefit of another person, with no anticipation of reward?
    a) altruism
    b) collectivism
    c) interdependence
    d) humanitarianism
    e) individualism

32. In a crowded mall parking lot, dozens of people hear a female voice yell, "He's killing me!" Yet no one calls the police. What is the reason for the lack of action, according to Darley and Latané?
    a) People are too busy to respond.
    b) Most people "do not want to become involved."
    c) The fight-or-flight response is not activated when others are in danger.
    d) There is a diffusion of responsibility.
    e) People are less likely to respond if they hear a female voice calling for help.

33. In Latané and Darley's classic 1969 study, they found that _____ of the participants reported the smoke in the room when the two confederates in the room noticed the smoke but then ignored it.
    a) all
    b) three-fourths
    c) one-half
    d) one-tenth
    e) none

34. All of the following are decision points in helping behavior EXCEPT _____.
    a) noticing
    b) defining an emergency
    c) taking responsibility
    d) diffusion of responsibility
    e) taking action

35.		The temporoparietal junction (TPJ) was named as one of the areas of the brain involved in _____.

> prosocial behavior
> prejudiced attitudes
> ethnocentric beliefs
> diffusion of responsibility
> social loafing in group situations

CHAPTER PRACTICE TEST ANSWERS

1.	c	Conformity involves going along with the group despite one's real opinion. Compliance would be the case if someone had asked him to voice an opinion in keeping with the previous speakers. In this case, Vince did it on his own as a result of internal pressure to conform.

2.	e	E is the correct answer. Asch conducted the well-known studies on conformity. Milgram studied obedience in his famous studies with electrical shock.

3.	d	Groupthink describes the thought processes that can dominate a group of individuals.

4.	a	Group polarization is the tendency for members involved in a group discussion to take somewhat more extreme positions.

5.	b	The groups shift toward aggression is best explained by the members increased sense of anonymity as a result of deindividuation.

6.	b	The door-in-the-face technique involves asking for a large request that you know will be refused followed up by a smaller request, which many people then agree to.

7.	b	Obedience involves changing your behavior due to an order from "above," while conformity involves changing your behavior to better "fit in" with others around you.

8.	a	The Milgram experiment has been repeated at various times, in the United States and in other countries, and the percentage of participants who went all the way consistently remained between 61 and 66 percent. In addition, few differences between males and females have been found.

9.	b	The teacher knows that some students will slack off if they are not being evaluated for their individual performance, due to a phenomenon known as social loafing.

10.	e	Social facilitation is the term for the positive effect on one's performance caused by the perception that others are watching.

11.	d	Writing is an action, or behavior. The fact that Bill struggled to understand indicates that what he is doing is cognitive.

12.	e	Attitude formation is believed to occur solely through the learning process and is not considered to be something that is inherited biologically.

13.	e	The fact that Kerry's mother talks about China all the time with Kerry and is Chinese indicates that her attitude is the result of interaction with her mother.

14.	a	Attractiveness and expertise have been shown to increase persuasiveness.

15.	e	In central-route processing, an individual pays attention to the content of the message, whereas in peripheral-route processing, an individual focuses on details other than the main content of the message.

16.	e	The group that got paid less used cognitive dissonance to justify their poor pay for telling a lie.

17.	d	Cognitive dissonance is an emotional disturbance that occurs when a person's actions don't match his or her statements.

18.	c	While stereotyping may be a component of impression formation, it is not the term for the process of developing an opinion about another person.

19.	b	Implicit personality theory represents the automatic associations a person makes about personality traits that are assumed to be related.

20.   b   An attribute is an explanation for a person's behavior. Stereotypes are preconceived ideas about a group of people.

21.   d   The driver attributed his error to something in his situation, the sun; whereas the officer attributed his error to something internal to him, his lack of attention.

22.   d   Your roommate attributed something that is situational (Trebek gets the answers ahead of time) to an internal characteristic (genius). Although internal attribution bias sounds correct, it is not a term used in social psychology.

23.   d   Prejudice is an unsupported, often negative belief about all people in a particular group, whereas discrimination is an action taken that is based on this belief. In this case, the action is the refusal to grant loans.

24.   d   Social identity refers to a person's identity with his or her social group. Ethnocentrism is the process of viewing the world from your own viewpoint and failing to see alternative perspectives.

25.   b   Simply bringing groups together normally does not reduce prejudice unless all the members of the group have equal status and power in the group.

26.   e   Social psychologists have found that we tend to like attractive people more than unattractive people.

27.   b   Things that "complement" each other tend to be opposites. The term proximity refers to nearness.

28.   b   Sternberg's theory of love includes the three components of intimacy, passion, and commitment, and when combined they form the triangular love theory.

29.   c   Aggression describes a type of behavior, whereas prejudice refers to a person's attitude.

30.   b   The impact of the social role points to learning and the influence of the surrounding environment on an individual's aggressive behavior.

31.   a   Altruism is defined as helping others for no personal benefit. Humanitarianism means almost the same thing as altruism but is not the term social psychologists use for the helping behavior that is performed voluntarily for the benefit of another person, with no anticipation of reward.

32.   d   According to Latané and Darley, most people say they do want to become involved, however often diffusion of responsibility occurs. Diffusion of responsibility is what occurs as each person thinks someone else will call for help, that is., take responsibility.

33.   d   About 1/10th of the participants reported smoke when the confederates in the room noticed the smoke but did nothing about it. This number was much higher when the participants were in the room alone.

34.   d   Diffusion of responsibility stops a person from helping and is not considered a decision point.

35.   a   The TPJ is linked with prosocial behavior as well as competitive behavior.

CHAPTER PRACTICE FREE RESPONSE QUESTION

You have 25 minutes to answer the following question. You must write in complete sentences and not just list facts. You should make your point clearly and use the language of psychology. Be sure to write legibly and respond to all parts of the question.

Alex volunteers during the summer as a lifeguard at the city pool. This summer Alex is being promoted to the position of shift leader. One of the duties included with being a shift leader is managing the five less experienced lifeguards that are assigned to the shift. Explain why Alex might need to be familiar with the following concepts from social psychology and make a suggestion that can help Alex minimize the impact they could have on the performance of the lifeguards.

- Groupthink
- Bystander effect
- Fundamental attribution error

- Conformity
- Social loafing

SUGGESTED RUBRIC—Students should provide specific details and examples to support their assertions; definitions alone are not sufficient. Information about each topic should be discussed in the context of the question rather than abstractly. Successful essays may include the following arguments:

10 points

- Groupthink
  - Score—Alex needs to be aware of groupthink because he is working with younger lifeguards. The younger lifeguards may be afraid to challenge the ideas of a senior lifeguard, and, as a result, they might just go along with a bad decision. Ex. Alex suggests that they move the diving tower to the shallow end of the pool. The younger lifeguards know this is a bad idea but they go along with it because they want Alex to think they are good "team players."
  - Score— Alex can tell one of the younger lifeguards that it is ok to question any idea that is suggested at the shift meetings. If one lifeguard shows that it is ok to challenge Alex the others will be more likely to share their ideas.
- Bystander effect
  - Score—Alex needs to be aware that when people are part of a group they are less likely to take the responsibility to act in an emergency situation. Ex. The lifeguards fail to respond to the needs of a swimmer in trouble because they each feel that someone else is going to respond.
  - Score—A suggestion for Alex would be to make sure that the lifeguards are not standing together as a group and are spread out around the pool. Also, Alex could give the team practice drills that require each lifeguard to respond to all threatening situations as an emergency rather than taking time to decide if it is an actual emergency. Finally, Alex can drill the lifeguards on their action plans and skills. This way they do not have to try to think of a plan during an emergency and they know they have the skills to help.
- Fundamental attribution error
  - Score—Alex should know that there is a tendency to overestimate the influence of internal factors on the behavior of other people while underestimating the influence of the situation. Ex. One of the lifeguards fails to see a child struggling and near drowning. Alex rescues the child and then blames the lifeguard for being lazy and inattentive. However, the situation was such that it would have been difficult for anyone on duty to see the child because the child was wearing a matching swim cap, suit, and shoes that were light blue in color.
  - Score—Before reprimanding the lifeguard Alex should ask, "What would I have done?" If Alex would have had the same difficulty and done the same thing then the outcome was probably situational.
- Conformity
  - Score—Alex should be aware that conformity is common and people tend to conform. Ex. One of the lifeguards brings ear buds and an MP3 player to the pool and listens to music during the shift. Soon all the lifeguards have their ear buds in and are listening to music. As a result of listening to music the lifeguards fail to hear the cries of a child in trouble in the water.

- o Score—Alex sees the other lifeguards conforming and must break the pattern of behavior by confronting the lifeguards and challenging their decisions to listen to music on the shift. If one person breaks the pattern of behavior it is likely that the others will do so as well.
- Social loafing
  - o Score—Alex should be aware that a person who is lazy will be even lazier when working in a group because they know that someone else will do the work to avoid a bad evaluation. Ex. One of the lifeguards rarely intervenes with the bad behavior of the swimmers because they know the other lifeguards will do so to avoid the shift getting a bad review.
  - o Score—Alex needs to make sure that all individuals know that they are individually responsible for the evaluation of the shift. Alex can make the shift evaluation a total of points earned by each lifeguard individually. That way each lifeguard is equally responsible for the success of the shift.

YOU KNOW YOU HAVE MASTERED THE MAIN TOPICS IN THIS CHAPTER IF YOU ARE ABLE TO . . .

- Define personality according to the various perspectives in psychology.
- Discuss Freud's psychoanalytical perspective on personality including the division of the mind, components of personality, stages of development, and modifications of his theory by the neo-Freudians.
- Describe the behaviorists' perspective on personality and the social cognitive theory, including Albert Bandura's model.
- Introduce the humanistic perspective of personality including Carl Rogers's view of the self and concept of unconditional positive regard.
- Discuss trait theory with regard to the description of personality.
- Explain what is known about the role of biology and heredity in personality development.
- Describe major methods of personality assessment including interviews, projective tests, behavioral assessment, and personality inventories.
- Outline the biological bases of the Big Five theory of personality.

RAPID REVIEW

Personality is the unique way in which each individual thinks, acts, and feels throughout life. Two components of personality are **character**, which refers to value judgments made about a person's morals or ethical behavior, and **temperament**, or the enduring characteristics a person is born with. There are at least four different perspectives regarding personality including the psychoanalytic, behaviorist, humanistic, and trait perspectives.

The **psychoanalytic perspective** originated with the theories of **Sigmund Freud** and focuses on the role of unconscious thoughts and desires in the development of personality. It is important to take into account the sexually repressed Victorian era in which Freud grew up when evaluating his theory or personality. Freud believed the mind was divided into three parts: the conscious mind contains all of the things a person is aware of at any given moment, the preconscious mind contains all the memories and facts that can be recalled with only minimal effort, and the **unconscious mind** is the part of our mind which remains hidden at all times. Freud believed the unconscious mind was the most important factor in directing behavior and personality. In addition to the divisions of the mind, Freud also believed that personality could be divided into three components: the id, ego, and superego. The **id** resides completely in the unconscious mind and represents the most primitive part of the personality containing all of the basic biological drives such as hunger, thirst, and sex. According to Freud, the id operates on the **pleasure principle**, which attempts to seek immediate gratification of needs with no regard for consequences. Freud referred to the psychological tension created by a person's unconscious desires as the **libido**. The **ego** represents the mostly conscious and rational aspect of personality, which operates on the **reality principle**, attempting to satisfy the desires of the id in a way that will minimize negative consequences. The **superego** is the last part of the personality to develop according to Freud's theory and represents the moral center of personality. The superego contains the **conscience**, or the part of personality that makes a person feel good or bad depending on whether they do the right or wrong thing. According to Freud, the id demands immediate satisfaction, while the superego places restrictions on which behaviors are morally acceptable, and the ego is left in the middle to come up with a compromise. Psychological defense mechanisms are ways of dealing with anxiety through unconsciously distorting one's perception of reality to manage the constant conflict among the three parts of the personality. The defense mechanisms used to deal with anxiety include denial, repression, and rationalization.

For Freud, the three components of personality develop in a series of **psychosexual stages** with each stage focused on a different **erogenous zone**, or area of the body that produces pleasurable feelings. Unresolved conflicts at any of the stages of development can lead to **fixation** and subsequent emotional or psychological problems as an adult. The first stage is called the **oral stage** because the erogenous zone is the mouth. Fixation can occur in this stage if the baby is weaned from the mother's breast too soon or too late. The second stage in Freud's theory is the **anal stage**, during which time period the anus serves as the erogenous zone and the conflict centers around toilet training. Fixation resulting from openly rebelling against the toilet training results in adults who are characteristically messy and are referred to as **anal expulsive personalities**. Fixation resulting from overly strict toilet training results in adults who are stingy, stubborn, and excessively neat and would be referred to as **anal retentive personalities**. The third stage is the **phallic stage** and focuses on the child's own genitals. During this stage the child develops a sexual attraction to the opposite-sex parent, becomes jealous of the same-sex parent, develops anxiety due to the attraction and the jealousy, and resolves the anxiety through sexual repression and identification with the same-sex parent. Freud referred to this process in boys as the **Oedipus complex** and suggested that girls go through a similar process called the **Electra complex** with their fathers as the target of their affection. The process of identification leads to the development of the superego so that by the end of Freud's third stage of development, all three components of personality are in place. The fourth stage, known as the **latency stage**, consists of repressed sexual feelings during which children focus on intellectual, physical, and social development but not sexual development. The final stage occurs around the start of puberty when sexual feelings can no longer be repressed and is referred to as the **genital stage**.

A number of psychologists, referred to as **neo-Freudians**, agreed with parts of Freud's theories but not all aspects. **Carl Gustav Jung** believed that there were two parts of the unconscious, a **personal unconscious** similar to the unconscious described by Freud and a **collective unconscious**, which contained universal human memories that Jung called **archetypes**. **Alfred Adler** felt that the motivating factor of behavior was not the pleasure-seeking drive of the libido suggested by Freud but rather the seeking of superiority through defense mechanisms such as compensation. **Karen Horney** disagreed with Freud's emphasis on sexuality and thought personalities were shaped more by a child's sense of **basic anxiety**, which if unattended to could lead to the development of **neurotic personalities**. **Erik Erikson** developed eight psychosocial stages of development which focused on the role of social relationships in the development of personality.

Although Freud's theory has had a significant impact on the culture of modern Western societies, his theory has been criticized on the scientific grounds due to the fact that it was not developed based on scientific experiments but rather on Freud's personal observations in his private practice as a psychiatrist, and that Freud's personal observations were limited to a specific group of wealthy Austrian women living in the sexually repressed Victorian era.

According to the behaviorists' perspective, personality consists of a set of learned responses or **habits**. A variation on the behaviorist perspective is that of the **social cognitive learning theorists**, who emphasize the role of conditioning along with an individual's thought processes in the development of personality. A strong proponent of the **social cognitive view**, **Albert Bandura**, suggested that the environment, behavior, and personal/cognitive factors all act together to determine an individual's actions in a process Bandura referred to as **reciprocal determinism**. An important component of the cognitive factors is the person's sense of **self-efficacy**, or perception of how effective a behavior will be in a particular context. Julian Rotter proposed that individuals develop a relatively set way of responding and this behavior represented "personality." An important determinant of the individual's response was his or her sense of **locus of control**. According to Rotter, the individual's **expectancy** and the response's reinforcement value were the two key factors that determined how an individual would react.

The **humanistic perspective** of personality focuses more on qualities that are considered uniquely human such as free will and subjective emotions. **Carl Rogers** proposed that humans are always striving to fulfill their innate capacities in a process known as the **self-actualizing tendency**. Rogers defined **positive regard** as warmth, affection, love, and respect that comes from significant others. In order for an individual to work towards self-actualization, they need to be exposed to a certain level of **unconditional positive regard** from the significant others in their lives. Rogers felt that **conditional positive regard** would restrict a person's ability to become a **fully functioning person**. Rogers believed an individual's image of oneself, or **self-concept**, also played a role in becoming fully functional. The self-concept was based on what an individual is told by others and also his or her own sense of **self**, an individual's awareness of his or her own Identity. According to Rogers, self-concept could be divided into a real self and an ideal self. If the real self and ideal self concept were too far apart, anxiety and neurotic behavior would result.

Trait theories of personality have focused on describing personality and predicting behavior based on that description. A **trait** is a consistent, enduring way of thinking, feeling, or behaving. Gordon Allport identified approximately 200 traits in the English language that he felt were "wired" into each person's nervous system. Raymond Cattell narrowed the number of traits down further by dividing traits into **surface traits**, such as the 200 traits described by Allport, and **source traits**, or the more basic traits that underlie the surface traits and form the core of personality. **Introversion** is an example of a source trait. Cattell believed that there were 16 basic, or source, traits. Later researchers including McCrae and Costa narrowed this list to five source traits and developed the personality model known as the **five-factor model**, or the Big Five. The five trait dimensions are **openness**, **conscientiousness**, **extraversion**, **agreeableness**, and **neuroticism**. Critics of the five-factor model have argued that the situation plays a more significant role in determining an individual's behavior than is suggested by trait theory and have proposed a theory that includes a **trait-situation interaction**.

The field of **behavioral genetics** studies the role of inherited traits in personality. Twin studies have found that identical twins are more similar than fraternal twins or unrelated people in certain aspects of personality such as intelligence, leadership, tendency to follow rules, assertiveness, and aggressiveness. Adoption studies have supported some of these findings and have suggested a biological basis for shyness and aggressiveness. **Heritability** is how much some trait within a population can be attributed to genetic influences, and the extent to which individual genetic variation impacts differences in observed behavior. Several studies have found that the five personality factors of the five-factor model have nearly a 50 percent rate of heritability across several cultures.

In an attempt to describe "national personalities," Geert Hofstede conducted a cross-cultural study for IBM which resulted in a description of each country along four basic dimensions. The dimensions Hofstede observed were individualism/collectivism, power distance, masculinity/femininity, and uncertainty avoidance.

Methods for assessing personality have been developed based on specific theories of personality as well as the various goals of classification, self-insight, and the diagnosis of psychological disorders. An **interview** is a method of personality assessment in which the professional asks questions of the client and allows the client to answer in either a structured or unstructured manner. Interviews are limited by the fact that clients can lie, intentionally or unintentionally, and the interviewers can bring their own biases into their interpretations including the **halo effect**, which is the tendency of a person's first impression to influence later assessments. Psychoanalysts have developed **projective tests** in an attempt to assess a person's unconscious conflicts or desires by having them projected onto an ambiguous visual stimulus. Two of the most commonly used projective tests are the **Rorschach inkblot test** and the **Thematic Apperception Test or TAT**. Projective tests are highly **subjective** and have been found to have very low reliability and validity. A behaviorist would be more likely to measure personality by directly observing an individual's actions. In **direct observation**, the psychologist would observe an individual in a specific setting and record his or her behaviors through the use of a **rating scale** or a **frequency count**. Critics of this approach have pointed out the possibility for both the observer effect and observer bias. Trait theorists would be most likely to use a **personality inventory**, which consists of a questionnaire that has a standard list of questions that require specific answers such as "yes" or "no." Examples of commonly used personality inventories include Cattell's 16 PF, the Neuroticism/Extraversion/Openness Personality Inventory (NEO-PI), the Myers-Briggs Type Indicator (MPTI) and the Minnesota Multiphasic Personality Inventory, Version II (MMPI-2). The advantage of personality inventories is that they are scored objectively, which eliminates the possibility of observer bias, and they have been found to have very high reliability and validity scores. However, the inventories are still based on self-report.

A large number of personality tests are accessible over the Internet; however, the results of such tests should be interpreted with an appropriate level of skepticism.

STUDY HINTS

1. Students often confuse the levels of awareness suggested by Freud with his three components of personality. The next two exercises should help you keep them straight. To start with, let's think about your levels of awareness. For each of the levels listed, list at least three examples of the information or memories that would be found there. Start with the conscious level.

My <u>conscious</u> level of awareness might contain the following:

_____

_____

My <u>preconscious</u> level of awareness might contain the following:

_____

_____

My <u>unconscious</u> level of awareness might contain the following:

_____

_____

2. Now think about the three components that Freud suggested make up an individual's personality: the id, the ego, and the superego. For each of the situations listed below, describe how a person's id, ego, and superego might respond. The first example has been completed for you. Notice how the ego always represents the compromise between the two extremes.

Situation	Id	Ego	Superego
Someone cuts you off in traffic as you are driving down the freeway.	*Speed up, cut in front of them, and then slow way down.*	*I'll yell a few words at the driver from my own car but remain driving at the speed limit.*	*It's wrong to break the law, and we don't know what is happening with that person; maybe they have an emergency.*
Your alarm goes off for school but you still feel completely exhausted.			
Your co-worker asks you to work her shift for you so that she can have the night off to go to a concert.			
Your roommate just made a batch of chocolate chip cookies and said he is going to take most of them to work with him tomorrow.			

You just finished watching two hours of TV and still have a lot of homework to do for tomorrow but you don't feel like doing it.			

LEARNING OBJECTIVES

12.1 What is personality, and how do the various perspectives in psychology view personality?

12.2 How did Freud's historical view of the mind and personality form a basis for psychodynamic theory?

12.3 How did the neo-Freudians modify Freud's theory, and how does modern psychodynamic theory differ from that of Freud?

12.4 How do behaviorists and social cognitive theorists explain personality?

12.5 How do humanists such as Carl Rogers explain personality?

12.6 How does the trait perspective conceptualize personality?

12.7 What part do biology, heredity, and culture play in personality?

12.8 What are the advantages and disadvantages of various measures of personality?

12.9 What are some biological bases of the Big Five theory of personality?

AP LEARNING OBJECTIVES

1. Compare and contrast the major theories and approaches to explaining personality (p. 476)
2. Describe and compare research methods that psychologists use to investigate personality. (p. 499)
3. Identify frequently used assessment strategies, and evaluate relative test quality based on reliability and validity of the instruments. (p. 500)
4. Speculate how cultural context can facilitate or constrain personality development, especially as it relates to self-concept. (pp. 497, 504)
5. Identify key contributors to personality theory. (pp. 477, 482, 483, 487, 488, 493)

CHAPTER GLOSSARY

agreeableness	the emotional style of a person which may range from easy-going, friendly, and likeable to grumpy, crabby, and unpleasant.
Albert Bandura	born 1925. Bandura developed the theory of reciprocal determinism to explain personality development.
Alfred Adler	1870–1937. one of the neo-Freudians who continued the pursuit of the unconscious. Adler focused on the need for power as a driving force in an individual's life.
anal expulsive personalities	a person fixated in the anal stage who is messy, destructive, and hostile.
anal retentive personalities	a person fixated in the anal stage who is neat, fussy, stingy, and stubborn.
anal stage	second stage occurring from about 1 to 3 years of age, in which the anus is the erogenous zone and toilet training is the source of conflict.
archetypes	Jung's collective, universal human memories.
basic anxiety	type of anxiety proposed by Karen Horney that is created when a child is born into the bigger and more powerful world of older children and adults.

behavioral genetics	field of study devoted to discovering the genetic bases for personality characteristics.
Carl Gustav Jung	1875–1961. Swiss psychiatrist who was a pioneer in the psychoanalytic school of thought and was heavily influenced by Freud.
Carl Rogers	1902–1987. humanist psychologist who focused on the role of the self-concept and positive regard on personality development.
character	value judgments of a person's moral and ethical behavior.
collective unconscious	Jung's name for the memories shared by all members of the human species.
conditional positive regard	positive regard that is given only when the person is doing what the providers of positive regard wish.
conscience	a person's sense of morality, or sense of right and wrong.
conscientiousness	the care a person gives to organization and thoughtfulness of others, dependability.
direct observation	assessment in which the professional observes the client engaged in ordinary, day-to-day behavior in either a clinical or natural setting.
ego	part of the personality that develops out of a need to deal with reality, mostly conscious, rational, and logical.
Electra complex	situation occurring in the phallic stage in which a female child develops a sexual attraction to the opposite-sex parent and jealousy of the same sex-parent.
Erik Erikson	1902–1994. developmental psychologist who believed that personality developed through a series of psychosocial crises.
erogenous zone	an area of the body especially sensitive to sexual stimulation.
expectancy	a person's subjective feeling that a particular behavior will lead to a reinforcing consequence.
extraversion	dimension of personality referring to one's need to be with other people.
five-factor model	also known as the Big Five, a model of personality traits that describes five basic trait dimensions.
fixation	disorder in which the person does not fully resolve the conflict in a particular psychosexual stage, resulting in personality traits and behavior associated with that earlier stage.
frequency count	assessment in which the frequency of a particular behavior is counted.
fully functioning person	a term proposed by Carl Rogers to describe a person who is in touch with and trusting of his or her own innermost urges and feelings.
genital stage	fifth stage of Freud's theory occurring from adolescence on; sexual energy is focused on sexual activity with others.
habits	in behaviorism, sets of well-learned responses that have become automatic.
halo effect	tendency of an interviewer to allow positive characteristics of a client to influence the assessments of the client's behavior and statements.
heritability	how much some trait within a population can be attributed to genetic influences, and the extent to which individual genetic variation impacts differences in observed behavior.
humanistic perspective	the "third force" in psychology that focuses on those aspects of personality that make people uniquely human, such as subjective feelings and freedom of choice.
id	part of the personality present at birth and completely unconscious.
interview	method of personality assessment in which the professional asks questions of the client and allows the client to answer, either in a structured or unstructured fashion.

introversion	dimension of personality in which people tend to withdraw from excessive stimulation.
Karen Horney	1885–1952. neo-Freudian who focused on more equal representation of men and women in psychoanalytic theory and also the role of basic anxiety as a motivating force.
latency stage	fourth stage occurring during the school years, in which the sexual feelings of the child are repressed while the child develops in other ways.
libido	the instinctual energy that may come into conflict with the demands of a society's standards for behavior.
locus of control	the tendency for people to assume that they either have control or do not have control over events and consequences in their lives.
neo-Freudians	followers of Freud who developed their own, competing theories of psychoanalysis.
neurotic personalities	personality type proposed by Karen Horney in which the individual is characterized by maladaptive ways of dealing with relationships.
neuroticism	degree of emotional instability or stability.
Oedipus complex	situation occurring in the phallic stage in which a male child develops a sexual attraction to the opposite-sex parent and jealousy of the same sex-parent.
openness	one of the five factors; willingness to try new things and be open to new experiences.
oral stage	first stage occurring in the first year of life, and in which the mouth is the erogenous zone and weaning is the primary conflict.
personal unconscious	Jung's name for the unconscious mind as described by Freud.
personality	the unique and relatively stable ways in which people think, feel, and behave.
personality inventory	paper-and-pencil or computerized test that consists of statements that require a specific, standardized response from the person taking the test.
phallic stage	third stage occurring from about 3 to 6 years of age, in which the child discovers sexual feelings.
pleasure principle	principle by which the id functions; the immediate satisfaction of needs without regard for the consequences.
positive regard	warmth, affection, love, and respect that come from significant others in one's life.
projective tests	personality assessments that present ambiguous visual stimuli to the client and ask the client to respond with whatever comes to mind.
psychoanalytic perspective	Freud's term for both the theory of personality and the therapy based upon it.
psychosexual stages	five stages of personality development proposed by Freud and tied to the sexual development of the child.
rating scale	assessment in which a numerical value is assigned to specific behavior that is listed in the scale.
reality principle	principle by which the ego functions; the satisfaction of the demands of the id only when negative consequences will not result.
reciprocal determinism	Bandura's explanation of how the factors of environment, personal characteristics, and behavior can interact to determine future behavior.
Rorschach inkblot test	projective test that uses 10 inkblots as the ambiguous stimuli.
self	an individual's awareness of his or her own identity.
self-actualizing tendency	the striving to fulfill one's innate capacities and capabilities.
self-concept	the image of oneself that develops from interactions with important, significant people in one's life.

self-efficacy	individual's perception of how effective a behavior will be in any particular circumstance.
Sigmund Freud	1856–1939. founder of the psychoanalytic school of thought which focuses on the role of the unconscious on behavior.
social cognitive learning theorists	theorists who emphasize the importance of both the influences of other people's behavior and of a person's own expectancies on learning.
social cognitive view	learning theory that includes cognitive processes such as anticipating, judging, memory, and imitation of models.
source traits	the more basic traits that underlie the surface traits, forming the core of personality.
subjective	referring to concepts and impressions that are only valid within a particular person's perception and may be influenced by biases, prejudice, and personal experiences.
superego	part of the personality that acts as a moral center.
surface traits	aspects of personality that can easily be seen by other people in the outward actions of a person.
temperament	the enduring characteristics with which each person is born.
Thematic Apperception Test (TAT)	projective test that uses twenty pictures of people in ambiguous situations as the visual stimuli.
trait	a consistent, enduring way of thinking, feeling, or behaving.
trait theories	theories that endeavor to describe the characteristics that make up human personality in an effort to predict future behavior.
trait-situation interaction	the assumption that the particular circumstances of any given situation will influence the way in which a trait is expressed.
unconditional positive regard	positive regard that is given without conditions or strings attached.
unconscious mind	level of the mind in which thoughts, feelings, memories, and other information is kept that is not easily or voluntarily brought into consciousness.

CHAPTER PRACTICE TEST

For the following multiple-choice questions, select the answer you feel best answers the question.

1. The unique way in which each individual thinks, acts, and feels throughout life is called
    _____.
    - a) character
    - b) collective unconscious
    - c) temperament
    - d) the unconscious
    - e) personality

2. One limitation of the trait perspective compared to the other perspectives is there is not much
    _____.
    - a) description
    - b) research
    - c) material
    - d) explanation
    - e) predicting of behavior

3. Many have compared Freud's idea of the mind to an iceberg. If that were the case and you were standing on the deck of a ship in Alaska, what part of the mind would you see above the water?
    a) ego
    b) superego
    c) id
    d) preconscious
    e) shadow

4. Information that cannot be recalled even when a person makes a determined effort to retrieve it would be said by Freud to be residing in the _____.
    a) conscious
    b) preconscious
    c) unconscious
    d) superego
    e) collective unconscious

5. In Sigmund Freud's theory, the _____ operates according to the pleasure principle.
    a) Oedipus complex
    b) ego
    c) thanatos
    d) superego
    e) id

6. According to Freud, the last component of an individual's personality to develop is the _____.
    a) ego
    b) superego
    c) id
    d) libido
    e) conscientiousness

7. What is Freud's term for the executive of the personality that has a realistic plan for obtaining gratification of an individual's desires?
    a) id
    b) ego
    c) superego
    d) preconscious
    e) central executive

8. Freud called the developmental stage in which the Oedipus/Electra complex occurs during the _____.
    a) oral stage
    b) anal stage
    c) phallic stage
    d) latency stage
    e) genital stage

9. Freud believed that the personality characteristics of overeating, gum chewing, being too dependent, or overly optimistic developed due to fixation during the _____.
    a) phallic stage
    b) anal stage
    c) genital stage
    d) latency stage
    e) oral stage

10. Which neo-Freudian viewed personality disturbances as resulting from the feelings of inferiority all people share?
    a) Carl Jung
    b) B.F. Skinner
    c) Carl Rogers
    d) Karen Horney
    e) Alfred Adler

11. Karen Horney disagreed with Freud about the unconscious force that influences behavior. She believed the force was not sexual desire but rather _____.
    a) feelings of inferiority
    b) basic anxiety
    c) the collective unconscious
    d) self-regard
    e) individuation

12. Which of the following is NOT a current criticism of Freud's psychoanalytic theory?
    a) the significant impact it has had on culture
    b) the lack of empirical evidence
    c) observations based on Freud's personal clients
    d) role of women in Freud's theory
    e) much was based on patient self-reports that were unverifiable

13. Albert Bandura's notion that people are affected by their environment but can also influence that environment is known as _____.
    a) self-efficacy
    b) locus of control
    c) phenomenology
    d) reciprocal determinism
    e) collective unconsciousness

14. A baseball player's son is quite talented; he has received lots of awards over the years. When he gets up to bat he expects to get a hit, and when he is in the field he expects to make every catch. According to Bandura, what characteristic does this young man seem to have?
    a) self-regard
    b) self-centeredness
    c) self-efficacy
    d) self-actualization
    e) self-determinism

15. _____ theory is called the third force in personality theory.
    a) Psychoanalytic.
    b) Behaviorist
    c) Cognitive
    d) Humanistic
    e) Neo-Freudian

16. In Carl Rogers's theory, our perception of our abilities, behaviors, and characteristics is known as
    _____.
    a) personality
    b) self-regard
    c) self-esteem
    d) self-concept
    e) ideal self

17. Which of the following represents an example of unconditional positive regard?
    a) a mother telling her son that she hopes he becomes an engineer like his father
    b) a father telling his daughter that he will really only be proud of her if she gets all As like she did last semester
    c) an owner only paying attention to her dog when he is well-behaved
    d) a parent telling his son he loves him even though he just wrecked the family car
    e) a husband telling his wife that he will love her if she gets a college education

18. What did Gordon Allport think about traits?
    a) He thought they were like stages.
    b) He thought they were wired into the nervous system.
    c) He thought they were learned.
    d) He thought they were the result of cognitive modeling.
    e) He thought they were internalized from the culture.

19. How many source traits did Raymond Cattell discover through the process of factor analysis?
    a) 5
    b) More than 10,000
    c) 4,500
    d) 200
    e) 16

20. What psychoanalytic theorist most notably influenced the Big Five theory of personality?
    a) Freud
    b) Jung
    c) Erikson
    d) Horney
    e) Allport

21. The fact that an outgoing extravert might be very talkative at a party but very quiet at a funeral is an example of _____.
    a) trait-situation interaction
    b) cross-cultural similarities
    c) source trait reliability
    d) neuroticism
    e) self-efficacy

22. What major conclusion about personality traits emerged from the Minnesota twin study?
    a) Identical twins are more similar than any other type of sibling.
    b) Siblings reared apart were much more similar than identical twins.
    c) Fraternal twins reared together were much more similar than identical twins.
    d) Personality scores for twins were not related in either case.
    e) Identical twins have the same degree of similarity as fraternal twins.

23. Which of the following countries would NOT be considered a collectivist country according to the studies by Geert Hofstede?
    a) Japan
    b) United States
    c) Mexico
    d) Korea
    e) China

24. Which of the following terms describes the cultural personality of the United States according to Hofstede's dimensions of cultural personality?
    a) high in individualism
    b) high in power distance
    c) low in individualism
    d) high in uncertainty avoidance
    e) low in masculinity

25. Which of the following is NOT considered a disadvantage in the use of interviews for personality assessment?
    a) halo effect
    b) answers are based on self-report
    c) bias of the interviewer
    d) natural flow of the questions
    e) client answers can be interpreted by the interviewer

26. Which personality test relies on the interpretation of inkblots to understand personality?
    a) MMPI
    b) 16PF
    c) TAT
    d) The Big Five
    e) Rorschach

27. Which of the following is NOT a criticism of projective tests?
    a) They are a projection of the person's unconscious concern.
    b) They are low in reliability.
    c) Their interpretation is more an art than a science.
    d) They lack validity.
    e) They are very subjective.

28. Direct observation is most like _____.
    a) case studies
    b) naturalistic observation
    c) experimental methods
    d) correlation
    e) survey methods

29. The most commonly used personality inventory is the _____.
   a) MMPI-2
   b) MBTI
   c) TAT
   d) CPI
   e) MCAT

30. Which of the following is an advantage to using personality inventories?
   a) They display observer bias.
   b) They are standardized.
   c) They show biases of interpretation.
   d) They rely on self-report.
   e) People have a tendency to answer in what they feel are the socially appropriate ways.

31. A personality test that results in statements that are so general that they could apply to just about anyone is a good example of _____.
   a) high validity
   b) the Barnum Effect
   c) observer bias
   d) inter-rater reliability
   e) the actor-observer effect

CHAPTER PRACTICE TEST ANSWERS

1. e   Temperament and character are both part of personality. Character refers to value judgments made about a person's morals, and temperament refers to the enduring characteristics that a person is born with.

2. d   Trait theories are descriptive and deal with the actual end result of personality.

3. a   The ego is the part of the mind that is conscious and in view.

4. c   Freud thought that information sometimes seeped out of the unconscious through our dreams or slips of the tongue, but for the most part the information was not readily available to our conscious awareness.

5. e   According to Freud, the id represents the most basic part of the personality and operates on the pleasure principle. The ego operates on the reality principle.

6. b   Freud's theory states that the superego develops during the phallic stage or when an individual is around 5–6 years old.

7. b   The ego is in charge of reality and decisions, and the superego is there for moral judgments, but the ego makes the decisions.

8. c   The Oedipus/Electra complex leads to the development of the superego and occurs during the phallic stage.

9. e   Freud described those personality traits as resulting from fixation during the oral stage of development.

10. e   Adler viewed personality disturbances as resulting from the feelings of inferiority all people share. Jung focused on archetypes in the collective unconscious.

11. b   Horney believed that basic anxiety was the unconscious driving force behind many of the behaviors people exhibited.

12. a   The impact of Freud's theory on culture is not considered a criticism.

13. d   Self-efficacy refers to one's perception of how effective a behavior will be in any particular circumstance, whereas reciprocal determinism is Bandura's notion that people are affected by their environment but can also influence that environment.

14. c   Self-efficacy refers to one's perception of how effective a behavior will be in any particular circumstance. Self-actualization has to do with self-fulfillment and reaching one's full potential.

15.   d   Humanistic theory is called the third force in personality theory; the first two are psychoanalytic theory and behaviorist theory.

16.   d   Self-esteem has more to do with one's sense of worth.

17.   d   Rogers defined unconditional positive regard as being love, affection, and respect with no strings attached.

18.   b   Allport thought traits were not learned, but rather were wired into the nervous system.

19.   e   Cattell proposed that there were 16 source traits of personality.

20.   b   Freud's views are not involved in trait theory, but Jung's theory mentioned extraversion, which is one of the Big Five traits.

21.   a   The trait-situation interaction focuses on the interaction of source traits with the specific environment or situation that a person is in.

22.   a   Identical twins, who share the same genes, are more similar in personality than are any other type of siblings.

23.   b   The Hofstede study found that the United States could be described as more of an individualistic culture.

24.   a   Americans expect power to be well distributed rather than held by an elite few; democracies are typically low in power distance.

25.   d   The natural flow of the interview process is one of the advantages of this method.

26.   e   The Rorschach is a projective test that relies on the use of inkblot interpretation.

27.   a   The reason a psychologist would use a projective test is in order to get a "projection" of that individual's unconscious concerns.

28.   b   In naturalistic observation, one directly observes behavior in a relatively natural environment. Doing case studies involves gathering information through interviews rather than through actually observing the individual in a natural setting.

29.   a   The MMPI-2 is used more than any other inventory.

30.   b   The fact that personality inventories are standardized represents one of the greatest advantages to using this assessment technique.

31.   b   The Barnum Effect can also be seen in daily horoscope readings.

CHAPTER PRACTICE FREE RESPONSE QUESTION

You have 25 minutes to answer the following question. You must write in complete sentences and not just list facts. You should make your point clearly and use the language of psychology. Be sure to write legibly and respond to all parts of the question.

Jordan is interviewing for a part time job at a fast food restaurant. Explain how the following could help Jordan make a positive impression with the person conducting the interview.
- Displaying the characteristics of an extraverted person
- Attaining a positive resolution to the identity versus role diffusion crisis
- Possessing a high degree of internal locus of control
- Being a fully functioning person
- High sense of self-efficacy

SUGGESTED RUBRIC—Students should provide specific details and examples to support their assertions; definitions alone are not sufficient. Information about each topic should be discussed in the context of the question rather than abstractly. Successful essays may include the following arguments:

5 points

- Score—Extraversion—An extravert is outgoing and talkative. Jordan may make a good impression with the interviewer because these are valuable characteristics for a person taking food orders or working with others.

- Score—Identity crisis—A positive resolution of the identity crisis indicates that Jordan will have a healthy sense of identity and have a strong basis for interaction with others.
- Score—Internal locus of control—A person that has a high degree of internal locus of control believes that they control their experiences and outcomes. Jordan believes this and is confident and assertive in the interview, thinking that being so will lead to getting the job. This helps Jordan make a good impression.
- Score—Fully functioning—A fully functioning individual is balanced and will trust their decisions and beliefs. Jordan is a fully functioning individual and trusts that the job is a good opportunity. As a result of being a balanced and confident person, Jordan gives a good interview.
- Score—Self-efficacy—A person with a high degree of self-efficacy uses strategies that were successful in the past. Jordan was successful in getting jobs in the past by being assertive and talkative; therefore, Jordan employs the same strategy with the current interviewer.

YOU KNOW YOU HAVE MASTERED THE MAIN TOPICS IN THIS CHAPTER IF YOU ARE ABLE TO. . .

- Define abnormality and briefly discuss the historical and cultural impact on defining psychological disorders.
- Present some of the models of psychopathology.
- Discuss the different types of disorders and their prevalence rates in the United States.
- Describe specific categories of psychological disorders including anxiety, mood, dissociative, schizophrenia, organic disturbances, and personality disorder.

RAPID REVIEW

The study of abnormal behavior, or **psychopathology**, can be traced to at least as early as 3000 B.C. from evidence of trepanning, or drilling some holes in the skull. Hippocrates (460–377 B.C.E.), a Greek physician, made the first, though incorrect, recorded attempt to explain abnormal thinking or behavior as due to some biological process involving the bodies fluids. People of the Middle Ages believed in spirit possession as one cause of abnormality. Presently, psychological disorders are often viewed from a medical model in that they can be diagnosed according to various symptoms and have an etiology, course, and prognosis. Abnormal behavior is considered to be any behavior that is rare, deviates from the social norm within the **situational context**, causes **subjective discomfort**, or is **maladaptive**. **Psychological disorders** are defined as a pattern of behavior that causes people significant distress, causes them to harm themselves or others, or interferes with their ability to function in daily life. *Insanity* is a legal term used to argue that a mentally ill person should not be held responsible for his or her situation.

The **biological model** of psychopathology proposes that psychological disorders arise from a physical or biological cause. The **psychodynamic model** suggests that disorders are the result of repressed thoughts in the unconscious mind, while the **behaviorist model** explains disorders as a set of learned behaviors. Cognitive psychologists have proposed the **cognitive model**, which describes psychological disorders as resulting from faulty thinking patterns. The **sociocultural perspective** of abnormality takes into account the effect of culture on behavior and suggests that psychological disorders should be assessed within the realm of **cultural relativity**. **Cultural syndromes** are certain psychological disorders that are only found in particular cultures. The **biopsychosocial model** proposes that abnormal behavior is the result of biological, psychological, social, and cultural influences.

Currently in the United States, psychological disorders are assessed by referring to the *Diagnostics and Statistical Manual of Mental Disorders, Fifth Edition* (**DSM-5**), which provides information about 250 different disorders including common symptoms, prevalence rates, and criteria for diagnosis. The *DSM-5* combines all disorders and diagnoses into a single list. A few of the 20 categories of disorders that can be diagnosed include depressive disorders, anxiety disorders, and schizophrenia spectrum disorders. In a given year, about 26.2 percent of adults in the United States could be diagnosed with a mental disorder, and it is quite common for people to suffer from more than one mental disorder at a time. In the world of psychological diagnosis and treatment, labels like *depression, anxiety*, and *schizophrenia* can be very helpful because they make up a common language in the mental health community. However, as discovered by researcher David Rosenhan, after admitting pseudopatients into a mental hospital, the labels changed the perceptions of the hospital staff on how they saw normal behaviors as pathological. Labels can bias us, affect our judgment, and give us preconceived notions that may very well turn out to be false.

Anxiety disorders include all disorders characterized by excessive or unrealistic anxiety. **Free-floating anxiety** is the term given to anxiety that seems to be unrelated to any realistic, known factor. **Phobias** are a specific form of anxiety disorder defined as an irrational and persistent fear of something and include **social phobias**, **specific phobias** such as **claustrophobia**, **acrophobia**, and **agoraphobia**, or fear of being in a place that would be difficult to escape from if something were to go wrong. **Panic disorder** is characterized by frequent occurrences of **panic attacks** or sudden onsets of extreme panic.

Individuals diagnosed with **generalized anxiety disorder** display excessive anxiety and worries with no real source that can be pinpointed as leading to the anxiety. Disorders in which people believe they are sick when they are not are called **somatoform disorders**. These disorders are different from **psychosomatic** or **psychophysiological disorders** in which an individual experiences an actual physical illness that is believed to be caused by psychological stress. Somatoform disorders include **hypochondrias**, a disorder in which a person worries excessively about becoming ill; **somatization disorder**, in which the person complains about a specific physical symptom for which there is no real physical cause; and **conversion disorder**, which includes the loss of motor and/or sensory function. Freud believed somatoform disorders were caused by the repression of unacceptable thoughts; behaviorists believe the disorders are learned through both positive and negative reinforcement; and cognitive psychologists point to faulty thinking such as magnification and false beliefs as the cause.

Obsessive-compulsive disorder now falls in the category of "Obsessive-Compulsive and Related Disorders" while *posttraumatic stress disorder* and *acute stress disorder* (*ASD*) are found under "Trauma- and Stressor-Related Disorders." **Obsessive-compulsive disorder** involves a reoccurring thought (or obsession) that causes extreme anxiety and leads to some repetitive or ritualistic behavior (or compulsion). **Acute stress disorder** and posttraumatic stress disorder are related to exposure to significant and traumatic stressors. The symptoms of ASD often occur immediately after the traumatic event and include anxiety, dissociative symptoms, sleep disturbances, and moments in which people seem to "relive" the event in dreams and flashbacks. When the symptoms associated with ASD last for more than 1 month, the disorder is then called **posttraumatic stress disorder (PTSD)**. The psychodynamic model states that anxiety disorders are caused by repressed urges or conflicts that are threatening to surface, while the behaviorist model sees anxious behavior as learned or conditioned responses. Cognitive psychologists believe that anxiety disorders are caused by illogical thinking including maladaptive thinking process such as **magnification**, **all-or-nothing thinking**, **overgeneralization**, and **minimization**. Evidence also supports biological factors, such as an imbalance in neurotransmitter levels, as playing a role in anxiety disorders. Anxiety disorders are found around the world although the particular form the disorder takes might be different in various cultures. *Ataque de nervios*, or "attack of nerves," found in Latin American cultures, and *taijin kyofusho* (TKS), found primarily in Japan, involve excessive fear and anxiety. These are examples of particular forms of disorders identified in different cultures.

In psychological terms, the word **affect** is used to mean "emotion" or "mood." **Mood disorders**, also referred to as affective disorders, represent a disturbance in emotion. The most common mood disorder is **major depression**, which is characterized by prolonged feelings of extreme sadness. **Bipolar disorder** involves all the symptoms of major depression in addition to brief periods of extreme **manic** episodes, or periods of excessive excitement, energy, and feelings of happiness. Behavioral theorists link depression to learned helplessness, whereas social cognitive theorists point to distortions of thinking.-Biological explanations have focused on the role of brain chemicals such as serotonin, norepiniphrine, and dopamine. The tendency of mood disorders to appear in genetically related individuals at a higher rate suggests rather strongly that genetics may play a significant part in these disorders.

Dissociative disorders involve a break, or dissociation, in a person's memory or sense of identity. In **dissociative amnesia**, an individual cannot remember information contained in long-term memory such as her own name or where she lives. A **dissociative fugue** occurs when a person suddenly travels away from his home and afterwards cannot remember the trip or even his own identity. In **dissociative identity disorder**, formerly referred to as multiple personality disorder, a person seems to experience at least two or more distinct personalities. According to the psychodynamic model, dissociation is a defense mechanism and is associated with emotional or physical trauma. Behaviorists believe that "not thinking" about certain events can be negatively reinforced by reducing anxiety and unpleasant feelings, while cognitive psychologists focus on the feelings of guilt, shame, or anxiety that may be avoided through "thought avoidance." Biological explanations for dissociative disorders also

exist. Researchers have found that individuals with **depersonalization disorder**, a disorder in which people feel detached and disconnected from themselves their bodies and their surroundings, also have lower brain activity in areas of the brain responsible for the sense of body awareness. Dissociative symptoms and features can also be found in other cultures such as the trancelike state known as *amok* in which a person suddenly becomes highly agitated and violent (found in Southeast Asia and Pacific Island cultures). This state is usually associated with no memory for the period during which the "trance" lasts.

Organic disturbances are disorders that result from physiological sources. They may be temporary or permanent. Examples include delirium, dementia, hallucinations, memory loss, and confused thought. Causes include epileptic seizure, Alzheimer's disease, brain surgery, drug withdrawal, head injury, and psychotropic drugs. Treatments focus on addressing the physiological basis for the disorder and include medical interventions like surgery, prescription drugs, detoxification, and managing the person's environment to minimize exposure to unpleasant stimuli such as loud noise and bright light and to ensure high-quality sleep along with familiar and comfortable surroundings. As a medical condition may pass over time, like the fading of a high fever that causes delirium, the symptoms of the organic disturbance can diminish. Other conditions are resistant to improvement because of permanent damage to the brain that leaves the person with long-term impairment.

Schizophrenia is a severe **psychotic** disorder in which the person is not able to distinguish fantasy from reality and experiences disturbances in thinking, emotions, behavior, and perception. Many people with schizophrenia experience **delusions** (false beliefs about the world), **hallucinations** (seeing or hearing things that are not really there), and **flat affect** (the display of little or no emotion). **Catatonia** is a symptom associated with schizophrenia in which the individual may sit without moving for hours or may move about wildly. Another way of describing symptoms in schizophrenia is to group them by the way they relate to normal functioning. **Positive symptoms** reflect an excess or distortion of normal functions, such as hallucinations, whereas **negative symptoms** reflect a decrease of normal functions. Medication appears to be more effective in treating the positive symptoms of schizophrenia. The biological model has attempted to explain the causes of schizophrenia. Increased levels of dopamine and brain structural defects are currently the two explanations with the strongest support. In addition, the **stress-vulnerability model** proposes that individuals may have a biological sensitivity which is then made worse by environmental stress.

In personality disorder, a person has an excessively rigid, maladaptive pattern of behavior and ways of relating to others. The *DSM-5* lists ten primary types of personality disorder. An individual with **antisocial personality disorder** typically feels no remorse and often behaves in an impulsive manner with no regard for the consequences. **Borderline personality disorder** is defined by moody, unstable behaviors in which the individual lacks a clear sense of identity. Cognitive-behavioral theorists suggest behaviors associated with personality disorder can be learned over time. Cognitive explanations involve the belief systems formed by the personality disordered persons, such as paranoia and extreme self-importance. Close biological relatives of people with personality disorders such as antisocial and borderline are more likely to have these disorders.

Common symptoms of *test anxiety* include the personal experience of possible negative consequences or poor outcomes on an exam or evaluation, accompanied by a cluster of cognitive, affective, and behavioral symptoms. While not yet recognized as a clinical disorder in the *DSM-5,* test anxiety has caused countless students considerable stress and agony over the years. Strategies for dealing with test anxiety include determining why you want to do well on the test, developing a strategy for controlling both your cognitive state and behavior before and during the exam, and using positive self-talk.

STUDY HINTS

1. Six different categories of psychological disorders are presented in this chapter. In order to help organize the new terms, try creating a table of the different disorders including a general description of each category and the specific disorders within the category. The first category has been completed for you as an example.

Disorder Type	General Description	Specific Examples
Anxiety disorders	*a psychological disorder in which the main symptom is an intense fear or anxiety*	*social phobias, specific phobias, agoraphobia, obsessive-compulsive disorder, generalized anxiety disorder, panic disorder*
Dissociative disorders		
Mood disorders		
Schizophrenia		
Personality disorder		

2. In addition to understanding the disorders themselves, it is important to understand the different theories as to the causes of each disorder. Your textbook discusses various explanations for each disorder. The models include the biological, psychodynamic, behavioral, and cognitive. In order to enhance your understanding of these models, briefly describe how each of them would explain the disorders listed below.

Model	Depression	Schizophrenia	Dissociative Identity Disorder
Behavioral			
Cognitive			
Biological			

Suggested Answers for Question 2

Model	Depression	Schizophrenia	Dissociative Identity Disorder
Behavioral	*learned helplessness*	*bizarre behavior that has been shaped through reinforcement*	*behavior shaped through positive reinforcement such as attention from others*
Cognitive	*negative and self-defeating thoughts*	*severe form of illogical thinking*	*thought avoidance*
Biological	*brain chemical imbalance (in neurotransmitters such as serotonin and dopamine)*	*chemical imbalance and brain structure abnormalities*	*variation in brain activity between different "personalities"*

LEARNING OBJECTIVES

13.1 How has mental illness been explained in the past, and how is abnormal behavior and thinking defined today?

13.2 What are some of the models used to explain psychological disorders?

13.3 What are the different types of psychological disorders, and how common are they?

13.4 What are the different types of anxiety disorders, obsessive-compulsive disorder, and stress related disorders, and what are their symptoms and causes?

13.5 What are the different disorders of mood disorders and their causes?

13.6 How do various dissociative disorders differ, and how do they develop?

13.7 What are the main symptoms and causes of schizophrenia?

13.8 How do the various personality disorders differ, and what is thought to be the cause of personality disorders?

13.9 What are some ways to overcome test anxiety?

AP LEARNING OBJECTIVES

1. Describe contemporary and historical conceptions of what constitutes psychological disorders. (p. 512)
2. Recognize the use of the *Diagnostic and Statistical Manual of Mental Disorders* (DSM) published by the American Psychiatric Association as the primary reference for making diagnostic judgments. (p. 518)
3. Discuss the major diagnostic categories, including anxiety and somatoform disorders, mood disorders, schizophrenia, organic disturbance, personality disorders, and dissociative disorders and their corresponding symptoms. (pp. 522, 527, 532)
4. Evaluate the strengths and limitations of various approaches to explaining psychological disorders: medical model, psychoanalytic, humanistic, cognitive, biological, and sociocultural. (p. 515)
5. Identify the positive and negative consequences of diagnostic labels. (p. 519)
6. Discuss the intersection between psychology and the legal system. (p. 514)

acrophobia	fear of heights.
acute stress disorder	is related to exposure to significant and traumatic stressors. Its symptoms often occur immediately after the traumatic event and include anxiety and flashbacks.
affect	in psychology, a term indicating emotion or mood.
agoraphobia	fear of being in a place or situation from which escape is difficult or impossible.
all-or-nothing thinking	the tendency to believe that one's performance must be perfect or the result will be a total failure.
antisocial personality disorder	disorder in which a person has no morals or conscience and often behaves in an impulsive manner without regard for the consequences of that behavior.
anxiety disorders	disorders in which the main symptom is excessive or unrealistic anxiety and fearfulness.
behaviorist model	explanation of disorder behavior as being learned just like normal behavior.
biological model	model of explaining behavior as caused by biological changes in the chemical, structural, or genetic systems of the body.
biopsychosocial model	perspective in which abnormal behavior is seen as the result of the combined and interacting forces of biological, psychological, social, and cultural influences.
bipolar disorder	severe mood swings between major depressive episodes and manic episodes.
borderline personality disorder	maladaptive personality pattern in which the person is moody, unstable, lacks a clear sense of identity, and often clings to others.
catatonia	a symptom associated with schizophrenia in which the person experiences periods of statue-like immobility mixed with occasional bursts of energetic, frantic movement and talking.
claustrophobia	fear of being in a small enclosed space.
cognitive model	model which explains abnormal behavior as resulting from illogical thinking patterns.
conversion disorder	Disorder that includes the loss of motor and/or sensory function.
cultural relativity	the need to consider the unique characteristics of the culture in which behavior takes place.
cultural syndromes	disorders found only in particular cultures.
delusions	false beliefs held by a person who refuses to accept evidence of their falseness.
depersonalization disorder	dissociative disorder in which individuals feel detached and disconnected from themselves, their bodies, and their surroundings.
dissociative amnesia	loss of memory for personal information, either partial or complete.
dissociative disorders	disorders in which there is a break in conscious awareness, memory, the sense of identity, or some combination.
dissociative fugue	traveling away from familiar surroundings with amnesia for the trip and possible amnesia for personal information.
dissociative identity disorder	disorder occurring when a person seems to have two or more distinct personalities within one body.
DSM	*Diagnostic and Statistical Manual of Mental Disorders.* Manual written and used primarily by psychologists and psychiatrists as a guide in diagnosing and assessing psychological disorders.
flat affect	a lack of emotional responsiveness.

free-floating anxiety	anxiety that is unrelated to any realistic, known source.
generalized anxiety disorder	disorder in which a person has feelings of dread and impending doom along with physical symptoms of stress which last six months or more.
hallucinations	false sensory perceptions such as hearing voices that do not really exist.
hypochondria	disorder in which a person worries excessively about becoming ill.
magnification	the tendency to interpret situations as far more dangerous, harmful, or important than they actually are.
major depression	severe depression that comes on suddenly and seems to have no external cause.
maladaptive	anything that does not allow a person to function within or adapt to the stresses and everyday demands on life.
manic	having the quality of excessive excitement, energy, and elation or irritability.
minimization	the tendency to give little or no importance to one's successes or positive events and traits.
mood disorders	disorders in which mood is severely disturbed.
negative symptoms	symptoms of schizophrenia that are less than normal behavior or an absence of normal behavior; poor attention, flat affect, and poor speech production.
obsessive-compulsive disorder	disorder in which intruding, recurring thoughts or obsessions create anxiety that is relieved by performing a repetitive, ritualistic behavior (compulsion).
overgeneralization	the tendency to interpret a single negative event as a never-ending pattern of defeat and failure.
panic attack	sudden onset of intense panic in which multiple physical symptoms of stress occur, often with feelings that one is dying.
panic disorder	disorder in which panic attacks occur frequently enough to cause the person difficulty in adjusting to daily life.
personality disorder	disorder in which a person adopts a persistent, rigid, and maladaptive pattern of behavior that interferes with normal social interactions.
phobias	an irrational, persistent fear of an object, situation, or social activity.
positive symptoms	symptoms of schizophrenia that are excesses of behavior or occur in addition to normal behavior; hallucinations, delusions, and distorted thinking.
posttraumatic stress disorder	related to exposure to significant and traumatic stressors. When the symptoms associated with ASD last for more than 1 month, the disorder is then called **posttraumatic stress disorder (PTSD)**.
psychodynamic model	model based on the work of Freud and his followers. Typically explains disorder behavior as the result of repressing thoughts and memories in the unconscious mind.
psychological disorders	any pattern of behavior that causes people significant distress, causes them to harm others, or harms their ability to function in daily life.
psychopathology	the study of abnormal behavior.
psychophysiological (or psychosomatic) disorder	Disorder in which an individual experiences an actual physical illness that is believed to be caused by psychological stress.
psychotic	term applied to a person who is no longer able to distinguish between fantasy and reality.

schizophrenia	severe disorder in which the person suffers from disordered thinking, bizarre behavior, and hallucinations and is unable to distinguish between fantasy and reality.
situational context	the social or environmental setting of a person's behavior.
social phobias	fear of interacting with others or being in social situations that might lead to a negative evaluation.
sociocultural perspective	perspective in which behavior is seen as the product of the learning within the context of the family, social group, and culture to which the individual belongs.
somatization disorder	disorder in which the person complains about a specific physical symptom for which there is no real physical cause.
somatoform disorders	disorders in which people believe they are sick when they are not.
specific phobias	fear of objects or specific situations or events.
stress-vulnerability model	explanation of disorder proposing that environmental stress can trigger the development of a disorder in an individual with a biological sensitivity.
subjective discomfort	emotional distress or emotional pain.

CHAPTER PRACTICE TEST

For the following multiple choice questions, select the answer you feel best answers the question.

1. It is probably accurate to assume that in ancient times signs of mental illness were believed to be caused by _____.
    a) imbalance of body fluids
    b) demons
    c) improper diet
    d) social forces
    e) chemical imbalances

2. What is the primary difficulty with applying the criterion of "social norm deviance" to define abnormal behavior?
    a) Norms are difficult to enumerate.
    b) Cultures accept and view all behaviors as normal.
    c) Behavior that is considered disordered in one culture may be acceptable in another.
    d) Norms do not guide behavior except in rare instances.
    e) Deviance in not found in all cultures.

3. Which of the following is NOT a criterion used to decide if a pattern of behavior should be considered to be a psychological disorder?
    a) The behavior is physically exhausting.
    b) The behavior causes subjective distress.
    c) The behavior goes against the norms of the society.
    d) The behavior is maladaptive.
    e) The behavior causes the person to be dangerous to self or others.

4. The biological model views psychological disorders as resulting from _____.

    a) distorted thought patterns
    b) repressed memories
    c) underlying behavioral issues
    d) physiological causes
    e) incongruence

18. Disorders characterized by disturbances in emotion are known as _____ disorders.
    a) conversion
    b) reflective
    c) somatoform
    d) dissociative
    e) mood

19. An individual diagnosed with major depressive disorder would most likely exhibit which of the following symptoms?
    a) cycles of being sad then happy then sad
    b) extreme sadness and despair
    c) lack of concern for the well-being of others.
    d) hallucinations and delusions
    e) increased anxiety when in open spaces

20. Which of the following is the biological explanation for mood disorders?
    a) They are a result of learned helplessness.
    b) They are a result of anger turned inward on oneself.
    c) They are a result of distortions in thinking.
    d) They are a result of an imbalance of brain chemicals.
    e) They are the result of childhood memories that are repressed.

21. Dissociative identity disorder is a psychological disorder that was commonly known as
    _____.
    a) amnesia
    b) fugue or flight disorder
    c) schizophrenia
    d) multiple personality disorder
    e) OCD

22. Which of the following perspectives claims that shaping may play a big role in the development of some cases of dissociative identity disorder?
    a) behavioral
    b) humanistic
    c) biological
    d) psychodynamic
    e) cognitive

23. Spanos conducted studies to determine the validity of dissociative identity disorder. He found that ordinary college students, under hypnosis, showed signs of a second personality. Based on his studies, what did he conclude about the disorder?
    a) Many of the diagnoses were incorrect, as professionals had been fooled by the clients' tendency to play the role of a multiple personality.
    b) Many cases had clearly been caused by childhood trauma.
    c) Many cases were a misdiagnosis of other psychological disorders.
    d) Very few cases had been misdiagnosed.
    e) College students suffer from dissociative identity disorder more than any other group of people.

24. A person suffering from disordered thinking, bizarre behavior, and hallucinations, who is unable to distinguish between fantasy and reality, is likely suffering from _____.
   a) cyclothymic personality disorder
   b) bipolar disorder
   c) a dissociative disorder
   d) passive-aggressive personality
   e) schizophrenia

25. The condition in which a person shows little or no emotion is referred to as _____.
   a) flat affect
   b) hallucinations
   c) delusions
   d) disorganization
   e) inappropriate affect

26. The primary feature of _____, a symptom associated with schizophrenia, is severe disturbance of motor behavior.
   a) disorganized
   b) catatonia
   c) residual
   d) paranoid
   e) hebephrenic

27. Which of the following symptoms would NOT be considered a symptom of schizophrenia?
   a) lack of affect
   b) poor attention
   c) delusions
   d) fugue
   e) hallucinations

28. Sal has decreased levels of the neurotransmitter dopamine in his prefrontal cortex. Which disorder might he be at risk of experiencing?
   a) antisocial personality disorder
   b) agoraphobia
   c) schizophrenia
   d) dissociative fugue
   e) depression

29. In _____, a person has an excessively rigid, maladaptive pattern of behavior and ways of relating to others.
   a) somatoform disorder
   b) dissociative disorder
   c) mood disorder
   d) personality disorder
   e) anxiety disorder

30. A person with antisocial personality disorder would be likely to engage in which of the following behaviors?
    a) lying to other people without worrying about the consequences
    b) display excessive and inappropriate emotions
    c) report hallucinations
    d) completely withdraw from society
    e) display excessive repetitive behaviors

31. Which of the following statements represents the more cognitive view of personality disorder?
    a) They are due to an inadequate resolution of the Oedipus complex.
    b) They are a result of repressed memories.
    c) They are due to instinctual responses to external stimuli.
    d) They are due the belief systems formed by the personality disordered person.
    e) They have physiological causes.

32. A strategy for dealing with test anxiety could include _____.

    a) focusing on how nervous you are and how sure you are that you aren't going to be able to remember anything
    b) using superficial processing to enhance memory retention
    c) studying in noisy areas
    d) cramming for hours the night before the test
    e) developing some type of strategy for controlling both your cognitive state and behavior, before and during the exam

CHAPTER PRACTICE TEST ANSWERS

1. b   b is the correct choice because people of ancient times perceived signs of mental illness as caused by demons. Hippocrates, a Greek physician, viewed the imbalance of body fluids as the cause of mental illness, but Hippocrates' time period is not considered "ancient times."

2. c   c is the correct answer, since behavior that is considered disordered in one culture may be acceptable in another. d is incorrect because most people do allow social norms to guide much of their behavior.

3. a   Four criteria characteristic of a psychological disorder are that it deviates from social norms, it is maladaptive, it causes the individual personal distress or discomfort, and/or it causes the person to be dangerous to self or others.

4. d   The biological model emphasizes physiological or physical causes for psychological disorders. The other choices represent the psychological models.

5. b   Originating with the theories of Freud, psychoanalysts view disorder behavior as resulting from thoughts that are below the level of conscious awareness.

6. a   Cognitive psychologists tend to treat disorders by attempting to change the person's thought patterns.

7. d   *Taijin-kyofu-sho*, *susto*, and *amok* are considered cultural disorders because they occur only in particular cultures.

8. e   The *DSM* helps psychological professionals diagnose psychological disorders, while the *Physician's Desk Reference* is used by medical professionals.

9. a   The *DSM-V* uses a single axis system for all disorders.

10. b   According to recent studies, approximately 22.6 percent of the U.S. adult population experiences a mental disorder in a given year.

11. b   This statement is true because some types of anxiety are normal.

12. d   Agoraphobia is an anxiety disorder characterized by an extreme fear of going in public places that would be difficult to escape from if necessary.

13. b   Cognitive psychologists view anxiety disorders as a result of distorted thought processes, while behaviorists view anxiety disorders as a result of learning.

14. e   Magnification is the tendency to interpret a situation as being far more harmful, dangerous, or embarrassing than it actually is, or in other words, making a big deal out of something that is actually very small.

15. a   Someone with hypochondriasis is excessively worried about getting ill and frequently goes to see doctors. People with somatization disorder do not worry so much about every aspect of their health; they complain in dramatic terms about one particular symptom.

16. c   The term "somatic" literally means bodily.

17. d   Dissociative disorders are characterized by a break in conscious awareness, memory, the sense of identity, or some combination.

18. e   Mood disorders are characterized by disturbances in emotion, while somatoform disorders take the form of bodily ailments that have no physical cause.

19. b   Major depressive disorder has a fairly sudden onset and is characterized by extreme sadness and despair with typically no obvious external cause.

20. d   The biological explanation emphasizes an imbalance of brain chemicals.

21. d   Multiple personality disorder is no longer used by psychologists but is still very common in the general public.

22. a   Behavioral psychologists emphasize shaping through positive and negative reinforcement as a factor in the development of some cases of dissociate identity disorder.

23. a   Spanos found that many supposed cases of dissociative identity disorder had been misdiagnosed.

24. e   Disordered thinking, bizarre behavior, hallucinations, and inability to distinguish between fantasy and reality are all symptoms of schizophrenia. Bipolar disorder is characterized by mood swings between depression and mania and does not involve hallucinations or inability to distinguish between fantasy and reality.

25. a   The word "affect" is used to mean emotion or mood.

26. b   Severe motor disturbance is a feature of catatonia, a symptom associated with schizophrenia.

27. d   Fugue, or flight, is a symptom found in a dissociative disorder.

28. c   Schizophrenia is associated with an imbalance of dopamine.

29. d   In personality disorder, a person has an excessively rigid, maladaptive pattern of behavior and ways of relating to others.

30. a   Antisocial personality disorder is characterized by an individual who acts "against society." For example, an individual might commit a crime without feeling any remorse.

31. d   The more cognitive explanations of personality disorder involve the belief systems formed by the personality disordered persons.

32. e   A strategy for dealing with test anxiety could include developing some type of strategy for controlling both your cognitive state and behavior, before and during the exam.

CHAPTER PRACTICE FREE RESPONSE QUESTION

You have 25 minutes to answer the following question. You must write in complete sentences and not just list facts. You should make your point clearly and use the language of psychology. Be sure to write legibly and respond to all parts of the question.

A. Taylor is authoring a graphic novel. The characters in the novel are designed around various symptoms of psychological disorders. Describe how the characters might behave if they are displaying symptoms associate with each of the following:

- Negative symptoms of schizophrenia
- Antisocial personality disorder
- Major depressive disorder

- Agoraphobia
- *Taijin kyofusho* (TKS)

SUGGESTED RUBRIC—Students should provide specific details and examples to support their assertions; definitions alone are not sufficient. Information about each topic should be discussed in the context of the question rather than abstractly. Successful essays may include the following arguments:

5 points

- Score—Negative symptoms of schizophrenia—Negative symptoms are experienced as losses. In the case of Taylor's graphic novel this character might display a flat affect, breakdown in language skills, apathy, and inability to concentrate.
- Score—Antisocial personality disorder—This character would likely show a lack of concern for the feelings or rights of others, indiscriminately break laws or rules, and show no remorse or guilt.
- Score—Major depressive disorder—This character might show symptoms like taking little or no pleasure in any activity, feeling tired, having trouble sleeping or sleeping too much, showing changes in appetite and significant weight changes, experiencing excessive guilt or feelings of worthlessness, and having trouble concentrating.
- Score—Agoraphobia—This character might show fear of being in a place or situation from which escape is difficult or impossible. Typical situations that agoraphobics fear include being in crowds, on bridges, or in cars or planes or even just leaving their homes.
- Score—*Taijin kyofusho*—This is a cultural syndrome found in Japan. This character might show excessive fear and anxiety, but in this case it is the fear that one will do something in public that is socially inappropriate or embarrassing, such as blushing, staring, or having an offensive body odor

YOU KNOW YOU HAVE MASTERED THE MAIN TOPICS IN THIS CHAPTER IF YOU ARE ABLE TO . . .

- Define two main types of theory and briefly discuss the history of treatment of the mentally ill.
- Introduce the major types of psychotherapy including psychoanalysis, humanistic, behavior, cognitive, and group therapy.
- Discuss the assessment and effectiveness of the psychotherapy treatments.
- Describe the biomedical approaches of treating psychological disorders including the use of drugs, electroconvulsive therapy, and psychosurgery.
- Discuss how computers are changing psychological therapy.

RAPID REVIEW

Therapy for psychological disorders consists of treatment methods aimed at making people feel better and function more effectively. The two main types of therapy are **psychotherapy**, which consists of talking things out with a professional, and **biomedical therapy**, which consists of using biological methods such as medication to treat a psychological disorder. Many psychological professionals today take an **eclectic** approach to psychotherapy which involves using a combination of methods to fit the particular client's needs. Psychotherapy techniques can be roughly divided into **insight therapies**, which have the goal of self-understanding, and **action therapies**, which focus on changing an individual's behaviors. Biomedical therapies consist mainly of the use of drugs, surgical techniques, or electroconvulsive therapy. Early treatment of the mentally ill often consisted of fatal attempts to "rid" the individual of the physical impurities causing the abnormal behavior. It was not until 1793 that Philippe Pinel began the movement of humane treatment of the mentally ill.

Psychoanalysis is an insight therapy developed by **Sigmund Freud** with the goal of revealing the unconscious conflicts, urges, and desires that Freud assumed were the cause of the psychological disorder. Freud utilized a number of techniques in his attempt to reveal the unconscious. **Dream interpretation** involved an analysis of the actual or **manifest content** of a dream as well as the hidden or **latent content**. Freud felt the latent content of dreams could reveal unconscious conflict. In addition, Freud used **free association**, or allowing the patients to freely say whatever came to their mind, to uncover the repressed material; **resistance**, in which the patient became unwilling to discuss a topic any further; and **transference**, in which the therapist became a symbol of a parental authority figure. Today, psychoanalytic therapy is often referred to as **psychodynamic therapy** and is **directive**, places more emphasis on transference, and is usually much shorter than traditional psychoanalysis. Individuals with anxiety, somatoform, or dissociative disorders are more likely to benefit from psychodynamic therapy than individuals with other types of disorders. **Interpersonal psychotherapy (IPT)** is a psychotherapy developed to address depression. It is an insight therapy focusing on relationships of the individual with others and the interplay between mood and the events of everyday life. Despite drawing ideas from psychodynamic thinking, IPT is not considered to be a psychodynamic therapy as it combines aspects of humanistic and cognitive–behavioral therapies, making it truly eclectic.

Humanistic therapy is also an insight therapy, but unlike psychoanalysis, humanistic therapy focuses on conscious experiences of emotion and an individual's sense of self. The two most common humanistic therapies are person-centered therapy and Gestalt therapy. **Carl Rogers** developed **person-centered therapy**, which has the goal of helping an individual get his or her real and ideal selves to more closely match up. According to Rogers, the role of the therapist is to provide the unconditional positive regard that was missing in the individual's life. He felt the therapy should be **nondirective** with the individual doing most of the work and believed the four key elements of **reflection**, **unconditional positive regard**, **empathy**, and **authenticity** were crucial for a successful person-therapist relationship. A variation of person-centered therapy is *motivational interviewing*. MI has specific goals to reduce ambivalence about change and to increase intrinsic motivation to bring that change about. For a therapist, the four principles of MI are to express empathy, develop discrepancy between the client's present behaviors and values, roll with resistance, and support the client's self-efficacy. **Fritz Perls** believed that people's problems arose from hiding important parts of their feelings from themselves and developed another humanistic therapy called **Gestalt therapy**, a directive form of insight therapy. Gestalt therapy focuses on the client's feelings and subjective experiences and uses leading questions and planned experiences such as role-playing to help the person reveal the feelings he or she may be hiding from him- or herself. Humanistic therapies have been found to be more successful with individuals who are able to express their thoughts and feelings in a logical manner and are not necessarily the best choice for individuals with more severe psychological disorders.

Behavior therapies use action-based therapy to change behavior based on basic principles of classical and operant conditioning. The abnormal behavior is not seen as a symptom but rather as the problem itself. **Behavior modification or applied behavior analysis** refers to the use of conditioning techniques to modify behavior. Behavior therapies that rely on classical conditioning include systematic desensitization, aversion therapy, and flooding. **Systematic desensitization** consists of a three-step process which utilizes **counter-conditioning** in order to reduce fear and anxiety. First the client learns deep muscle relaxation techniques, then the client creates a list of anxiety-producing events called a hierarchy of fear, and finally the client confronts the anxiety-producing event while remaining in a relaxed state. **Aversion therapy** uses classical conditioning to decrease a behavior by pairing an aversive (unpleasant) stimulus with the stimulus that normally produces the unwanted behavior.

For example, someone who wants to stop smoking might go to a therapist who uses a *rapid-smoking* technique, in which the client is allowed to smoke but must take a puff on the cigarette every 5 or 6 seconds. As nicotine is a poison, such rapid smoking produces nausea and dizziness, both unpleasant effects. Behavioral techniques that introduce the client to situations, under carefully controlled conditions, which are related to their anxieties or fears are called **exposure therapies**. **Flooding** involves rapid and intense exposure to an anxiety-producing object in order to produce extinction of the conditioned fear response. Behavior therapies that utilize operant conditioning include participant modeling, token economies, contingency contracts, and extinction techniques such as the use of a time-out. **Eye-movement desensitization reprocessing (EMDR)** is a therapy technique in which clients attempt to decrease their fears, anxieties, and disturbing thoughts by moving their eyes rapidly back and forth. As a topic of ongoing investigation and debate, recent studies of EMDR have suggested eye movements or other dual-attention tasks interfere with working memory processes and may decrease the vividness or emotional impact of negative memories. **Modeling**, or learning through the observation and imitation of a model, is a therapy based on the work of Albert Bandura. **Participant modeling** has been used to successfully treat phobias and obsessive-compulsive disorders by having the client watch and mimic a model demonstrating the desired behaviors. In a **token economy**, clients are reinforced with tokens for behaving correctly and can later exchange the tokens for things they want such as food, candy, or special privileges. A **contingency contract** is a written statement of specific required behaviors, contingent penalties, and subsequent rewards. **Extinction** involves the removal of a reinforcer to reduce the frequency of a particular response. Extinction techniques such as **time-outs** work by removing the reinforcement for a behavior. In adults, simply refusing to acknowledge a person's behavior is often successful in reducing the frequency of that behavior. Behavior therapies have been effective in the treatment of disorders including overeating, drug addictions, and phobias.

Cognitive therapy is an action therapy that focuses on helping people change the distorted thinking and unrealistic beliefs that lead to maladaptive behaviors. Common distortions in thought include **arbitrary inference** (or "jumping to conclusions"), **selective thinking**, **overgeneralization**, **magnification and minimization**, and **personalization**. **Cognitive behavioral therapy (CBT)** is a type of cognitive therapy in which the goal is to help clients overcome problems by learning to think more rationally and logically. Albert Ellis developed a version of CBT called **rational-emotive behavioral therapy (REBT)** in which clients are taught to replace their own irrational beliefs with more rational, helpful statements. Cognitive therapies have considerable success in treating disorders such as depression, stress disorders, anxiety disorders, and some types of schizophrenia.

An alternative to individual therapy is **group therapy**, in which a group of clients with similar problems gather together and discuss their problems under the guidance of a single therapist. Types of group therapies include **family counseling or family therapy** and **self-help (or support) groups**. The goal in family therapy, then, is to discover the unhealthy ways in which family members interact and communicate with one another and change those ways to healthier, more productive means of interaction. **Self-help groups** or **support groups** are usually formed around a particular problem. Some examples of self-help groups are Alcoholics Anonymous, Overeaters Anonymous, and Narcotics Anonymous. The advantages of self-help groups are that they are often free and provide the social and emotional support that a group session can provide. Self-help groups do not have leaders but instead have people who volunteer monthly or weekly to lead individual meetings. The advantages of group therapy are the lower cost, exposure to the ways other people handle the same kinds of problems, the opportunity for the therapist to see how that person interacts with others, and the social and emotional support from the people in the group. The disadvantages are that the person may not feel as free to reveal embarrassing or personal information, the therapist's time must be shared during the session, a shy person may have difficulty speaking up in the group setting, and people with severe disorders such as schizophrenia may not tolerate a group setting. Group therapy seems to be most successful as a long-term treatment intended to promote the development of skilled social interactions.

The effectiveness of the various psychotherapy techniques is difficult to determine due to various timeframes required for the different therapies, alternate explanations of "effectiveness," the lack of adequate control groups, experimenter bias, and the inaccuracies of self-report information. The most important aspect of successful psychotherapy appears to be the relationship between the client and the therapist, also referred to as the **therapeutic alliance**. In light of managed health care and tight budgets, clients benefit through *evidence-based practice*. Empirically supported or **evidence-based treatment (EBT)** refers to techniques or interventions that have produced desired outcomes or therapeutic change in controlled studies. Some examples of evidence-based, or empirically supported, treatments are exposure therapies, cognitive–behavioral therapies, and cognitive processing for PTSD. Differences in culture between the therapist and the client can make it difficult for the therapist to understand the exact nature of the client's problems. Several studies have found that members of minority racial or ethnic groups drop out of therapy at significantly higher rates than the majority group clients. Traditional forms of psychotherapy, developed mainly in Western, individualistic cultures, may need to be modified to fit the more collectivistic, interdependent cultures. Barriers to effective psychotherapy include differences in language, cultural values, social class, and nonverbal communication. A new form of therapy that is delivered via the Internet, called **cybertherapy**, is now available. Although this method of delivery may have the advantages of lower or no cost, availability of therapy opportunities for those unable to get to a therapist easily (such as people living in a remote or rural area), access to support groups online, and relative anonymity, there are dangers. There is no guarantee that the cybertherapist has any credentials or training in psychotherapy.

Biomedical therapies directly affect the biological functions of the body and include the three categories of drug therapy, shock therapy, and surgical treatments. **Psychopharmacology** refers to the use of drugs to control or relieve the symptoms of a psychological disorder and is often combined with psychotherapy for a more effective outcome. Psychopharmacological drugs can be divided according to the disorders they treat including drugs for psychotic disorders, anxiety disorders, manic symptoms of mood disorders, and depression. Drugs used to treat psychotic symptoms such as hallucinations, delusions, and bizarre behaviors are called **antipsychotic drugs** and include typical neuroleptics, atypical neuroleptics, and partial dopamine agonists. In general, these drugs work to decrease dopamine levels in the brain. Side effects of typical antipsychotic drugs include extrapyramidal symptoms and tardive dyskinesia. Side effects of atypical antipsychotic drugs include weight gain, diabetes, blood lipid level changes, and changes in the electrical rhythms of the heart. The newer drugs tend to have fewer negative side effects than the older typical neuroleptics. The two kinds of drugs currently used to treat anxiety disorders include the traditional **antianxiety drugs** such as the minor tranquilizers, or benzodiazepines, including Xanax, Ativan, and Valium. Concerns with the use of benzodiazepine drugs include their potential for addiction and abuse in the form of "escape" behavior. The most common treatment for the manic symptoms of bipolar disorder is the mood-stabilizing drug lithium. The exact mechanism of lithium is still not clearly understood. The use of lithium has been associated with weight gain, and diet needs to be controlled when taking lithium because lowered levels of sodium in the diet can cause lithium to build up to toxic levels. **Antidepressant drugs** can be divided into three separate categories: the monamine oxidase inhibitors (MAOIs) such as Marplan and Nardil, tricyclic antidepressants such as Tofranil and Elavil, and the selective serotonin reuptake inhibitors (SSRIs) such as Prozac and Zoloft. MAOIs may produce unwanted side effects, although in most cases the side effects decrease or disappear with continued treatment: weight gain, constipation, dry mouth, dizziness, headache, and drowsiness or insomnia are possible. Side effects of tricyclic antidepressants, which may also decrease over the course of treatment, are very similar to those of the MAOIs but can also include skin rashes, blurred vision, lowered blood pressure, and weight gain. Overall, many psychological professionals today believe that combining psychotherapy with medical therapies—particularly drug therapy—is a more effective approach to treating many disorders.

        Electroconvulsive therapy (ECT), also known as shock therapy, is still in use today to treat severe cases of depression, schizophrenia, and mania. The treatment involves delivery of an electric shock to one or both sides of a person's head, causing a release of neurotransmitters and almost immediate improvement in the individual's mood. One of the main side effects of ECT is at least a short-term loss of memory. **Psychosurgery** involves operating on an individual's brain to remove or destroy brain tissue for the purpose of relieving symptoms of psychological disorders. One of the earliest psychosurgery techniques is the **prefrontal lobotomy**, which is no longer performed today. The main psychosurgery technique in use today is the **bilateral anterior cingulotomy** which destroys the cingulated gyrus and has been shown to be effective in about one-third of cases of depression, bipolar disorder, and obsessive-compulsive disorder. This procedure is only performed with the patient's full and informed consent after all other treatment options have been exhausted.

        Virtual reality is being used in therapy. One of the main uses of VR as a therapy incorporates exposure therapy of some form. Exposure therapy involves preventing a person with a phobia, for example, from avoiding the presentation of the phobic object. Posttraumatic stress disorder (PTSD) is another mental health issue benefiting from the use of VR psychotherapy. Although still a relatively new area of research, evidence suggests virtual reality psychotherapy may be as effective as traditional exposure methods in the treatment of PTSD. One advantage is the more vivid and realistic imagery produced by VR as opposed to asking patients to imagine the scenarios that disturb them.

STUDY HINTS

1. An important task in this chapter is to understand the differences among the multiple types of therapy. Listed below are several of the psychotherapies discussed in the chapter. For each therapy, indicate the type of therapy (insight or action), the role of the therapist (directive or nondirective), the school of thought most likely to use this technique, and the overall goal of the therapy. The first psychotherapy has been filled in as an example.

Therapy	Type of Therapy	Role of Therapist	School of Thought	Goal of Therapy
Traditional psychoanalysis	*Insight*	*Nondirective*	*Psychoanalysis*	*Uncover unconscious conflicts*
Person-centered therapy				

Gestalt therapy				
Rational-emotive behavioral therapy (REBT)				
Systematic desensitization				

Suggested Answers

Therapy	Type of Therapy	Role of Therapist	School of Thought	Goal of Therapy
Traditional psychoanalysis	*Insight*	*Nondirective*	*Psychoanalysis*	*Uncover unconscious conflicts*
Person-centered therapy	*Insight*	*Nondirective*	*Humanistic*	*Bring ideal self and real self into congruence*
Gestalt therapy	*Insight*	*Directive*	*Humanistic*	*Increase self awareness*
Rational-emotive behavioral therapy (REBT)	*Action*	*Directive*	*Cognitive–Behavioral*	*Replace irrational beliefs with more rational, helpful statements*
Systematic desensitization	*Action*	*Directive*	*Behaviorist*	*Reduce fear and anxiety*

Which of the therapies listed above would you find most helpful? _____

Why? _____

_____

_____

_____

_____

2. Rational-emotive behavioral therapy is commonly used for individuals with depression and anxiety. The therapy is based on the idea that an individual has adopted irrational beliefs that have in turn led to his or her condition of anxiety and depression. The goal of the therapy is to identify the irrational beliefs and teach the individual how to respond with more rational thought processes. In order to better understand the process, assume you are a therapist using the REBT technique and your client makes the following irrational statements. List a suggestion for a rational belief the client could adopt instead. The first one has already been completed.

Irrational Belief	Rational Belief
1. I must be loved, or at least liked, and approved by every significant person I meet.	*I want to be loved or liked by some of the people in my life, and I know I may feel disappointed or lonely when that doesn't happen, but I can cope with those feelings.*
2. I must be completely competent, make no mistakes, and achieve in every possible way if I am to be worthwhile.	
3. It is dreadful, nearly the end of the world, when things aren't how I would like them to be.	
4. Human unhappiness, including mine, is caused by factors outside of my control, so little can be done about it.	

5. If something might be dangerous, unpleasant, or frightening, I should worry about it a great deal.	
6. My problem(s) were caused by event(s) in my past, and that's why, I have my problem(s) now.	
7. I should be very upset by other people's problems and difficulties	

LEARNING OBJECTIVES

14.1   *How have psychological disorders been treated throughout history, and what are two modern ways they are treated today?*

14.2   *What were the basic elements of Freud's psychoanalysis, and how do psychodynamic approaches differ today?*

14.3   *What are the basic elements of the humanistic therapies known as person-centered therapy and Gestalt therapy?*

14.4   *How do behavior therapists use classical and operant conditioning to treat disordered behavior, and how successful are these therapies?*

14.5   *What are the goals and basic elements of cognitive therapies such as cognitive–behavioral therapy and rational emotive behavior therapy?*

14.6   *What are the various types of group therapies and the advantages and disadvantages of group therapy?*

14.7   *How effective is psychotherapy, and what factors influence its effectiveness?*

14.8   *What are the various types of drugs used to treat psychological disorders?*

14.9   *How are electroconvulsive therapy and psychosurgery used to treat psychological disorders today?*

14.10   *How might computers be used in psychotherapy?*

AP LEARNING OBJECTIVES

1. Describe the central characteristics of psychotherapeutic intervention. (p. 548)
2. Describe major treatment orientations used in therapy and how those orientations influence therapeutic planning. (p. 549)
3. Compare and contrast different treatment formats. (p. 562)
4. Summarize effectiveness of specific treatments used to address specific problems. (pp. 551, 563, 565, 570)
5. Discuss how cultural and ethnic context influence choice and success of treatment. (p. 568)
6. Describe prevention strategies that build resilience and promote competence. (pp. 553, 568)
7. Identify major figures in psychological treatment. (pp. 549, 552, 556, 557, 560, 561, 569)
8. Identify major historical figures in psychology. (p. 548)

9. Evaluate the strengths and limitations of various approaches to explaining psychological disorders: medical model, psychoanalytic, humanistic, cognitive, biological, and sociocultural. (p. 549)

CHAPTER GLOSSARY

action therapies	therapies in which the main goal is to change disordered or inappropriate behavior directly.
antianxiety drugs	drugs used to treat and calm anxiety reactions, typically minor tranquilizers.
antidepressant drugs	drugs used to treat depression and anxiety.
antipsychotic drugs	drugs used to treat psychotic symptoms such as delusions, hallucinations, and other bizarre behavior.
arbitrary inference	distortion of thinking in which a person draws a conclusion that is not based on any evidence.
authenticity	the genuine, open, and honest response of the therapist to the client.
aversion therapy	form of behavioral therapy in which an undesirable behavior is paired with an aversive stimulus to reduce the frequency of the behavior.
behavior modification or applied behavior analysis	the use of learning techniques to modify or change undesirable behavior and increase desirable behavior.
behavior therapies	action therapies based on the principles of classical and operant conditioning and aimed at changing disordered behavior without concern for the original causes of such behavior.
bilateral anterior cingulotomy	surgical technique that destroys part of the cingulate gyrus. Used to treat obsessive-compulsive disorder, depression, and bipolar disorder.
biomedical therapy	therapy for mental disorders in which a person with a problem is treated with biological or medical methods to relieve symptoms.
Carl Rogers	1902–1987. humanist psychologist who focused on the role of the self-concept and positive regard on personality development.
cognitive behavioral therapy (CBT)	action therapy in which the goal is to help clients overcome problems by learning to think more rationally and logically.
cognitive therapy	therapy in which the focus is on helping clients recognize distortions in their thinking and replace distorted, unrealistic beliefs with more realistic, helpful thoughts.
contingency contract	a formal, written agreement between the therapist and client (or teacher and student; parent and child) in which goals for behavioral change, reinforcements, and penalties are clearly stated.
counter-conditioning	replacing an old conditioned response with a new one by changing the unconditioned stimulus.
cybertherapy	psychotherapy that is offered on the Internet. Also called online, Internet, or Web therapy or counseling.
directive	therapy in which the therapist actively gives interpretations of a client's statements and may suggest certain behavior or actions.
dream interpretation	the analysis of the elements within a patient's reported dream as a means of revealing unconscious conflicts and desires.
eclectic	therapy style that results from combining elements of several different therapy techniques.
electroconvulsive therapy (ECT)	form of biomedical therapy to treat severe depression in which electrodes are placed on either one or both sides of a person's head and an electric current is run through the electrodes that is strong enough to cause a seizure or convulsion.
empathy	the ability of the therapist to understand the feelings of the client.

evidence-based treatment (EBT)	refers to techniques or interventions that have produced desired outcomes or therapeutic change in controlled studies.
exposure therapies	behavioral techniques that introduce the client to situations, under carefully controlled conditions, which are related to their anxieties or fears.
extinction	using techniques in therapy that involve the removal of a reinforcer to reduce the frequency of a particular response, usually an inappropriate or undesirable behavior.
eye-movement desensitization reprocessing (EMDR)	controversial form of therapy for posttraumatic stress disorder and similar anxiety problems in which the client is directed to move the eyes rapidly back and forth while thinking of a disturbing memory.
family counseling or family therapy	a form of group therapy in which family members meet together with a counselor or therapist to resolve problems that affect the entire family.
flooding	technique for treating phobias and other stress disorders in which the person is rapidly and intensely exposed to the fear-provoking situation or object and prevented from making the usual avoidance or escape response.
free association	Freudian technique in which a patient was encouraged to talk about anything that came to mind without fear of negative evaluations.
Fritz Perls	developed and popularized Gestalt therapy.
Gestalt therapy	form of directive insight therapy in which the therapist helps the client to accept all parts of his or her feelings and subjective experiences, using leading questions and planned experiences such as role-playing.
group therapy	type of therapy in which a group of clients meet together with a therapist.
humanistic therapy	psychotherapy focused on conscious, subjective experiences of emotion and a person's sense of self.
insight therapies	therapies in which the main goal is helping people to gain insight with respect to their behavior, thoughts, and feelings.
interpersonal psychotherapy (IPT)	an insight therapy focusing on relationships of the individual with others and the interplay between mood and the events of everyday life.
latent content	the symbolic or hidden meaning of dreams.
magnification and minimization	distortions of thinking in which a person blows a negative event out of proportion to its importance (magnification) while ignoring relevant positive events (minimization).
manifest content	the actual content of one's dream.
modeling	learning through the observation and imitation of others.
nondirective	therapy in which the therapist remains relatively neutral and does not interpret or take direct actions with regard to the client, instead remaining a calm, nonjudging listener while the client talks.
overgeneralization	distortion of thinking in which a person draws sweeping conclusions based on only one incident or event and applies those conclusions to events that are unrelated to the original.
participant modeling	technique in which a model demonstrates the desired behavior in a step-by-step, gradual process while the client is encouraged to imitate the model.
personalization	distortion of thinking in which a person takes responsibility or blame for events that are unconnected to the person.
person-centered therapy	a nondirective insight therapy based on the work of Carl Rogers in which the client does all the talking and the therapist listens.
prefrontal lobotomy	psychosurgery in which the connections of the prefrontal lobes of the brain to the rear portions are severed.
psychoanalysis	an insight therapy based on the theory of Freud, emphasizing the revealing of unconscious conflicts.

psychodynamic therapy	a newer and more general term for therapies based on psychoanalysis, with an emphasis on transference, shorter treatment times, and a more direct therapeutic approach.
psychopharmacology	the use of drugs to control or relieve the symptoms of psychological disorders.
psychosurgery	surgery performed on brain tissue to relieve or control severe psychological disorders.
psychotherapy	therapy for mental disorders in which a person with a problem talks with a psychological professional.
rational-emotive behavioral therapy (REBT)	cognitive–behavioral therapy in which clients are directly challenged in their irrational beliefs and are helped to restructure their thinking into more rational belief statements.
reflection	therapy technique in which the therapist restates what the client says rather than interpreting those statements.
resistance	occurs when a patient becomes reluctant to talk about a certain topic, either changing the subject or becoming silent.
selective thinking	distortion of thinking in which a person focuses on only one aspect of a situation while ignoring all other relevant aspects.
self-help groups (support groups)	a group composed of people who have similar problems and who meet together without a therapist or counselor for the purpose of discussion, problem solving, and social and emotional support.
Sigmund Freud	1856–1939. founder of the psychoanalytic school of thought which focuses on the role of the unconscious on behavior.
systematic desensitization	behavior technique used to treat phobias, in which a client is asked to make a list of ordered fears and taught to relax while concentrating on those fears.
therapeutic alliance	the relationship between therapist and client that develops as a warm, caring, accepting relationship characterized by empathy, mutual respect, and understanding.
therapy	treatment methods aimed at making people feel better and function more effectively.
time-out	an extinction process in which a person is removed from the situation that provides reinforcement for undesirable behavior, usually by being placed in a quiet corner or room away from possible attention and reinforcement opportunities.
token economy	the use of objects called tokens to reinforce behavior in which the tokens can be accumulated and exchanged for desired items or privileges.
transference	in psychoanalysis, the tendency for a patient or client to project positive or negative feelings for important people from the past onto the therapist.
unconditional positive regard	referring to the warmth, respect, and accepting atmosphere created by the therapist for the client in client-centered therapy.

CHAPTER PRACTICE TEST

For the following multiple-choice questions, select the answer you feel best answers the question.

1. Therapies directed at changing disordered behavior are referred to as _____.
    a)   action therapies
    b)   insight therapies
    c)   biomedical therapies
    d)   relationship therapies
    e)   intuitive therapies

2.   Which of the following is the best example of biomedical therapy?
     a)   use of antidepressants to treat depression
     b)   use of insight therapy for social phobia
     c)   psychoanalysis to help treat an anxiety disorder
     d)   flooding treatment for an individual with obsessive-compulsive disorder
     e)   systematic desensitization

3.   Approximately how long ago were the first efforts made to treat the mentally ill with kindness rather than subjecting them to harsh physical treatment?
     a)   500 years ago
     b)   100 years ago
     c)   20 years ago
     d)   50 years ago
     e)   200 years ago

4.   Psychoanalysis was a therapy technique designed by _____.
     a)   Alfred Adler
     b)   Carl Rogers
     c)   Fritz Perls
     d)   Sigmund Freud
     e)   B.F. Skinner

5.   Freud believed one of the indications that he was close to discovering an unconscious conflict was when a patient became unwilling to talk about a topic. He referred to this response in the patient as _____.
     a)   transference
     b)   latent content
     c)   dream analysis
     d)   resistance
     e)   catharsis

6.   Which of the following individuals would be *least* likely to benefit from psychoanalysis?
     a)   Mary, who has a somatoform disorder.
     b)   Kaleem, who suffers from a severe psychotic disorder.
     c)   Pasha, who has panic attacks.
     d)   Lou, who suffers from anxiety.
     e)   Jeff, who suffers from agoraphobia.

7.   The modern psychoanalyst provides more guidance to the patient, asks questions, suggests helpful behaviors, and gives opinions and interpretations. This type of role for the therapist is described as a _____ approach.
     a)   free association
     b)   directive
     c)   biomedical
     d)   nondirective
     e)   eclectic

8. What did Carl Rogers view as a cause of most personal problems and unhappiness?
   a) reinforcement of maladaptive behavior patterns
   b) unrealistic modes of thought employed by many people
   c) a neurochemical imbalance
   d) unresolved unconscious conflicts occur between the id and superego
   e) mismatch between an individual's ideal self and real self

9. Which of the following was NOT one of the four key elements Rogers viewed as necessary for a successful person–therapist relationship?
   a) reflection
   b) unconditional positive regard
   c) authenticity
   d) resistance
   e) empathy

10. What is a major goal of Gestalt therapist?
    a) to facilitate transference
    b) to eliminate the client's undesirable behaviors
    c) to provide unconditional positive regard
    d) help repressed memories emerge from the unconscious
    e) to help clients become more aware of their own feelings

11. Which of the following is a limitation of humanistic therapy?
    a) Clients do not need to be verbal.
    b) There is not enough empirical research to support its basic ideas.
    c) It cannot be used in a variety of contexts.
    d) The therapist runs the risk of having his or her words misinterpreted by the client.
    e) It is only useful with psychotic clients.

12. In the aversion therapy technique known as rapid smoking, the client takes a puff on a cigarette every five or six seconds so that the nicotine now produces unpleasant responses such as nausea and dizziness, so that eventually the cigarette itself produces a sensation of nausea in the client. In terms of classical conditioning, the cigarette functions as the _____ and the nicotine is the _____.
    a) UCS; CS
    b) UCR; CS
    c) CR; UCS
    d) CS; UCR
    e) CS; UCS

13. Which method of treating phobias involves progressive relaxation and exposure to the feared object?
    a) extinction
    b) punishment
    c) token economy
    d) systematic desensitization
    e) aversion therapy

14. In a token economy, what role does the token play in shaping behavior?
   a) The tokens are used as punishment to decrease the maladaptive behavior.
   b) The tokens are used to reinforce the desired behavior.
   c) The token is the actual behavior itself.
   d) The token represents the written contract between the client and therapist.
   e) The token is an unconditioned stimulus.

15. What is an advantage of using operant conditioning in treating undesirable behaviors?
   a) The undesirable behaviors can be treated with defense mechanisms.
   b) Clients can get an understanding of the underlying cause of the problem.
   c) Unconscious urges of clients are revealed.
   d) Clients can change distorted thought patterns that affect behavior.
   e) The results are usually quickly obtained.

16. Which of the following is one of the criticisms of behavior therapy?
   a) It focuses on the underlying cause of behavior and not the symptoms.
   b) Therapy typically lasts for several years and is very expensive.
   c) It focuses too much on the past.
   d) It only relieves some symptoms of schizophrenia but does not treat the overall disorder.
   e) It depends on insight, and it is difficult to apply with disorders like schizophrenia.

17. What is the goal of cognitive therapy?
   a) to help clients gain insight into their unconscious
   b) to help people change their ways of thinking
   c) to change a person's behavior through shaping and reinforcement
   d) to provide unconditional positive regard for the client
   e) to interpret dreams for their latent content

18. Which of these clients is the most likely candidate for Aaron Beck's form of cognitive therapy?
   a) Albert, who suffers from mania.
   b) Barbara, who suffers from depression.
   c) Robert, who suffers from schizophrenia.
   d) Virginia, who has been diagnosed with dissociative identity disorder.
   e) Camia, who suffers from panic attacks.

19. Which approach assumes that disorders come from illogical, irrational cognitions and that changing the thinking patterns to more rational, logical ones will relieve the symptoms of the disorder?
   a) cognitive-behavioral
   b) person-centered
   c) psychoanalytic
   d) Gestalt
   e) analytic psychology

20. According to Albert Ellis, we become unhappy and depressed about events because of
   _____.
   a) our behaviors
   b) our irrational beliefs
   c) the events that happen to us
   d) other people's irrational beliefs
   e) repressed memories

21. Which of the following is the best example of an irrational belief that a therapist using rational-emotive behavioral therapy would challenge you to change?
    a) It is disappointing when things don't go my way.
    b) If I fail this test, it will hurt my grade in this class, but I will try to make it up on the next exam.
    c) There must be something wrong with Bob since he turned down my invitation for a date.
    d) Everyone should love and approve of me, and if they don't, there must be something wrong with me.
    e) If I work hard at my studies, I have a good chance of being successful in school.

22. Which of the following is an advantage of cognitive and cognitive–behavioral therapies?
    a) Clients do not need to be verbal.
    b) They treat the underlying cause of the problem.
    c) They are less expensive and short-term than typical insight therapies.
    d) The therapist decides which of the client's beliefs are rational and which are irrational.
    e) It is nondirective.

23. An advantage to group therapy is that groups _____.
    a) are a source of social support
    b) allow countertransference to occur
    c) provide unconditional approval to the group members
    d) allow an extremely shy person to feel more comfortable speaking up
    e) increase dependency on the therapist

24. In family therapy, the therapist would most likely
    a) focus on one individual who has been identified as the source of the problem.
    b) have each family member come in for therapy individually.
    c) provide unconditional approval to all the family members.
    d) focus on the entire family system to understand the problem.
    e) direct a client to speak to a chair as if a family member were seated in the chair listening.

25. Which of the following is NOT true about self-help support groups?
    a) Self-help groups do not have leaders.
    b) Currently there are only a limited number of self-help groups operating in the United States.
    c) Self-help groups are typically not directed by a licensed therapist.
    d) Self-help groups are usually free to attend.
    e) Self-help groups are usually formed around a particular problem.

26. An advantage of group therapy is that it _____.
    a) can provide help to individuals who may be unable to afford individual psychotherapy
    b) can be helpful to individuals who are uncomfortable in social situations
    c) can only be used alone and not in combination with any other form of therapy
    d) can be helpful to those who have difficulty speaking in public
    e) forces individuals to reveal personal information to others

27. _____ is a controversial form of therapy in which the client is directed to move the eyes rapidly back and forth while thinking of a disturbing memory.
    a) Eye-movement desensitization reprocessing
    b) Systematic desensitization
    c) Eye-memory therapy
    d) Eye therapy

e) Systematic reprocessing

28. Most psychological professionals today take a(n) _____ view of psychotherapy.
    a) group treatment
    b) humanistic
    c) eclectic
    d) behavioral
    e) psychoanalytic

29. The most important aspect of a successful psychotherapy treatment is _____.
    a) the length of the session
    b) the specific approach of the therapist
    c) the relationship between the client and the therapist
    d) the severity of the disorder
    e) the rate the therapist charges for each session

30. Studies that have examined cultural and ethnic factors in the therapeutic relationship have found that _____.
    a) members of minority racial or ethnic groups are more likely to continue treatment until the problem has been resolved
    b) members of the majority racial or ethnic group usually have lower prevalence rates of disorders
    c) members of minority racial or ethnic groups prefer group therapy
    d) members of minority racial or ethnic groups rarely or never seek therapy
    e) members of minority racial or ethnic groups drop out of therapy at a higher rate than members of the majority group

31. Which of the following has NOT been found to be a barrier to effective psychotherapy when the cultural background of client and therapist is different?
    a) language differences
    b) differing cultural values
    c) nonverbal communication
    d) severity of the disorder
    e) social class

32. Antipsychotic drugs treat symptoms such as _____.
    a) hopelessness, sadness, and suicide ideations
    b) excessive worry, repetitive thoughts, and compulsive behavior
    c) hallucinations, delusions, and bizarre behavior
    d) manipulation, lying, and cheating
    e) wearing a "mask" of socially appropriate behavior

33. In what way is the new class of antidepressants known as the SSRIs an improvement over the older types of antidepressants?
    a) They work faster.
    b) They are more effective.
    c) They target a larger number of different neurotransmitters.
    d) They have fewer side effects.
    e) They increase reuptake and reduce the transmission of serotonin.

34. For which disorder was electroconvulsive therapy originally developed as a treatment?
    a) panic
    b) schizophrenia
    c) bipolar disorder
    d) cyclothymia
    e) multiple personality disorder

35. Which of the following is the appropriate definition of psychosurgery?
    a) information given to a patient about a surgical procedure before the surgery in order to prevent anxiety
    b) surgery performed on a patient that was under hypnosis instead of under anesthesia
    c) surgery that severs the spinal cord of the patient
    d) a procedure in which a brief current of electricity is used to trigger a seizure that typically lasts one minute, causing the body to convulse
    e) surgery that is performed on brain tissue to relieve or control severe psychological disorders

36. Psychosurgery is no longer performed in the United States.
    a) True; long-term studies highlighting the serious negative side effects of lobotomies led to the discontinuation of all psychosurgery techniques in the United States.
    b) False; although frontal lobotomies are no longer performed, bilateral anterior cingulotomies are still carried out on patients that have not been helped by any other treatment.
    c) False; frontal lobotomies are still performed on a small number of patients in the United States today.
    d) True; all forms of psychosurgery have been banned in the United States.
    e) True: the threat of a malpractice lawsuit has led to the banning of psychosurgery by the American Medical Association.

37. Which of the following is most likely to be treated with therapy involving the use of virtual reality?
    a) schizophrenia
    b) bipolar disorder
    c) antisocial personality disorder
    d) posttraumatic stress disorder (PTSD)
    e) dissociative identity disorder

CHAPTER PRACTICE TEST ANSWERS

1. a Action therapy emphasizes changing behavior, whereas insight therapy emphasizes understanding one's motives and actions.
2. a Any medical treatment that is directed at changing the physiological functioning of an individual is classified as a biomedical therapy. All of the remaining choices are examples of types of psychotherapy treatments.
3. e In 1793, Philippe Pinel unchained the mentally ill inmates at an asylum in Paris, France, and began the movement of humane treatment for the mentally ill.
4. d Freud was the founder of psychoanalysis, while Rogers developed person-centered therapy.
5. d Resistance occurred when a patient became unwilling to discuss a concept. In transference the patient would transfer positive and negative feelings for an authority figure in his or her past onto the therapist.
6. b People with severe psychotic disorders are less likely to benefit from psychoanalysis than are people who suffer from somatoform or anxiety disorders.

7.   b   A directive approach involves asking questions and suggesting behaviors. The more traditional psychoanalyst typically takes a more nondirective approach in which the therapist remains neutral and does not interpret or take direct actions with regard to the client.

8.   e   Rogers believed the closer the match between a person's ideal and real selves, the happier the person. It was Freud, not Rogers, who viewed unresolved unconscious conflicts between the id and superego as the cause of personal problems.

9.   d   Rogers felt a therapist must provide the four elements of reflection, unconditional positive regard, empathy, and authenticity in order for successful treatment to occur.

10.   e   The major goal of Gestalt therapists is to help clients become more aware of their feelings. Providing unconditional positive regard is the primary goal of person-centered therapy, not Gestalt.

11.   b   The humanistic therapist does not run the risk of having his or her words misinterpreted by the client because the therapist uses reflection as the main means of communication. However, unfortunately at this point there is not enough empirical evidence to support or refute the basic ideas of humanistic therapy.

12.   e   Both the cigarette and nicotine are stimuli, so choices b, c, and d can be immediately eliminated. In rapid smoking, the cigarette serves as the conditioned stimulus and the nicotine serves as the unconditioned stimulus.

13.   d   Systematic desensitization involves progressive relaxation and exposure to the feared object, while extinction involves the removal of a reinforcer to reduce the frequency of a particular response.

14.   b   In a token economy, the tokens are the reinforcers used to shape and strengthen the desired behaviors.

15.   e   Operant conditioning is not concerned with the cause of the problems; rather it is concerned with changing behavior. However, operant conditioning does provide rapid change in behavior in comparison to other therapies.

16.   d   Behavior therapy may help relieve some symptoms but does not treat the overall disorder of schizophrenia.

17.   b   Cognitive therapy focuses on changing an individual's cognitions or thought processes.

18.   b   Beck's cognitive therapy is especially effective in treating distortions related to depression.

19.   a   Cognitive behavioral therapists are concerned with helping clients change their irrational thoughts to more rational and positive thoughts. A person-centered therapist believes disorders come from a mismatch between the ideal self and the real self and a lack of unconditional positive regard.

20.   b   Ellis believes irrational beliefs cause dissatisfaction and depression.

21.   d   Irrational beliefs typically have one thing in common: they are all-or-none types of statements.

22.   c   Cognitive and cognitive–behavioral therapies are relatively inexpensive and are short-term.

23.   a   Group therapy provides social support for people who have similar problems. However, an extremely shy person is not likely to do as well in group therapy.

24.   d   Family therapy focuses on the entire family as a part of the problem.

25.   b   Currently there are an extremely large number of self-help groups in the United States.

26.   a   Group therapy can provide help to those who may be unable to afford individual psychotherapy.

27.   a   EMDR is a form of therapy in which the client is directed to move the eyes rapidly back and forth while thinking of a disturbing memory. Systematic desensitization gradually exposes the client to the feared object while using relaxation techniques to reduce anxiety.

28.   c   An eclectic view is one that combines a number of different approaches to best fit the needs of the client.

29.   c   A number of studies have found that the client-therapist relationship (also called the therapeutic alliance) is the best predictor of successful treatment.

30.   e   Members of minority groups are much more likely to drop out of therapy when compared to members of majority racial and ethnic groups.

31.   d   The severity of the disorder has not been found to be a cultural barrier for treatment.

32.   c   Hallucinations, delusions, and bizarre behaviors are defined as psychotic behaviors and are treated with antipsychotic drugs. Antidepressant drugs, not antipsychotic drugs, treat feelings of hopelessness, sadness, and suicide ideations.

33.   d   The speed of action and effectiveness is similar among the three classes of antidepressants but the main difference is the number of negative side effects. The SSRIs actually target only one neurotransmitter: serotonin.

34.   b   ECT was originally designed to induce seizures in schizophrenics.

35.   e   Severing the spinal cord would lead to the very negative side effect of paralysis of the body. Psychosurgery is performed on brain tissue.

36.   b   Frontal lobotomies are no longer performed; however, bilateral anterior cingulotomies are still performed on severe cases in which no other treatments have been found to be effective.

37.   d   VR is currently being used to treat posttraumatic stress disorder as well as phobias.

CHAPTER PRACTICE FREE RESPONSE QUESTION

You have 25 minutes to answer the following question. You must write in complete sentences and not just list facts. You should make your point clearly and use the language of psychology. Be sure to write legibly and respond to all parts of the question.

The various approaches to psychotherapy can be described as directive or nondirective. Also, therapies tend to be focused more heavily on insight or on action. Describe the following therapies in terms of how directive they are and on their focus, insight, or action. Use techniques from each approach to support your position.

- Rational-emotive behavior therapy
- Modern psychoanalytic therapy
- Person-centered therapy
- Gestalt therapy

SUGGESTED RUBRIC—Students should provide specific details and examples to support their assertions; definitions alone are not sufficient. Information about each topic should be discussed in the context of the question rather than abstractly. Successful essays may include the following arguments:

8 points

- Rational-emotive behavior therapy
  - Score—directive—REBT is very directive because the therapist challenges the client's thinking and points out where the client is not thinking rationally. For example, by pointing out that a situation is "inconvenient" and not "terrible" and directing the client to stop thinking in "catastrophic" terms the REBT therapist is being directive.
  - Score—action—REBT is focused on changing the client's behavior of irrational thinking. New understanding or insight into how his or her thinking is irrational helps, but the end goal is to help the client refrain from practicing the same behaviors. For example, challenging "my way or nothing" statements points out the weaknesses in thinking in absolute terms and strives to reduce the client's behavior of using this pattern of thinking.

- Modern psychoanalytic therapy
  - Score—directive—Modern psychoanalytic therapy is more directive than Freudian therapy. Instead of waiting for information to be "revealed" the therapist will ask questions. For example, the therapist suspects that the client had a bad relationship with a parent. Instead of waiting for the client to reveal information through free association, the therapist asks the client specifically to discuss the parent–child relationship he or she experienced.
  - Score—insight—The focus of modern psychoanalytic therapy is on bringing information to light so the client can have insight. For example, pointing out that the client is transferring anger that he or she is really feeling toward a parent onto the therapist can help the client understand that he or she is hurt and angry toward that parent.
- Person-centered therapy
  - Score—nondirective—Rogerian therapy focuses on facilitating the client's progress toward bringing the real self and ideal selves closer together. Rogerian therapists will not tell the client what to do but rather support the self-exploration by the client.
  - Score—insight—Rogerian therapy is designed to help the client recognize the factors that result in incongruence between the real self and ideal self. Person centered therapy is designed to help clients recognize these barriers and work toward a new understanding of how to approach them.
- Gestalt Therapy
  - Score—directive—Gestalt therapy, as in person-centered therapy, works on helping clients match the real self to the ideal self; however, rather than just reflecting back to the client, a Gestalt therapist prompts the client and plans experiences to help the client gain insight.
  - Score—insight—An important aspect to Gestalt therapy is to help the client understand that his or her real feelings may be held behind a mask of socially acceptable behaviors. The therapist leads the client to a better understanding of his or her feelings and behaviors.

Sample AP Psychology Exam 1

General Instructions for the AP Psychology Multiple Choice Exam

Work efficiently, watch the time, and do not dwell too long on any one question. Come back to questions you skipped and look at them again. No one can be expected to know everything on the exam. If you are unfamiliar with the topic in a question, do not become anxious or upset. Just move on to the next question, and come back to it if you have time.

Psychology
Section 1
Time—1 hour and 10 minutes
100 Questions

Directions: Each question is followed by five choices. Select the choice that best answers the question and enter your choice on the answer sheet.

AP MC Exam 1

Multiple Choice
Identify the letter of the choice that best completes the statement or answers the question.

_____ 1. All of the following are challenges that a researcher can face when conducting an experiment except:
   a. the high degree of reactivity that a participant in an experiment can experience.
   b. having an IRB evaluate his or her research proposal.
   c. eliminating possible confounding variables.
   d. being identified while the experimenter observes people in a natural environment.
   e. finding participants to study.

_____ 2. A person that experiences cycles of sadness and happiness interspersed with normal mood is likely to be diagnosed as:
   a. dysthymic.
   b. manic.
   c. bipolar.
   d. cyclothymic.
   e. hypomanic.

_____ 3. One questionable aspect of Terman's longitudinal study on the gifted is that:
   a. a longitudinal study cannot provide information about the same cohort of subjects over time.
   b. the study did not use a random sample and consisted of almost entirely white, urban, and middle-class children.
   c. Terman did not interfere with the lives of the subjects and try to help them outside of the experiment.
   d. the cross-sectional design of the study was not able to reveal difference in the same individual over time.
   e. the definition of *gifted* was weak because it did not include mathematical abilities.

_____ 4. Correlations can be positive or negative:
   a. but only positive correlations show the inverse relationship between two variables.
   b. and negative correlations are always weaker than positive correlations.
   c. therefore, positive correlations show the effect of the independent variable and negative correlations show the effect of the dependent variable.
   d. and, as a result, negative correlations and positive correlations can be used to make a prediction about how two variables are related.
   e. but only positive correlations can be used to make a prediction.

_____ 5. One difference between the Stanford-Binet and the Wechsler intelligence tests is that:
   a. the Stanford-Binet test uses only a pencil and paper test and the Wechsler uses only a set of performance based activities.
   b. the Stanford-Binet test was developed for use with children while the Wechsler test was the first to develop variations for all ages.
   c. the Stanford-Binet test measures vocabulary and the Wechsler does not.
   d. the Stanford-Binet test uses 200 as a mean score and the Wechsler test uses 100.
   e. the Wechsler test measures vocabulary and the Stanford-Binet test does not.

_____ 6. Structuralism and functionalism are competing schools of thought because:
   a. structuralism focused on the body and functionalism focused on the mind.
   b. structuralism focused on the behaviors of individuals and functionalism focused on internal experiences of individuals.
   c. structuralists were interested in how humans adapted to the environment and functionalists were primarily interested in sensation and perception.
   d. structuralism tried to break consciousness down into elements and functionalism studied the purpose of consciousness.
   e. structuralism investigated internal experiences and functionalism investigated unconscious experiences.

_____ 7. When a miscarriage occurs, it is most likely caused by:
   a. a genetic defect in the way the embryo or fetus is developing that will not allow the infant to survive.
   b. exercise.
   c. stress.
   d. physical trauma to the mother.
   e. environmental factors such as pollution, water contamination, or pesticides.

_____ 8. Inferential statistics consist of statistical techniques that allow researchers to: .
   a. determine the difference between results of a study that are meaningful and those that are merely due to chance variations.
   b. determine the mathematical average of a set of data.
   c. determine if a set of data is positively or negatively skewed.
   d. determine how much the scores in a distribution vary from the central tendency of the data.
   e. determine the score that falls in the middle of an ordered distribution of scores.

_____ 9. The survivor of a bad car accident now has difficulty coordinating muscle movements. The part of the brain most likely injured in the accident is the:
   a. medulla.
   b. thalamus.
   c. pons.
   d. cerebellum.
   e. temporal lobe.

_____ 10. All of the following are concerns raised about dissociative identity disorder except:
   a. Dissociative identity disorder may actually be a misdiagnosis of borderline personality disorder or some other form of anxiety disorder.
   b. The alarming increase in the number people diagnosed in the 1980s gave it the appearance of being a "fad" disorder.
   c. Clients who demonstrate different "personalities" may be simply acting to get attention.
   d. Therapists may be "creating" the disorder in their clients.
   e. People that are faking their symptoms don't need help.

_____ 11. An EEG of a brain displays delta waves. The person that is being given the EEG is most likely:
   a. daydreaming.
   b. awake.
   c. in a light sleep.
   d. in a deep sleep.
   e. brain dead.

_____ 12. Glutamate is:
   a. a depressant.
   b. a narcotic.
   c. an endorphin.
   d. a major excitatory neurotransmitter.
   e. an inhibitory neurotransmitter.

_____ 13. One strength of Costa and McCrae's NEO-PI is that:
   a. taking the test requires a long period of direct contact between the psychologist and the client, which provides ample time for an in-depth understanding of the client to be gained.
   b. there is growing evidence of a cross-cultural basis for the Big Five traits.
   c. the answers are based on self-reports, and the results cannot be manipulated by the client.
   d. the 16 factors assessed by the NEO-PI are comprehensive.
   e. its use of ambiguous pictures promotes projection from the unconscious mind.

_____ 14. After receiving nerve damage in his face from a serious car accident, a police officer lost the ability to move his cheek muscles. According to the facial feedback hypothesis:
   a. the people in the park will think the police officer is kind and friendly.
   b. the police officer will receive positive emotional feedback from others.
   c. the police officer should be feeling an enhanced sense of happiness.
   d. the people in the park will see feedback cues in the officer's uniform and know how to respond emotionally.
   e. the police officer should have a slightly flat affect due to his inability to "put on a happy face."

_____ 15. According to Edward Thorndike, if an action is followed by a pleasurable consequence, it will tend to be repeated. This is known as:
   a. Weber's law.
   b. the law of averages.
   c. the pleasure principle.
   d. the secular trend.
   e. the law of effect.

_____ 16. A normal distribution curve is:
   a. symmetrical, bimodal, and has a standard deviation of 1.
   b. asymmetrical, has a standard deviation of 1, and the mean is a different number than the mode.
   c. symmetrical, has a standard deviation of 1, and the mean is the same number as the mode, but the mean is a different number than the median.
   d. symmetrical, has a standard deviation of 1, and the mean, median, and mode are the same number.
   e. symmetrical, has a standard deviation of 1, and the mean is a different number than the median.

_____ 17. Vibrations of fluid in the cochlea:
   a. can stimulate signals to the brain about frequency of the sound wave but not amplitude.
   b. triggers efferent neural signals about hearing that are sent to the brain.
   c. causes movement that stimulates the hair like cells in the cochlea to send signals about hearing to the brain.
   d. stimulate the hammer, anvil, and stirrup and send signals about hearing to the brain.
   e. stimulate the tympanic membrane and send signals about hearing to the brain.

_____ 18. According to Weber's law of just noticeable differences:
   a. the just noticeable difference grows as humans progress from age 10 to age 20.
   b. the just noticeable difference in not constant as the intensity of the stimulus increases.
   c. the just noticeable difference cannot be determined when working with weak sensory stimuli.
   d. the just noticeable difference is the smallest difference between two stimuli that is detectable 50 percent of the time.
   e. the just noticeable difference is smaller with intense stimuli.

_____ 19. A student enjoys reading, attends class on a regular basis, engages in class discussions, and seeks extra time to discuss topics from class with the teacher. However, the student does not turn in assignments and seems indifferent about grades. It is most likely that this student is:
   a. intrinsically motivated to learn.
   b. extrinsically motivate to learn.
   c. high in need for achievement.
   d. unmotivated to learn.
   e. low in need for achievement.

_____ 20. The boy sitting in the next seat on the bus is pretending that a mitten is a cell phone, believes that rabbits deliver candy and eggs to children in the spring, argues that Mount Rushmore can fit into a lunch box, and believes that flowing water is alive. This child is most likely in the:
   a. sensory-motor stage of cognitive development.
   b. preoperational stage of cognitive development.
   c. proximal stage of cognitive development.
   d. concrete operations stage of cognitive development.
   e. post-formal stage of cognitive development.

_____ 21. The ancient surgical practice of cutting holes in skulls is known as:
   a. humor identification.
   b. phrenology.
   c. mesmerism.
   d. trephining.
   e. agoraphobia.

_____ 22. A person begins jogging, and after the first mile, his or her heart rate and respiration is elevated and he or she is perspiring. The system responsible for the physiological response to the exercise is:
a. the sympathetic nervous system.
b. the limbic system.
c. the olfactory system.
d. the gustatory system.
e. the parasympathetic nervous system.

_____ 23. If new parents were purchasing a mobile to hang above a newborn's crib, which of the following would be a characteristic the baby would prefer?
a. low contrasts in color
b. simple patterns
c. two dimensions
d. positioned at least three feet away from the baby's face
e. complex patterns

_____ 24. Watching violence on television causes children to behave violently. This statement can be challenged because:
a. children do not behave violently.
b. not all children watch television.
c. cause is inferred from correlation.
d. violence on television has no influence on the behavior of children.
e. violent television programs also contain love scenes.

_____ 25. Which of the following is the correct order for the levels of intellectual disability from most limited to least limited?
a. severe, profound, mild, moderate
b. severe, profound, moderate, mild
c. mild, moderate, profound, and severe
d. profound, severe, moderate, mild
e. mild, moderate, severe, profound

_____ 26. Evidence that suggests a need for REM sleep includes research indicating that:
a. people deprived of REM sleep will experience REM rebound once they are allowed a normal night of rest.
b. when infants are in REM sleep they cannot move around and are safer during sleep.
c. physical changes in the brain associated with storing a memory are more common during REM sleep.
d. a physically demanding day leads to a night of sleep with increased time in REM sleep.
e. people deprived of REM sleep become paranoid.

_____ 27. Recent developments in psychology are prompting researchers to:
a. study women and minority groups less and shift to a growing focus on men of European descent.
b. study the unconscious mind to determine if rewards and punishments change human behavior.
c. study human factors psychology less and human instincts more.
d. study non-Western cultures to determine if the research from western cultures is valid to more diverse populations.
e. develop tests that are biased against populations from agrarian cultures.

_____ 28. According to Joan Freeman's longitudinal study of 210 gifted and non-gifted children in Great Britain:
   a. the level of giftedness found in children correlates with the level of happiness experienced later in life.
   b. gifted children need to be pushed into taking advanced exams.
   c. the greater the challenges faced in childhood, the greater the levels of success achieved by gifted individuals in adulthood.
   d. gifted children pushed into taking advanced exams early often grow up to be disappointed, somewhat unhappy adults.
   e. there is no difference between gifted and non-gifted children when examined later in life as adults.

_____ 29. When giving responses in private:
   a. women will give conforming responses at a higher rate than they give conforming responses in public.
   b. women are less likely to give conforming responses than men.
   c. women will give conforming responses at the same rate they give conforming responses in public.
   d. women will give conforming responses at the same rate as men.
   e. women are more likely to give conforming responses than men.

_____ 30. Which of the following tasks involves the use of semantic memory?
   a. riding a bicycle
   b. roller skating
   c. washing your hands
   d. eating potato chips
   e. answering trivia questions

_____ 31. Infants are born with the ability to recognize all phonemes; however, after about nine months:
   a. they have the ability to recognize and to babble all phonemes.
   b. that ability has expanded to include all phonemes, morphemes, and pragmatics.
   c. the phoneme-based language has expanded into semantics that babies use when communicating with each other.
   d. recognizing phonemes is replaced with the ability to recognize morphemes.
   e. that ability has deteriorated and the infant recognizes only the phonemes of the language to which the infant is exposed.

_____ 32. Humanistic therapy is:
   a. directive toward the client and non-directive toward the therapist.
   b. client centered and directive.
   c. non-directive and client centered.
   d. therapist centered and directive.
   e. non-directive and therapist centered.

_____ 33. A set of characteristics believed to be shared by all members of a particular category is a:
   a. prejudice.
   b. dispositional cause.
   c. situational cause.
   d. stereotype.
   e. scapegoating.

_____ 34. A perfect positive correlation is signified by the correlation coefficient of:
   a. +10.00.
   b. +1.00.
   c. -1.00.
   d. -10.00.
   e. 0.00.

_____ 35. A difference between psychotherapy and biomedical therapy is:
   a. psychotherapy relies on talking with people about their thoughts, and biomedical therapy relies on talking with people about their behaviors.
   b. a psychotherapist listens and tries to help people understand their problems or change the behavior that causes them while biomedical therapy uses medical interventions to bring the symptoms under control.
   c. psychotherapy relies on talking with people about their thoughts and behaviors while biomedical therapy relies on projective tests for information.
   d. psychotherapy focuses only on behaviors, and biomedical therapy focuses only on thoughts.
   e. psychotherapy employs the use of drugs, and biomedical therapy does not.

_____ 36. The concept of instinctive drift is best illustrated by:
   a. a squirrel that returns to the same place it found an acorn last year.
   b. a raccoon that rubs coins together and "dips" them into a coin slot without dropping them.
   c. a child that puts his or her laundry away for an ice cream cone.
   d. a dog that sits, shakes hands, and rolls over before getting a treat.
   e. a cat that stays off the kitchen counter after being squirted with a spray of water.

_____ 37. The difference between manifest and latent content in dreams is:
   a. manifest content is the symbolic meaning of the dream content, but latent content is the actual dream and its events.
   b. manifest content is rare in dreams, and latent content is common.
   c. some dreams contain manifest content, but all dreams contain latent content.
   d. manifest content is the actual dream and its events, but latent content is the symbolic meaning of the dream.
   e. manifest content reveals unconscious conflicts, and latent content reveals conscious conflicts.

_____ 38. At $p < .01$ the probability that the results of an experiment were due to chance is 1 out of 100. At $p < .05$ the probability that the results of an experiment were due to chance is:
   a. more likely than at $p < .10$
   b. greater than the probability the results were due to the change in the independent variable in the experiment.
   c. impossible to determine because of the standard error of measurement.
   d. greater than at $p < .01$
   e. less than at $p < .01$

_____ 39. A person who has the use of only one eye is standing still and looking down the center of a long and straight section of railroad track. Which of the following cues could most likely be applied to visual perception in this situation by a person with the use of only one eye?
   a. motion parallax
   b. binocular disparity
   c. convergence
   d. linear perspective
   e. binocular cues of perception

_____ 40. In researching age-related changes the longitudinal research design is:
    a. structured so that different age groups are sampled and studied at one time.
    b. constructed in such a way as to include participants with long term goals.
    c. structured so that one group of people is followed and assessed at different times as the group ages.
    d. used because of its advantages, such as taking less time to complete than cross sectional research.
    e. organized so that groups are selected from different regions in the world from east to west.

_____ 41. Elizabeth Loftus studied eye witness testimony and found that:
    a. people have hindsight bias, which is the tendency to falsely believe they would correctly predict the outcome of a event in advance.
    b. there is little reason to be concerned about eye witnesses testimony because of the "memory construction" process.
    c. giving eye witnesses misinformation about an event can increase the inaccuracy of their testimony.
    d. eye witness testimony rarely includes false information.
    e. hypnotized people have more accurate memories than people that are fully awake.

_____ 42. The dopamine hypothesis suggests that:
    a. a change in dopamine levels is linked to a change in behavior; therefore it can be concluded that dopamine causes schizophrenia.
    b. increased dopamine is linked to negative symptoms of schizophrenia.
    c. there are two types of dopamine, and one causes negative symptoms of schizophrenia.
    d. decreased dopamine is linked to negative symptoms of schizophrenia.
    e. increased dopamine is linked to positive symptoms of schizophrenia.

_____ 43. Which of the following is true of cultural syndromes?
    a. Cultural syndromes are not found in Asian cultures.
    b. Depression is a culture bound syndrome associated with Western cultures.
    c. Cultural syndromes are primarily established by genetic differences.
    d. Cultural syndromes are found specifically in particular cultures.
    e. Schizophrenia is not found in Eastern cultures and is a culture bound syndrome in Western cultures.

_____ 44. When listening to a lecture, which of the following is used to keep the beginning of a sentence in your mind until the end of a sentence is reached?
    a. iconic memory
    b. flashbulb memory
    c. procedural memory
    d. echoic memory
    e. elaborate encoding

_____ 45. An example of Elkind's idea of a "personal fable" is:
    a. "I am being under utilized in this job."
    b. "I am special and it can't happen to me."
    c. "Life is too short to spend it waiting for something good to happen."
    d. "Good grades in school will help me get into college."
    e. "I am taller than you."

46. A child is interested in the differences between boys and girls, is attracted to the opposite sexed parent, and considers the same sexed parent an anxiety causing force. According to Freud, this child is in the psycho-sexual stage known as:
   a. Oedipal.
   b. phallic.
   c. genital.
   d. latent.
   e. oral.

47. Kosslyn (1983) asked subjects questions such as the following: "Do frogs have lips and a stubby tail?" Kosslyn was researching the idea of:
   a. concepts.
   b. mental imagery.
   c. network model of language.
   d. mechanical solutions.
   e. the network model of memory.

48. Research on how well attitude can predict behavior indicates that:
   a. attitude can predict behavior in all situations.
   b. economic factors do not influence the continuity between attitude and behavior.
   c. the more important the attitude appears, the more likely the behavior will match the attitude.
   d. attitude cannot be used to predict behavior.
   e. general attitudes predict behavior better than specific attitudes.

49. Which of the following is not one of Gardner's multiple intelligences?
   a. logical/mathematical
   b. visual/spatial
   c. environmental
   d. musical
   e. gustatory

50. The number of tickets a police officer writes is going up each month. Which of the following could best explain this increase through negative reinforcement?
   a. The police chief yells at the officers when they let people off with a warning after stopping them for speeding.
   b. The police officer hears complaints from every person that receives a ticket.
   c. The police chief gives officers in the top 10 percent of ticket writing each month a gift certificate.
   d. The police officer receives time off work for writing the most tickets in a month.
   e. The police officer feels good about keeping the roads safe for other drivers after writing a ticket.

51. After several hours of trying and experimenting with a puzzle, a student suddenly gets the solution and solves the puzzle. This is a good example of:
   a. insight.
   b. drive reduction.
   c. functional fixedness.
   d. meta analysis.
   e. mental set.

_____ 52. Humanism, as a theoretical perspective in psychology, challenged the behavioral and psychoanalytic perspectives because:
    a. they both did not have a research base to support their perspectives.
    b. they both put too much emphasis on external factors of human behavior.
    c. they both put too much emphasis on biological drives.
    d. they did not give enough attention to important human qualities and the human potential for growth.
    e. they both did a great amount of research studying animals, which reduced the amount of time and money spent on studying humans.

_____ 53. Which of the following is most characteristic of a prototype of bird?
    a. ostrich
    b. emu
    c. kiwi
    d. penguin
    e. robin

_____ 54. Two groups of rats are put in identical mazes every day for ten days. One group is reinforced with food for learning the maze. The other group is left to wander the maze without reinforcement. According to Edward Tolman:
    a. the reinforced group is learning the maze but the non-reinforced group is not learning the maze.
    b. the rats are showing instinctive drift by wondering through the maze tunnels.
    c. both groups of rats are learning the maze, but the second group isn't demonstrating their latent learning.
    d. both groups of rat are learning the mazes at the same pace.
    e. reinforcement is necessary for learning to take place.

_____ 55. The type of processing in which people attend to the content of the message is known as:
    a. affective processing.
    b. un-encoded processing.
    c. dual processing.
    d. peripheral-route processing.
    e. central-route processing,

_____ 56. Which of the following is the best example of an operational definition?
    a. Rhonda is studying love, which she operationally defines as "caring."
    b. Jon is studying happiness, which he operationally defines as "number of smiles per minute."
    c. Debbie is studying anger, which she operationally defines as "hurting others feelings."
    d. Susie is studying achievement, which she operationally defines as "trying hard."
    e. Lana is studying hunger, which she operationally defines as "wanting food."

_____ 57. According to Dweck, a person that believes intelligence is fixed and unchangeable:
    a. values the learning process more than "looking smart" by always having the right answer.
    b. is likely to have a strong internal locus of control.
    c. is likely to engage in intelligence building activities.
    d. may demonstrate an external locus of control, give up easily, or avoid situations in which failure is possible.
    e. considers an internal locus of control over intelligence a valuable personal asset.

_____ 58. All of the following are anxiety-based disorders except:
   a. schizophrenia.
   b. agoraphobia.
   c. panic disorder with agoraphobia.
   d. panic disorder.
   e. obsessive-compulsive disorder.

_____ 59. The three elements of emotion are:
   a. subjective experience, social, and informational.
   b. physiological, behavioral, and subjective experience.
   c. physiological, social, and behavioral.
   d. behavioral, cognitive, and social.
   e. cultural, genetic, and social.

_____ 60. Maslow, Alderfer, and Ryan and Deci have all incorporated which need into their theories?
   a. challenge
   b. work
   c. relatedness
   d. laughter
   e. exercise

_____ 61. The tendency of one's expectations to affect one's behavior in such a way as to make the expectations more likely to occur is known as:
   a. the realistic conflict theory.
   b. a stereotype vulnerability.
   c. the social cognitive theory.
   d. the social identity theory.
   e. a self-fulfilling prophecy.

_____ 62. Afferent and efferent neurons:
   a. link the spinal cord to the brain.
   b. process information in the brain.
   c. carry messages to and from the spinal cord.
   d. form the neural network in the neocortex.
   e. are found mainly in the brain and the spinal cord.

_____ 63. People who are high in nAch are likely to:
   a. look for careers and hobbies that allow others to evaluate them.
   b. show signs of Parkinson's disease.
   c. show little persistence in difficult activities.
   d. are only driven by external motivation.
   e. tend to select very easy tasks instead of very difficult tasks.

_____ 64. On the Wechsler Intelligence Scales the mean is 100 and the standard deviation is 15. This means that:
   a. a score of 112 is within one standard deviation of the mean.
   b. a score of 131 is within one standard deviation of the mean.
   c. scores greater than 15 and less than 115 are within one standard deviation of the mean.
   d. a score of 80 is within one standard deviation of the mean.
   e. a score of 15 is within one standard deviation of the mean.

_____ 65. Antisocial personality disorder is associated with:
   a. extreme suspicion of others.
   b. showing habitual disregard for both the law and rights of others.
   c. a strong sense of conscience or morals.
   d. a tendency to overact and draw attention from others.
   e. being moody and unstable.

_____ 66. The effects of heroin on an addict's body include:
   a. a reduction of norepinephrine followed by activation of the sympathetic nervous system.
   b. an excitatory affect on the body's pain receptors.
   c. elevated levels of dopamine.
   d. a disruption of the body's natural endorphin system.
   e. an intense release of glutamate.

_____ 67. Regarding the effectiveness of psychotherapy, it is most accurate to say that:
   a. few people found psychotherapy to be effective.
   b. the effectiveness of psychotherapy is easy to study.
   c. gaining insights and feelings of control are easily evaluated.
   d. no one psychotherapy is the most effective or works for every type of problem.
   e. staying in therapy longer does not result in greater improvement for a client.

_____ 68. According to Rotter, people who assume that their own actions and decisions directly affect the consequences they experience are said to be:
   a. internal in cognition but external in control.
   b. cognitive in locus of control.
   c. generally low in their sense of self efficacy.
   d. unclear about the relationship between expectancy and behavior.
   e. internal in locus of control.

_____ 69. Two people are standing near one another at a distance from an observer. When asked to describe the two people, the observer describes the two people as a "couple." This best illustrates the Gestalt principle of:
   a. proximity.
   b. closure.
   c. similarity.
   d. common fate.
   e. continuity.

_____ 70. Which of the following phrases best applies to mental abilities in old age?
   a. "Use it or lose it."
   b. "Stop and smell the roses."
   c. "Less is more."
   d. "You get what you pay for."
   e. "A penny saved is a penny earned."

_____ 71. Erik Erikson would likely agree that:
   a. babies should not be left to "cry it out" when they want attention.
   b. babies should be left to cry out their anxieties of being alone.
   c. social development is complete by puberty.
   d. psycho-sexual development is more important than psycho-social development.
   e. clinging to power and control is a positive way to spend the latter years of a career.

_____ 72. There are more men with color blindness than women because:
  a. color blindness is a recessive trait. Men have only one X chromosome and are more vulnerable to recessive genes.
  b. women have two Y chromosomes, and they are protected by the second one.
  c. males experience greater prenatal exposure to teratogens and as a result contract color blindness more often.
  d. women are genetically predisposed to have better vision than men.
  e. color blindness is a recessive trait and needs only one gene to be present.

_____ 73. Which of the following could most likely be determined from an MRI scan?
  a. activity in the visual cortex
  b. the location of emotional responses in the brain
  c. which lobe of the brain is activated when thinking about the melody of a song
  d. the location of a tumor in the brain
  e. the location of Broca's area

_____ 74. According to the research by Stanley Milgam on obedience:
  a. none of the "teachers" would give a "shock" to the "learners."
  b. 100 percent of the "teachers" would give the most severe "shock" to the "learners."
  c. only female "teachers" would give a "shock" to the "learners."
  d. around 65 percent of the "teachers" would give the most severe "shock" to the "learners" even when the "learner" made a protest.
  e. very few of the "teachers" would give a "shock" to the "learners."

_____ 75. Habituation is experienced when:
  a. sensory receptors are still responding to stimulation, but the lower centers of the brain are not sending the signals from those receptors to the cortex.
  b. a person performs a behavior automatically without thinking.
  c. a drug addiction becomes a part of a person's daily habits.
  d. mild sensations are experienced but are consciously ignored.
  e. sensory receptors are no longer sending signals to the brain.

_____ 76. Which of the following statements is most characteristic of projection?
  a. "When I go to my parents' house I feel uneasy."
  b. "That cloud looks like George Washington's picture on a dollar bill."
  c. "I feel like I am trying to live up to my parents' goals for my life, when I would rather be surfing."
  d. "I will give you a cookie if you do your homework."
  e. "I like ice cream."

_____ 77. An example of a discriminative stimulus is:
  a. checking for change in a vending machine.
  b. turning in an assignment for a treat.
  c. smiling at a person after giving them a hug.
  d. complaining about receiving homework.
  e. a dog only checks its food dish for food when it sees the dog food bag is open.

_____ 78. If a person participates in a group that shares beliefs about an issue, the person will most likely:
  a. experience no effect on his or her personal beliefs.
  b. experience a weakening of the shared beliefs.
  c. experience a strengthening, or polarization, of his or her personal beliefs.
  d. begin to question the beliefs he or she shares with the group.
  e. experience a weakening in his or her personal beliefs, but the group will experience a strengthening overall in shared beliefs.

_____ 79. A personality theorist explains that an individual's personality is the result of certain traits being reinforced and others being punished. This personality theorist explains personality development from the:
a. evolutionary view.
b. humanistic view.
c. psychodynamic view.
d. biological view.
e. behaviorist view.

_____ 80. One drawback to humanistic therapies is:
a. there is little experimental research to support the basic ideas on which this type of therapy is founded.
b. it is unethical to be so non-directive.
c. it doesn't work with intelligent clients.
d. it only works with schizophrenic clients.
e. the comments from the therapist are often misinterpreted because they are original thoughts.

_____ 81. REBT can be described as a:
a. directive therapy.
b. non-directive therapy focused on insight.
c. a humanistic approach to therapy.
d. non-directive therapy focused on identifying unconscious conflicts.
e. directive therapy focused on identifying unconscious conflicts.

_____ 82. Classical conditioning is limited in its ability to explain learning because:
a. it does not work on adults and can only explain the learning behavior of children.
b. generalization does not occur in the case of second-order conditioning.
c. it can only be used to teach new associations to old behaviors, and it does not explain how new behaviors are learned.
d. learning by association only works on animals.
e. the unconditioned stimulus must be a visual stimulus.

_____ 83. According to the evolutionary perspective in psychology:
a. the behaviors of humans and their responses to rewards and punishments should be the primary focus of study.
b. the influence of forces like poverty and crime on people should be the primary focus of study.
c. the unconscious mind and the influence of early childhood experiences should be the primary focus of study.
d. the adaptive quality of human characteristics like aggression and language should be the primary focus of study.
e. the stresses and worries of everyday life as people strive to achieve their full potential should be the primary focus of study.

_____ 84. Each of the following is a component of language except:
a. phonemes.
b. pragmatics.
c. morphemes.
d. generativity
e. semantic.

85. As people age their vision changes because:
    a. the cornea becomes overly flexible, which makes it difficult to focus on distant objects.
    b. microsaccadic movements stop and sensory adaptation increases.
    c. the cornea hardens and makes it difficult to focus on distant objects.
    d. the cornea hardens and becomes less flexible, which leads to the onset of presbyopia.
    e. the ability to focus an objects that are near becomes more difficult because the size of the blind spot increases.

86. The myelin that coats the axons of neurons:
    a. contains the neurotransmitters for inhibitory neural activity.
    b. is generated by afferent neurons.
    c. is completely developed at birth.
    d. speeds up the transmission of neural impulses.
    e. contains the neurotransmitters for excitatory neural activity.

87. Standardizing a test would include all of the following except:
    a. using a sample of people from the group for whom the test was designed.
    b. giving the test to groups for whom the test was designed.
    c. giving the test to a non-random sample of the group for whom the test was designed.
    d. having all test subjects take the test under the same conditions.
    e. following a set procedure for administering the test.

88. The adaptive theory of sleep suggests that:
    a. prey animals sleep more and during the day while predators sleep less and during the day.
    b. animals higher up on the food chain need less sleep.
    c. prey and predator animals have similar sleeping patterns.
    d. prey animals sleep less and at night while predators sleep more and during the day.
    e. predator animals sleep less than prey animals.

89. Chemical substances that can mimic or enhance the effects of neurotransmitters on the receptor sites of the next cell are known as:
    a. protagonists.
    b. antagonists.
    c. agonists.
    d. geons.
    e. transducers.

90. Two unhappy campers are sitting in the rain on a neatly stacked pile of bricks. The campers are not happy because they were unable to pitch their tent before the rain started. The sad campers forgot to bring a hammer along and didn't have anything to drive the tent stakes into the ground. The campers are experiencing functional fixedness because:
    a. they didn't keep an emergency tool kit in the car.
    b. they failed to realize that while a brick is typically used for construction, it could also be used to pound in a tent stake.
    c. rain was in the weekend's weather forecast but they went to the campground anyway.
    d. they should have made a list of things needed when camping before packing up and driving to the campground.
    e. they could have borrowed a hammer form a neighboring camp site.

91. All of the following are associated with recessive genes except:
   a. cystic fibrosis.
   b. brown hair.
   c. blond hair.
   d. red hair.
   e. sickle cell anemia.

92. Terms like "unconscious," "repression," and "psycho-sexual" are best associated with:
   a. trait theorists.
   b. humanistic psychology.
   c. the psychodynamic perspective.
   d. the biological perspective.
   e. the behaviorists.

93. One way to use operant conditioning to modify behavior is to:
   a. use flooding to get clients to face their fears.
   b. interpret the symbolic meaning of clients' dreams to reveal unconscious conflicts.
   c. challenge the irrational thinking of the client.
   d. model the correct behavior for the client.
   e. create a token economy and let clients earn tokens for behaving correctly.

94. All of the following are considered by Ekman and Friesen to be universal emotions except:
   a. sadness.
   b. shame.
   c. disgust.
   d. anger.
   e. contempt.

95. The tendency for people to overestimate the influence of another person's internal characteristics on behavior and underestimate the influence of their situation is called:
   a. stereotyping.
   b. the fundamental attribution error.
   c. the central route to persuasion.
   d. cognitive dissonance.
   e. the halo effect.

96. Volunteers who spent several days without information about day or night:
   a. experienced a higher degree of anxiety because of a need to know the time of day.
   b. began to have sleep wake cycles of less than 24 hours.
   c. shifted in their sleep routines to a pattern of micro sleeps.
   d. saw no change in their sleep wake cycles.
   e. experienced a slightly longer sleep wake cycle of 25 hours.

97. Which of the following questions is least culturally biased?
   a. "Who was the first president of the United States?"
   b. "How do you catch a fish?"
   c. "Where is your heart?"
   d. "Which is better to eat, pork or beef?"
   e. "How long do you cook spaghetti?"

_____ 98. Which of the following is true about case studies?
    a.   Case studies are not vulnerable to bias by the person conducting the study.
    b.   Researchers can apply the information from a case study to similar people.
    c.   A case study can be used to make predictions about other people.
    d.   A case study uses an experimental group and a control group.
    e.   A case study is used to gather in depth information about a single person.

_____ 99. The villain in the latest graphic novel doesn't wait for a pause in a conversation to begin talking, stands uncomfortably close to others in a conversation, uses gestures in ways that are difficult to understand, and speaks to everyone as if he were speaking to a child. Clearly, as it applies to the use of language, this villain has a lot to learn about:
    a.   grammar.
    b.   deep structure.
    c.   relativity.
    d.   syntax.
    e.   pragmatics.

_____ 100.   One thing that intelligence tests do well is:
    a.   predict academic success for those who score at the higher and lower ends of the normal curve.
    b.   assess the differences in intelligence between cultures.
    c.   provide reliable data for the placement of students in the fine arts.
    d.   predict the ability to be resilient and strive for success in life.
    e.   measure the ability for creativity and self-expression.

Psychology
Section II
Time—50 minutes
Percent of total grade—33 1/3

Directions: You have 50 minutes to answer both questions. You must do more than list facts. Present your answers in complete sentences based on your analysis of the questions. Use the appropriate psychological terminology.

AP Style FRQ 1

Terri lives in Los Angeles and Jamie lives in New York City. Terri decides to fly to New York City and spend spring break with Jamie. Describe and give an example of how the following could apply to Terri's experiences while on spring break in New York.

- Circadian rhythm
- Schema
- Internal locus of control
- Extraversion
- Positive reinforcement
- Confirmation bias

AP Style FRQ 2

It is after dark and Chitkala is waiting at a bus stop. Chitkala sees two people walking side by side and heading in the direction of the bus stop. One person is tall and is wearing a hat and the other person is of average height and is not wearing a hat. Unexpectedly, the tall person with a hat runs forward, grabs a purse from a women standing near Chitkala, and races around the corner and out of view. The person without a hat immediately turns around, runs in the opposite direction, and also disappears out of view. Shortly after the incident the police arrive and question Chitkala.

(A) Give an example of how the following could contribute to Chitkala giving an ACCURATE account of the events at the bus stop to the police.
- Limbic system
- Social facilitation
- Elaborative rehearsal

(B) Give an example of how the following could contribute to Chitkala giving an INACCURATE account of the events at the bus stop to the police.
- Cones and color vision
- Gestalt Law of Proximity
- Fundamental attribution error

MULTIPLE CHOICE

1. ANS: D

    An experimenter would not be using naturalistic observation so being discovered is not a challenge of an experiment.

2. ANS: D

    A person who experiences cycles of sadness and happiness interspersed with normal mood is likely to be diagnosed as cyclothymic. Bipolar involves extreme mood swings ranging from severe depression to manic episodes.

3. ANS: B

    Once questionable aspect of Terman's longitudinal study on the gifted is that the study did not use a random sample and consisted of almost entirely white, urban, and middle-class children.

4. ANS: D

    Correlations, whether positive or negative, can be used to predict a relationship between two variables.

5. ANS: B

    One difference between the Stanford-Binet and the Wechsler intelligence tests is the Stanford-Binet test was developed for use with children while the Wechsler test was the first to develop variations for all ages.

6. ANS: D

    Structuralism was focused on internal experiences and used introspection as their method of studying the mind. Structuralists tried to break consciousness down into elemental forms of emotion, and sensation. Functionalism was more practical and looked at the "whys" of human behavior.

7. ANS: A

    When a miscarriage occurs, it is most likely caused by a genetic defect in the way the embryo or fetus is developing that will not allow the infant to survive.

8. ANS: A

    Inferential statistics consist of statistical techniques that allow researchers to determine the difference between results of a study that are meaningful and those that are merely due to chance variations.

9. ANS: D

    The cerebellum plays a primary role in coordinating muscle movements.

10. ANS: E

    There are a number of concerns surrounding the status of dissociative identity disorder; however, whether or not the person is faking their symptoms, he or she may be in deep psychological trouble and need real help.

11. ANS: D

    Delta waves are associated with deep sleep. A waking brain is associated with beta waves.

12. ANS: D

    Glutamate is the brain's most common excitatory neurotransmitter.

13. ANS: B

A strength of Costa and McCrae's NEO-PI is that there is growing evidence of a cross-cultural basis for the Big Five traits.

14. ANS: E

According to the facial feedback hypotheses, the police officer should have a slightly flat emotional affect because of the inability to express a smile.

15. ANS: E

Thorndike developed the idea of the "law of effect" to help explain behavior of cats when they learn to escape from his "puzzle" boxes.

16. ANS: D

On a standard curve the mean, median, and mode are the same number. A standard curve is symmetrical, and it also has a standard deviation of 1. Skewed curves have a standard deviation of more or less than one.

17. ANS: C

Vibrations of fluid in the cochlea causes movement that stimulates the hair-like cells in the cochlea to send signals about hearing to the brain. Efferent neural signals are motor signals sent from the brain to the body.

18. ANS: D

According to Weber's law of just noticeable difference, the just noticeable difference is the smallest difference between two stimuli that is detectable 50 percent of the time.

19. ANS: A

This student is most likely intrinsically motivated to learn. There is not enough information in the question to determine the achievement needs in the student.

20. ANS: B

This child is most likely in the preoperational stage of cognitive development.

21. ANS: D

The practice of cutting holes in skulls is known as trephining. Phrenology is the study of bumps on the skull.

22. ANS: A

The sympathetic nervous system is responsible for body arousal, and the parasympathetic system is for restoring the body to homeostasis.

23. ANS: E

Newborns prefer complex patterns and three dimensions. Also, their vision for low contrasts in colors is limited, and they can only see clearly from about 7 to 12 inches from their face.

24. ANS: C

The statement is best challenged by the error of inferring cause from correlation. The other items may or may not be true, but it is always an error in thinking to infer cause from correlation.

25. ANS: D

The correct order from most limited to least limited is profound, severe, moderate, mild.

26. ANS: A

Evidence that suggests a need for REM sleep includes research that indicates people deprived of REM sleep will experience REM rebound when allowed a normal nights rest. REM rebound is an increase in the percentage of sleep spent in REM sleep after a period of REM deprivation.

27. ANS: D

A growing interest in cultural diversity is prompting researchers to challenge traditional perspectives in psychology. Now investigations are being conducted to see if the findings from research in Western cultures apply to all humanity.

28. ANS: D

According to Joan Freeman, gifted children pushed into taking advanced exams early often grow up to be disappointed, somewhat unhappy adults.

29. ANS: D

In private, women will give conforming responses at the same rate as men; however, women will give conforming responses at a higher rate than men when giving responses in public.

30. ANS: E

Semantic memory is information like the meanings of words, concepts, and terms as well as names of objects and math skills. The other choices involve implicit memory.

31. ANS: E

Infants are born with the ability to recognize all phonemes; however, after about nine months that ability has deteriorated and the infant recognizes only the phonemes of the language to which the infant is exposed.

32. ANS: C

Humanistic therapy is non-directive and client centered. Rogers believed that the goal of the therapist should be to provide the unconditional positive regard that has been absent from the client's life.

33. ANS: D

A set of characteristics believed to be shared by all members of a particular category is a stereotype. An often negative attitude based on a stereotype is prejudice.

34. ANS: B

Because it is a direct and perfect relationship between two variables, a positive correlation is shown by a straight line that angles upward from left to right, and the correlational coefficient is +1.

35. ANS: B

A difference between psychotherapy and biomedical therapy is a psychotherapist listens and tries to help people understand their problems or change the behavior that causes them while biomedical therapy uses medical interventions to bring the symptoms under control. Biomedical therapists may prescribe drugs, electro-shock, or surgery to help patients.

36. ANS: B

When a pattern of behavior mirrors an instinctive behavior, like a raccoon "washing" a coin, it is an example of instinctive drift.

37. ANS: D

The difference between manifest and latent content in dreams is manifest content is the actual dream and its events, but latent content is the symbolic meaning of the dream. According to Freud, the latent content must be interpreted to reveal unconscious conflicts.

38. ANS: D

At $p < .05$ the chance of an erroneous conclusion is 5 out of 100 and is greater than the chance at $p < .01$

39. ANS: D

When looking down a long and straight section of railroad, the two sides of the tracks appear to merge together in the distance producing the illusion that the rails converge. The other choices are binocular cues and would be less relevant for a person that only has one eye.

40. ANS: C

In researching age-related changes the longitudinal research design is structured such that one group of people is followed and assessed at different times as the group ages.

41. ANS: C

Loftus found that by giving eye witnesses misinformation about an event can increase the inaccuracy of their testimony.

42. ANS: E

The dopamine hypothesis suggests that increased dopamine is linked to positive symptoms of schizophrenia. However, this is a correlation, and cause cannot be inferred from correlation.

43. ANS: D

Culture bound syndromes are found specifically in particular cultures.

44. ANS: D

Echoic memory is the ability to keep a sound or voice in your memory for brief period before it is processed.

45. ANS: B

"I am special and it can't happen to me" is an example of a "personal fable" because is reflects the person has become convinced that he or she is special, one of a kind, and that no one else has ever had these thoughts and feelings before them.

46. ANS: B

This child is in the phallic stage. Oedipal is not a stage of development because it is a "complex" used by Freud to explain gender identification.

47. ANS: A

Kosslyn was studying the idea of mental imagery and the rotation of mental images.

48. ANS: C

Research on how well attitude can predict behavior indicates that the more important the attitude appears, the more likely the behavior will match the attitude. Economic factors do influence the connection between attitude and behavior.

49. ANS: E

Gustatory is the sense of taste and is not identified by Gardner as a separate intelligence yet.

50. ANS: D

Receiving time off work is an example of negative reinforcement. Receiving a gift certificate for writing the most tickets is an example of positive reinforcement.

51. ANS: A

Suddenly understanding the solution to the puzzle is a good example of achieving insight.

52. ANS: D

The humanist perspective criticized the behavioral and psychoanalytic perspectives for ignoring the qualities that make people human and focusing too much on forces like animalistic drives and environmental forces on human behavior.

53. ANS: E

A robin is a prototypical bird because it most closely matches the defining characteristics of a bird, such as feathers, wings, and the ability to fly.

54. ANS: C

According to Edward Tolman both groups of rats are leaning the maze, but the second group isn't demonstrating their latent learning.

55. ANS: E

The type of processing in which people attend to the content of the message is known as central-route processing. Peripheral-route processing relies on cues outside the message, such as the expertise of the message source.

56. ANS: B

An operational definition specifically names the procedure to measure a variable. Jon can count the number of smiles per minute his participants display. The other choices do not include a way to measure the variable.

57. ANS: D

According to Dweck, a person who believes intelligence is fixed and unchangeable may demonstrate an external locus of control, give up easily, or avoid situations in which failure is possible.

58. ANS: A

Schizophrenia is the only disorder listed that is not considered an anxiety disorder.

59. ANS: B

The three elements of emotion are physiological, behavioral, and subjective experience.

60. ANS: C

Maslow, Alderfer, and Ryan and Deci have all incorporated relatedness (affiliation) in their theories of motivation.

61. ANS: E

The tendency of one's expectations to affect one's behavior in such a way as to make the expectations more likely to occur is known as a self-fulfilling prophecy.

62. ANS: C

Afferent and efferent neurons transmit neural information to and from the spinal cord.

63. ANS: A

People who are high in nAch (need for achievement) are likely to look for careers and hobbies that allow others to evaluate them because they are interested in feedback on their performance.

64. ANS: A

On the Wechsler Intelligence Scales the mean is 100 and the standard deviation is 15. This means that a score of 112 is within one standard deviation of the mean.

65. ANS: B

Antisocial personality disorder is associated with habitual disregard for both the law and rights of others.

66. ANS: D

The effect of heroin addiction is a reduction in the body's production of endorphins and a painful withdrawal experience.

67. ANS: D

It is most accurate to say that no one approach to psychotherapy is the most effective or works for every type of problem.

68. ANS: E

According to Rotter, people who assume that their own actions and decisions directly affect the consequences they experience are said to be internal in locus of control.

69. ANS: A

This best illustrates the Gestalt principle of proximity. The two people are associated with being a couple because they are near one another.

70. ANS: A
"Use it or lose it" is the phrase to remember because people who exercise their mental abilities have been found to be far less likely to develop memory problems and even senile dementias such as Alzheimer's in old age.

71. ANS: A
Erik Erikson would likely agree that babies should not be left to "cry it out" when they may need attention.

72. ANS: A
There are more men with color blindness than women because color blindness is a recessive trait. Men have only one X chromosome and are more vulnerable to recessive genes.

73. ANS: D
An MRI scan shows very small details in the structure of the brain. Activity in the brain is not imaged by an MRI scan.

74. ANS: D
Milgram found that around 65 percent of the "teachers" would give the most severe "shock" to the "learners" even when the "learner" made a protest. While 100 percent of the "teachers" gave at least the mildest "shock" during the experiment, only around 45 percent of the "teachers" refused to be obedient enough to "go all the way."

75. ANS: A
Habituation is experienced when sensory receptors are still responding to stimulation but the lower centers of the brain are not sending the signals from those receptors to the cortex. Sensory adaptation is experienced when sensory receptors are no longer sending signals to the brain.

76. ANS: B
Looking at an ambiguous image and interpreting it is characteristic of projection.

77. ANS: E
The dog checks its food dish for food, a reinforcer, only when it sees a cue, the dog food bag.

78. ANS: C
By spending time in a group that shares beliefs on an issue, the members of the group will become more polarized, or strengthened in their shared beliefs.

79. ANS: E
Environmental factors like rewards and punishments are emphasized in the behaviorist view.

80. ANS: A
One drawback to humanistic therapies is there is little experimental research to support the basic ideas on which this type of therapy is founded. Humanistic therapists do not interject their ideas or thoughts into the clients thinking, and it is considered a very ethical form of therapy.

81. ANS: A
REBT is a very directive therapy and it is focused on changing behavior. Unconscious conflicts are a focus in psychoanalytic therapy.

82. ANS: C
Classical conditioning is limited in its ability to explain learning because it can only be used to teach new associations to old behaviors, and it does not explain how new behaviors are learned. Operant conditioning is used to elicit new behaviors through learning.

83. ANS: D
The evolutionary perspective has moved toward a refocus on the adaptive qualities of human behavior.

84. ANS: D

Generativity is associated with Erikson's stages of development and is not a component of language.

85. ANS: D

As people age, their vision changes because the cornea hardens and becomes less flexible. This condition leads to the onset of presbyopia.

86. ANS: D

The myelin coating on axons speeds up the transmission of neural impulses. The process of myelinization continues into young adulthood.

87. ANS: C

Standardizing a test would include all of the following except giving the test to a non-random sample of the group for whom the test was designed.

88. ANS: D

The adaptive theory of sleep suggests that prey animals sleep less and at night while predators sleep more and during the day.

89. ANS: C

Agonists are chemicals that mimic the effects of neurotransmitters. Antagonists block the effects of neurotransmitters.

90. ANS: B

Functional fixedness is the failure to see that something could be used for a purpose other than the one it was designed to serve.

91. ANS: B

Brown hair is the result of a dominant gene.

92. ANS: C

Terms like "unconscious," "repression," and "psycho-sexual" are best associated with the psychodynamic perspective.

93. ANS: E

One way to use operant conditioning to modify behavior is to create a token economy and let clients earn tokens for behaving correctly.

94. ANS: B

Shame is not considered a universal emotion.

95. ANS: B

The tendency for people to overestimate the influence of another person's internal characteristics on behavior and underestimate the influence of the situation is called the fundamental attribution error.

96. ANS: E

Volunteers that spent several days without information about day or night experienced a slightly longer sleep wake cycle of 25 hours.

97. ANS: C

"Where is your heart?" is the least culturally biased question because the location of your heart is not dependent on information that may be culturally specific.

98. ANS: E

A case study is used to gather in-depth information about a single person. However, it is difficult to generalize the information to others.

99. ANS: E
    Pragmatics are the "niceties" of language that facilitate communication, such as taking turns in a conversation.

100. ANS: A
    Intelligence tests predict academic success for those who score at the higher and lower ends of the normal curve.

FRQ 1 SCORING RUBRIC

12 points—must correctly address both parts of each topic to score

2 points—circadian rhythm—score—circadian rhythms are rhythms based on a 24-hour cycle. Example: Terri will have difficulty getting up in the morning after first arriving because New York is in an earlier time zone, which interferes with the sleep-wake cycle.

2 points—schema—score—a schema consists of generalizations about objects, persons, or events. Example: Terri has a schema of how cities are organized with grid like streets and numbered blocks. Terri is able to locate sites around the city by using a schema of "city."

2 points—internal locus of control—an assumption that a person makes about having control over what happens in their lives. Example: Terri believes that personal actions and choices will improve an individual's circumstances and not fate or chance. After becoming very lost while looking for the Empire State Building, Terri takes personal initiative, walks around, and asks questions until becoming reoriented.

2 points—extraversion—being an outgoing, affectionate, talkative, and social person—Terri is outgoing and talkative while on the flight to New York and talks to the passenger in the next seat, the flight attendant, the cab driver, and the tour guides at the tourist attraction. By being talkative and affectionate, Terri makes friends with other tourists. Terri is being an extravert.

2 points—positive reinforcement—a pleasant stimulus added to a situation to increase a behavior—Terri walks into an expensive restaurant and sees an attractive celebrity seated across the room. Terri returns to the restaurant every day for the rest of the vacation because seeing the attractive celebrity was a positive experience that reinforced returning to the restaurant.

2 points—confirmation bias—the tendency to search for evidence that fits one's beliefs while ignoring any evidence that does not fit those beliefs. Terri will remember information that supports her ideas and ignore information that conflicts with her ideas.

FRQ 1 SAMPLE STUDENT RESPONSE

Circadian rhythm

A circadian rhythm is a rhythm that repeats on a 24-hour cycle. A common circadian rhythm for humans is the sleep-wake cycle. Terri is vacationing in a different time zone. Because Terri's 24-hour cycle is adapted to the Pacific time zone, Terri will have difficulty during the first few days of vacation getting up in the morning because the Eastern time zone is 3 hours ahead.

Schema

A schema is a generalized idea about something. Terri has a schema about how cities are organized and will use the schema to navigate around the city. Terri knows that streets are often ordered by numbers or letters and that the numbers go up in one direction and down in the other. With the help of a schema, Terri is able to find the tourist attractions around the city.

Internal locus of control

An internal locus of control means that Terri believes that fate or chance is not responsible for things happening to a person, but instead personal choices and decision drive what happens to a person. As a result, after getting lost, Terri asks for directions to the Empire State Building instead of waiting to stumble across it by chance.

Extraversion

Extraversion is a characteristic that means a person is outgoing. By talking to every new person she met on the trip, Terri is being extraverted and making friends with the tourists.

Positive reinforcement

A positive reinforcement is something pleasant that is added to a situation to increase the likelihood that a behavior will be repeated. Terri goes to a nice restaurant for dinner and meets an attractive celebrity. For the rest of the vacation Terri goes back to the restaurant because of the pleasant experience of meeting the celebrity.

Confirmation bias

Confirmation bias is the tendency to ignore information that conflicts with previously held notions and seek information that supports them. Terri believes cities are dangerous and crime is rampant in the streets. Even though Terri has a good time during her vacation, witnesses no criminal activity, and remembers that she saw many policeman present on the streets of the city, Terri still believes that cities are dangerous and crime ridden. When writing her journal about the trip, Terri included in her comments what she just saw in the evening news that crime was up in New York City.

FRQ 2 SCORING RUBRIC

6 points—must correctly provide a relevant example of each topic to score

(A)
1 point—limbic system—score—the limbic system is engaged with emotions and memory. Example: Chitkala is very scared by the incident, and the limbic system is stimulated by the fear. As a result, Chitkala's memory of the event is very vivid and contains details the might be forgotten.

1 point—*social facilitation* is the tendency for the presence of other people to have a positive impact on the performance of an easy task. Because there is a group of people at the bus stop, just enough increased arousal is caused, and Chitkala is able to perform the relatively easy task of describing the event with accuracy.

1 point—elaborative rehearsal—score—using elaborative rehearsal is a way of linking and making meaning out of information. Example: Chitkala makes up a song about using the details of the event as lyrics to the song and links the information to a song that is already familiar.

(B)

1 point—cones and color vision—score—cones are used in the retina for color vision; however, in low light the ability to process color is diminished. Example: Chitkala tells the police that the hat the tall person was wearing was black, but the hat was actually a dark green.

1 point—Gestalt Law of Proximity—score—proximity is the tendency to associate things that are near one another as a group. Example: Chitkala noticed that the tall person and the person without a hat were near each other as they walked closer to the bus stop. Chitkala associated the two individuals as a couple and assumed they were together which might not be accurate.

1 point—fundamental attribution error—score—this is the error of thinking that people are more responsible for what happens to them than the situation. Example: Chitkala blames the person that lost his or her purse for being careless when it was just as likely that there was little the person could have done to prevent the theft.

FRQ 2 SAMPLE STUDENT RESPONSE
(A)

Limbic system

The limbic system is related to emotion and memory. If Chitkala was scared by the incident and the limbic system was aroused, then Chitkala would have vivid memories of the event and would be able to accurately recall details of the incident.

Social facilitation

Social facilitation is how the presence of others can help improve performance on an easy task. Because there were a number of people at the bus stop and they were present when Chitkala was questioned by the police, she is given affirmation and support as she answers the questions and does a good job describing the events.

Elaborative rehearsal

Elaborative rehearsal is a way to add meaning to information and keep the details clear. If Chitkala were to make up a song with the details of the event as words in the lyrics and link the information to a familiar melody, the report given to the police would be more accurate.

(B)

Cones and color vision

Cones are used for color vision and are less effective in distinguishing color in low light. Since the event took place after dark it is likely that some details about colors might be inaccurate. For example Chitkala might report the hat as being black when it was actually dark green.

Gestalt Law of Proximity

This Gestalt law indicates that objects that are near one another are associated as a group. In the case of the bus stop incident Chitkala saw the two people walking together and assumed they were together and reported so to the police. This could be inaccurate because there is no way of knowing if the two people were together or not.

Fundamental attribution error

This is the tendency toward error by thinking that people are more responsible for what happens to them than the situation. If Chitkala blames the person that lost his or her purse for being careless as the reason for the theft and doesn't consider the fact that it could happen to anyone, then the report to the police might be inaccurate.

Sample AP Psychology Exam 2

General Instructions for the AP Psychology Multiple Choice Exam

Work efficiently, watch the time, and do not dwell too long on any one question. Come back to questions you skipped and look at them again. No one can be expected to know everything on the exam. If you are unfamiliar with the topic in a question, do not become anxious or upset. Just move on to the next question, and come back to it if you have time.

Psychology
Section 1
Time—1 hour and 10 minutes
100 Questions

AP MC Exam 2

Multiple Choice
Identify the letter of the choice that best completes the statement or answers the question.

_____ 1. Which of the following is the best example of Seligman's idea of learned helplessness?
   a. A person learns to stay on the couch and tell other people to get them things because he or she doesn't like to get up.
   b. Several opportunities for a promotion are passed up by employees because they don't like the boss they would have to work for.
   c. Even though the job listings are full of employment opportunities, a person stays in a bad job because previous interviews for a new job failed.
   d. A teacher stops coming to work because the students in class do not turn in their assignments.
   e. A cat never comes down stairs because the dog is always chasing it around the main level of the house.

_____ 2. Which of the following is the best example of top-down processing?
   a. guessing the name of a person before he or she tells you
   b. listening to the sounds of individual letters and then understanding the word that they make
   c. saying the alphabet backward
   d. using the picture of a jigsaw puzzle as a guide when putting it together
   e. reading words in a random order and then realizing that they are the words to "The Star Spangled Banner"

_____ 3. Very fast, life-saving reflexes are processed in the:
   a. spinal cord.
   b. afferent neurons.
   c. brain.
   d. sensory nervous system.
   e. efferent neurons.

4. If you stare for a short period of time at a "flag" that is yellow, green, and black, and then shift your gaze to a white screen, you should see a flag with the usual red, white, and blue colors. This afterimage phenomenon is best explained by the:
   a. process of visual transduction.
   b. opponent-process theory of color vision.
   c. process of sensory adaptation.
   d. Ganzfeld effect.
   e. trichromatic theory of color vision.

5. The need for power differs from the need for achievement because:
   a. power is directed by reaching a goal and achievement is directed by reaching a new level of control over people.
   b. the need for achievement is directed toward accumulating external evidence of achievement and the need for power is directed toward accumulating internal evidence of achievement.
   c. the need for achievement is not as strong a motivational force as the need for power.
   d. a need for achievement is directed by reaching a goal and power is directed by gaining control over people.
   e. a need for power is stronger in a person that has an internal locus of control and weaker in a person that has an external locus of control.

6. The visual cliff is a test used to determine:
   a. if an infant has developed nearsightedness.
   b. if an infant has developed depth perception.
   c. stages of cognitive development in children.
   d. if appropriate motor movement is developing in infants.
   e. when an infant has developed the Babinski reflex.

7. An EEG of a brain displays delta waves. The person that is being given the EEG is most likely:
   a. awake.
   b. brain dead.
   c. daydreaming.
   d. in a deep sleep.
   e. in a light sleep.

8. In predicting how successful any persuasive effort at attitude change might be, it is true that:
   a. the message should only present one side of an argument.
   b. people in their mid-twenties are less susceptible to persuasion than are older people.
   c. more weight is given to people who are perceived as experts.
   d. the clarity and organization of the message does not change the effectiveness of a message.
   e. the characteristics of the targeted group of the message are not relevant.

9. During a night of sleep:
   a. more sleep is spent in Stage Four sleep early, and less later in the night.
   b. more sleep is spent in REM sleep early, and less later in the night.
   c. the number of hypnagogic images reported increases as REM sleep increases.
   d. REM sleep will correlate most likely with beta wave patterns.
   e. hypnic jerks are more likely to occur in Stage Four sleep.

____ 10. Which series of numbers, regarding the number of factors in intelligence, correlates best with the following list of names: Spearman, Guilford, Sternberg, Gardner?
    a. 120, 2, 3, 9
    b. 1, 120, 3, 9
    c. 120, 9, 3, 1
    d. 2, 120, 3, 7
    e. 1, 2, 9, 120

____ 11. All of the following are uncontrolled variables except:
    a. an interfering variable.
    b. a confounding variable.
    c. a lurking variable.
    d. an extraneous variable.
    e. a dependent variable.

____ 12. A variable ratio schedule of reinforcement is like:
    a. finding a request for a friend on your social networking web page.
    b. answering the doorbell every time it rings.
    c. playing a slot machine.
    d. getting paid for every ten widgets you make.
    e. getting paid on every Saturday.

____ 13. Which of the following best describes the way a neuron fires?
    a. "all or nothing"
    b. "above and beyond"
    c. "inside or out"
    d. "back and forth"
    e. "baby steps"

____ 14. Freud designed a technique to help his patients feel more relaxed, open, and able to explore their innermost feelings without fear of embarrassment or rejection. This method was called:
    a. analytic psychology.
    b. the Ganzfeld approach.
    c. Gestalt therapy.
    d. psychoanalysis.
    e. behavioral therapy.

____ 15. Neurotransmitters that remain in the synaptic cleft and do not engage with a receptor site:
    a. build up in the synapse until they create a stronger transmission of their signal.
    b. are converted into polytransmitters by enzymes, change polarity, and trigger a neural impulse.
    c. most often go through reuptake.
    d. combine with other neurotransmitters to create a synapse.
    e. are acted upon by enzymes and converted into hyperactive transmitters.

_____ 16. A teacher tells the class, "I am thinking of something that has a large head, cries often, spends most of the day sleeping, does not walk, and is fed with a bottle." If a student raises his or her hand and says, "You are thinking of a baby" the student is using:
 a. a representative heuristic.
 b. mechanical solution.
 c. means-end analysis.
 d. an algorithm.
 e. artificial intelligence.

_____ 17. The employees in an office know that the boss only shows up once a week and usually around noon on Friday. As Friday approaches, the employees in the office start becoming busier and more on task. Friday comes and the boss visits shortly, hands out paychecks, and then leaves. After the boss leaves, the employees go back to their habits of loafing. Which schedule of reinforcement best applies to activities at the office?
 a. variable interval
 b. variable ratio
 c. fixed ratio
 d. fixed interval
 e. continuous reinforcement

_____ 18. According to Hobson and McCarley:
 a. dreams contain latent content that can be interpreted to determine the nature of unconscious conflicts.
 b. dreams contain random images and meaningful bits and pieces of a person's experiences from previous days that are synthesized into a storyline for the dream.
 c. the interpretation of dreams must be conducted as a scientific process.
 d. symbols, numbers, and themes of dreams contain archetypes that cross cultures and eras.
 e. the basis of dreaming is found in the active regions of the frontal lobes during sleep.

_____ 19. Every time a person takes a painkilling medication, the pain he or she is experiencing goes away. As a result, addiction to the painkillers is best explained by the concept of:
 a. positive reinforcement.
 b. negative punishment.
 c. negative reinforcement.
 d. neutral reinforcement.
 e. positive punishment.

_____ 20. One way the possibility of groupthink can be minimized by group leaders is to:
 a. make it clear that group members will be held responsible for decisions made by the group.
 b. exert pressure on individual members to conform to group opinion.
 c. seek the opinions of only group members and not of people outside the group.
 d. promote the idea that the group is morally correct.
 e. make the group vote by a show of hands and not by secret ballot.

_____ 21. The difference between two data sets is statistically significant if:
 a. one data set has a large number of data points.
 b. both data sets have a small number of data points.
 c. the researcher is careful and makes precise calculations.
 d. the difference is found on more than one test.
 e. the difference between the data sets is larger than chance variation.

_____ 22. One research group that is particularity useful when examining the nature versus nurture question is:
    a. identical twins raised apart.
    b. cousins raised apart.
    c. siblings raised together.
    d. single child families.
    e. dizygotic twins raised together.

_____ 23. The tendency for people to put less effort into a simple task when working with others is known as:
    a. social loafing.
    b. habituation.
    c. social facilitation.
    d. avoidance-avoidance conflict.
    e. compliance.

_____ 24. Imagine a person who has suffered a brain injury cannot remember any information from the time before the injury, not even his or her name. However, he or she can remember how to tie his or her shoes. The ability to remember how to tie shoes is best described as:
    a. semantic memory.
    b. procedural memory.
    c. declarative memory.
    d. episodic memory.
    e. iconic memory.

_____ 25. The regions of the brain that seem to control aggressive responses are:
    a. the amygdala and other structures of the limbic system.
    b. influenced more by high levels of testosterone and serotonin.
    c. not influenced by alcohol because it is a depressant.
    d. less developed in identical twins and more developed in fraternal twins.
    e. found to change as the brain matures.

_____ 26. A second-grade teacher gives students "classroom dollars" for reading books. The students can use the "classroom dollars" to buy items from the class store. This is an example of which behavior modification technique?
    a. shaping
    b. a token economy
    c. classical conditioning
    d. ABA technique
    e. primary reinforcement

_____ 27. Which of the following is an example of Piaget's idea of assimilation?
    a. forgetting about a ball that rolled under a couch
    b. calling a donkey a horse
    c. not being able to see things from another person's point of view
    d. gaining the ability to think about abstract ideas
    e. thinking a complete graham cracker broken into two pieces is a greater amount of cracker than a complete and unbroken graham cracker.

_____ 28. In a prolonged, stressful situation the parasympathetic nervous system may over respond and cause:
   a. an increase in heart rate.
   b. fainting.
   c. a dramatic increase in blood flow to the brain.
   d. an adrenaline rush.
   e. exhaustion.

_____ 29. Statements such as, "I am embarrassed because my face is red," "I am nervous because my stomach is fluttering," and "I am in love because my heart rate increases when I look at her or him" are examples of which theory of emotion?
   a. Lazarus and the cognitive-mediational theory
   b. Schachter-Singer and cognitive arousal theory
   c. James-Lange theory
   d. Cannon-Bard theory
   e. facial feedback hypothesis

_____ 30. One factor that limits the ability to determine heritability of intelligence with twins raised apart is that:
   a. twins learn to adapt in ways that are different from non-twins.
   b. even twins reared apart are usually placed in homes that are similar in socioeconomic and ethnic background, opening the door to environmental influences.
   c. the variations in geographic distance between the twins is a known confounding variable that has now been determined to directly influence the results of intelligence testing on twins.
   d. identical twins are not genetically similar in any way that can be used to distinguish them from the genetic similarity of non-twin siblings.
   e. twins are often already more intelligent than the general population and skew the results of intelligence tests.

_____ 31. Which of the following is an example of a positive symptom associated with schizophrenia?
   a. flat affect
   b. apathy
   c. disorganized thinking
   d. hallucinations
   e. problems with producing speech

_____ 32. Which of the following is not a part of Hofstede's dimensions of cultural personality?
   a. individualism/collectivism
   b. industry/inferiority
   c. power distance
   d. masculinity/femininity
   e. uncertainty avoidance

_____ 33. According the research of Hermann Ebbinghaus:
   a. retrieval failure leads to the construction of false memories.
   b. it is better to distribute study time into shorter sessions over a semester than to have a "cram" session at the end.
   c. repressed memories are accurate and can be accessed through hypnosis.
   d. encoding failure makes it difficult to recall details like the face of a penny.
   e. the recollection of an event will be more accurate if the person giving the account is under hypnosis.

____ 34. If a person is hearing a high-pitched sound, all of the hair cells near the oval window will be stimulated, but if the sound is low-pitched, all of the hair cells that are stimulated will be located farther away on the organ of Corti. The theory of hearing that best fits this description is:
  a. particle theory.
  b. place theory.
  c. resistance theory.
  d. volley theory.
  e. frequency theory.

____ 35. Which of the following would most likely be associated with the effects of GABA?
  a. fight or flight
  b. waking up
  c. falling asleep
  d. eating
  e. an adrenaline rush

____ 36. IQ scores of 130 and 70 share what characteristic?
  a. They are both two standard deviations away from the mean of intelligence scores on the Wechsler IQ test.
  b. They are typical differences in intelligence scores found when testing the same person as a child and as an adult.
  c. They are both above the mean of intelligence scores on the Wechsler IQ test.
  d. They are both considered within the normal range of intelligence on the Wechsler IQ test.
  e. They are both below the mean of intelligence scores on the Wechsler IQ test.

____ 37. Bandura's Bobo doll experiment is best described by the phrase:
  a. "footloose and fancy free."
  b. "locking the barn door after the horse has bolted."
  c. "monkey see, monkey do."
  d. "fortune favors the bold."
  e. "a penny saved is a penny earned."

____ 38. Critics of Gardner's theory of multiple intelligences point out that:
  a. there is no way to determine if one person is more musical than another.
  b. Gardner's support for the idea of a G-factor is weakened by the idea of "street smarts."
  c. there is little scientific evidence to support the concept of multiple intelligences.
  d. environmental intelligence is found only in industrial cultures.
  e. taste and smell are not classified as separate intelligences.

____ 39. The word "kiss" is made up of three:
  a. phonemes.
  b. concepts.
  c. heuristics.
  d. prototypes.
  e. morphemes.

____ 40. Which region of the brain is associated with the ability to interpret the facial expressions of others as a particular emotion?
  a. the right and left temporal lobes
  b. the right hemisphere
  c. Broca's area
  d. Wernicke's area
  e. the left parietal lobe

____ 41. During a surgery to remove a brain tumor, a person experiences trauma to the brain. After the surgery the person no longer has the ability to create new memories. The part of the brain most likely injured is the:
  a. brain stem.
  b. cerebellum.
  c. thalamus.
  d. hippocampus.
  e. medulla.

____ 42. The "foot-in-the-door-technique" is used to acquire another person's:
  a. reciprocity.
  b. cognitive dissonance.
  c. compliance.
  d. vicarious conditioning.
  e. social facilitation.

____ 43. In collectivist cultures:
  a. negative emotions are displayed in public but positive emotions are only displayed in private.
  b. display rules typically allow for public expression of emotion.
  c. display rules are designed to facilitate public expression of emotion.
  d. only positive emotions are displayed.
  e. display rules typically do not allow for public expression of emotion.

____ 44. Members of in-groups tend to stereotype members of out-groups by:
  a. deep ideological issues.
  b. social factors such as religion but not by physical factors such as weight.
  c. getting to know the members of the out-groups on an individual basis.
  d. by physical factors such as weight but not by social factors such as religion.
  e. superficial characteristics such as skin or hair color.

____ 45. The "Robbers Cave" study showed that:
  a. competitive activities helped to reduce in-group member prejudice toward out-group members.
  b. non-competitive activities conducted jointly between two opposed groups immediately decreased hostility between the groups.
  c. out-group members are rarely shown prejudice or discrimination by in-group members when the in-group members have higher status than the out-group members.
  d. forcing groups to work together toward resolving a "crisis" situation increases hostility and prejudice between groups.
  e. equal status contact between groups helps reduce prejudice and discrimination.

46. Treatment of psychological disorders with a medical approach would likely be a practice of:
    a. behavioral and humanistic psychologists.
    b. psychiatric nurses and humanistic psychologists.
    c. most psychiatrists but not all psychologists.
    d. humanistic but not behavioral psychologists.
    e. few clinical psychologists and few psychiatrists.

47. The Rorschach inkblot test would most likely be used to:
    a. measure a person's intelligence.
    b. assess a person's sensitivity to light.
    c. determine if a person has a deficit in color vision.
    d. find the extent to which heritability plays a role in language development.
    e. explore a person's personality or uncover problems in personality.

48. All of the following are an infant reflex except:
    a. the turning reflex.
    b. the rooting reflex.
    c. the Moro reflex.
    d. the grasping reflex.
    e. the stepping reflex.

49. The neurotransmitter most associated with sensations of pleasure is:
    a. dopamine.
    b. GABA.
    c. acetylcholine.
    d. norepinephrine.
    e. endorphin.

50. For most people, a missed night of sleep will likely result in:
    a. inability to do complex tasks, such as math problems.
    b. weakened sensory responses.
    c. a reduction of microsleep episodes during the following day.
    d. concentration problems and the inability to do simple tasks that normally would take no thought at all.
    e. improved concentration on simple tasks.

51. In the early 1900s women in psychology, like Mary Whiton Calkins, had a difficult time establishing academic careers because:
    a. women were not allowed to study psychology.
    b. there were discriminatory practices in place that made it difficult for women to participate in academic fields.
    c. they were not allowed to attend college.
    d. entrance tests for colleges were intentionally designed to favor men.
    e. colleges did not offer psychology as a course of study.

52. Projective tests are considered by psychologists to be:
    a. high in validity because of their objective approach.
    b. low in validity and low in reliability.
    c. low in validity and high in reliability.
    d. high in validity and high in reliability.
    e. low in reliability because of their objective approach.

53. You are studying sleep and reaction time in mice. You find a –.65 correlation between hours of sleep per night and reaction time in mice. Next you are studying diet and reaction time in mice. You find a +.65 correlation between the number of calories consumed per day and reaction time. Which of the following statements is true regarding your findings?
    a. Sleep and reaction time have a stronger correlation than calories and reaction time.
    b. There is no way to determine if sleep and reaction time have a stronger or weaker correlation than calories and reaction time.
    c. Sleep and reaction time have the same strength of correlation as calories and reaction time.
    d. Sleep and reaction time have a direct relationship, and calories and reaction time have an inverse relationship.
    e. Sleep and reaction time have a weaker correlation than calories and reaction time.

54. Gender differences in the rates of depression are best described as:
    a. decreasing, possibly because of more recent improvements in the roles of women.
    b. decreasing, possibly because of effective hormone treatments.
    c. increasing, possibly because of increases in stress reactivity due to genetic differences.
    d. increasing, possibly because of increasing levels of steroids in food.
    e. decreasing, possibly because the rate of depression is in decline in all groups.

55. The removal of a reinforcement to reduce the frequency of an undesired response is:
    a. a way of using negative reinforcement to modify behavior.
    b. a variation on the idea of flooding.
    c. a method of applying positive punishment to modify behavior.
    d. a way of using extinction to modify behavior.
    e. characteristic of the humanistic approach.

56. As the amount of light in a room goes down:
    a. bipolar cells in the retinal begin to increase their rate of firing.
    b. younger people will adapt to the darkness more slowly than older people.
    c. cones are more active and increase clarity in low light conditions.
    d. the differences in colors are easier to distinguish.
    e. rods become more active to help a person see in low light conditions.

57. Each of the following is an example of a secondary sex characteristic except:
    a. menarche.
    b. a deeper voice.
    c. an increase in height.
    d. the appearance of body hair.
    e. breast development.

58. One reason that the likelihood of a bystander to help someone in trouble decreases as the number of bystanders increases is because of:
    a. the elaboration likelihood model.
    b. the reciprocity theory.
    c. the diffusion of responsibility.
    d. the social facilitation effect.
    e. the cognitive dissonance theory.

_____ 59. According to the research of Terman, which of the following is characteristic of exceptionally gifted people?
   a. They tend to be more susceptible to mental illnesses.
   b. They tend to be socially maladjusted.
   c. They tend to be above average in physical attractiveness.
   d. They tend to be less financially successful than the average adult.
   e. Then tend to not have a consistent sense of self.

_____ 60. Which of the following is an example of an approach–approach conflict?
   a. deciding between mowing the lawn or taking a nap
   b. looking for a certain friend in a crowd and finding a different friend instead
   c. needing to buy food and needing to pay for vehicle repairs
   d. driving in the direction of school and getting closer to home at the same time
   e. having to choose between a vacation in Hawaii or a vacation in Europe

_____ 61. According to Noam Chomsky:
   a. the brain is like an empty dictionary that needs words entered into it before language can be developed.
   b. the size of the average teenager's vocabulary has increased since 1940 because of all the words invented for new technology.
   c. speaking in a native language activates the left side of Broca's area and speaking in a second language activates the right side of Broca's area.
   d. language is learned through a system of reinforcements and punishments.
   e. humans have an innate ability to understand and produce language that he named the language acquisition device or LAD.

_____ 62. Which of the following was an attachment style identified by Mary Ainsworth?
   a. controlled
   b. disorganized-disoriented
   c. avoidant
   d. stranger oriented
   e. slow to warm up

_____ 63. Rosenhan's research, in which he asked healthy participants to enter psychiatric hospitals and complain that they were hearing voices, illustrates the power of assigning labels to people because:
   a. the "pseudopatients" were then able to better explain their symptoms to the hospital workers.
   b. once the participants in his research were admitted with a diagnosis, the "pseudopatients" began to display even more advanced symptoms of their disorder.
   c. once the participants were admitted with a diagnosis, it was easier for the hospital workers to determine that the participants were pretending to be ill.
   d. after the participants in the study were given labels, they received better care.
   e. once the participants in his research were admitted for a disorder, the "pseudopatients" stopped pretending to be ill, but the hospital workers interpretations of their normal behavior was skewed.

64. All of the following are Freudian techniques except:
    a. free association.
    b. transference.
    c. systematic desensitization.
    d. analysis of resistance.
    e. dream interpretation.

65. The work of Collins and Quillian examined the organization of information in the brain. Their findings suggest that:
    a. semantic memories can be forgotten, but implicit memories are resistant to forgetting.
    b. information in the brain is organized in a connected form described as a semantic network.
    c. memories are processed in the limbic system and encoded in the frontal lobe.
    d. information processing goes from sensory memory, to short-term memory, and then to long-term memory.
    e. most forgetting of information takes place quickly and tapers off over time.

66. The correct order of prenatal developmental stages from earliest to latest is:
    a. germinal, fetal, and embryonic.
    b. embryonic, germinal, and fetal.
    c. fetal, embryonic, and germinal.
    d. fetal, germinal, and embryonic.
    e. germinal, embryonic, and fetal.

67. A side effect associated with prolonged use of typical neuroleptics is:
    a. retrograde amnesia.
    b. tardive dyskinesia.
    c. an increase in positive symptoms of schizophrenia.
    d. excessively high transmission of dopamine.
    e. lowered levels of sodium.

68. Which of the following is not included in the domains tested by the Wechsler Intelligence Scale for Children (WISC)?
    a. verbal comprehension
    b. perceptual reasoning
    c. working memory
    d. processing speed
    e. emotional intelligence

69. The cognitive perspective can be thought of as a return to the 19th century in psychology because:
    a. it is based on the idea that instincts direct human behavior.
    b. it is a movement that is working to advance research in phrenology.
    c. it revived an interest in thinking and internal processes of the mind.
    d. it seeks to explain how biology leads to heritable characteristics.
    e. it is based on a renewed interest in observable behavior.

70. All of the following are considered in the diagnosis of intellectual disability except:
   a. the age of the person when the deficit occurs.
   b. deficits in intellectual functioning.
   c. skills in the conceptual domain.
   d. skills in the social domain.
   e. skills in the practical domain.

71. Volume, tone, and pitch of sound can also be described as:
   a. distance, loudness, and complexity.
   b. resonance, warmth, and control.
   c. warmth, strength, and control.
   d. amplitude, timbre, and frequency.
   e. intensity, warmth, and resonance.

72. Each of the following are characteristics associated with antisocial personality disorder except:
   a. impulsivity.
   b. borrowing money and not repaying the debt.
   c. keeping commitments.
   d. exploiting people without remorse.
   e. disobeying rules and laws.

73. The perspective in psychology that emphasizes personal growth, choices, and potential is the:
   a. genetic perspective.
   b. biological perspective.
   c. humanistic perspective.
   d. evolutionary perspective.
   e. behavioral perspective.

74. All of the following are true about survey research except:
   a. surveys can be used to study private or covert behavior.
   b. people tend to misremember things, answer inaccurately, purposefully lie, or show a courtesy bias in their answers.
   c. people tend to give socially appropriate answers.
   d. the wording of the questions can affect the outcome.
   e. the order in which the questions appear on the survey cannot affect the outcome.

75. Each of the following are characteristic of client-centered therapy except:
   a. authenticity.
   b. transference.
   c. reflection.
   d. unconditional positive regard.
   e. empathy.

76. The test scores from a standardization group are called norms. This means that:
   a. the scores from the standardization group are the highest scores that can be archived and will now help encourage others that take the test to try and achieve similar scores.
   b. scores from others that take the test are expected to be higher than those of the standardization group.
   c. test scores from others are normal if they fall more than one standard deviation below the mean of the standardization group.

d.   only scores form the standardization group will be accurate.
e.   the scores from the standardization group are the standards against which all others who take the test will be compared.

_____ 77. The person who has the greatest risk for developing schizophrenia is:
a.   the child of a parent that is schizophrenic.
b.   the dizygotic twin of a schizophrenic raised apart.
c.   the sibling of a schizophrenic.
d.   the dizygotic twin of a schizophrenic raised together.
e.   the monozygotic twin of a schizophrenic raised together.

_____ 78. According to cross-cultural research on the fundamental attribution error by Masuda and Kitayama:
a.   Japanese participants are more likely to overestimate the influence of internal characteristics of a person on behavior.
b.   Americans and Japanese participants are equally susceptible to the fundamental attribution error.
c.   Japanese participants are less likely to overestimate the influence of internal characteristics of a person on behavior.
d.   Americans or Japanese participants are not prone to committing the fundamental attribution error because of the high levels of education in each country.
e.   Americans are more likely to overestimate the influence of the situation on a person's behavior.

_____ 79. If your test score is between the +2 to +3 standard deviation range and the scores on the test produce a standard curve:
a.   your test score is higher than 90 percent of the test scores and lower than 5 percent of the other test scores.
b.   your test score is lower than 95 percent of the other test scores.
c.   your test score is higher than 15 percent of the test scores and lower than 20 percent of the other test scores.
d.   your test score is higher than at least 95 percent of the other test scores.
e.   your test score is higher than 80 percent of the test scores but lower than 10 percent of the other test scores.

_____ 80. A quiz was taken in class, and the teacher analyzed the scores. A negatively skewed distribution will be produced from the quiz scores if:
a.   the correlation coefficient between the scores on the quiz and the students GPA is –.75.
b.   the mode of all the test scores is less than 50 percent of the highest test score in the class.
c.   all the students earned perfect scores.
d.   the standard deviation of the scores is +1.
e.   the scores include several extremely low values.

_____ 81. A dog learns to sit at the low pitched sound of a dog trainer's whistle. A tea kettle heats up on the stove, starts making a high-pitched whistle. The dog hears the whistling sound of the tea kettle and sits. This is best explained by the concept of:
a.   shaping.
b.   discrimination.
c.   counter conditioning.
d.   spontaneous recovery.
e.   generalization.

_____ 82. An important distinction between personality theorists and trait theorists is that:
   a.   personality theorists agree that characteristics are inborn; trait theorists agree that characteristics are shaped by genetics and environment.
   b.   personality theorists emphasize the characteristics of personality and the extent to which they are evident in a person.
   c.   trait theorists emphasize the origins and development of personality.
   d.   trait theorists focus on identifying what characteristics a person has but not how strongly the characteristics are expressed.
   e.   personality theorists emphasize the origins and development of personality, but trait theorists focus on the characteristics themselves.

_____ 83. The lobe of the brain associated with processing sensations of touch is:
   a.   the parietal lobe.
   b.   the temporal lobe.
   c.   the frontal lobe.
   d.   the occipital lobe.
   e.   the prefrontal lobe.

_____ 84. Each of the following characterizes the use of severe punishment except:
   a.   it can serve as a model for aggression if hitting is involved.
   b.   it can lead to avoidance.
   c.   it can lead to lying.
   d.   it decreases the undesired behavior and it increases the desired behavior.
   e.   it creates fear and anxiety.

_____ 85. The Yerkes-Dodsen law indicates that:
   a.   all tasks require a high level of arousal to make sure the task is completed.
   b.   maintaining a high level of arousal increases concentration when working on a difficult task.
   c.   tasks that require concentration should be accompanied by a very high level of arousal.
   d.   the relationship between task performance and arousal suggests that there is an optimal level of arousal.
   e.   low levels of arousal are better than high levels of arousal.

_____ 86. Researchers have gathered scientific evidence that subliminal perception:
   a.   stimulates the frontal lobes when presented to a person's visual field.
   b.   has a weak but long-term effect when repeated exposures are used.
   c.   has a strong but short-term effect when used in movie theaters.
   d.   does not work in advertising.
   e.   is a confirmed phenomenon that induces powerful responses in children but weak responses in adults.

_____ 87. The concept of homeostasis is illustrated by which of the following?
   a.   A teacher becomes distracted by hunger from the day's lesson, finds and eats a candy bar, and then goes back to teaching class.
   b.   A baby pushes a bowl of cereal off the tray of the high chair onto the floor and makes a mess.
   c.   A person is very busy and works through lunch to complete a project.
   d.   A person is interested in going to a movie and asks a friend if he or she thought the movie was good.
   e.   A group of friends put their money together to buy a birthday cake for a friend who is living in a foster home.

88. According to research on parenting styles:
   a. authoritative parents tend to be overly concerned with rules.
   b. authoritarian parents combine firm limits on behavior with love, warmth, affection, respect, and a willingness to listen to the child's point of view.
   c. children from permissive parenting tend to be selfish, immature, dependent, lacking in social skills, and unpopular with peers.
   d. authoritarian parents put very few demands on their children for good behavior.
   e. children raised by authoritative parents are often insecure, timid, withdrawn, and resentful.

89. Festinger's research on cognitive dissonance indicates that:
   a. the more boring a task was, the more people would lie and say it was fun.
   b. cognitive dissonance is strongly linked with neural activity in the right frontal cortex.
   c. cognitive dissonance was only experienced by people performing boring tasks.
   d. no amount of payment could get people to say a boring task was fun.
   e. people paid $1 to lie and say a boring task was fun experienced more cognitive dissonance than people paid $20 to lie and say a boring task was fun.

90. To help reduce a client's overeating, the therapist pairs junk food with a noxious smell. This aversion therapy technique is using:
   a. unconditional positive regard to modify the client's behavior.
   b. observational learning to modify the client's behavior.
   c. operant conditioning to modify the client's behavior.
   d. classical conditioning to modify the client's behavior.
   e. transference to modify the client's behavior.

91. A person with conversion disorder:
   a. usually experiences a fugue episode as a symptom of their disorder.
   b. typically complains of the same physical symptoms when under hypnosis.
   c. often complains of hallucinations.
   d. is experiencing physical symptoms without any physical reason.
   e. experiences intruding thoughts followed by ritualistic, repetitive behaviors.

92. One way to control for the placebo effect is to:
   a. conduct a longitudinal study.
   b. use random sampling to select participants.
   c. use a control group and an experimental group.
   d. calculate a correlational coefficient.
   e. use a balanced design method.

93. The venom of a black widow spider causes a flood of acetylcholine to be released into the body's muscles. The most likely response is:
   a. reduced neural activity.
   b. inhibitory neural activity.
   c. sleepiness.
   d. muscle convulsions.
   e. a weakened sense of touch.

94. According to the Sapir-Whorf linguistic relativity hypothesis:
   a. private speech is a way to formulate concepts and thoughts.
   b. collective monologue predicts the size of a child's vocabulary.
   c. the thought processes and concepts within any culture are determined by the words of the culture.
   d. the number of morphemes in a language is relative to the number of phonemes.
   e. linguistic relativity may limit the number of words a culture has for a color.

95. The titles of the chapters in a book that is now the latest best seller are: Brainstorming, Keeping a Journal, Freewriting, and Mind Mapping. Which of the following titles would be the best choice for the book?
   a. Convergent Thinking: Inside the Life of a CEO
   b. Mental Set: A Handbook for Concrete Thinkers
   c. Divergent Thinking: An Artist's Guide to New Ideas
   d. Using Heuristics: One Teacher's Shortcut to a Thinking Classroom
   e. Functional Fixedness: The Glue for Making Ideas Stick

96. "Effective personality development is dependent on unconditional positive regard." This statement is characteristic of the:
   a. biological perspective.
   b. neo-Freudian perspective.
   c. Freudian perspective.
   d. behavioral perspective.
   e. humanistic perspective.

97. A criticism of Kohlberg's stages of moral development is that:
   a. post-conventional morality is practiced by only a small percentage of the population.
   b. part of the population reaches moral development above Kohlberg's highest stage.
   c. most people don't make it to the conventional stage.
   d. Kohlberg only studied women.
   e. what people say they will do and what people actually do when faced with a real dilemma are often two different things.

98. One advantage of naturalistic observation as a research method is:
   a. that the researcher can manipulate the independent variable to see if it produces a change in the dependent variable.
   b. that a high degree of control is obtained for the study.
   c. that only people interested in the research are studied.
   d. that the potential for confounding variables is eliminated.
   e. that there is a low degree of reactivity produced by the researcher.

99. From the behavioral view:
   a. disorders are the result of differences between the real self and the ideal self.
   b. disorders are learned.
   c. disorders are the result of evolutionary trends.
   d. disorders are the result of genetics.
   e. disorders are the result of unconscious conflict.

_____ 100. One advantage to using an algorithm instead of a heuristic is that:
  a. it is a way to use a shortcut to get the solution to a problem.
  b. it always produces faster and more accurate solutions.
  c. when it can be applied, an algorithm will produce the correct answer every time.
  d. it can be used to solve a problem with an infinite number of solutions.
  e. it may require the consideration of every possible solution.

Directions: You have 50 minutes to answer both questions. You must do more than list facts. Present your answers in complete sentences based on your analysis of the questions. Use the appropriate psychological terminology.

AP Style FRQ 1

Danica, a student at Glacier High School (home of the Grizzlies), is walking in the hallway during passing time on her way to AP Psychology class. Danica walks into the AP Psychology classroom just as the passing bell rings and unexpectedly sees a bear. Danica is startled at first, but she quickly realizes that it is not a real bear, and she laughs. The "bear," luckily, was just a friend in the school's mascot costume. Describe each of the following and give an example of how they could apply to Danica as a result of her episode with the "bear" in the classroom.

- Parasympathetic nervous system
- Schachter-Singer theory of emotion
- Flashbulb memory
- Narcolepsy
- Classical conditioning
- Cognitive dissonance

AP Style FRQ 2

Akil is sitting on the roof of the apartment building he lives in and looking up at the stars in the night sky. Akil's science class assignment is to find six major constellations and identify the brightest star in each constellation. While he is looking for the constellations, he sees a meteor make a bright streak across the night sky. Akil finishes his assignment in about 30 minutes and goes inside. On the way inside he says to himself, "I knew I was going to see a meteor tonight!" Explain how the following could apply to Akil as he completed his assignment.

- Dark adaptation
- Gestalt principal of closure
- Weber's law
- Bottom-up processing
- Iconic memory
- Hindsight bias

MULTIPLE CHOICE

1. ANS: C

   Even though the job listings are full of employment opportunities, a person stays in a bad job because previous interviews for a new job failed. This illustrates learned helplessness because the person could get out of the bad work environment if he or she kept applying for new jobs.

2. ANS: D

   The best example of top-down processing is using the picture of a jigsaw puzzle as a guide when putting it together.

3. ANS: A

   Because you don't have time to think and need to act fast, reflexive actions are processed in the spinal cord.

4. ANS: B

   This afterimage phenomenon is best explained by opponent-process theory of color vision. The afterimage effect is not explained by trichromatic theory of color vision.

5. ANS: D

   The need for power differs from the need for achievement because a need for achievement is directed by reaching a goal and power is directed by gaining control over people.

6. ANS: B

   The visual cliff is a test used to determine if an infant has developed depth perception.

7. ANS: D

   Delta waves are associated with deep sleep. A waking brain is associated with beta waves.

8. ANS: C

   In predicting how successful any persuasive effort at attitude change might be, it is true that more weight is given to people who are perceived as experts. People in their mid-twenties are more susceptible to persuasion than are older people.

9. ANS: A

   During a night of sleep, REM sleep increases and Stage Four sleep decreases.

10. ANS: B

    1 Spearman (2 abilities combined for the G-factor), 120 Guilford, 3 Sternberg, 9 Gardner (Gardner started with 7, added an eight and proposed a ninth)

11. ANS: E

    A dependent variable is controlled for in an experiment.

12. ANS: C

    Playing a slot machine is a variable ratio schedule because you don't know how many times you have to play to get a reinforcer, but you do know that you have to play if you are going to win anything.

13. ANS: A
"All or nothing" best describes the way a neuron fires because neurons either fire at their full strength or don't fire at all.

14. ANS: D
Freud designed a technique to help his patients called psychoanalysis. Jung developed analytic psychology.

15. ANS: C
Most often neurotransmitters that remain in the synaptic cleft go through reuptake. Some of the neurotransmitters that remain are inactivated by enzymes.

16. ANS: A
A baby shares characteristics with the description and is representative of the description, so the student is using a representative heuristic.

17. ANS: D
The appearance of the boss is on a fixed interval schedule.

18. ANS: B
According to Hobson and McCarley, dreams contain random images and meaningful bits and pieces of a person's experiences from previous days that are synthesized into a storyline for the dream.

19. ANS: C
Because the painkillers take the unpleasant experience of pain away, they are an example of negative reinforcement.

20. ANS: A
Group leaders should make it clear that group members will be held responsible for decisions made by the group to prevent group members from differing responsibility to the group.

21. ANS: E
The difference between two data sets is statistically significant if the difference between the data sets is larger than chance variation. Repeating the test and careful calculations can confirm the data, but that is not enough to determine whether or not the results are a product of chance.

22. ANS: A
Identical twins raised apart can help gain insight into the nature versus nurture question because they share the same genes but have different environments.

23. ANS: A
The tendency for people to put less effort into a simple task when working with others on that task is social loafing. A person who is lazy will tend not to do as well when working on a group task.

24. ANS: B
The ability to tie your shoes is an example of procedural memory, also known as non-declarative memory. These types of memories are implicit and are not easily retrieved into conscious awareness.

25. ANS: A

The regions of the brain that seem to control aggressive responses are the amygdala and other structures of the limbic system. The aggressive responses are influenced by high levels of testosterone and low levels of serotonin.

26. ANS: B

Using classroom dollars to buy items from a classroom store is an example of a behavior modification technique known as a token economy.

27. ANS: B

Calling a donkey a horse is an example of assimilation because two similar objects are processed with the same scheme. Altering a scheme to include new characteristics is accommodation.

28. ANS: B

An over response of the parasympathetic nervous system can cause fainting as the result of a sudden loss of blood pressure to the brain.

29. ANS: C

In each statement, the physical response precedes the emotional response. This order of events is characteristic of the James-Lange theory of emotion.

30. ANS: B

One factor that limits the ability to determine heritability of intelligence with twins raised apart is that even twins who are reared apart are usually placed in homes that are similar in socioeconomic and ethnic background, opening the door to environmental influences.

31. ANS: D

Hallucinations are a positive symptom. All the other symptoms listed are examples of negative symptoms because they are associated with a decrease of normal functions.

32. ANS: B

Industry/inferiority is part of Erikson's psycho-social stage theory.

33. ANS: B

Ebbinghaus found that it is better to use distributed practice than massed practice to remember information, for example breaking study time into shorter sessions over a semester instead of having a "cram" session at the end.

34. ANS: B

The theory of hearing that best fits this description is the place theory. The frequency theory suggests that the faster the cells fire, the higher the pitch of the sound is being perceived.

35. ANS: C

GABA is a major inhibitory neurotransmitter and would be associated most with falling asleep.

36. ANS: A

An IQ of 130, for example, would be two standard deviations above the mean, whereas an IQ of 70 is two standard deviations below the mean.

37. ANS: C

Bandura's Bobo doll research was about observational learning and is best described by the phrase "monkey see, monkey do."

38. ANS: C

Critics of Gardner's theory of multiple intelligences point out that there is little scientific evidence to support the concept of multiple intelligences.

39. ANS: A

The word "kiss" is made up of three phonemes or basic units of sound in speech.

40. ANS: B

The right hemisphere is associated with the ability to interpret the facial expressions of others as a particular emotion.

41. ANS: D

The part of the brain most associated with the formation of new memories is the hippocampus.

42. ANS: C

The "foot-in-the-door technique" is used to acquire another person's compliance by asking for a small request followed by a larger request.

43. ANS: E

In collectivist cultures display rules typically do not allow for public expression of emotion.

44. ANS: E

Members of in-groups tend to stereotype members of out-groups by superficial characteristics such as skin or hair color. Getting to know the members of the out-groups on an individual basis is a way to break down stereotypes.

45. ANS: E

The "Robbers Cave" study showed that equal status contact between groups helped reduce prejudice and discrimination. Simply putting groups together for non-competitive activities was not sufficient in reducing negative attitudes and hostility between groups.

46. ANS: C

Psychiatrists can and often do prescribe medication to help treat disorders. Most psychologists do not have a medical degree and cannot prescribe medicine; however, in some states a small number of psychologists have a certification to legally prescribe medicine.

47. ANS: E

The Rorschach inkblot test is a projective test that would most likely be used to explore a person's personality or uncover problems in personality.

48. ANS: A

Turning is not categorized as a reflex.

49. ANS: A

Dopamine is associated with sensations of pleasure and simulates the regions of the brain associated with pleasure.

50. ANS: D

For most people, a missed night of sleep will most likely result in concentration problems and the inability to do simple tasks that normally would take no thought at all.

51. ANS: B
In the early 1900s, Harvard, Columbia, and other schools did not allow women the same academic status as men, and women had disadvantages to overcome in pursuit of academic careers.

52. ANS: B
Projective tests are considered by psychologists to be low in validity and low in reliability.

53. ANS: C
The correlation coefficient's positive or negative sign does not indicate strength. The more the correlation is near 1 or –1 the stronger the correlation. In this case, the correlations are equidistant from zero and have the same strength.

54. ANS: A
Gender differences in the rates of depression are decreasing, possibly because of more recent improvements in the roles of women.

55. ANS: D
The removal of a reinforcement to reduce the frequency of an undesired response is a way of using extinction to modify behavior. Negative reinforcement is designed to increase a desired behavior not reduce a behavior.

56. ANS: E
As the amount of light in a room goes down, rods become more active to help a person see in low light conditions.

57. ANS: A
Menarche is a primary sex characteristic because it is directly related to sexual maturation.

58. ANS: C
One reason that the likelihood of a bystander to help someone in trouble decreases as the number of bystanders increases is the diffusion of responsibility.

59. ANS: C
According to Terman's research, the gifted tend to be above average in physical attractiveness.

60. ANS: E
Having to choose between a vacation in Hawaii or a vacation in Europe is an example of an approach-approach conflict because both choices are attractive.

61. ANS: E
According to Noam Chomsky, humans have an innate ability to understand and produce language, which he named the language acquisition device or LAD.

62. ANS: C
Ainsworth identified the avoidant attachment style. Later, researchers identified the disorganized-disoriented attachment style.

63. ANS: E
Rosenhan's research illustrates the power of assigning labels to people because once the participants in his research were admitted for a disorder the "pseudopatients" stopped pretending to be ill, but the hospital workers' interpretations of their normal behavior was skewed.

64. ANS: C

Systematic desensitization is a behavioral technique.

65. ANS: B

Collins and Quillian's work indicated that information was organized in a connected manner that involved categories and subgroups.

66. ANS: E

The correct stages of prenatal development from earliest to latest are germinal, embryonic, and fetal.

67. ANS: B

A side effect associated with prolonged use of typical neuroleptics is *tardive dyskinesia*, a syndrome causing the person to make repetitive, involuntary jerks and movements. Typical neuroleptics lower the transmission of dopamine, and lower levels of sodium are associated with taking lithium.

68. ANS: E

The WISC does not measure emotional intelligence.

69. ANS: C

The cognitive perspective focuses on thinking and consciousness and is a reaction to the overemphasis on behavior characteristic of psychology in the 1950s.

70. ANS: A

The age of the person when the deficit occurs is not considered in the diagnosis of intellectual disability, only the developmental period when the symptoms begin..

71. ANS: D

Volume, tone, and pitch of sound can also be described as amplitude, timbre, and frequency.

72. ANS: C

Not keeping commitments is characteristic of a person with antisocial personality disorder.

73. ANS: C

The perspective in psychology that emphasizes personal growth, choices, and potential is the humanistic perspective.

74. ANS: E

Not only can the wording of the questions affect the outcome of the survey, but the order in which the questions appear on the survey can affect the outcome as well.

75. ANS: B

Transference is part of psychoanalysis. Transference would not be encouraged in client-centered therapy because the client should direct his or her feelings to the appropriate target.

76. ANS: E

Norms are the scores from the standardization group, the standards against which all others who take the test would be compared.

77. ANS: E

The monozygotic twin of a schizophrenic twin is identical in genetics and has a risk factor of 50 percent. Dizygotic twins have no greater risk than non-twin siblings.

78. ANS: C

Japanese participants are less likely to overestimate the influence of internal characteristics of a person on behavior and are more open to the idea that a person may have situational factors governing their behavior.

79. ANS: D

On a standard curve the +2 to +3 range of scores is above 97.73 percent of the scores and below 0.13 percent of the scores.

80. ANS: E

The mean is sensitive to extreme values. Several extremely low scores would lead to a negatively skewed distribution.

81. ANS: E

The best explanation for the dog's behavior is generalization.

82. ANS: E

An important distinction between personality theorists and trait theorists is personality theorists emphasize the origins and development of personality, but trait theorists focus on the characteristics themselves.

83. ANS: A

The parietal lobe is associated with the processing touch because it contains the sensory strip.

84. ANS: D

While punishment can decrease the undesired behavior, it does not necessarily increase a desired behavior.

85. ANS: D

The Yerkes-Dodsen law indicates that maintaining a high level of arousal increases concentration when working on a difficult task. Typically, an easy task requires higher levels of arousal to achieve optimal performance than a difficult task.

86. ANS: D

Researchers have gathered scientific evidence that subliminal perception does not work in advertising.

87. ANS: A

The concept of homeostasis is illustrated by the teacher's behavior because the hunger is a drive, and the candy bar is food taken to reduce the hunger and bring the teacher's systems back to homeostatic levels.

88. ANS: C

According to research on parenting styles, children from permissive parenting tend to be selfish, immature, dependent, lacking in social skills, and unpopular with peers.

89. ANS: E

Festinger's research on cognitive dissonance indicates that people paid $1 to lie and say a boring task was fun experienced more cognitive dissonance than people paid $20 to lie and say a boring task was fun.

90. ANS: D

This aversion therapy technique uses classical conditioning to modify the client's behavior. Notice that the noxious smell is intended to elicit an involuntary response of nausea.

91. ANS: D

People with conversion disorder describe a physical concern like blindness, but they do not have a physical basis for the symptoms. Hallucinations, fugue, and ritualistic behaviors are not symptoms associated with conversion disorder.

92. ANS: E

The balanced design method uses a placebo group to control for the placebo effect.

93. ANS: D

Acetylcholine stimulates the muscles, so a flood of acetylcholine is likely to produce muscle convulsions.

94. ANS: C

According to the Sapir-Whorf linguistic relativity hypothesis, the thought processes and concepts within any culture are determined by the words of the culture.

95. ANS: C

Since the chapters are titled with ways to be creative and think in a divergent manner, the best title is Divergent Thinking: An Artist's Guide to New Ideas.

96. ANS: E

This statement is characteristic of the humanistic perspective because unconditional positive regard supports the congruence between the ideal self and the real self.

97. ANS: E

A criticism of Kohlberg's stages of moral development is that what people say they will do and what people actually do when faced with a real dilemma are often two different things. Kohlberg could be criticized for only studying men.

98. ANS: E

Naturalistic observation is used as a research method because it has a low degree of reactivity. The reason low reactivity is important is that people will behave in a more "natural" way than if they are in a highly controlled environment.

99. ANS: B

Behaviorists believe that disorders are learned and the result of experiences.

100. ANS: C

When they can be applied, algorithms are more accurate, but not always faster, than heuristics.

FRQ 1 SCORING RUBRIC

12 points—must correctly address both parts of each topic to score

2 points—parasympathetic nervous system—score—the parasympathetic nervous system restores the body to normal functioning after arousal. Example: This applies to Danica because when she is startled, her physiology is elevated, and the parasympathetic nervous system will bring her back to normal functioning.

2 points—Schachter-Singer theory of emotion—score—the Schachter-Singer theory of emotion says that a label is added to bodily arousal and an emotional reaction is experienced. Example: Danica sees the bear and her heart races. Danica thinks, "My heart is racing and I am in possible danger from this bear; therefore, I must be afraid." As a result of the label, Danica experiences fear. Danica then sees that it is actually her friend in a bear costume and her physiology changes. Now Danica thinks, "My heart rate is a little elevated, and I see my friend in a costume; therefore, I am amused and laughing."

2 points—flashbulb memory—score—flashbulb memories are encoded automatically with great detail and associated with highly emotional events. Example: Because Danica was scared by the sight of a bear, she will have a flashbulb-type memory of the event and remember the event with great detail.

2 points—narcolepsy—a sleep disorder that causes a person to uncontrollably fall into REM sleep, often as a result of experiencing strong emotions. Example: If Danica was a narcoleptic and she was scared by the sight of the bear, she might fall uncontrollably into REM sleep.

2 points—classical conditioning—Danica heard the bell just before she saw the bear. Pairing the bell (conditioned stimulus) with the bear (unconditioned stimulus) elicits fear (unconditioned response). The next time the bell rings (conditioned stimulus) Danica might experience fear (conditioned response). The AP Psychology classroom could also be used as the conditioned stimulus.

2 points—cognitive dissonance—the emotional discomfort experienced when a person has inconsistency between what he or she believes and what he or she does. Example: Danica believes that the person in the bear costume is her friend, but she is experiencing fear and anger about being afraid. Now Danica feels cognitive dissonance because she is afraid or mad at a person she considers a friend.

FRQ 1 SAMPLE STUDENT RESPONSE

Parasympathetic nervous system

The parasympathetic nervous system brings you back to normal or homeostatic levels of arousal. In the case of Danica, when she is afraid her heart races, and she is ready for a fight-or-flight response toward the bear. However, she realizes it is just her friend so the parasympathetic system starts to slow her down to normal levels.

Schachter-Singer theory of emotion

This is the two-factor or cognitive arousal theory of emoting where a person sees a stimulus; then, at the same time, he or she experiences a physical change, does a cognitive appraisal, and applies a label. After the label is applied the person has an emotional reaction. In the case of Danica, when she thinks she sees a bear, she has a physical change and thinks bears are dangerous so she must be afraid. Then she experiences the fear emotion. After she sees it is really her friend, she calms down and a second cognitive appraisal is made—this is my friend and I was silly to be afraid—she then is amused and laughs.

Flashbulb memory

Flashbulb memories are memories that are automatically encoded, usually as part of a highly emotional event. Danica becomes very afraid by seeing the bear. It is likely that she will now have a vivid memory of the "bear in the classroom" event for a long time to come.

Narcolepsy

Narcolepsy is a sleep disorder that causes a person to fall uncontrollably into REM sleep, and this often happens as a response to an exciting event. If Danica is a narcoleptic, then she might be so afraid at the sight of a bear that she could fall uncontrollably into REM sleep.

Classical conditioning

Classical conditioning is a type of learning that occurs when a new stimulus is paired with a stimulus that already causes an involuntary response. After several pairings, the new stimulus now causes the involuntary response. Danica heard the bell ring just before she saw the bear. This could cause an association to be made between the bell and the bear. Now when Danica hears the passing bell ring she has a fear response.

Cognitive dissonance

This is an uncomfortable emotional feeling that a person has when he or she believes one thing and does another. Danica believes the person in the bear costume is a friend, but she is afraid of bears, and now she feels cognitive dissonance about being afraid or mad at her friend.

FRQ 2 SCORING RUBRIC

6 points—must correctly provide a relevant example of each topic to score

1 point—dark adaptation—score—this is when your rods adjust to low light conditions. Example: For Akil, when he first starts looking at the stars he might be able to only see the brightest stars, but after a while he can see more of the dim stars because his eyes adapted to the low light of the night sky.

1 point—Gestalt principal of closure—score—closure is filling in the gaps of a partial figure. Example: In the case of the constellations, it is seeing a figure in the night sky by filling in the gaps between the stars.

1 point—Weber's law—this is the law of the just noticeable difference. Example: In the case of the science assignment, Akil will have to look for the differences between the brightness of the stars. If Akil cannot see a difference in the brightness of the stars in a constellation, he will be unable to identify the brightest star. However, since the intensity of the light is low, the just noticeable difference should be small, and it will be easy to select the brightest star.

1 point—bottom-up processing—this is starting with the small parts and combining them to create a larger whole. Example: Akil is looking for constellations. If he has to find the Big Dipper, he could start with the North Star and then locate a star in the Big Dipper and so on until he has found the entire constellation.

1 point—iconic memory—this is the sensory memory of vision that is very brief. Example: In the case of Akil, he is able to hold in his iconic memory the beginning of the bright light the meteor makes while it travels across the sky creating the illusion of a "streak."

1 point—hindsight bias— this is the tendency to believe you could have predicted an event after the fact. (Note: meteors are common, but seeing one is not.) Example: Akil said he knew he was going to see a meteor. This is after the fact that he saw one. The actual case is that Akil did not know with any greater degree of certainty that he was going to see a meteor and now is showing a hindsight bias.

FRQ 2 SAMPLE STUDENT RESPONSE

Dark adaptation

Akil will experience dark adaptation for about 30 minutes after coming into the darkness of the night sky. As a result of the adaptation, he will be able to only see the brighter stars at first, but as time passes he can see more of the dim starts while looking for the constellations.

Gestalt principal of closure

Closure is filling in the gaps, so once Akil sees a constellation he will, in his mind, fill in the gaps and be able to see the figure that is associated with the configuration of the stars.

Weber's law

Weber's law says that the greater the intensity of the stimulus, the greater the just noticeable difference becomes. In the case of Akil, the light of the stars is quite low in intensity, and he should be able to notice small differences in their brightness and identify the brightest star in the constellation.

Bottom-up processing

This is building up to a greater idea from the parts. In the example of a constellation, the individual stars are put together and become a recognizable configuration in the sky. Akil could start by looking for three stars in a row, and after he finds that, he could look for the rest of the stars in the constellation Orion.

Iconic memory

This is visual sensory memory. Iconic memory holds sensory information for less than a second but long enough to see the bright light at the beginning of the meteor's path as it travels across the sky for Akil to see a "streak" of light made by the meteor.

Hindsight bias

It is the bias that Akil has about his greater chances of seeing a meteor AFTER seeing one. Typically, seeing meteors in the night sky is not that common, and Akil did not have very good odds of seeing one, but after seeing the meteor, he was convinced that he "knew" he was more likely to see one at that time.